This celebratory book in his honour is a veritable attestation by its various contributors, who have known him over the years and benefitted from his works and experience. The book documents various aspects of intellectual property law, reform and administration in Nigeria. Its content is a valuable contribution to knowledge, in general, and intellectual property, in particular, world-wide. It is a 'must read' and I fully endorse it."

Johnson A. Ekpere, *Former Executive Secretary, Organization of African Unity (now African Union) Scientific, Technical and Research Commission (OAU/STRC), and Retired Professor, University of Ibadan, Ibadan, Nigeria*

"It has been a while now since we first met, and he has done many things since, but I will always think of Prof. Adewopo as 'D.G.'. Prof. Adebambo Adewopo served as Director General of the Nigerian Copyright Commission for six years, just one of the many respected stops in his distinguished career. For me personally, his able leadership and depth of copyright expertise were surpassed only by his kindness and generosity, making a space for a young foreign law student with big dreams. I learned immensely from him and from the opportunity to work alongside Dr. Yemi Lawal-Arowolo and now D.G. himself, John Asein. It is wonderful to see Prof. Adewopo appropriately honored with this work, to collect together in one volume illustrations of his influence, and to put in place another thread that will continue his inspiration of attorneys and scholars, from copyright experts down to young students with big dreams, both in Nigeria and abroad. Congratulations to Prof. Adewopo and all the contributing authors, and from me personally, Ẹ ṣeun pupọ."

Aurelia Schultz, *Counsel for Policy and International Affairs U.S. Copyright Office*

"This title, which covers topical issues with an eye to reform, is designed for people interested in a broad range of intellectual property issues across many areas of business, community and government. The book is dedicated to Professor Adebambo Adewopo who has been a leading figure in the development of Nigerian Intellectual Property Law and Policy. He has displayed the unique ability to combine practice of the law, academic research and investigation of the law and policy development in the many significant roles he has held in Nigeria and beyond. Importantly, he has mentored a new generation of IP scholars that are now based around the globe. Many are contributors to this volume of essays published in Honour of Professor Adewopo. He has been an important and influential voice for Nigeria and Africa and is respected at an international level as an expert in his field and distinguished administrator. I trust you will enjoy this Festschrift for Professor Adewopo."

Brian Fitzgerald, *Barrister at Law, Australia*

"This volume in honor of Professor Adebambo Adewopo is a must-read for those interested in contemporary issues in Nigerian Intellectual Property Law. It considers a broad array of issues including patents and designs in relation to Genomic Research; COVID-19, patents and medicinal uses of Plants and the relevance of the AfCFTA to MSMEs."

Caroline B Ncube, *SARChI Research Chair in Intellectual Property, Innovation and Development and Professor, Department of Commercial Law, University of Cape Town, South Africa*

"This book honors the notable contributions of Professor Adewopo to intellectual property law teaching, research, and administration in Nigeria. His contributions have inspired this important work, which gives a good overview of intellectual property issues in Nigerian contexts. This book also provides a needed background for understanding intellectual property legal reform efforts in Nigeria. This book should be a required reading for those with an interest in intellectual property law and legal reform in Nigeria."

Olufunmilayo B. Arewa, *Shusterman Professor of Business & Transactional Law, Temple University Beasley School of Law, USA*

"This edited collection is a welcome addition to the emerging school of scholarship on intellectual property law in Nigeria. More importantly, this body of essays in honour of Prof Bambo Adewopo is no less than he deserves. His visionary, collegial, and innovative approach to the teaching, administration, and practice of intellectual property law is amply reflected in the various chapters of this body of work. This volume has blazed the trail in collaborative and synergistic academic interventions on the peculiarities, opportunities and challenges in Nigerian intellectual law and practice. I commend this collection of essays to every student, practitioner, and academic."

Ikechi Mgbeoji, *Professor, Osgoode Hall Law School, York University, Canada*

"This publication is an invaluable contribution to the expansion of knowledge in the ever-growing field of IP in Nigeria, Africa and the developing world. It is even more remarkable bearing the honour of a leading figure in IP, Professor Adebambo Adewopo. I have the privilege of working with him at the Nigerian Institute of Advanced Legal Studies (NIALS). An outstanding IP Scholar of repute, he is highly regarded for his role as Director General of the Nigerian Copyright Commission. His idea of introducing a journal of intellectual property at NIALS is a legacy that will endure for many years. Professor Adewopo's scholarship and diverse capacities as policy maker, regulator, legal counsel and de facto leader in facilitating the development of intellectual property are well known and deserving of this publication in his honour."

Epiphany Azinge SAN, OON, *Former Director General, Nigerian Institute of Advanced Legal Studies*

"I have known Professor Adebambo Adewopo for several years, but more intimately during his tenure as Director General, Nigeria Copyright Commission. He is an intellectual property expert of international repute who has contributed immensely to the understanding of intellectual property law and practice in Nigeria through teaching, research and administration.

Nigerian Intellectual Property Law

This book reflects on the development of Nigeria's intellectual property law and outlines the urgent need for reform.

Bringing together expert contributors from around the world, the book identifies and discusses the inadequacies and lacunas in current intellectual property law, and how it is practiced and applied in Nigeria. The book argues that the revision and reform of Nigeria's intellectual property law will be vital for the country's development and national interests, whilst also recognising that Nigeria's legal provisions must sit within a broader global context. Divided into three parts, the book discusses patents, trademarks, and copyright in the context of broad overarching themes affecting all aspects of intellectual property law.

Honouring Professor Adebambo Adewopo SAN, the pioneering thinker in Nigerian intellectual property law, this book will be an important resource for researchers working on African Law.

Ayoyemi Lawal-Arowolo is Professor in the Department of Jurisprudence and Public Law, Babcock University School of Law and Security Studies, Nigeria.

Kunle Ola is a Senior Lecturer at the Thomas More Law School (TMLS), Australian Catholic University.

Routledge Studies on Law in Africa

Series Editor: Makau W. Mutua

The Constitution and Governance in Cameroon
Laura-Stella E. Enonchong

Internally Displaced Persons and the Law in Nigeria
Romola Adeola

Nigerian Intellectual Property Law
Reform and Development
Edited by Ayoyemi Lawal-Arowolo and Kunle Ola

Nigerian Intellectual Property Law

Reform and Development

Edited by
Ayoyemi Lawal-Arowolo and Kunle Ola

Routledge
Taylor & Francis Group
LONDON AND NEW YORK

First published 2022
by Routledge
4 Park Square, Milton Park, Abingdon, Oxon OX14 4RN

and by Routledge
605 Third Avenue, New York, NY 10158

Routledge is an imprint of the Taylor & Francis Group, an informa business

British Library Cataloguing-in-Publication Data
A catalogue record for this book is available from the British Library

Library of Congress Cataloging-in-Publication Data
A catalog record has been requested for this book

ISBN: 978-1-032-16899-9 (hbk)
ISBN: 978-1-032-16903-3 (pbk)
ISBN: 978-1-003-25088-3 (ebk)

DOI: 10.4324/9781003250883

Typeset in Times New Roman
by codeMantra

Contents

Contributors

Faith Aboyeji, Doctoral Researcher, Graduate School of Business and Law, RMIT University, Australia.

A.A. Adedeji, PhD, BL, Faculty of Law, Obafemi Awolowo University, Ile-Ife Osun State Nigeria.

Olumayowa O. Adesanya, PhD candidate in Centre for Law and Genetics, University of Tasmania Australia.

Ayodele A. Adewole, LLB, BL, LLM, PhD, Lecturer, University of Jos, Nigeria.

Emeka Polycarp Amechi, LLM & PhD (Wits), Senior Lecturer/Ag HoD, Commercial and Industrial Law, University of Port Harcourt, Port Harcourt Nigeria.

Christian Aniukwu, LLB (Nig.) BL, LLM, Associate Intellectual Property Department, Aluko & Oyebode, Lagos State Nigeria.

Faith K. Bamidele, Lecturer II, Department of Private and Business Law, Afe Babalola University (ABUAD), Ado-Ekiti, Nigeria.

Omolara 'bisi Olabanji, IP Advisor, US Consulate Abuja, Nigeria.

Helen Chuma-Okoro, Senior Research Fellow, Nigerian Institute of Advanced Legal Studies, Lagos, Nigeria.

O. Durotolu, MPhil, BL, Lecturer at Bowen University College of Law, Iwo, Osun State.

Jane Ezirigwe, Doctoral Scholar, University of Cape Town, South Africa; Research Fellow, Nigerian Institute of Advanced Legal Studies.

Nkem Itanyi, LLB (Ife), LLM (London), BL, Lecturer in Law, Faculty of Law, University of Nigeria, and Doctoral Researcher, Queen's University Belfast, United Kingdom.

Ridwan 'Lanre Ajetunmobi, Research Fellow, Nigerian Institute of Advanced Legal Studies Abuja, Nigeria.

Ayoyemi Lawal-Arowolo, LLB, LLM, PhD (Kent), Lecturer at Babcock University School of Law and Security Studies, Ilishan, Ogun State.

Dorcas A. Odunaike, PhD, Associate Professor, School of Law and Security Studies, Babcock University, Ilishan Remo, Ogun State.

Somto David Ojukwu, Lecturer, Faculty of Law, Nnamdi Azikiwe University, Awka Nigeria.

Amarachi Chizaram Okonkoh, BL, LLM, Lecturer at Babcock University School of Law and Security Studies, Ogun State Nigeria.

Kunle Ola, LLB, LLM, PhD, Senior Lecturer | Discipline Leader at Brisbane Campus, Thomas More Law School, Australian Catholic University, Australia.

Oluwatobiloba O. Olanrewaju, Doctoral Candidate, Babcock University School of Law and Security Studies, Iperu Campus, Ogun State.

Ifeoluwa A. Olubiyi, Senior Lecturer, Department of Private and Business Law, Afe Babalola University, Ado-Ekiti (ABUAD), Ekiti State, Nigeria.

Ifeoma Anne Oluwasemilore, LLB, BL, MLS, LLM, PhD, Lecturer, Department of Commercial and Industrial Law, Faculty of Law, University of Lagos, Akoka, Nigeria.

Olasupo Owoeye, LLB, PhD, Senior Lecturer in Law, College of Law, Criminology and Justice, CQ University, Australia.

Bankole Sodipo, PhD (London) BL, Professor of Law, Babcock University School of Law and Security Studies Iperu Campus Ogun State Nigeria.

Foreword

Chidi Oguamanam

Nigeria – and certainly most developing countries – has had a troubled relationship with intellectual property. Intellectual property is rooted in colonial relations of power, the capitalist-centred worldview of knowledge production, and the privileging of western science over disdain for alternative knowledge systems. On that premise, developing countries and their informal knowledge-producing communities are located at the periphery of intellectual property. Moreover, at independence, most African countries, including Nigeria, have continued to run on the inherited colonial intellectual property systems in their statute books. Those laws were made primarily for the economic interest of the colonial powers, reflecting sensitivity neither to developing countries' postcolonial economic priorities nor to those countries' cultural aspirations as independent states in the new global economic order.

Over the past several decades, a complex combination of factors has forced intellectual property into the forefront of trade and economic development. With the onset of the technology-driven information and communication revolution and its spill-over effect into life sciences and biotechnology, intellectual property affects every facet of human existence and the quality of life in both the developed and developing world. Intellectual property has since ceased to be an arcane subject navigated only by sophisticated lawyers. It is now, in the words of a scholar, a matter of life and death. The defining technology revolutions of our time in the digital and biological domains have required compulsory multidisciplinary interest in intellectual property. From health, medicines, agriculture, food security, logistics, data, media, arts and crafts, music, and indeed all sites of innovation and creativity, these technologies have disrupted knowledge production, lowering the entry barrier for many stakeholders.

For Nigeria and African countries, the initial trepidation to embrace intellectual property has turned into pragmatism for strategic engagement. Nigeria is Africa's largest economy, the home to the continent's most skilled human capital at home and abroad. Constituting more than half of the Economic Community of West African States' (ECOWAS) subregional economic bloc, and the hub of Africa's creative and entertainment industry, how has Nigeria – with all its factor endowments in human capital, innovation, and creativity – (re)positioned intellectual property as a tool to harness its economic and associated potentials? This is the central question the editors and contributors to *Reform and Development of Intellectual Property Law in Nigeria* have spotlighted in this volume. In the title of this collection lies the contributors' unequivocal answer to that important question. A tour of the entire collection demonstrates widening gaps and astounding deficits in intellectual property reform in Nigeria.

The three sections of the book focus on the three classical regimes of conventional intellectual property: patents and designs; copyrights and trademarks without discountenancing cross-cutting, newer regimes and issues such as traditional knowledge; domain names; and intellectual property administration. Within the copyright section, the contributors engage with the imperative for a strategic balancing of interest to entrench open access culture toward mainstreaming online publications. They also explore opportunities for liberalized trade regimes pursuant to the African Continental Free Trade Area, through proactive policymaking, with a focus on small and medium enterprises. That section further highlights gaps in Nigerian intellectual property and entertainment law over rights to one's images, arguing for judicial inspiration from more progressive jurisdictions given existing legislative lethargy.

All the chapters in this collection highlight a disappointing irony. Despite the exponential rise in technology and innovation across diverse domains since the mid-twentieth century, most of Nigeria's intellectual property laws are stuck in their colonial versions frozen in time. Nigeria Patents and Designs Act of 1970 is the colonial version, the same is true of the Trademark Act of 1965. Notwithstanding a comparatively progressive, but hardly satisfactory, tenor of the copyright regime, Nigerian courts are not proactive in their approach to copyright law. Generally, the contributors stress a range of gaps in the law as well as areas of opportunity for legislation and policymaking. Those include the need for patent examination, especially for biotechnology-related patents and indigenous knowledge, specialist skill in intellectual property contracting including patent licencing, intellectual property response to biopiracy, leveraging Trade-Related Aspects of Intellectual Property Rights (TRIPS) flexibilities, calibrating trademark law to digital realities (including cybersquatting), and addressing a host of internet-related phenomena, such as "revenge porn."

Like most developing countries, one of the weaknesses that Nigeria faces in the area of the rapid transformations in intellectual property at the cusp of technological revolution is the shortage of manpower and expertise. The dearth of developing country manpower during the negotiations of the TRIPS Agreement was evident to stakeholders; hence, capacity-building and technology transfer have since been entrenched as a norm of intellectual property development. From the early 1990s to date, however, Nigeria has, relative to other countries in Africa, cultivated critical manpower in intellectual property and across related disciplines, legal practice and academia, and general intellectual property policy R&D. Arguably, Nigeria now has the largest African manpower base in the field at home and in the diaspora, even though much expertise is needed at practical, judicial, and administrative levels.

The foundation of that progress was laid by outstanding professional and academic leaders dedicated to the hitherto obscure field of intellectual property. The editors – and indeed virtually all the contributors to this volume – reflect a new generation of intellectual property academics and practitioners who have benefited from the mentorship of one of the leading champions of intellectual property law reform and development in Nigeria – Professor Anthony Adebambo Adewopo, SAN. For over three decades, Professor Adewopo has been in the trenches digging for intellectual property law reform and development in all spheres of influence, including through the practising Bar, the legal academy, and at the highest level of intellectual property administration in Nigeria. He was one of the most impactful Directors General of Nigerian Copyright Commission. He is on record as the first intellectual property specialist academic to be conferred with the rank of Senior Advocate of Nigeria. His life's work has been on the reform and development of intellectual property law in Nigeria. Irrespective of the slow legislative, judicial, and policy embrace of intellectual property reform, he has cultivated and enlisted an army of the next generation of change-makers to that very cause. Perhaps Professor Adewopo's most important investment is his contribution as a teacher, mentor, and role model in handing the torch to the next generation. Even though it is hard to tackle in any exhaustive manner all the gaps in intellectual property reform and development in Nigeria in one single collection, this volume attests to the primacy, urgency, and sustainability of that struggle. I have the permission of the editors to fête Professor Adewopo for being their inspiration and pathfinder on this specialist's professional and increasingly interdisciplinary trajectory, which is crucial for Nigeria's economic development.

I commend this volume to all stakeholders in intellectual property: lawyers, innovators, industry, governments, legislators, knowledge and content producers, academics, students, and the general public who appreciate how high the stakes are in intellectual property reform and development. Nigeria has yet to learn that intellectual property is the starting point for taking the knowledge economy seriously. It is about time.

Chidi Oguamanam, PhD Professor
Faculty of Law University of Ottawa, ON Canada

Introduction

Nigerian IP Experience: Past and Present

Ayoyemi Lawal-Arowolo and Kunle Ola

Intellectual property experience in Nigeria: the past, present and future

Given that definitions are meant, as far as possible, to clarify or simplify concepts, intellectual property (IP) or intellectual property rights (IPR) has been universally adopted as a generic or all-encompassing term. IPR, in the words of Professor William Cornish, safeguards 'some of the finer manifestations of human achievement'[1]and as a dynamic concept, has endured as 'a convenient genus, but its various species remain distinct.'[2] World Intellectual Property Organization (WIPO) perceives intellectual property rights (IPRs) 'as any other property right. They allow the creators or owners of IP to benefit from their work or from their investment in a creation by giving them control over how their property is used.'[3] At the core of those and other authoritative definitions is the concept of a 'bundle of exclusive rights' in intangible property that embodies IP, whether copyright, patent or trademark.

The combination of exclusivity and diversity of legal rights which underpins the conceptual foundations of IP have shaped not only its fundamental principles but also its historical and normative development. However, in the rise of global economy and in many contexts, IP as the dominant legal framework for protection of knowledge assets and the rights over them has

1 W R Cornish, *Intellectual Property*, 3rd edition, Sweet & Maxwell, 3 (In defining the term, Professor Cornish does not give a single generic definition rather, he segregated the three primary forms of IP;

> patents give temporary protection to technological inventions and designs rights to the appearance of mass-produced goods; copyright gives longer-lasting rights in, for instance, literary, artistic and musical creations; trademarks are protected against imitation so long at least as they continue to be employed in trade)

2 See William Cornish, Intellectual Property *Omnipresent, Distracting, Irrelevant*, Clarendon Law *Lectures* (Oxford University Press, 2004) 5.

3 World Intellectual Property Organization *What is Intellectual Property,* 2020 WIPO Booklet 3.

DOI: 10.4324/9781003250883-1

assumed more complexity and notoriety than any singular definition may simply convey.

It is no exaggeration to say that IP has risen to a phenomenon of global renown, indeed, one cannot agree more that IP has become economically and politically relevant today than ever before. Conventional understanding has always cast IP as the authentic incentive system for creators without which creativity and innovation cannot be sustained. However, a more informed position finds a flexible and balanced IP system a better or superior view. Theoretically, this shift implies that IP should not be addressed from a superficial perception if it must produce desired objectives. Hence, countries or organizations who utilize and view IP from a narrow vision are not likely to design IP policies and standards that fit the peculiarity of their environment and needs or likely to enjoy the benefits that IPR protection guarantees every faithful adherent to its tenets and nuances. More than a century of the advent of IP laws as part of the introduction of received English law to Nigeria, IP has gradually emerged from a relatively obscure subject matter into a notable field of law that has generated considerable debates across scholarship, policy and practice spheres. Yet it is ironic for an increasingly dynamic legal field like IP to hold such an unenviable pedigree of one of the least revised or improved pieces of legislation in the gazettes of the Nigerian law. If there was nothing else to add, the Nigerian IP journey is best captured in those statements.

While the pioneer set of IP laws, comprising trademark, patent and copyright acts,[4] were reputed to have served imperial interest, subsequent replacements, with the emergence of local industry, did not make much impact in the legal and commercial environment.[5] That trend neither has significantly changed nor has come into full circle. The Nigerian IP experience can be seen around four important narratives that have combined as the main features of IP regime in Nigeria. For the most part, the first noticeable feature has been its slow and protracted growth.[6] Indeed, in its historical evolution, IP has mainly occupied the fringes of legal development and jurisprudence, and for some, this narrative has still remained substantially correct. At least in the last two or three decades, there is no doubt that IP and the momentum of awareness of its importance to national development,

4 During the colonial era, the first pieces of IP legislation include, for trademark, trademark proclamation of 1900 applicable to the then southern protectorate of Nigeria and subsequent to the amalgamation of 1914, trademark ordinance 1914 applicable to the whole of Nigeria; for patent, patent proclamation ordinances of 1900 and 1902 applicable to the colony of Lagos and southern Nigeria, and the Northern protectorate respectively and then post-amalgamation, UK patent ordinance of 1925; and for copyright, copyright order-in-council 1912 which extended English copyright act 1911 to Nigeria).

5 Adebambo Adewopo, Role of the Court in the Interpretation and Development of Intellectual Property Law: The Nigerian Experience (2015) 6 *GRBPL* No.1, 1, 2–6.

6 Adebambo Adewopo, *Intellectual Property Rights in Nigeria, Law and Development* (NIALS Press, 2015), Chapter 10, 301–19.

particularly in the context of developing countries, have engaged robust attention in both industry and policy landscape in Nigeria.

In more recent years, the growing significance of IP has been a subject of study in its doctrinal, empirical and interdisciplinary contexts, affirming that IP has truly emerged not only as a major currency of the digital age but also as indispensable to national development in our country and region. Policymakers, legal industry, academics, development experts and the public have risen to narratives of the strategic role of IP in emergent digital economy, and accompanying consensus on IP reform has resonated across board. This book reinforces that narrative and brings together contributions from Nigerian IP scholars who understand the nuances of the subject and application of its principles in national contexts. The array of authors in a single volume is provided by the idea to produce a collection of essays in honor of Professor Adebambo Adewopo who is one of the fathers of IP teaching and scholarship,[7] and has contributed to the development of IP law and policy in Nigeria.

There is no doubt that IP debate in Nigeria has been sustained and is getting even more intense by the day particularly from the body of IP scholars who have continued to grow in number and quality. Substantive questions around tenor, scope and adequacy of specific and general aspects of IP law in the contexts of the local creative and innovation industries continue to be discussed among IP experts. What can be considered as the two eras of IP, namely, the first generation or preindependence era of IP laws and postindependence era and still subsisting, have shaped the foundations of IP law in Nigeria and given rise to the call, now an urgency for a new IP dispensation or era as the case may be. This singular theme – IP reform – has defined the works and contributions of Professor Adewopo both as a scholar and as a policymaker. For a country with fertile creative roots that predates colonization, which has gradually grown into modern industries requiring IPR protection, reform can no longer be ignored in many material respects. In the above regard, reform of IP law has become a unifying theme among the generality of IP scholars in Nigeria today.

Discussions whether on copyright, patent or trademark have traversed different aspects of the sub-discipline and have continued to contribute to the growing awareness and knowledge base in the expansive field. In one breath, IP is both vast and highly specialized as it connects with other fields across humanities, social, economic, technology, sciences and more. Yet it is no more arcane just as it has rapidly developed to one of the contemporary

7 Delivering the citation at the Inaugural Lecture of professor Adebambo, professor Obiora Okafor stated that 'it will not be an exaggeration at all to say that he is one of the intellectual fathers of this sub-discipline in Nigeria'. See *According to Intellectual Property: A Pro-Development Vision of the Law and the Nigerian Intellectual Property Law and Policy Reform in the Knowledge Era*, 5th Inaugural Lecture, Nigerian Institute of Advanced Legal Studies, 5th October 2012 at p. 85 (Reprint)

fields such that, economists, policymakers and administrators, engineers, scientists, creatives, innovators and entrepreneurs and specialists in other fields, apart from lawyers, have courted the cross-cutting appeal of IP. More than ever before, its interdisciplinary reach to both economic and political power of industries and nations has been acknowledged. This narrative helps explain why IP debate cannot be allowed to diminish in our country notwithstanding the inability of our legal system to actively respond to the significance of IP. Professor Adewopo puts this in the following context:

> The whole debate about how developing countries like Nigeria are faring in the knowledge economy revolves around important questions on how these countries can engage not as consumers but as net producers of knowledge assets and cultural products in the emergent marketplace, which is where the real wealth of nations reside.[8]

The second feature is the shared impact of national and global IP system on IP developments in Nigeria and the controversy it has engendered over the years. In a large measure, the interaction of the two perspectives constitutes a significant part of the challenges of protecting IPRs in Nigeria. With respect to national IP space, the conversation has focused around domestic environment in which IP law operates and for the most part, the context in which the development role of IP has been scrutinized. The domestic environment has been recognized as the most decisive factor for the development of IP regime, a 'necessary part of the evolution of states from being under developed to becoming developed,'[9] and which can only thrive in a conducive and enabling environment for creativity and innovation. This is particularly so in the case of Nigeria, with a promising and vibrant creative sector that relies on a suitable IP regime for sustenance and growth.[10]

8 Keynote delivered at IP Symposium 'The Bane of Counterfeit Pharmaceuticals and Piracy: building respect for IPRs as a strategic resource for economic growth' hosted by the Office of International Intellectual Property and Computer Hacking Attorney Advisor, Department of Justice and Embassy of the United States in association with key public, private and international institutions, Lagos, 16–17 September 2018. See Adebambo Adewopo, Keynote: IP Symposium, NJIP, 6 (2019) 155–65.

9 Rami Olwan and Brian Fitzgerald, 'Intellectual Property and Development-A Road Map for Developing Countries in the 21st Century' (2012) 1(2) *NIALS Journal of Intellectual Property* 44, 47. See also Ruth L. Gana (Okediji, 'The Myth of Development, the Progress of Rights: Human Rights to Intellectual Property and Development' (1996) 18 *Law and Policy Law Journal* 315, 331.

10 Ayoyemi Lawal-Arowolo, 'Constructing a Model Intellectual Property Policy for Nigeria' (2015) *NIALS Journal of Intellectual Property* (noting a bottom-up approach,130–147, 136.

an active process of public deliberations where a diversity of views and interests is represented is more beneficial. An arena for IP to thrive can be created only if more people are aware of how to earn an income by being creative or innovative.

Part of the national system is the IP institutional and regulatory framework which implicates the role of institutions such as the Nigerian Copyright Commission (NCC) and Industrial Property registries in the administration and enforcement of IPRs. This comprises in the regulatory coverage, and capacities that are consistent with prevailing domestic needs and environment. For example, even with a relatively inadequate copyright law, the strategic action against piracy (STRAP) initiative in 2005 which 'succeeded in redesigning and strengthening the Commission's regulatory measures to serve as credible structures for the realization of the gains of the copyright system by genuine right owners and the creative industries'[11] always provides a reference point in what unarguably can be referred to as the golden era of copyright in Nigeria. The concrete achievements of that era especially in the context of extensive regulatory and institutional reforms geared toward enhancing the Commission's mechanisms for promotion, administration and enforcement of copyright bear an eloquent testimony to what dynamic and innovative leadership can do even with a seemingly obsolete law.

At the international level, global IP norm and norm setting have impacted national IP reforms or better still provided informed perspectives in which to examine IP law in many jurisdictions, especially for developing countries like Nigeria. Notably, under WIPO instruments and World Trade Organization/Trade-Related Aspects of Intellectual Property Rights (TRIPs) Agreement, among other sites, it has influenced IP developments and reform across countries. From the standpoint of trade, TRIPs Agreement particularly has dominated the global space since its inception in 1994 and has dictated emergent IP reform agenda across the North and South hemispheres. Nigeria is not an exception, only which it has not, like other countries, succeeded in reforming its IP laws although its IP reform initiative predated TRIPS itself.

The reasons range from slow law reform process, lack of coordination and political will, non-priority of IP and more, all of which speak to exigency more than mere necessity particularly in an era of digital transformation that has continued to shape the current global economy. Significantly, expanding international regime complex on intersections of IP, for example, with human rights, trade, health, food and agriculture, environment and genetic resources, digital technologies and more recently autonomous intelligence systems and the overarching dynamics of the sustainable development goals (SDG) and impact of COVID-19 pandemic have coalesced to shape IP landscape at national, regional and global levels.

In Africa, the African Continental Free Trade Agreement (AfCFTA) has come on board to facilitate African integration and transborder trade with the prospects for IP protection for goods and services for the 55 African Union member states. With a combined population of over 1.3 billion and

11 Adebambo Adewopo, *Nigerian Copyright System* (Odade Publishers, Lagos 2012) 138.

gross domestic product (GDP) valued at US$3.4 trillion, AfCFTA has effectively established the world's largest free trade area,[12] and with the protocol for IPRs, among other proposed protocols, in the second negotiation phase, the role of IP has never been more strategic to the growing momentum of African economic growth. The impact of digital revolution has continued to shape African IP and innovation landscape. In Nigeria, from the advent of creative sector to the expanding ICT frontiers, impact of rapid digital transformation has continued to shape the development of local industries and emerging national digital economy. IPR framework remains central to the legal, regulatory and policy environment, particularly in leveraging the use and exploitation of Nigerian IP assets such as traditional knowledge, plant and genetic resources and cultural expressions, among others, much of which have been unprotected and susceptible to misappropriation.

There is no doubt that with the combination of the domestic, multilateral and global developments that have continued to establish the historic role and potential contribution of IP to economic growth and development, IP conversation in Nigeria in many circles can only gather more momentum until the desired goal is achieved. In his inaugural lecture, Professor Adewopo explored those dynamics in the development of IP and their impact on the impetus for and prospects of reform in Nigeria.[13] He argued that as socioeconomic value of IP has defined IP law reform along developmental lines, the structure of IP law in the context of prodevelopment reform should focus on four key elements, namely, IP subject matter with accompanying standard of IP rights, digital IPRs and IPR administration including enforcement.[14]

From the foregoing, it is evident that the highlighted features have characterized existing IP landscape in the last 100 years of IP law in Nigeria. To be clear, they have involved sluggish growth both in the context of law and policy reform, and jurisprudence, combined impact of domestic and global development and IP institutional frameworks. For the most part, lack-luster legal reform ranks as the most notorious, having engendered other elements of IP developments. As it has been the most desirable and significant factor in IP reform, adapting IP law to prevailing commercial and technological environment has been the most potent drawback in the recent attempts at reform. Today, IPRs are mostly defined in the digital context. This leads to the fifth principle or narrative that is meant to usher the present Nigerian IP experience into the future. From the wave of emerging digital IP agenda and this applies across jurisdictions in both the North and South divide, digital

12 World Bank, https://www.worldbank.org/en/topic/trade/publication/the-african-continental-free-trade-area accessed 13 April 2021.

13 Adebambo Adewopo, *According to Intellectual Property: A Pro-Development Vision of the Law and the Nigerian Intellectual Property Law and Policy Reform in the Knowledge Era* (Nigerian Institute of Advanced Legal Studies 2012) 12–44.

14 Ibid 50–69.

technology and the Internet have by far created the most transformative impact on diffusion of knowledge and information since the invention of printing.

Consequently, IP law and policy response have been driven by the paradigm shift of universal access to cultural works that has shaken the foundations of IP law and law-making nationally and globally. With the birth of Fourth Industrial era, it is well understood that creativity and innovation are best harnessed in the IP legal architecture that is carefully adapted to digital economy. This imperative completes above highlighted narratives or better still the Nigerian IP experience to introduce this book, and which the following chapters address in varying degrees and context.

This book contributes to the current discussion and to a large extent offers a useful resource to the reform process. It covers topics examined under broad areas of IP, patent, copyright and trademark. They reflect some of the important and engaging areas that have featured in the debates of the past two decades, for instance, copyright in the digital era, image right, patent and access to medicines, patent and genomic research, traditional medicinal knowledge, open access and copyright, including case law development. The book is arranged around three broad themes of conventional IP: **Part I** – *Patent and design,* **Part II** – Trademark, and **Part III** – Copyright.

In Part I, Olasupo Owoeye and Faith Aboyeji, Olumayowa Adesanya, Emeka Polycarp Amechi and Jane Ezirigwe, Amarachi Chizaram Okonkoh and Ayodele Adewole, in the respective five chapters, explore different aspects of patent law, discussing comparative approaches to patent licensing, relevance and propriety of Nigerian patentability to genomic research, deconstructing Nigerian patent system for medicinal uses of plants in the context of COVID-19 era, and recalling the debate over patent and access to medicine and the controversy over employee invention, all vital to initiatives that have informed the reform of patent law in Nigeria.

In Part II, trademark in its digital context is addressed: trademark in the digital age and domain name are examined by Ifeoma Anne Oluwasemilore and Somto David Ojukwu, respectively. Ayoyemi Lawal-Arowolo adds to this trademark discourse with an insight on the applicability of registrable trademark from traditional knowledge to digital age.

In Part III, Kunle Ola revisits the access to knowledge debate in the discussion of open access 'quagmire' in the context of availability, accessibility and impact of scholarly works in developing countries like Nigeria. Odunaike and Olanrewaju discuss the evolution of digital performances and the Rights in performances. Helen Chuma-Okoro and Olabisi Olabanji examine the ongoing debate on the prospects of leveraging AfCFTA in the protection of Nigeria's creative sector in digital economy. Nkem Itanyi and Christian Aniukwu discuss image rights, one of the contentious areas at the intersection of IP. Ifeoluwa A Olubiyi and Faith K Bamidele, Ridwan Lanre Ajetunmobi, and A A Adedeji and O. Durotolu survey the expanse of copyright. In three separate chapters, pornographic works, the issue of registration of copyright and bargaining power between artistes and recording companies in transactional copyright are examined.

Bankole Sodipo concludes the compendium with an overview of existing gaps in the IP legal frameworks across the creative and innovation landscape and the imperatives that have rendered reform the most compelling in the entire IP reform enterprise in Nigeria.

On the whole, this book and the contributions demonstrate that ultimately the goals and objectives of IP law are best served in the context of prevailing domestic environment and development aspiration. This context is represented in the following chapters that cut across various aspects of IP regime in Nigeria.

Part I

Patents

1 Patent licensing contracts under Nigerian and US law

The operation of exhaustion doctrine in Nigeria

Olasupo Owoeye and Faith Aboyeji

Introduction

Patents generally confer monopoly rights in relation to the manufacture, sale, and general exploitation of patented articles. Given the fact that patented products are usually highly valuable commodities, those seeking to trade in them will need the consent of the patent holder to sell or exploit the products for commercial purposes. The patentee's consent is a licence to use the product. Patent licences embody the terms of the agreement between the patent holder and the licensee and cover the scope of the rights and obligations conferred on the licensee. There are however limits to what a licensee may do under a patent licence given that a licence is not an assignment of rights. The Nigerian law on patents raises thorny questions on what restrictions may be validly imposed by a licence as section 23(3) of the Nigerian Patents and Designs Act 1970 ('PDA')[1] prohibits restrictions that are 'unnecessary' for safeguarding the rights conferred by patent protection.

Patent licensing occurs when a patent holder grants authority or permission to another (the licensee) to use some or all of the rights conferred by the patents. Thus, imposing contractual obligations which are generally non-exclusive and non-transferable.[2] It is important to note that patent licences differ from patent assignments. A patent assignment normally involves the full legal transfer of patent rights, privileges, and obligations to the assignee who will then assume full and exclusive entitlements to all the rights conferred by the patent. Patent licensing plays a very important role in promoting the advancement of scientific knowledge, technology transfer, and the enhancement of technological progress in virtually every field of scientific endeavour.[3]

1 Cap. P2 Laws of the Federation of Nigeria 2004.

2 *Agreement on Trade-Related Aspects of Intellectual Property Rights* (as amended on 23 January 2017), Annex 1C of the *Marrakesh Agreement Establishing the World Trade Organization*, opened for signature 15 April 1994, 1867 UNTS 3 (entered into force 1 January 1995) ('TRIPS Agreement'), art 31(c) and (d).

3 Rodney Ho, 'Patents Hit Record in '98 as Tech Firms Rushed to Protect Intellectual Property' *Wall Street Journal* (January 15, 1999).

DOI: 10.4324/9781003250883-3

This chapter examines patent licensing restrictions in American jurisprudence and the extent to which these restrictions may be validly imposed on patent licensees under Nigerian law. The chapter discusses the validity of 'assignment-back' and 'licence-back' grant-back clauses under US and Nigerian law. The chapter considers the validity of conditions in licences that impose obligations beyond the patent term and the right of licensees to challenge the validity of the patent in the US and Nigeria. The chapter notes that section 23(3) of the PDA is designed to strike a fair balance between the rights of patent holders and licensees. The chapter equally evaluates the extent to which patent licensing restrictions may affect the operation of the exhaustion doctrine under Nigerian patent law and highlights the need for Nigeria to amend the PDA to allow for international exhaustion of patent rights.

Patent licensing and grant-back clauses

Patent licences often include provisions that restrain patent licensees from using improvements made to the licensed patents in a manner that would be detrimental to the commercial interest of the licensee.[4] This inclusion is known as the grant-back or improvement clause.[5] A grant-back is defined as 'an arrangement under which a licensee agrees to extend to the IP licensor the right to use the licensee's improvements to the licensed technology'.[6] The essence of a grant-back clause is to ensure the patent holder's intellectual property is not rendered completely redundant or otiose by improvements made by the licensee. While grant-back clauses serve the desired purpose of protecting the interest of licensors in the process of licensing their patent rights, they can raise significant anti-trust concerns.[7] Some of the anti-trust concerns relating to grant-back clauses include the fact that (i) they can disincentivise innovation when licensees feel they would not be able to recoup the cost of investment in improvement should patent for improvements be shared with the licensor; (ii) exclusive grant-back clauses would normally prevent parties to the licensing agreement from granting further licences to third parties thereby limiting third-party market entry; and (iii) exclusive grant-back clauses may in some cases restrain the licensee from retaining any right in the improvement patent, thereby reinforcing the market monopoly of the licensor.[8]

4 John M Murray, 'Antitrust and Patent License Agreements: A New Look at the Grantback Clause in High Technology Markets' (2012) 3(2) *Case Western Reserve Journal of Law, Technology and the Internet* 299, 300.

5 Ibid.

6 Pedro Caro de Sousa, *Licensing of IP Rights and Competition Law* (Organisation for Economic Co-operation and Development, 2019) [DAF/COMP(2019)3] 22.

7 Murray (n 4) 299; Sol M Linowitz and George W F Simmons, 'Antitrust Aspects of Grant Back Clauses in License Agreements' (1958) 43 *Cornell Law Review* 217.

8 Ibid 307–9.

Thus, grant-back clauses have the negative effect of expanding the monopoly of the patentee (licensor) in a manner that may be contrary to the foundational objectives of the patent system, and they can, as already mentioned, have significant anti-competitive effects.[9] Grant-back clauses may come in the form of an 'assignment-back' or a 'licence-back' clause.[10] Where the patentee acquires full rights to the improvement patents with the licensee having to relinquish all rights in the improvement patents to the licensor patentee, then the grant-back clause is an 'assignment-back' clause.[11] However, if the licensee only grants the licensor patentee a right to use the improvement patent without relinquishing their exclusive rights to the subject matter of the patent that is a licence-back clause.[12] Licence-back clauses are a form of cross-licensing. Patent cross-licensing is a well-recognised and accepted practice in the field of patent law.[13]

One must however add that a grant-back clause can offer the advantage of encouraging technology transfer through the benefit it offers to the patentee. Without grant-back clauses, patentees may be reluctant to license their patented technologies as the licensees' exclusive control over the improvement patent may ultimately drive the original patent licensor out of the market.[14] Grant-back clauses are equally used to ensure a unified control over the entire manufacturing process in complex inventions and this can also significantly foster the overall efficiency of the invention and the relationship between the collaborators.[15]

In *Transwrap Corp. v. Stokes Co.*, the US Supreme Court had an opportunity to determine the validity of 'assignment-back' grant-back clauses conferring exclusive rights on improvement patents on the patentee licensor.[16] The patent licensing agreement in question was an exclusive licence granted to the respondents, *Stokes Co*, to manufacture and sell the *Transwrap* invention in the United States, Canada, and Mexico.[17] The exclusive licence granted to the respondent included a condition mandating the respondents' licensees to transfer and assign all improvements patents made during the exploitation of the licensed patents to *Transwrap*, the patentee licensor.[18] The US District Court upheld the validity of the exclusive 'assignment-back', grant-back clause. This was reversed on appeal to the US Court of Appeals.[19]

9 Richard Schmalbeck, 'The Validity of Grant-Back Clauses in Patent Licensing Agreements' (1975) 42(4) *University of Chicago Law Review* 733, 733–4.

10 Ibid.

11 Ibid.

12 Ibid.

13 TRIPS Agreement, art 31(l).

14 Schmalbeck (n 9) 733, 735.

15 Ibid.

16 Transwrap Corp. v. Stokes Co. 329 U.S. 637 (1947).

17 Ibid 637.

18 Ibid.

19 Stokes Smith Co. v. Transparent-Wrap Mach. Corp., 2 Cir., 156 F.2d 198 (2nd Cir. 1946).

On further appeal to the US Supreme Court, an order of certiorari was granted, quashing the decision of the Court of Appeals and holding that exclusive grant-back clauses are neither illegal nor unenforceable. The US Supreme Court observed that a long line of cases had established the principle that a patent holder should not use licensing conditions to expand the monopoly rights conferred by a patent.[20] The US apex court however held that exclusive grant-back clauses are not illegal or an undue extension of a patent monopoly.[21]

The court advanced three main justifications for this conclusion. First, the court took the view that patents are legally assignable and there are no statutory limits on the consideration for assignability.[22] Thus, a patent licensing agreement may require a grant-back clause as consideration for the agreement. Second, the court opined that a patent is a limited monopoly that may be lawfully purchased.[23] The court went on to hold thus: *One who uses one patent to acquire another is not extending his patent monopoly to articles governed by the general law and as respects which neither monopolies nor restraints of trade are sanctioned. He is indeed using one legalized monopoly to acquire another legalized monopoly.*[24]

Thus, the court held that using one patent to acquire another would not constitute an unlawful expansion of the patentee's monopoly. The justification adduced is that while a patent licensing agreement could contain provisions that might violate anti-trust laws, there was no statutory prohibition against exclusive grant-back clauses.[25] The court however refrained from making a pronouncement on whether exclusive grant-back clauses violate anti-trust laws. The court remanded the anti-trust question to the US Court of Appeals. The US Supreme Court, while noting that the anti-trust question remained open to the lower court to determine, concluded thus: *We only hold that the inclusion in the license of the condition requiring the licensee to assign improvement patents is not per se illegal and unenforceable.*

On remand from the Supreme Court to the US Court of Appeals, the Court of Appeals affirmed the decision of the District Court upholding the validity of the exclusive grant-back clause.[26] The Court of Appeals in discountenancing the arguments of *Stoke Co* and summarily dismissing the action thus observed:

> The plaintiff's effort to avoid the result of the Supreme Court's reversal is an afterthought — a tabula in naufragio. Its complaint, its evidence

20 Transwrap Corp. v. Stokes Co. 329 U.S. 637 (1947), 640–1.
21 Ibid 641–2.
22 Ibid 642.
23 Ibid 644.
24 Ibid.
25 Ibid 647–8.
26 Stokes Smith Co. v. Transparent-Wrap Machine 161 F.2d 565 (2d Cir. 1947).

> and its arguments in all three courts were based upon the point on which it has lost; it was the only point upon which it meant to stake the result, and that result it must abide.[27]

The US Supreme Court's decision in *Transwrap Corp. v. Stokes Co* has since been followed in a long line of cases. Some recent decisions adopting the position in *Transwrap Corp. v. Stokes Co* include *Icon Health & Fitness, Inc. v. True Fitness Tech., Inc.*[28] and *Dodocase VR, Inc. v. MerchSource, LLC.*[29]

Legality of patent grant-back clauses in Nigeria

The question for consideration is whether patent grant-back clauses are valid under the Nigerian patent law regime. The relevant provision here is section 23(3) of the PDA.[30] There is no doubt that the right to licence a patent flows from the patent and to that extent, non-exclusive licensing rights are very legal. Thus, non-exclusive 'licence-back' grant-back clauses are legal and valid under Nigerian law. In fact, the right to 'licence-back' grant-back clauses is fully recognised under section 23(1)(a) of the PDA which provides thus: *a patentee or design owner may by a written contract signed by the parties grant a licence to any person to exploit the relevant invention or design.*[31]

The right to transfer or assign a patent flows from the patent. However, the validity of exclusive 'assignment-back' grant-back clauses in licensing agreements under the PDA is at best suspect. The relevant point to consider is whether the US jurisprudence on the validity of exclusive 'assignment-back' grant-back clauses in patent licensing has support under section 23(3) of the PDA. It is submitted that section 23(3) constitutes a statutory prohibition against exclusive grant-back clauses and should be interpreted as such.

27 Ibid 568.

28 Icon Health and Fitness, Inc. v. True Fitness Tech., Inc. Case No. 4:18CV00439 SRC (E.D. Mo. Aug. 2, 2019).

29 Dodocase VR, Inc. v. MerchSource, LLC Case No. 17-cv-07088-JCS (N.D. Cal. Jan. 22, 2020).

30 Section 23 (3): Any clause in a contract for a licence under subsection (1) of this section is null and void in so far as it imposes on the licensee in the industrial or commercial field restrictions which do not derive from the rights conferred by the relevant patent or design or are unnecessary for the safeguarding of those rights: Provided that (a) limitations concerning the scope, extent, territory, or duration of the exploitation of the patent or design or the quality of the products in connection with which the patent or design may be exploited; (b) obligations imposed on the licensee to abstain from all acts capable of prejudicing the validity of the patent or the validity of the registration of the design; and (c) in the case of a patent, limitations justified by the interest of the licensor in the technically efficient exploitation of the subject of the patent, are not restrictions of the kind mentioned in this subsection.

31 Patents and Designs Act 1970, section 23(1)(a).

Exclusive 'assignment-back' grant-back clauses imposing an obligation to fully assign improvement patents obtained by the licensee through the exploitation of the patents are restrictions that 'are unnecessary for the safeguarding of those rights' and are as such, not supportable under the provisions of section 23 of the PDA. This is particularly so because the 'assignment-back' clause is seeking full and exclusive ownership of a new patent that is independent of the licensed patent. It is thus not a right flowing from the licensed patent nor is it necessary for safeguarding the rights conferred by the patent of the patentee seeking the 'assignment-back' grant-back for the improvement patent.

The licence-back clause on the other hand seeks a non-exclusive right to use the new patent in consideration of the authorisation to use the original patent. This is a well-recognised international practice and is a requirement even for non-voluntary licences under section 31 of the TRIPS Agreement. While the 'licence-back' clause cannot be said to be a right flowing from the original patent, it is sometimes important to protect the original patent from being rendered prematurely obsolete. It can, therefore, be supported as necessary for safeguarding the rights of the patentee requesting the grant-back clause. Without such cross-licensing arrangements, patent holders would be more reluctant to offer licences as new improvements may render their inventions otiose if they cannot get a licence to exploit the new inventions.

While cross-licensing through licence-back clauses are reasonably necessary measures for safeguarding patents, exclusive assignment-back clauses are generally egregious and superfluous. They will therefore not satisfy the 'necessary for safeguarding the rights of the patentee' test under section 23 of the PDA. The US jurisprudence is therefore of little help in Nigeria as the statutory framework for patent protection in Nigeria does not provide support for the recognition of exclusive 'assignment-back' grant-back clauses.

Patent trolls and provision for royalties after the expiration of patents in patent licences

Patent licensing may be used to promote technology transfer and it can also be used merely to generate revenue in return for a forbearance to sue as is often the case with patent trolls.[32] Patent trolls are natural or juristic entities that acquire patent rights without working the patents and they are particularly focused on exploiting the monopoly power conferred by patents through licensing royalties or infringement litigation.[33] Patent trolls have been described as a tax on innovation as they often use patent monopoly

32 Robin Feldman and Mark A Lemley, 'Do Patent Licensing Demands Mean Innovation?' (2015) 101 *Iowa Law Review* 137, 138.

33 Eric Rogers and Young Jeon, 'Inhibiting Patent Trolling: A New Approach for Applying Rule 11' (2014) 12(4) *Northwestern Journal of Technology and Intellectual Property* 291, 293.

to obtain substantial infringement settlements without contributing to the advancement of technology.[34]

Companies tend to pay licence fees to patent trolls to avoid expensive lawsuits even when such patents are real impediments to innovation.[35] Patent trolls generally tend to make patented inventions more expensive to use and this has the undesirable effect of inhibiting the use of patented inventions.[36] While the objective of the patent system is to promote innovation, patent trolls generally tend to stifle innovation by unduly increasing the transactional costs of making improvements on the prior art base. It has been argued that the majority of patent cases involve independent inventions and not copying.[37] Thus, where companies seek to license to avoid patent infringement actions on inventions they develop independently, this has the undesirable consequence of impeding rather than fostering technological progress.[38]

Patent trolls, however, can only exercise licensing rights to the extent that there are valid patents under their control and their rights are inexorably circumscribed by the patent term. It is also pertinent to add that the challenges normally associated with patent trolls are unlikely to exist in Nigeria given the fact that patent enforcement actions are not particularly common in the country and the operation of section 23(3) of the PDA should be sufficient to limit the abuse of patent rights even by a patent troll.

A term in a patent licensing agreement that imposes an obligation on the licensee to continue paying royalties after the expiration of the patent term is *ipso facto* void and unenforceable.[39] In *Scheiber v Dolby Lab's, Inc.*,[40] the plaintiffs brought an action against the defendants, Dolby, to enforce a licensing agreement for audio system patents owned by the plaintiff. Scheiber owned the US and Canadian patents on the audio system invention.[41] The licensing agreement was made in 1983. The US patent was to expire in May 1993 while the expiration date for the Canadian patent was September 1995. At the time of negotiating the contract, it was agreed between parties and made a term of the licensing agreement that in consideration of lower licensing fees payable by Dolby, the patent royalties would continue to be paid on all patents until the Canadian patent expired.[42] Dolby subsequently

34 Feldman and Lemley (n 32) 137, 140.

35 Ibid.

36 Eric Rogers and Young Jeon, 'Inhibiting Patent Trolling: A New Approach for Applying Rule 11' (2014) 12(4) *Northwestern Journal of Technology and Intellectual Property* 291, 294.

37 Feldman and Lemley (n 32) 137, 142.

38 Ibid.

39 Matthew Antonelli and Bernadette McCann Ezring, 'Patent License Requiring Royalties to Be Paid after Patent Expiration Unenforceable' (2002) *Intellectual Property and Technology Law Journal* 17, 17.

40 Scheiber v Dolby Lab's, Inc., 293 F.3d 1014 (7th Cir. 2002).

41 Ibid 1016.

42 Ibid.

refused to pay a royalty on expired patents and Scheiber brought an action to enforce the terms of the licensing agreement.[43] The trial court found for the defendants and an appeal was made to the US Court of Appeals, Seventh Circuit.

It was contended by Dolby that the obligation to pay royalties on patents under the licensing agreement ceased to exist the moment the patent expired notwithstanding the clause in the licence that imposed continuing liability for royalties payment until the expiration of the last Canadian patents.[44] In canvassing this position, Dolby placed reliance on the decision of the US Supreme Court in *Brulotte v. Thys Co.*,[45] to the effect that a licensor may not enforce an agreement for the patent royalties payment beyond the subsistence of the patent. The US Court of Appeals expressed concerns on the reasoning of the Supreme Court in *Brulotte* by opining thus:

> The Supreme Court's majority opinion reasoned that by extracting a promise to continue paying royalties after expiration of the patent, the patentee extends the patent beyond the term fixed in the patent statute and therefore in violation of the law. That is not true. After the patent expires, anyone can make the patented process or product without being guilty of patent infringement. The patent can no longer be used to exclude anybody from such production. Expiration thus accomplishes what it is supposed to accomplish. For a licensee in accordance with a provision in the license agreement to go on paying royalties after the patent expires does not extend the duration of the patent either technically or practically, because, as this case demonstrates, if the licensee agrees to continue paying royalties after the patent expires the royalty rate will be lower.[46]

The Court of Appeals on Scheiber thus expressed the view, as an *obiter dictum*, that an agreement for good consideration for the payment of patent royalties for longer than the patent term would not extend the term of patent monopoly and where parties voluntarily enter such arrangements, they ought ordinarily to be bound by it.[47] Nonetheless, the US Court of Appeals felt constrained by the decision in *Brulotte* and expressed its helplessness on the issue in the following terms: *However, we have no authority to overrule a Supreme Court decision no matter how dubious its reasoning strikes us, or even how out of touch with the Supreme Court's current thinking the decision seems.*[48]

The court went further to express the view that Scheiber could have been entitled to a compensatory relief in quantum meruit in the circumstances of

43 Ibid.
44 Ibid 1017.
45 Brulotte v. Thys Co., 379 U.S. 29, 85 S.Ct. 176, 13 L.Ed.2d 99 (1964).
46 Ibid.
47 Scheiber v Dolby Lab's, Inc., 293 F.3d 1014 (7th Cir. 2002) 1018.
48 Ibid.

the case should it be shown that Dolby had paid less than the market value for the use of Scheiber's patents. Nonetheless, the court followed the authority in *Brulotte* and affirmed the decision of the lower court while dismissing the appeal.[49] Since section 23(3) of the Nigerian Patents and Designs Act explicitly render null and void 'restrictions which do not derive from the rights conferred by the relevant patent or design or are unnecessary for the safeguarding of those rights', patent licensing contracts cannot include provisions that impose royalty obligations on licensees beyond the term or validity period of the licence as that would clearly be beyond the entitlements and rights conferred by the patent. Such an obligation will also be completely unnecessary for protecting the rights conferred by patents. The decision of the US Supreme Court in *Brulotte* is thus fully countenanced under section 23(3) of the Nigerian Patents and Designs Act.

The right of a licensee to challenge the validity of a patent

There was a time legal practitioners held the view that patent licensees acting in line with the terms of a patent licensing agreement could seek a declaratory relief to challenge the validity of the patent under US law.[50] While a licensee is generally bound by the licensing agreement under the principles of contract law, until the decision of the US Federal Circuit Court in *Gen-Probe, Inc. v. Vysis, Inc.*,[51] it was generally believed that a licensee could challenge the validity of the licensor's patent and still revert to the terms of the licence agreement should the action fail.[52] Should the challenge against the patent's validity be successful, the licensee would be able to use the invention without being bound by the obligations imposed by the licence agreement.

The decision in *Gen-Probe, Inc. v. Vysis, Inc.* has however shown that a licensee may not question or challenge the validity of the licensor's patent while still bound by the terms. In this case, Vysis, the defendant-appellant held a patent (the '338 patent) for 'methods and kits for use in nucleic acid diagnostic assays' for testing blood for HIV and hepatitis C viruses.[53] At the time the '338 patent was issued, both parties were involved in litigation with respect to other patents. The plaintiff-cross appellant, Gen-Probe, was planning to develop blood testing technology using methods that might fall within the scope of the Vysis patent.[54]

To avoid a real likelihood of infringement on the Vysis patent, Gen-Probe decided to take a licence from Vysis, and the latter granted a non-exclusive

49 Ibid 1023.

50 Victoria F Maroulis and Anthony P Alden, 'Litigating Patent License Disputes: Licensees' Challenges to Validity' (2006) *The Licensing Journal* 9, 9.

51 Gell-Probe, 359 F.3d I 376.

52 Maroulis and Alden (n 50) 9, 9-10.

53 Gell-Probe, 359 F.3d I 376, 1377.

54 Ibid 1377.

licence for the use of the '338 patent.[55] The plaintiff-cross appellant subsequently filed an action for a declaratory judgement to the effect that its invention did not infringe the '338 patent and that the patent was in fact invalid.[56] While the matter was pending before the court, the plaintiff-cross appellant wrote to the defendant-appellant that they believed the '338 patent was invalid. However, given the fact that their position was being strongly contested by the patent holder, they were going to fully adhere to the terms of the license pending the resolution of the legal challenge.[57]

Following a jury trial, the trial court found for the plaintiff-cross appellant and held that the '338 patent was invalid for obviousness and non-enablement'.[58] The defendant-appellant appealed to the US Court of Appeals, Federal Circuit on different grounds including subject matter jurisdiction. In holding that the court lacked the jurisdiction to entertain the suit, the court held that because the plaintiff-cross appellant was a licensee in good standing, there could be no likelihood of an infringement suit. Thus, the action for declaratory relief was incompetent and the judgement given for the plaintiff-cross appellant should be overturned.[59] The court thus opined:

> Moreover, permitting Gen-Probe to pursue a lawsuit without materially breaching its license agreement yields undesirable results. Vysis voluntarily relinquished its statutory right to exclude by granting Gen-Probe a nonexclusive license. In so doing, Vysis chose to avoid litigation as an avenue of enforcing its rights....[60]
>
> Under these circumstances, there is not a reasonable apprehension of suit. Therefore, this court holds that no actual controversy supports jurisdiction under the Declaratory Judgment Act for Gen-Probe's suit against Vysis over the '338 patent. Accordingly, this court vacates the district court's judgment and remands with instructions to dismiss.[61]

This decision implies that a licensee in good standing is estopped from challenging the legal validity of the licensor's patent. Thus, a licensee wishing to challenge the validity of the licensor's patent will either have to breach the terms of the licensing agreement and assume the full risk of infringement liability should the action fail, or the licensee may continue to pay royalties under the licence agreement and remain barred from challenging the agreement for the duration or term of the patent licence.[62] It is important to note

55 Ibid 1377–8.
56 Ibid 1378.
57 Ibid 1378–9.
58 Ibid 1376.
59 Ibid 1382.
60 Ibid.
61 Ibid.
62 Maroulis and Alden (n 50) 9, 12.

that this position finds no support under the Nigerian patent law. Section 9 of the *Patents and Designs Act* explicitly provides that anyone, including a licensee in good standing, may apply for the nullification of a patent where they contest the validity or patentability of the patented invention.

A careful review of section 23(3) of the PDA clearly indicates an attempt by the legislature to strike a fair balance between the rights of patentees and licensees. It would appear section 23(3) provides a strong statutory framework that can protect licensees from exploitation by patent rights holders while still offering sufficient protection to patentees. Section 23(3)(a) however raises a knotty point that does not seem to have received any attention or consideration in the Nigerian intellectual property literature. This is with respect to the extent to which patentees may use their rights to control or prohibit parallel importation under the PDA. To understand how this may operate in relation to patent licensing, it is first important to understand the doctrine of exhaustion which is briefly discussed below.

Exhaustion of rights in patent law

Patent exhaustion is a common law doctrine.[63] The doctrine states that once the subject matter of a patent has been lawfully distributed, whether by sale or otherwise, the purchaser has the right to use the patented product in any way they deem fit, and also the right to sell the product without any encumbrance from the patentee.[64] Also, going by this doctrine, when a patented product is released into the stream of commerce in a country by the patentee or under the authorisation of the patentee, the exclusive rights of the patentee to distribute the product by way of sale becomes exhausted in that country after the first sale of the product.[65] This means that every subsequent sale of non-infringing copies of the patented product cannot be controlled by the patentee. Both the seller and purchasers of the products are shielded from patent infringement in so far as the acts of selling and reselling the products are concerned. The patentee's exclusive right to make the product is however not exhausted by sale; as such, any unlawful reproduction of the patented product without the authorisation of the patentee would amount to infringement.[66]

The scope of the exhaustion rules in a country depends on the exhaustion regime operating in that country. There are three possible exhaustion

63 Andrew T Dufresne, 'The Exhaustion Doctrine Revived? Assessing the Scope and Possible Effects of the Supreme Court's Quanta Decision' (2009) 24(1) *Berkeley Technology Law Journal* 11, 11-12.

64 Shubha Gosh, 'Incentives, Contracts, and Intellectual Property Exhaustion' in Irene Caboli and Edward Lee (eds) *Research Handbook on Intellectual Property Exhaustion and Parallel Imports* (Edward Elgar Publishing Limited, 2016) 3, 17.

65 Gosh (n 64) 3, 17 17.

66 Ibid 17.

regimes: national, regional, and international.[67] Where a national exhaustion regime is in place, the exclusive rights of the patentee become exhausted in a country with the first authorised sale of the patented product in that country's market. With respect to regional exhaustion, the rights of the patentee are exhausted in a country with the first authorised sale of the patented product in any market within the regional bloc of the country. Where a country has an international exhaustion regime, the first sale of the patented product authorised by the patentee in any country in the world would exhaust the rights of the patentee in such a country.

The exhaustion regime in a country determines whether the parallel importation of a patented production from another country would be allowed without the need to obtain the consent of the patentee. Parallel importation (also known as parallel trade) 'allows the importation of products manufactured and marketed by the patent owner in another country without the approval of the right holder, usually with the objective of making the market for the goods more competitive in the importing country'.[68] The patented products are usually imported from a market abroad where they are sold at a lower price and compete with the primary authorised market of the products in the importing country.[69] If a country operates a national exhaustion regime, there can be no parallel importation and a patentee, therefore, has exclusive control over the importation of the patented products into that country. Where it is a regional exhaustion regime, parallel importation becomes possible once the product is put on sale by the patentee in any country within the region of the importing country. And where there is an international exhaustion regime, parallel importation is allowed upon the first sale authorised by the patent owner in any country in the world.

There is no international restriction on the patents exhaustion regime a country can adopt and as such, countries are free to opt for any of these regimes and determine the rules on parallel importation.[70] The PDA does not explicitly provide for an operative exhaustion regime in Nigeria. However, the PDA gives a patentee the right to preclude any other person from importing the patented product.[71] The Nigerian patent law does not provide for international or regional exhaustion. The law in Nigeria thus supports a national exhaustion regime. This position is further reinforced by the provision of section 6(1) of the PDA which confers on the patentee the exclusive rights to import the patented products into the country. An international

67 Olasupo Owoeye, 'Access to Medicines and Parallel Trade in Patented Pharmaceuticals' (2015) 37(6) *European Intellectual Property Review* 359, 360.

68 Ibid 359.

69 Ariel Katz, 'The Economic Rationale for Exhaustion: Distribution and Post-sale Restraints' in Irene Caboli and Edward Lee (eds) *Research Handbook on Intellectual Property Exhaustion and Parallel Imports* (Edward Elgar Publishing Limited, 2016) 23, 30.

70 TRIPS Agreement, art 6. See also Owoeye (n 67) 359, 360.

71 Patents and Designs Act 1970, section 6(1).

exhaustion regime is however more in line with Nigeria's development interests. An international exhaustion regime allows traders to import from the cheapest market in which a patent product is available and this allows for a robust competition that can drive down prices in the local market.[72]

Exhaustion of rights and patent licensing

A patentee may enter into a licensing contract with a licensee to make the patented product and offer the products for sale in a territory. The licensing contract may contain a term restricting the use of the licence to that territory, in which case the licensee may not be able to offer the products for sale outside the designated territory. Considering the doctrine of exhaustion of rights and the statutory protection for licensees in section 23(3) of the PDA, can a licensee who is subject to a restriction on territorial use of the licence offer the patented products for sale outside the designated territory? There are at least two possible scenarios – where a licensee outside of Nigeria seeks to engage in parallel importation to Nigeria (a territory outside the scope of the licensing contract); and where a licensee in Nigeria seeks to use the licence to operate outside the territory authorised by the patentee (exportation to another country). These scenarios will be explored seriatim.

The first possible scenario involves an inventor who has patented the same invention in Nigeria and another country (for instance, Ghana) and has entered into a licensing contract with a company in Ghana, authorising the company to use the licence for manufacturing and selling products in Ghana only. Despite the clause in the contract restricting the use of the licence to Ghana, the company may want to import the patented products into Nigeria. Since the products were made under a licence in Ghana, they would not be infringing products for domestic sales in Ghana. However, whether the parallel importation of these non-infringing patented products can be made to Nigeria is a different question – the answer to which is dependent on the patent exhaustion regime in Nigeria.

Where the patented product has not been first offered for sale in Nigeria by the patentee or under the authorisation of the patentee, the rights of the patentee to control the sale of the patented product in Nigeria subsists until the first authorised sale. Only a first sale of a product in Nigeria as authorised by the patentee exhausts the right to control the subsequent sale. Given the national exhaustion principle applicable in Nigeria, the release of the products into the market in Nigeria under a patent licence does not make an importation from a licensee in another country or even an unauthorised trader in Nigeria legal. Thus, the framework of the Nigerian patent law

72 Susy Frankel and Daniel Gervais, 'International Intellectual Property Rules and Parallel Imports' in Irene Caboli and Edward Lee (eds) *Research Handbook on Intellectual Property Exhaustion and Parallel Imports* (Edward Elgar Publishing Limited, 2016) 85, 87.

provides no legal basis for parallel importation and such importation may be challenged under the law.

Conversely, if the patentee has distributed or authorised the distribution of the patented products in the Nigerian market, the products from the local licensees or authorised agents are allowed to move freely in the domestic market as the patent monopoly on sales is thereby exhausted. Thus an importer of the patented product may be liable for patent infringement if the importation was not authorised by the patentee. Section 6(1) of the PDA confers on a patentee the right to preclude any other person from importing into Nigeria for sale or use, a product for which the patentee has been granted a patent in Nigeria. This means a patentee has the right to control the parallel importation of the patented products in Nigeria. Thus, there is no limitation on the right of the patentee to limit, prohibit, or control importation under the PDA.

The second possible scenario is where a patentee in Nigeria enters into a licensing contract with a licensee in Nigeria to make the patented product and offer the same for sale in Nigeria only. Section 23(3) renders void any clause in a licensing contract that imposes on the licensee any restrictions 'which do not derive from the rights conferred by the relevant patent or design or are unnecessary for the safeguarding of those rights'. This is, however, followed by a proviso that 'limitations concerning the scope, extent, territory or duration of the exploitation of the patent' are valid under the law.[73] In light of this proviso, a clause in a patent licensing contract that limits the territory in which the licence may be used is valid and a violation of the clause would amount to a breach of contract which would be actionable in Nigeria. Thus, a licensee in Nigeria whose licence limits the rights to sell or exploit the patented product to Nigeria could be found liable for patent infringement and breach of the patent licence should the licensee sell or exploit the products without authorisation outside of Nigeria.

Conclusion

Patentees may offer licences for the exploitation of their inventions and they may include conditions and obligations necessary for protection and enjoyment of their exclusive rights for the term of the contract. The law in the US allows patentees to include 'assignment-back' and 'licence-back' grant-back clauses in patent licence contracts. Under Nigerian law, while patentees may make arrangements for licence-back agreements in line with recognised and generally accepted international practices on cross-licensing of patents, the imposition of 'assignment-back' grant-back clauses would be indefensible under section 23(3) of the PDA. It is also important to note that the rights or obligations conferred under a patent term cannot extend beyond the patent

73 Patents and Designs Act 1970, section 23(3)(a).

term. Furthermore, nothing restricts a licensee who considers the validity of the patent to be suspect from taking legal action to challenge the patent under Nigerian law even though a non-exclusive licensee lacks the right to do so under US law.

The operation of exhaustion doctrine in relation to patent licences in Nigeria is guided by section 23(3) of the PDA. While the Nigerian law makes no express provision for an exhaustion regime, the effect of section 6(1) of the PDA and the generally territorial nature of intellectual property rights support the conclusion that international or regional exhaustion would not be legal under Nigerian law. A statutory framework would, therefore, be required for giving effect to an exhaustion regime beyond a national exhaustion system under Nigerian law.

Given the economic challenges of Nigeria, the patent system should be designed to respond adequately to the economic and development interests of the nation. Even though the restrictions imposed on patent licensees under section 23 of the PDA serve the purpose of striking a balance between the rights of the patentees and licensees seeking to exploit such inventions, the law in Nigeria should create a robust regime for parallel importation that allows for an international exhaustion regime. This will greatly help in enhancing competition and promoting greater access to the benefits of scientific progress in the nation.

2 The patent system and access to essential medicine (HIV and cancer) in Nigeria

Overcoming the challenges of unsustainable donor funding and impaired access

Amarachi Chizaram Okonkoh

Introduction

Payments for healthcare is made primarily through out of the pocket expenses, which further impoverishes the already poor, and less than 5% of Nigerians are enrolled under the National Health Insurance Scheme.[1] For example, out of the total healthcare expenditure made in 2016, payment through health insurance was only 3%.[2] The prohibitive cost of accessing treatments, especially for cancer, makes many people shy away from the orthodox healthcare system. This leads to late presentation at the hospital, which in turn acutely increases cancer morbidity and mortality. Cancer patients and survivors alike have decried the prohibitive cost of treating cancer. A cancer survivor stated that 'For anyone to survive cancer in Nigeria, you must spend through your nose. My husband sold all his properties to fund my treatment… I'm not sure how much we spent but it was well over N5 million.'[3]

Increased access to essential medicine for the treatment and management of cancer and a sustained HIV intervention lie in the optimal use of the

1 PWC, 'Sustainability of State Health Insurance Schemes in Nigeria: Beyond the Launch' (2019) 2.

2 PWC, 'Sustainability of State Health Insurance Schemes in Nigeria: Beyond the Launch' (2019) 2.

3 Tobi Awodipe, 'Two Breast Cancer Survivors: "The Cost of Cancer Treatment Is Killing Most People"' *The Guardian Newspaper* (Nigeria, 26 October 2019) https://guardian.ng/guardian-woman/two-breast-cancer-survivors-the-cost-of-cancer-treatment-is-killing-most-people/ accessed 4 August 2020.

In 2017, it was reported that women in Nigeria need between #2.1 million and #29.2 million Naira to treat breast cancer. The cost of chemotherapy alone was estimated to be around #916,000. When this is contrasted with the minimum national wage of #30,000, it becomes clear that cancer treatment is out of the reach of the average Nigerian. See Paul Adepoju, 'Nigeria Is Buying Radiotherapy Machines, but Most Patients Cannot Afford Cancer Drugs' (*Health News.ng*, 2019) http://www.healthnews.ng/nigeria-is-buying-radiotherapy-machines-but-most-patients-cannot-afford-cancer-drugs/ accessed 4 August 2020.

DOI: 10.4324/9781003250883-4

patent system and the flexibilities it offers. While this is not the only way to enhance access, this chapter focuses on compulsory license as tool for enhancing access to essential medicines in Nigeria. It appraises the extent to which the Nigerian legal framework permits Trade-Related Aspects of Intellectual Property Rights (TRIPS) Agreement flexibilities to be explored domestically in order to develop a more sustained structure for access to anti-retroviral drugs and access to cancer drugs. The chapter is divided into seven parts. Part 1 examines the incidence of HIV and cancer in Nigeria and appraises the way essential healthcare services are funded for these two diseases. Part 2 succinctly discusses the right to health in Nigeria and identifies the right to essential medicines as a component of that right. Part 3 examines the extent to which there is access to anti-retroviral drugs and cancer medication in Nigeria and discusses the international legal framework for access to essential medicine. Part 4 examines the extent to which the Nigerian Patents and Designs Act accommodates the use of TRIPS flexibilities. Part 5 traces the development of Nigeria's patent law and the use of compulsory licenses and government use of patent in Nigeria and makes a case for its use under the extant patent system. Part 6 identifies some of the challenges that may result from the use of compulsory licenses by a state and Part 7 concludes the chapter and makes recommendations on how access to essential medicine can be enhanced in Nigeria, through the patent system.

In Nigeria, the right to health is not a constitutional right. This, however, does not mean that the right to access essential health services is not recognised and provided for under the Nigerian law. Section 17(3)(d) of the Nigerian Constitution enjoins the Nigerian government to ensure that there are adequate medical and health facilities for all persons, but the failure of the government to provide adequate healthcare facilities is unenforceable.[4] The National Health Act[5] provides that the National Health System[6] shall provide access to the best possible health services within the limits of available resources for persons living in Nigeria.[7] The duty to provide health services is subject to the availability of resources. Implicit in the duty to provide access to health services, is the duty to ensure access to essential drugs for persons resident in Nigeria. It is from the provisions of the National Health Act that the right to essential medicines is derived in Nigeria. This does not detract from the right as fundamental to the right to life recognised by

4 Constitution of the Federal Republic of Nigeria 1999 (As amended 2011), section 6(6)(c). This is often referred to as the non-justiciability clause.

5 National Health Act 2014, section 1(2).

6 The National Health System is comprised of: the Federal Ministry of Health; the Ministry of Health in every State and the Federal Capital Territory Department responsible for Health; parastatals under the federal and state ministries of health; all local government health authorities; the ward health committees; the village health committees; the private health care providers; traditional health care providers; and alternative healthcare providers.

7 National Health Act, section 1(1) (c).

the Nigerian Constitution. Access to essential medicine is a corollary of the right to health and is one which is recognised in international law.

International framework on access to essential medicines

'Essential medicines are those that satisfy the priority health care needs of the population.'[8] Drugs that fall into the category of essential medicines are so classified based on the following factors: disease prevalence and public health relevance; evidence of clinical efficacy and safety; and comparative costs and cost-effectiveness.[9] Availability and access to essential medicine are hallmarks of a functional healthcare system[10]; they enhance health equity and ensure citizens and residents of a state have access to essential healthcare services.

Drugs relevant for the prevalent diseases in every health system, must be readily available and affordable. If they are readily available but not affordable; access is impaired. WHO recognises four components of access to essential medicine to include rational use, affordable prices, sustainable financing and reliable health and supply system.[11] In Nigeria, there is access to antiretroviral drugs, but there are concerns as to sustainability of its continued availability and affordability. Meanwhile in the case of cancer treatment, there is impaired access, as the drugs are unaffordable.

In accordance with the WHO's policy that all states develop a National Health policy and a National Essential Medicine List, Nigeria has its Essential Medicines List (EML).[12] WHO advises that essential medicines list should be 'forward-looking'[13] and should be updated regularly to reflect new therapeutic options, changing therapeutic needs, drug quality, emerging diseases and medicines that can meet the changing resistance patterns.[14] This places an obligation on the government to ensure that drugs that are on its EML are affordable and accessible.

8 World Health Organization (WHO), 'Essential Medicines and Health Products' http://www.who.int/medicines/services/essmedicines_def/en/ accessed 5 August 2020.

9 Ibid.

10 Dipika Basnsal and Vilok k Purohit, 'Accessibility and Use of Essential Medicines in Health Care: Current Progress and Challenges in India' (2013) 4(1) *Journal of Pharmacology and Pharmacotherapeutics* 13.

11 Socorro Z Escalant, 'Access to Essential Medicines' Office of the WHO Representative in the Philippines https://www.who.int/medicines/areas/nextgen_essentialmeds/1accessadditionalmaterials.pdf?ua=1 slide 17.

12 Essential Medicines List, 6th edition, 2016. https://www.medbox.org/document/nigeria-essential-medicines-list#GO accessed 16 September 2020.
The EML provides for antiretroviral drugs (for the treatment of HIV/AIDS) and antineoplastic and immunosuppressive medicines (used for the treatment of cancer). See Nigeria's Essential Medicines List, 5, 13.

13 World Health Organization (WHO) (n 8).

14 Ibid.

Access to essential drugs is a public health problem in Nigeria.[15] However, the proper use of compulsory license can enhance access. Compulsory license is a term that is used to describe any non-voluntary authorisation (especially when employed by the state) to authorise a non-voluntary use of patent.[16] Before the TRIPS,[17] there was more access to drugs particularly by low and medium income countries who traded freely in generic drugs with countries where patent was not recognised for pharmaceutical products.[18] It was therefore argued that 'TRIPS enhanced the interests of transnational pharmaceutical companies and industrialised countries with large pharmaceutical industries, notably the US, Japan and European Union, at the expense of access to affordable medicines by millions in genuine need'.[19]

The public outcry in favour of public health and the right to access essential medicine over the right of pharmaceutical industries as set out in TRIPS led to an attempt to remedy the situation and enhance access to drugs through the DOHA Declaration of 2001,[20] six years after TRIPS and the implementation of Paragraph Six Decision in 2003,[21] eight years after TRIPS (these are discussed below). These form the international framework for access to essential medicine. Article 31(f) of TRIPS, which provides that a compulsory license can only be granted for domestic use; that is use within a country, was suspended to allow the production of generic drugs for exportation to countries that lack manufacturing capacity for pharmaceutical products.[22] This was done to enhance access and promote public health. Zimbabwe, Zambia, Mozambique and Malaysia have all granted compulsory licenses under the flexibilities available in the post-TRIPS era, while Nigeria remains shy and unwilling to exploit this tool, which will undoubtedly improve public health of Nigerians.[23] Thailand is particularly notable

15 Ibid.

16 James Packard Love, 'Recent Examples of the Use of Compulsory Licenses on Patents' (2007) 2 Knowledge Ecology International Research Notes 1.

17 Annex 1C of the Marrakesh Agreement Establishing the World Trade signed in Marrakesh, Morocco on 15 April 1994 and amended in January 2017.

18 Vanessa Bradford Kerry and Kelley Lee, 'TRIPS, The Doha Declaration and Paragraph 6 Decision: What Are the Remaining Steps For Protecting Access to Medicines?' (2007) 3(3) *Globalization and Health* 2.

19 Kerry and Lee (n 18) 2.

20 Declaration on The Trips Agreement And Public Health (Doha Declaration), WT/MIN(01)/DEC/2 20 November 2001, adopted 14 November 2001.

21 Implementation of Paragraph 6 of the Doha Declaration on the TRIPS Agreement and Public Health, WT/L/540 and Corr.1, 1 September 2003 (Decision of the General Council of 30 August 2003). Hereinafter, Paragraph 6 Decision.

22 See the newly inserted Article 31bis of TRIPS, pursuant to the January 2017 amendment.

23 Zimbabwe in May 2002 issued a compulsory license to produce seven generic versions of ARVs; Malaysia in November 2003 issued a compulsory license to import ARVs from India for two years from 1 November 2003;
Mozambique in April 2004 issued a compulsory license authorising the local manufacture of ARVs; in September 2004, Zambia issued a compulsory license to locally

for its use of compulsory licenses. In November 2006, it issued a license for government use of Patents of three drugs; Efavirenz (Stocrin) of (Merck Sharp and Dohme), Lopinavir+Ritonavir (Kaletra) of Abbott Laboratory) and Clopidogrel (Plavix) of SanofiAventis).[24]

The African group and the developing countries have been instrumental to the development of the public health aspect of intellectual property rights. Their request for clarity on the flexibilities provided by TRIPS led to the Doha Declaration of 2001 and the Paragraph 6 Solution of 30 August 2003 (this is discussed below), which balance private right, trade and public health. The extent to which this is applicable to national systems is dependent on the degree to which these provisions have been incorporated by the states in their domestic laws.

Vanessa and Kelley opine that 'there remains general reluctance among LMICs to fully test the flexibilities for compulsory licensing available under TRIPS'.[25] This is particularly true for Nigeria whose law, makes extensive provisions for the use of compulsory licenses and government use of patent in order to facilitate access to essential medicines. Nigeria's reluctance to explore TRIPS flexibilities and the flexibilities under its law are linked to the absence of political will on the part of its government. Political consideration and the unwillingness to invoke the wrath of big pharmaceutical companies and sanctions from the country of nationality of the pharmaceutical companies remain critical factors for developing countries, such as Nigeria in the use of compulsory licenses. Since the Doha Declaration, multinational pharmaceutical companies and developed countries continue to exert commercial and political pressure on developing countries not to make use of TRIPS flexibilities for public health'.[26] Nigeria, like the most developing African countries is a consumer country, inordinately reliant on imported generic pharmaceuticals from India and China. It lacks the capacity to manufacture pharmaceutical products on a wide scale.[27] This has an adverse effect on its willingness to issue a compulsory licence. It is

manufacture ARVS; Indonesia in October 2004 issued a compulsory license for the manufacture of ARVs; Eritrea in June 2005 issued a compulsory license for the importation of generic ARVs; while Ghana in October 2005 issued a compulsory license to authorise the importation of generic ARVs. All these show that several countries are utilising the flexibilities in TRIPS to enhance access to essential medicines.

24 Vichai Chokevivat (ed), 'Facts and Evidences on the 10 Burning Issues Related to the Government Use of Patents on Three Patented Essential Drugs in Thailand: Document to Support Strengthening of Social Wisdom on the Issue of Drug Patent by the Ministry of Public Health and The National Health Security Office Thailand' (Sangsue 2007) 3.

25 Kerry and Lee (n 18) 4.

26 South Centre, 'The Doha Declaration on TRIPS and Public Health Ten Years Later: The State of Implementation' (2011) 7 *Policy Brief* 1, 6.

27 Adebambo Adewopo, 'Intellectual Property Rights, Pharmaceutical Patents and Public Health: Adopting Compulsory and Government Use Licences in COVID-19 Emergency' (2020), 4 https://nials.edu.ng/pdf/PROF_ADEWOPO_IPR_PHAMACEUTICAL__COVID-19_BREIFS.pdf

time for the provisions of the Nigerian Patents and Designs Act (PDA),[28] on compulsory license to be acknowledged or be put to use to enhance access to essential drugs in Nigeria.

TRIPS, the Doha declaration and the paragraph 6 decision

TRIPS sets out the minimum standards that the states must comply with, in the protection of intellectual property rights (IPRs). States have no obligation to provide more extensive protection than is required under TRIPS. However, the protection granted by members must not contravene TRIPS.[29] It is from this provision that the obligation on states to become 'TRIPS compliant' is derived. Nigeria is a member of the World Trade Organization and has an obligation to bring its national laws in compliance with TRIPS. The provisions of TRIPS and the PDA will be considered to determine the extent to which Nigeria's patent law conforms to TRIPS and to determine the extent to which Nigeria can utilise TRIPS flexibilities to safeguard public health.

A principle under TRIPS is that members are at liberty to adopt measures that are necessary to protect public health and nutrient in the formulation or amendment of their laws and regulations.[30] Thus, in the protection of IPRs, states are at liberty to make provisions which can safeguard and better serve the public health of their citizens. This right must, however, be exercised within the scope of the agreement and its generally agreed exceptions.

The Doha Declaration made several proclamations, which affirm its stance on advancing public health. The opening paragraph acknowledges this and declares that: 'We recognize the gravity of the public health problems afflicting many developing and least-developed countries, especially those resulting from HIV/AIDS, tuberculosis, malaria and other epidemics'.[31] It also stresses that TRIPS is a part of the wider national and international action to address those problems and not an impediment to it. It went further to state that:

> We agree that the TRIPS Agreement does not and should not prevent members from taking measures to protect public health. Accordingly, while reiterating our commitment to the TRIPS Agreement, we affirm that the Agreement can and should be interpreted and implemented in a manner supportive of WTO members' right to protect public health and, in particular, to promote access to medicines for all In this connection, we reaffirm the right of WTO members to use, to the full, the provisions in the TRIPS Agreement, which provide flexibility for this purpose.[32]

28 Cap P2 Laws of the Federation of Nigeria (LFN) 2004.
29 TRIPS, Article 1(1).
30 TRIPS, Article 8(1).
31 Doha Declaration, Paragraph 1.
32 Doha Declaration, Paragraph 4.

The Doha Declaration recognises the right of member states to grant compulsory license,[33] and the freedom to determine the grounds upon which to grant the license, the right to determine what constitutes a national emergency or other circumstances of extreme urgency. Public health crisis is recognised as national emergency or other circumstances of extreme urgency.[34] This affirmation was essential in the light of the responses of pharmaceutical companies and their countries of nationality, when states such as South Africa and Thailand issued compulsory licenses.[35] With this clarity, states are less likely to engage in reprisal actions over the grant of a compulsory license.

The Doha declaration reaffirmed the right of states to issue compulsory licenses when they feel the need to do so in the light of prevailing public health concerns.[36] The authority to determine if the prevailing public health concerns are such that warrant the grant of compulsory license is vested in the issuing state. Thus, a third-party state cannot allege that there are no circumstances in a country justifying the grant of a compulsory license.

The Paragraph 6 decision of the General Council of 30 August 2003 is a waiver of the obligations under paragraph (f) of Article 31 of TRIPS, which provides that a compulsory license or government use of a patent shall be authorised predominantly for the authorising state's domestic market and not for export. Paragraph (h) of Article 31 provides that the patent holder shall be paid adequate remuneration for a compulsory or government use of his patent. Under TRIPS, member states are permitted to issue compulsory licenses or licenses for government use, but such licenses are to be used strictly for their domestic markets. This was criticised as capable of creating hardship on countries with little or no manufacturing capacity. It was because of the need to alleviate this hardship that the paragraph 6 decision was made, creating a waiver of the obligations under TRIPS.[37] The Decision was made by the TRIPS Council in exercise of the mandate given it under the Doha Declaration to find an expeditious solution to the difficulties countries with little or no manufacturing power might encounter in the use of compulsory licensing under the TRIPS Agreement.[38]

The waiver provided under the said provisions extends to only pharmaceutical products. Pharmaceutical product is defined under the Paragraph 6 Decision as:

> Any patented product, or product manufactured through a patented process, of the pharmaceutical sector needed to address the public

33 Compulsory license as used in this context should be understood to include government use of a patent.

34 Doha Declaration, Paragraph 5.

35 See generally William W Fisher III and Cyrill P Rigamonti, 'The South Africa AIDS Controversy A Case Study in Patent Law and Policy' 2005 Harvard Law School https://cyber.harvard.edu/people/tfisher/South%20Africa.pdf accessed 16 September 2020.

36 Doha Declaration, Paragraph 5(b).

37 Paragraph 6 Decision, Paragraph 2(a) (ii).

38 Doha Declaration, Paragraph 6.

health problems as recognized in paragraph 1 of the Declaration. It is understood that active ingredients necessary for its manufacture and diagnostic kits needed for its use would be included.[39]

The right to utilise the provisions of the decision is reserved for any least developed country (LDC) that seeks to import pharmaceutical product and any other country that notifies the TRIPS Council of its intention to import pharmaceutical products under the decision.[40] This provision benefits LDCs and developing countries that generally lack the capacity to manufacture pharmaceutical products and even active pharmaceutical ingredients.[41] A country may opt to produce and export pharmaceutical products to an importing state under the provisions of the Decision.

Certain conditions are expected to be fulfilled by countries intending to produce any pharmaceutical product for exportation. It is required that the TRIPS Council is notified by the importing country of its intention to import a pharmaceutical product from an exporting country and the notification must state the following:

i The name and expected quantities of the pharmaceutical product sought to be imported;
ii Establish, where it is not a least developed country, that it has insufficient or no manufacturing capacities in the pharmaceutical sector for the product it seeks to import under the Decision;
iii Confirm that, in the case of a product patented in its territory, it has granted or intends to grant a compulsory licence in accordance with Article 31 of the TRIPS Agreement and the provisions of this Decision.[42]

It is a prerequisite of the Paragraph 6 Decision that the exporting country also issues a compulsory license in its own country to the extent necessary for it to be able to produce and export the same. It is when this is done that its obligations under Article 31(f) may be waived. Such a compulsory license should contain the following conditions in accordance with the Decision:

i that only the quantity necessary to meet the needs of the eligible importing country will be manufactured under the license, and all the products manufactured under the license will be exported to the importing country which has notified the TRIPS Council of its need for the product;
ii That the products produced under the licence will be clearly identified as being produced under the system set out in the Decision through specific labelling or marking and that the suppliers of the product will take

39 Paragraph 6 Decision, Paragraph 1.
40 Paragraph 6 Decision, Paragraph 1 (b).
41 Carlos M Correa, 'Will the Amendment to the TRIPS Agreement Enhance Access to Medicine?' (2019) *South Centre, Policy Brief* 57, 2.
42 Paragraph 6 Decision, Paragraph 2 (a) (i–iii).

special steps for the special packaging, provided that such distinguished packaging is feasible and does not have a significant impact on the price and;

iii That the following information must be posted on a website before shipment begins: the quantities being supplied to each destination and the distinguishing features of the products.[43]

When an exporting country grants a compulsory license, it is also required to notify the TRIPS Council and such notification should include general information such as the name and address of the licensee, the product in respect of which the license is granted, the quantities to be produced under the license, the country to which the products are to be exported and the duration of the license and the website that contains information of the products produced under the license.[44]

It is expected that where a compulsory license is granted in an exporting country, adequate remuneration will be paid to the patentee in accordance with Article 31(h) of TRIPS, while, where the license is granted for the same product in an importing country, the obligation under Article 31(h) may be waived in respect of the product, where remuneration has been paid in the exporting country.[45] Importing states are also expected to take reasonable measures proportionate to their administrative capacities to prevent a trade diversion and re-exportation of pharmaceutical products that have been imported into their country. This is to ensure that the public health purposes for which such drugs are imported are achieved.[46] The further flexibilities and waivers granted by the Decision do not prejudice the other obligations provided for under TRIPS, [47] and it is also 'without prejudice to the extent to which pharmaceutical products produced under a compulsory licence can be exported under the present provisions of Article 31(f) of the TRIPS Agreement'.[48]

TRIPS and the Nigerian law on compulsory license and government use of patent

In accordance with Article 27 of TRIPS, pharmaceutical products as well as processes are patentable under the Nigerian Patent and Designs Act.[49] TRIPS vests certain exclusive rights on the patent holder, including the right to prevent third parties from making, using, offering for sale or importing

43 Paragraph 6 Decision, Paragraph 2 (b) (i–iii).
44 Paragraph 6 Decision, Paragraph 2(c).
45 Paragraph 6 Decision, Paragraph 3.
46 Paragraph 6 Decision, Paragraph 4.
47 Paragraph 6 Decision, Paragraph 9.
48 Paragraph 6 Decision, Paragraph 9.
49 Patents and Designs Act, section 3(3).

for the aforementioned purposes the product; in the case of a product patent. A patent holder also has the right to prevent third parties from using the process and from using, offering for sale, selling, or importing for the aforementioned purposes the product obtained directly from the patented process.[50]

The same bundle of rights are conferred on a patent holder in Nigeria by the PDA, which provides that in respect of a product patent, a patentee shall have the right to restrain the doing of the following acts; the making of the product, importing, selling or using the product, or stocking it for the purpose of sale or use.[51] In the case of a process patent, it includes the right to restrain anybody from applying the process, or making, importing, selling or using a product derived by means of the process.[52] The patent subsists for 20 years from the date of the filling of the patent application.[53] This is also the case under TRIPS. In terms of the rights conferred on a patentee and the duration of those rights, the Nigerian patent law is in harmony with TRIPS.

Compulsory license means government authorisation granted to a person other than the patentee or right holder to reproduce a patented product or to use a patented process.[54] TRIPS makes provisions for compulsory licenses and government use of patent. The PDA also makes extensive provisions for the issuance of a compulsory license and government use of patent. The extent to which the Nigerian law accommodates the use of TRIPS flexibilities to enhance access to essential drugs will be examined.

Sometimes, the issuance of a compulsory license by the government or government use of a patent could be prejudicial to the interest of a patentee. Yet, the exercise of this right by the government is permitted by law and recognised in international instruments such as TRIPS and the Doha Declaration, as essential for balancing private and public interests; in this case, furthering and enhancing access to medicine as a safeguard of public health.

Article 31 of TRIPS provides for compulsory licenses and government use of patent. It sets out principles that should guide any state that chooses to exercise its right to use a patent or issue a compulsory license. The first consideration is that an authorisation for government use or compulsory license must be considered on its individual merit.[55] Government use or a compulsory license may be issued where a voluntary license has been denied by the patent holder. That is, where efforts have been made by the proposed user to obtain a license from the right holder on reasonable commercial

50 TRIPS, Article 28(1) (b).

51 Patents and Designs Act, section 6(1) (a).

52 Patents and Design Act, section 6(1) (b).

53 Patents and Designs Act, section 7(1).

54 Y Shao, 'A Practical Way to Improve Access to Essential Medicines against Major Infectious Diseases' (2013) 57, 58.

55 TRIPS, Article 31(a).

terms and conditions and such efforts have been unsuccessful within a reasonable period of time.[56] A state can grant a compulsory license or use a patent without first attempting to obtain a voluntary license in the case of a national emergency, other circumstances of extreme urgency, or in cases of public non-commercial use. However, it is a requirement of TRIPS that the right holder be notified as soon as practicable.[57] To ensure that the use of compulsory licenses by states is not hindered, it is provided that where a state alleges that there is no national emergency or case of extreme urgency necessitating the use of a patent by a state, the burden shall be on that state to prove its assertion and not on the state that has issued the license to justify its use.[58] This provision is significant as it grants wide discretion and opportunity for a state to utilise TRIPS flexibilities in order to protect the public health of its citizens. A compulsory license or government use of a patent should be non-exclusive and its scope and duration is to be limited to the purpose for which it was authorised.

The provisions of TRIPS are broad enough to permit the unilateral grant of a compulsory license by a government authority with or without a referral to a judicial body for determination. However, there remains a right for the challenge of the legal validity of the grant of a compulsory license or a government use of a patent.[59] TRIPS does not provide for a retroactive grant of a compulsory license. It requires a state to first issue a compulsory license before exploiting a patent, this will be contrasted with the Nigerian position.

Compulsory license and government use of patent under the Nigerian patents and designs act

The use of patents for the services of government agencies and the grant of compulsory licenses are recognised by the PDA. Elaborate provisions are made under the Nigerian law for the issuance of a compulsory license and the use of patent for the services of government agencies. The provisions of the PDA are wider than that under TRIPS, such that it raises the question of compliance with TRIPS. The Nigerian law makes a distinction between government use and a compulsory license, as the processes of obtaining both vary under the law. A compulsory license can only be granted by the courts in Nigeria upon the application of a person who asserts that:

- i the patented version capable of being worked in Nigeria, has not been so worked;
- ii the extent to which it has been worked, or is being worked in Nigeria does not meet on reasonable terms the demand for the product;

56 TRIPS, Article 31(b).
57 TRIPS, Article 31 (b).
58 Doha Declaration, Paragraph 5(c).
59 TRIPS, Article 31(i).

iii the working of the patented invention is being hindered by the importation of the patented article; and
iv by reason of the patentee's refusal to grant a voluntary license on reasonable grounds, the establishment or development of industrial and commercial activities in Nigeria is unfairly and substantially prejudiced.[60]

A person who applies for the grant of a compulsory license in Nigeria must establish any of the facts in paragraphs i to iii, in addition to the last fact in paragraph iv. An application for a compulsory license will not be granted by the court unless the applicant establishes that he has requested a contractual license but has been unable to obtain the license within a reasonable time and on reasonable terms.[61] It is also required that the applicant satisfies the court that he will work the invention in respect of which a compulsory license is sought, sufficiently to remedy the deficiencies or satisfy the requirements upon which his application for the grant of a compulsory license is based. An application for the grant of a compulsory license can only be made at any time after the expiration of four years after the filing of a patent application or three years after the grant of a patent, whichever last expires.[62] The essence of this provision is to enable the patentee reap exclusively the dividend of his research and innovation for a period of time. A grant of compulsory license may be made before the expiration of the stipulated time in certain cases. The PDA provides as follows:

> The Minister by order in the Federal Gazette may provide that, for certain patented products and processes (or for certain categories thereof) declared by the order to be of vital importance for the defence or the economy of Nigeria or for public health, compulsory licences may be granted before the expiration of the period mentioned in paragraph 1 above and may permit importation.[63]

This provision, therefore, gives room for a compulsory license to be granted even before the expiration of four years after the period of filing or three years after the grant of a patent, depending on the period which first expires, to entertain emergency situations such as defence, the economy of Nigeria or the public health of Nigerians. The minister referred to in this provision is the Minister of Industry, Trade and Investment.[64]

60 Patents and Designs Act, Paragraph 1 of the First Schedule.
61 Patent and Designs Act, Paragraph 5 (a) of the First Schedule.
62 Patent and Designs Act, Paragraph 5 (a) of the First Schedule.
63 Patent and Designs Act, Paragraph 13 of the First Schedule.
64 Note the use of the definite article 'The', this supposes that 'The Minister' in question is the minister in charge of Industry, Trade and Investment (the Trademarks, Patent and Designs Registry is domiciled under the commercial department of the Ministry of Industry, Trade and Investment). This should be compared with the provisions of

TRIPS does not stipulate any time frame within which a compulsory license can be granted. It can be granted at any time when the factors justifying its grant exists. TRIPS also requires that a compulsory license and even government use of a patent should be granted only where attempts to obtain same on reasonable commercial grounds and terms have been unsuccessful.[65] However, as earlier stated, a compulsory license or license for government use may be granted where there are prevailing circumstances such as a national emergency, cases of extreme urgency or in cases of public non-commercial use, obviating the need to attempt obtaining a voluntary license first.[66] When the court grants a compulsory license, it could leave the parties to agree on the terms, where the parties are unable to reach the terms, the court will fix the terms of the grant, including adequate royalties to be paid.[67]

The representative of the Minister of Industry, Trade and Investment Minister of Trade has a right to be heard in a hearing for an application for a grant of compulsory license.[68] The implication of recognising the right of the Minister to be heard is that his position will be instrumental to the consideration of the court in granting or refusing to grant a compulsory license.

Government use of patent under the patents and designs act

The PDA provides that where a minister is satisfied that it is in the interest of the public, he/she may authorise any person to purchase, make, exercise or vend any patented article or invention for the service of a government agency in the Federal Republic of Nigeria.[69] This refers to government use of patent. The powers of a Minister to authorise the use of patent are very wide under the Nigerian law and can be exercised:

- i before or after the relevant patent has been granted;
- ii before or after the doing of the act in respect of which the authority is given; and
- iii to any person whether or not he is authorised directly or indirectly by the patentee to make, use, exercise or vend the relevant article or invention.[70]

The power to authorise government use of any patent registered in Nigeria can be exercised by a minister either before the doing of the acts or after the

Paragraph 15 and 16 of the First Schedule where 'a Minister' is used to indicate that any Minister could exercise the authority provided for in those Paragraphs. See Paragraph 23 of the First Schedule where Minister was defined.

65 TRIPS, Article 31 (b).
66 TRIPS, Article 31 (b).
67 Patents and Designs Act, Paragraph 8 of the First Schedule.
68 Patents and Designs Act, Paragraph 12 of the First Schedule.
69 Patents and Designs Act, Paragraph 15 of the First Schedule.
70 Patents and Designs Act, Paragraph 16 of the First Schedule.

act (which would ordinarily be an infringement of patent) has been done to validate the acts and bring them within the purview of government use. Government could also use a patent where it considers that it would be in the interest of the public to do so, before the patent itself is granted to an applicant. An authority given by a minister for the use of a patent for government use would absolve any authorised person from liability and from the payment of royalty. Accordingly, the following persons are deemed to be exempted from liability for government use of a patent:

- i the government;
- ii any person authorised by a minister in exercise of the power to permit government use;
- iii any supplier of the government or of any such person; and
- iv any agent of any supplier.[71]

From the foregoing, persons who directly or indirectly do acts which would ordinarily constitute an infringement of patent would be protected under government use of the patent if their acts can be shown to be of some benefit to the government, even if they were not expressly authorised to do the act. Consequently, an agent of a supplier who infringes patent rights would be held to be protected by government use, if he can prove that his actions were done in execution of his obligations to the government or the supplier of a government.

The instances in which a minister may authorise the use of a patent are very wide, so much so that in virtually any situation, the power can be invoked. The authority to issue a license for government use can be exercised if any minister considers it to be in the public interest to do so.[72] This power may also be exercised in a period of emergency in relation to a patented article or invention by a minister for any purpose that appears to the minister necessary or expedient:

- i for the maintenance of supplies and services essential to the life of the community[73]; or
- ii for securing a sufficiency of supplies and services essential to the well-being of the community[74]; or
- iii generally, for ensuring that the whole resources of the community are available for use, and are used, in a manner best calculated to serve the interests of the community.[75]

71 Patents and Designs Act, Paragraph 17 of the First Schedule.
72 Patents and Designs Act, Paragraph 15 of the First Schedule.
73 Patents and Designs Act, Paragraph 20 (b) of the First Schedule.
74 Patents and Designs Act, Paragraph 20 (c) of the First Schedule.
75 Patents and Designs Act, Paragraph 20 (f) of the First Schedule.

The law recognised patented articles to include pharmaceutical products such as drugs, [76] and any 'plant, machinery or apparatus, whether fixed to the land or not after importation, patented under the law of a country other than Nigeria'.[77] This definition is broad enough to include machines and equipment used in the delivery of healthcare services. This provision can support the replication of patented radiotherapy machines, to improve access to cancer treatments. Thus, the provisions of the law can be utilised to enhance access to essential medicine and healthcare services.

A minister of the federal cabinet or any commissioner of any state in Nigeria can grant a valid license for government use of a patent. The use must however be for the benefit of a 'government agency in the Federal Republic'. Government agency has been defined as 'any Federal or State Ministry or department of government and includes:

i a voluntary agency hospital, that is, a hospital in Nigeria (not being a hospital operated by the government) that is wholly or partly maintained by the Federation or a State by way of grant in aid or otherwise;
ii a local authority, that is to say, any administration, council or other authority exercising limited governmental powers in a defined area within a State;
iii a statutory corporation, that is to say, a body corporate directly established by law to which in the performance of its functions the Government or a Minister is empowered by law to give directions; and
iv Any company that is owned or controlled by the Government.[78]

Federal Republic is defined as the Federal Republic of Nigeria and includes any of the states of the federation,[79] while 'government' means the Federal Government of Nigeria and includes the governor of any state of the federation.

The power to issue an authorisation for government use of patent is very wide under the Nigeria law. For instance, if a Commissioner for Health of Lagos State decides to issue authorisation for the generic production of a patented cancer drug for the treatment of patients at the Lagos State University Teaching Hospital, it would amount to a valid exercise of that authority for several reasons. First, he is a minister within the contemplation of the law. Second, it is for the purpose of securing a sufficiency of supplies essential for the well-being of the community. Third, it is for the use of the state hospital that is a statutory corporation. Fourth, the drug in respect of which authority for government use was given is a patented article.

76 Patents and Designs Act, Paragraph 23 (a) of the First Schedule.
77 Patents and Designs Act, Paragraph 23(b) of the First Schedule.
78 Patents and Designs Act, Paragraph 23 of the First Schedule.
79 Patents and Designs Act, Paragraph 23(b) of the First Schedule.

The broad provisions of the Nigerian law on who may exercise the power to authorise the use of a patent for government use does not offend against TRIPS. However, it would be ideal to put in place some checks to avoid abuse. There is no requirement on the part of the minister to notify the Registrar of Patents about an authorisation for government use of patent, but there is an obligation under the law for a minister who issues authorisation for the use of patent for government use to notify the patentee of the extent of the authorised use of his patent upon the request of the patentee.[80] However, the duty to furnish the patentee information of the extent of the usage of his patent may be waived by the minister if it appears that it would be contrary to public interest to do so.[81] This is clearly contrary to Article 31(b) of TRIPS, which requires that a right holder whose patent is the subject of a compulsory license or government use should be notified as soon as it is practicable.

The use of compulsory license in Nigeria

To lay a proper foundation for the appraisal of the use of the flexibilities provided under TRIPS, it is essential to briefly describe the development of the Nigeria's Patent law. The Patents Ordinance of 1916,[82] which was essentially a law that provided for the reregistration of the United Kingdom Patents in Nigeria, was applicable to Nigeria until the Registration of United Kingdom Patents Ordinance 1925[83] replaced it.[84] Under the Registration of United Kingdom Patents Ordinance, no provision was made for the grant of a compulsory license or for government use of patent. Thus, the Nigerian Government unlike its United Kingdom counterpart lacked authority to issue compulsory licenses. This came to the fore in the case of *Rhone Poulenc and anor v Lodeka Pharmacy*.[85] In that case, the defendant had supplied the Federal Ministry of Health with a drug whose patent was held by the plaintiff, when the defendant attempted to make further supplies, the plaintiff sought an injunction restraining the defendant from infringing its patent. The defendant relied on government use of patent provided for by section 46(1) of the UK Patent Act 1949, but the court held that the provisions of section 46(1) of the UK Patent Act 1949 did not extend to Nigeria and the rights could not be exercised by the Nigerian government.[86] The Nigerian

80 Patents and Designs Act, Paragraph 18 of the First Schedule.
81 Patents and Designs Act, Paragraph 18 of the First Schedule.
82 No 30 of 1916, Cap 141, Laws of Nigeria.
83 No 6 of 1925, Cap 182, 1958 Laws of Nigeria and Lagos.
84 Bankole Sodipo, *Piracy and Counterfeiting: GATT TRIPS and Developing Countries* (Kluwer Law International 1997) 33.
85 (1965) LLR9.
86 A similar case occurred in Ghana; *Rhone Poulenc SA V The Ghanaian National Corporation* [1972] 2 GLR 109. The Ghanaian court also held that the Ghanaian Government could not issue a compulsory license under its laws, which merely provided for the reregistration of UK patent in Ghana.

government responded by enacting the Patents Rights (Limitation) Act of 1968, which empowered it to grant compulsory licenses. Shortly after the decision in *Rhone Poulenc and anor v Lodeka Pharmacy*, the provisions of the Patents Rights (Limitation) Act 1968 were tested in *Welcome Foundation Ltd v Lodeka Pharmacy Ltd & Kayode Fashina*.[87] In that case, the plaintiff contested the validity of the exercise of the right to authorise government use of a patent by the Commissioner for Health of the defunct Northern Nigeria, on the basis that the power was not exercised in strict compliance with the law. Rather than issue, the defendants with a letter of authority to use the plaintiff's patent for the benefit of the government, the Commissioner issue a letter of exemption from liability for patent infringement, to the defendants. The court in its judgment agreed with the submissions of the plaintiff that the Commissioner had not strictly complied with the directive of the statute in authorising government use of a patent. However, it held that to insist that such irregularity nullified the authorisation granted would work great hardship on the defendants. The Patents and Designs Act 1970 is the extant law governing patents in Nigeria.[88]

Nigeria's HIV burden, its unsustainable donor funding, the HIV funding gap and its growing cancer burden, indicate that the time is ripe for the use of compulsory licenses and the authorisation of government use of patents in Nigeria. This will provide easy access to much needed drugs that are unaffordable by many Nigerians. In view of Nigeria's historic background in relation to the patent system and the right to issue compulsory licenses and authorise government use of patents, it is astonishing that since the enactment of the PDA, Nigeria is yet to issue a compulsory license to enhance access to essential drugs. States of the federation have a responsibility to develop policies to safeguard the health of their citizens. It is not a duty to be abandoned for the federal government alone. Abia, Taraba, Benue, Enugu, Anambra, Akwa Ibom and Rivers State have the highest prevalence of HIV in Nigeria.[89] The government of these states, working closely with the Federal and State Ministries of Health may issue a compulsory license or authorise government use of patent to improve the availability of antiretroviral drugs and cancer drugs within their states.

Challenges to the deployment of TRIPS flexibilities

One of the challenges which the issuance of a compulsory license/government use of patents may pose, is that, while access to certain essential drugs may be enhanced, it could also hinder access to other essential drugs. The case of

87 (1971) All NLR 536.

88 It is contained in Cap P2 of the Laws of the Federation of Nigeria (LFN) 2004.

89 National Agency for the Control of AIDS (NACA), 'Revised National HIV and AIDS Strategic Framework 2019–2021: Future Directions for the HIV AIDS Response in Nigeria' 12.

Thailand illustrates this. In November 2006, Thailand granted a compulsory license to the Government Pharmaceutical Organisation to manufacture generic versions of HIV/AIDS drug efavirenz, whose patent was held by the pharmaceutical company Merck in Thailand until the year 2011.[90] The government also authorised the importation of generic versions of the drug from India. The Thai government in defence of its actions stated that the compulsory license would reduce the cost of providing treatment to patients under Thai's Universal HIV/AIDS treatment Scheme.[91] In January 2007, Thailand also issued a compulsory license for the HIV/AIDS drug, Kaletra patented by Abbott, Plavix, a heart disease medication manufactured by Sanofi-Aventis and marketed by Bristol-Myers Squibb.[92] In response to the government's compulsory license, Abbott's spokeswoman was quoted as saying 'Thailand has chosen to break patents on numerous medicines, ignoring the patent system. As such, we've elected not to introduce new medicines there'.[93] Abbott withdrew applications for the registration of some of its new drugs and stated that the withdrawal of its applications was warranted by Bangkok's disrespect for western companies' intellectual property'.[94] Dirk van Eeden, Abbott's public affairs director further stated that '[a]ctions that don't respect patents make it difficult to justify bringing forward new medicines in Thailand'.[95] The compulsory license granted by Thailand, therefore, had the negative effect of robbing the country of the opportunity of having seven other drugs that would have been beneficial to it, if patented in the country.

Before the advent of TRIPS, Abbott's refusal to patent its new drugs in Thailand would not have posed any problem as the generic versions could easily be gotten from countries such as India and Brazil, but since the advent of TRIPS, there exists only a restricted window for the generic production and export of patented drugs. The stringent rules under TRIPS

90 International Centre for Trade and Sustainable Development, 'Thailand Issues Compulsory License for Patented AIDS Drug' (2006) 2(42) *Bridges* https://ictsd.org/bridges-news/bridges/news/thailand-issues-compulsory-license-for-patented-aids--drugs accessed 5 August 2020.

91 Ibid.

Thai government argued that the cost of providing treatment using Merck's drug efavirenz costs 1,500 bahts (USD 41) in a month, while India's generic efavirenz would cost half almost half of that at 800 bahts (USD 22).

92 Darren Schuettler, 'Angered U.S Firm Excludes Thailand from New Drugs' *Reuters* (Bangkok, 14 March 2007) https://www.reuters.com/article/us-thailand-drugs-abbott/angered-u-s-firm-excludes-thailand-from-new-drugs-idUSBKK27714620070314 accessed 5 August 2020.

93 Thomas Fuller, Thailand Takes on Drug Industry, and May be Winning' *The New York Times* (11 April 2007) https://www.nytimes.com/2007/04/11/world/asia/11iht-pharma.4.5240049.html accessed 5 August 2020.

94 Amy Kazmin and Andrew Jack, 'Abbott Pulls New HIV Drug in Thailand' *Financial Times* (Bangkok, 13 March 2007) https://www.ft.com/content/5a5a88c2-d1a6-11db-b921-000b5df10621 accessed 5 August 2020.

95 Kazmin and Jack (n 94).

flexibilities, and the need to comply with the legal requirements of both the exporting and importing countries could make the process cumbersome.[96] Nonetheless, TRIPS flexibilities can still be positively exploited to enhance access to drugs even when a pharmaceutical company refuses to patent a new drug in a country in protest of its issuance of a compulsory license. The approval and cooperation of the country from which drugs are sought to be imported, must be gotten and the TRIPS Council will need to be notified under Paragraph 2(a) of Paragraph 6 Decision.[97] The challenge this option presents are that it could take a long time to sort out all the paper work and get the necessary approvals and cooperation.

The issuance of a compulsory license may also pith the state which seeks to grant the compulsory license or license for government use against the home country of the patent-holder pharmaceutical company. Some states have resorted to the use of unilateral sanctions and coercion to compel a state to reverse its actions. This has had the ultimate effect of straining diplomatic relations and trade between states. Again, the South African experience[98] and the Thailand case illustrate this. Thailand's actions were in compliance with TRIPS. The United States was displeased and it was reported that the Deputy United States Trade Representative, Karan Bhatia, expressed his government's displeasure over the Thai's government's grant of compulsory license. The United States took further retaliatory steps against Thailand; the Office of the United States Trade Representative (USTR) in its Special 301 Report of 2007, elevated Thailand from its Watch List to its Priority Watch List stating the rationale for that thus:

> Thailand will be elevated to the Priority Watch List in 2007, reflecting a concern that the past year has been characterized by an overall

96 For example, when Canada and Rwanda chose to explore the Paragraph 6 option, it took over two years to finally send the last batch of drugs to Rwanda from the time Rwanda notified the TRIPS Council of its intention to import a generic version of a patented drug. See 'Canada's Intervention to TRIPS Council: Experience Using the System (Apotex -Rwanda Case)' (*Knowledge Ecology International* 31 October 2010) https://www.keionline.org/21413 accessed 25 September 2020.

97 Implementation of Paragraph 6 of the Doha Declaration on the TRIPS Agreement and public health Decision of the General Council of 30 August 2003. General Council WT/L/540 and Corr.1 1 September 2003.

98 In 1997, South Africa amended its Medicines Act 90 of 1997 to make provisions for the manufacture of generic drugs and for the importation of cheaper versions of patented drugs, to meet its national need for antiretroviral drugs. The United States in a reprisal action and in an attempt to protect its national trade interest and that of its industries enacted the US Public Law 105–277 (105th Congress, 1999), which provided that:

> None of the funds appropriated under this heading may be available for assistance for the central Government of the Republic of South Africa, until the Secretary of State reports in writing to the appropriate committees of the Congress on the steps being taken by the United States Government to work with the Government of the Republic of South Africa to negotiate the repeal, suspension, or termination of section 15 (c) of South Africa's Medicines and Related Substances Control Amendment Act No. 90 of 1997.

> deterioration in the protection and enforcement of IPR in Thailand … In addition to these longstanding concerns with deficient IPR protection in Thailand, in late 2006 and early 2007, there were further indications of a weakening of respect for patents, as the Thai Government announced decisions to issue compulsory license for several patented pharmaceutical products. While the United States acknowledges a country's ability to issue such licenses in accordance with WTO rules, the lack of transparency and due process exhibited in Thailand represents a serious concern.

It is worthy of note that the United States in its Special 301 Report of 2007 did not dispute the fact that Thailand's actions were in compliance with the World Trade Organization rules, TRIPS and the Doha Declaration. Its contention is that there was no transparency and due process. However, that was not the case. Thailand's compulsory license steps have been described as 'the first stern test of article 31'.[99] It appears that there is no stopping of Thailand in the optimisation of the flexibilities presented by TRIPS as Thailand has gone further to grant more compulsory licenses and government use of patents. In 2007, Thailand issued a compulsory license for a heart disease drug clopidogrel and in 2008, it issued yet another compulsory license in respect of four anti-cancer drugs.[100]

Another challenge that could militate against its use in Nigeria is the gap between available data that can help in planning and identifying challenges of access to drug, determining disease burden and determining the quantity of drugs needed. The absence of reliable data is a problem, because Paragraph 6 Decision requires that states intending to import generic versions of drugs should state the quantity of drugs needed in the notification to the TRIPS Council. With the dearth of reliable statistics, a country such as Nigeria might have challenges ascertaining the quantity of drugs needed. Nigeria is an aid-dependent country and is a beneficiary of funding from countries such as the United States. It is believed that if Nigeria issues a compulsory license in respect of patents held by indigenous American companies, it may strain Nigeria's diplomatic relations with such countries. It may even result in the withdrawal of foreign funding to Nigeria.

The Nigerian state and its people can learn a thing or two from the Thai experience. The decision of the Thai government to grant a compulsory license was as a result of years of lobbying by civil societies such as Thai Network of People Living with HIV/AIDS (TNP+), AIDS ACCESS

99 Kristina M Lybecker and Elisabeth Fowler, 'Compulsory Licensing in Canada and Thailand: Comparing Regimes to Ensure Legitimate Use of the WTO Rules' (2009) *Journal of Law, Medicine and Ethics* 222, 223.

100 Program on Information Justice and Intellectual property Law (PIJIL), 'Timeline for US-Thailand Compulsory License Dispute' (2009) 3 http://infojustice.org/wp-content/uploads/2012/11/pijip-thailand-timeline.pdf accessed 26 September 2020.

Foundation, Médecins Sans Frontières (MSF), academics, etc.[101] In the wake of Abbott's refusal to register essential medicines in the country, civil societies organised protests demanding that Abbott registers essential drugs manufactured in Thailand. Whether the protests resulted in the subsequent registration of essential drugs in the country is not of much consequence to this research; what is of importance is the fact that Thais are alive to their responsibility and recognise that civil action can influence the development of laws and policies that can enhance public health and access to medicine in a post-TRIPS era.

Conclusion

This chapter discussed the prevalence and funding of two major public health issues in Nigeria, HIV/AIDS and cancer. It examined the right to health and identified the right to access essential medicines as a component of the right to health in Nigeria. It explored how the international and domestic legal framework can be utilised to enhance access to antiretroviral drugs and cancer drugs in Nigeria.

The Nigerian government is encouraged to make optimal use of the international framework and its domestic framework for access to essential medicine to advance the health of Nigerians by ensuring the availability of effective drugs at affordable prices. Nigeria's growing cancer burden, and the number of lives at risk of being cut short by cancer make this imperative. There is no guarantee of continued donor funding for HIV treatment, especially in light of the new Covid-19 pandemic, however, the IP system offers Nigeria an opportunity to assume control and responsibility for its HIV intervention.

The issuance of a compulsory license should be the last resort for Nigeria. First, the government should negotiate with patent owners, so as to work out the production and supply of essential drugs at a more affordable rate. In order to ensure, this is achieved without prejudicing the commercial interest of right holders, incentives such as tax relief, concessions and waivers and the reduction of the cost of running a business, where possible should be given to pharmaceutical industries that manufacture essential drugs. This will make it possible for patent owners to accept a cut in profit, while reducing production and running cost, without operating at a loss. The government can also consider obtaining a voluntary license from right owners on mutually beneficial terms. Where all of these fail, the government may issue a compulsory license. The objective of the flexibilities in TRIPS is not the exploitation of patent holders, but the balancing of private rights and public interests by enhancing access to drugs.

101 Make Medicines Affordable, 'The Campaign for Use of Compulsory Licensing in Thailand' (18 February 2015) makemedicinesaffordable.org/en/the-campaign-for-use-of-compulsory-licensing-in-thailand/ accessed 11 November 2018.

It is also desirable for Nigeria to develop a compulsory license/government use of patent policy for pharmaceutical products. Representatives of the pharmaceutical industry should also be involved in the policy development process. This is an effective way of getting pharmaceutical industries who are the key players in the patent system involved in the use of compulsory licenses. This also has the added advantage of ensuring that a proper balance is struck between the private rights of patents holders and the public interest. It is also important for the Nigerian government to invest in health and place less reliance on donor funding for the health needs of its citizens. The health needs of Nigerians will be better met if Nigeria builds its pharmaceutical manufacturing capacity, because without that, very limited benefit will be derived from the issuance of a compulsory license.

3 Rethinking the Patents and Designs Act in the era of genomic research

Olumayowa O. Adesanya

Introduction

Decades ago, the year 2020 seemed like such a distant vision filled with immense possibilities including the laudable goal of eliminating avoidable blindness.[1] Today, the year 2020 has been marred by the emergence of a global pandemic – the coronavirus disease 2019 (COVID-19) – which has resulted in a global socio-economic and health crisis. Amongst other things, the pandemic has led to a renewed focus on the prospects of genomics.[2] In Australia, for instance, genomic sequencing of the virus has been instrumental in developing public health policies pending the availability of an effective vaccine.[3] Previously, genomic sequencing had been used to trace food poisoning outbreaks as well as the transmission of tuberculosis.[4]

1 The International Agency for the Prevention of Blindness, 'What Is VISION 2020?' (*The International Agency for the Prevention of Blindness*, 2020) https://www.iapb.org/global-initiatives/vision-2020/what-is-vision-2020/ accessed 22 August 2020.

2 Rebecca Rockett, 'Genomic Fingerprinting' Helps Us Trace Coronavirus Outbreaks. What Is It and How Does It Work?' (*The Conversation*, 21 July 2020) https://theconversation.com/genomic-fingerprinting-helps-us-trace-coronavirus-outbreaks-what-is-it-and-how-does-it-work-142917 accessed 22 August 2020.

3 Rockett (n 3); John-Sebastian Eden and others, 'An Emergent Clade of SARS-CoV-2 Linked to Returned Travellers from Iran' (2020) 6(1) *Virus Evolution* https://academic.oup.com/ve/article/6/1/veaa027/5818738 accessed 22 August 2020; R J Rockett and others, 'Revealing COVID-19 Transmission in Australia by SARS-CoV-2 Genome Sequencing and Agent-Based Modeling' (2020) *Nature Medicine* https://www.nature.com/articles/s41591-020-1000-7 accessed 22 August 2020.

4 Rockett (n 3); Qinning Wang and others, 'It Is Not All About Single Nucleotide Polymorphisms: Comparison of Mobile Genetic Elements and Deletions in Listeria *monocytogenes* Genomes Links Cases of Hospital-Acquired Listeriosis to the Environmental Source' (2015) 53 *Journal of Clinical Microbiology* 3492; Elena Martinez and others, 'Whole-Genome Sequencing of Mycobacterium Tuberculosis for Rapid Diagnostics: Feasibility of a Decentralised Model' (2016) 4 *The Lancet Respiratory Medicine* e13; C Thompson and others, 'Epidemiology and Whole Genome Sequencing of an Ongoing Point-Source *Salmonella* Agona Outbreak Associated with Sushi Consumption in Western Sydney, Australia 2015' (2017) 145 *Epidemiology and Infection* 2062.

DOI: 10.4324/9781003250883-5

In itself, genomics refers to 'the study of all of a person's genes (the genome), including interactions of those genes with each other and with the person's environment'.[5] Through genomic sequencing (that is, mapping the exact order genomes in an organism), researchers are able to investigate genetic variations and/or mutations that may impact the development or progression of a disease.[6] This is especially important in the development of improved diagnostics as well as effective therapeutic strategies.[7]

Despite the growing importance of genomic research, it has been noted that less than 2% of the genomes studied globally come from Africans with Caucasian genetic data making up 90% of the available data and samples.[8] This is notwithstanding the fact that Africans are more genetically diverse than all of the other populations in the world combined.[9] This dearth of information is especially problematic because of its potential implications on the availability of medical treatments suited to the genetic compositions of Africans as well as the control of infectious diseases on the continent.[10]

To this end, there has been a growing push for the inclusion of African populations in global genomic research. In Nigeria, examples abound in the activities of the National Reference Laboratory in analysing deoxyribonucleic acid (DNA) from 200,000 blood samples stored in its biobank,[11] the Institute of Human Virology of Nigeria (IHVN) Human Heredity and Health in Africa (H3Africa) Biorepository (I-HAB) initiative aimed at supporting 'multiple H3Africa investigators to conduct high quality genomics and translational research in Africa',[12] and 54gene – a private genetics company

5 National Human Genome Research Institute, 'A Brief Guide to Genomics' (*National Human Genome Research Institute*, 15 August 2020) https://www.genome.gov/about-genomics/fact-sheets/A-Brief-Guide-to-Genomics accessed 22 August 2020.

6 National Human Genome Research Institute (n 6).

7 Ibid.

8 Jonathan Shieber, 'Only 2% of Genomic Material Available for Research Comes from Africa; 54gene Wants to Change That' (*Tech Crunch*, 3 July 2019) https://techcrunch.com/2019/07/02/only-2-of-genomic-material-available-for-research-comes-from-africa-54gene-wants-to-change-that/ accessed 22 August 2020; Amy Maxmen, 'The Next Chapter for African Genomics' (2020) 578 *Nature* 350.

9 S A Tishkoff and others, 'The Genetic Structure and History of Africans and African Americans' (2009) 324 *Science* 1035; Shieber (n 9).

10 Shieber (n 9); Maxmen (n 9); Alison Buckholtz, 'New Nigerian Biobank Advances Africa's Genomic Revolution' (International Finance Corporation, July 2020) https://www.ifc.org/wps/wcm/connect/news_ext_content/ifc_external_corporate_site/news+and+events/news/insights/i14-54gene accessed 22 August 2020; O A Folarin, A N Happi and C T Happi, 'Empowering African Genomics for Infectious Disease Control' (2014) 15 *Genome Biology* https://genomebiology.biomedcentral.com/articles/10.1186/s13059-014-0515-y accessed 22 August 2020.

11 Maxmen (n 9); Buckholtz (n 11).

12 The Human Heredity and Health in Africa, 'Our History' (*The Human Heredity and Health in Africa*) https://h3africa.org/index.php/about/ accessed 22 August 2020; The Human Heredity and Health in Africa, 'IHVN H3 African Biorepository (I-HAB) Initiative' (*The Human Heredity and Health in Africa*) https://h3africa.org/index.php/ihvn-h3-african-biorespository-i-hab-initiative/

established in 2019 with the objective of increasing access to highly curated genomic data from African populations stored in its biobank.[13]

Additionally, there is also the Africa Centre for Infectious Genomics Disease (ACEGID) genomics facility located at Redeemer's University which is aimed at conducting translational genomics-based research on health in Africa.[14] In particular, ACEGID has been instrumental in the genomic sequencing of Ebola[15] and Lassa fever viruses,[16] which have been endemic in Nigeria in the past decade. Currently, it is involved in the fight against COVID-19 having played a significant role in sequencing the whole genome of the first SARS-CoV-2 in Africa from the index case of COVID-19 in Nigeria.[17]

Encouraging as it is for genomic research to be gaining ground in Nigeria, the ethical, legal and social implications associated with such research must not be overlooked if we are to truly enjoy the benefits of such research. This is especially in light of historical exploitation of research participants and African researchers by international health collaborators.[18] Already, a framework has been developed for the ethical conduct of genomic research in Africa.[19] However, another important consideration which must

---

accessed 22 August 2020; O Nnamuchi, 'Biobank/Genomic Research in Nigeria: Examining Relevant Privacy and Confidentiality Frameworks' (2015) 43 *Journal of Law, Medicine and Ethics* 776; T Croxton and others, 'H3Africa Partnerships to Empower Clinical Research Sites to Generate High-Quality Biological Samples' (2020) 9 *African Journal of Laboratory Medicine*; Folarin, Happi and Happi (n 11).

13 Shieber (n 9); Maxmen (n 9); Buckholtz (n 11); 54gene, 'About Us' (*54gene*) https://www.54gene.com/about-us#sub-nav-bar accessed 22 August 2020.

14 African Higher Education Centres of Excellence, 'ACEGID' (*African Higher Education Centres of Excellence*) https://ace.aau.org/ace-1-centers/acegid/ accessed 22 August 2020; Folarin, Happi and Happi (n 11).

15 Munyaradzi Makoni, 'Africa Contributes SARS-CoV-2 Sequencing to COVID-19 Tracking' (*The Scientist*, 30 March 2020) https://www.the-scientist.com/news-opinion/africa-contributes-sars-cov-2-sequencing-to-covid-19-tracking-67348 accessed 22 August 2020; 'Q and A with Fogarty, NIH Grantee Christian Happi, MSc, PhD' (2020) 19 *Global Health Matters* 5; Stephen K Gire and others, 'Genomic Surveillance Elucidates Ebola Virus Origin and Transmission During the 2014 Outbreak (2014) 345 *Science* 1369.

16 K J Siddle and others, 'Genomic Analysis of Lassa Virus during an Increase in Cases in Nigeria in 2018' (2018) 379 *The New England Journal of Medicine* 1745.

17 'Q and A with Fogarty, NIH Grantee Christian Happi, MSc, PhD' (n 16); Paul Oluniyi, 'First African SARS-CoV-2 Genome Sequence from Nigerian COVID-19 Case' (*Virological*, 6 March 2020) https://virological.org/t/first-african-sars-cov-2-genome-sequence-from-nigerian-covid-19-case/421 accessed 22 August 2020; Makoni (n 16).

18 A R Bentley, S Callier and C Rotimi, 'The Emergence of Genomic Research in Africa and New Frameworks for Equity in Biomedical Research' (2019) 29 *Ethnicity and Disease* 179; N S Munung, B M Mayosi, and J de Vries, 'Equity in International Health Research Collaborations in Africa: Perceptions and Expectations of African Researchers' (2017) 12 *PLoS ONE* https://journals.plos.org/plosone/article?id=10.1371/journal.pone.0186237 accessed 22 August 2020.

19 'An Ethics and Governance Framework for Best Practices in Genomic research and Biobanking in Africa' (2017) https://h3africa.org/wp-content/uploads/2018/05/Final-Framework-for-African-genomics-and-biobanking_SC-.pdf accessed 22 August 2020; Clement Adebamowo, African Researchers Weigh in on Ethics of Genomic Research on African

equally not be overlooked is how the resulting inventions are protected and accessed.

Accordingly, this chapter examines the existing legal framework for the protection of inventions in Nigeria – the Patents and Designs Act[20] (the Act or PDA), and considers whether the Act in its current form is poised to deal with the challenges associated with patenting inventions arising from genomics research and indeed the growing field of biotechnology as a whole.

The Nigerian patent system

The earliest patent laws in Nigeria were the Patent Proclamation Ordinances of 1900 and 1902 which applied to the colony of Lagos and Southern Nigeria and the Northern Protectorate, respectively.[21] These were subsequently repealed by the Patent Ordinance of 1916, which in itself was repealed by the Registration of UK Patents Ordinance of 1925.[22] The 1925 Ordinance essentially provided for a re-registration of patents first registered in the United Kingdom in Nigeria.[23]

By 1970, however, a new PDA[24] was enacted which allowed for the grant of patents and designs right in Nigeria without recourse to the United Kingdom patent law.[25] This Act which has never been repealed or amended remains in force in its current form till this day.[26]

Like most patent legislations, the PDA provides that an invention is patentable if it is new, results from inventive activity and is capable of industrial application.[27] Principles and discoveries of a scientific nature are, however, specifically excluded from being categorised as inventions for the purposes of the Act.[28] The Act further provides for two main exceptions

Continent (*National Human Genome Research Institute*, 5 February 2014) https://www.genome.gov/27546350/african-researchers-weigh-in-on-ethics-of-genomic-research-on-african-continent accessed 22 August 2020; Bentley (n 19); A Yakubu and others, 'Model Framework for Governance of Genomic Research and Biobanking in Africa – A Content Description' (2018) 1 *AAS Open Research* https://aasopenresearch.org/articles/1-13/v2 accessed 22 August 2020; P Tindana and others, 'Engaging Research Ethics Committees to Develop an Ethics and Governance Framework for Best Practices in Genomic Research and Biobanking in Africa: The H3Africa Model' (2019) 20 *BMC Medical Ethics* https://bmcmedethics.biomedcentral.com/articles/10.1186/s12910-019-0398-2 accessed 22 August 2020.

20 Cap P2 Laws of the Federation of Nigeria 2004.

21 Adebambo Adewopo, *Intellectual Property Rights in Nigeria: Law and Development* (Nigerian Institute of Advanced Legal Studies, Abuja 2015) 13.

22 Adewopo (n 22) 13.

23 Ibid.

24 Cap P2 Laws of the Federation of Nigeria 2004.

25 Adewopo (n 22) 14; F O Babafemi, *Intellectual Property: The Law and Practice of Copyright, Trademarks, Patents and Industrial Designs in Nigeria* (Justinian Books, Ibadan 2007) 346.

26 Adewopo (n 22) 14; Babafemi (n 26) 346.

27 Patents and Designs Act s 1(1).

28 Patents and Designs Act s 1(5).

to patentability, namely, plant or animal varieties, or essentially biological processes for the production of plants or animals (other than microbiological processes and their products)[29]; and inventions the publication or exploitation of which would be contrary to public order or morality.[30]

With regard to the grant of a patent, patents are generally valid for 20 years.[31] However, by virtue of section 4 of the Act, the Registrar is not required to make inquiries into whether an invention satisfies the patentability requirements in so far as the application satisfies the statutory requirements as to form. In other words, only a formal examination, as opposed to a substantive examination, is contemplated by the Act. It is therefore not unsurprising to note that the Act specifically provides that patents are granted at the risk of applicants without guarantee as to validity.[32]

The absence of a substantive examination process has often been levelled as a criticism against the Act.[33] While it might appear that the rationale for this approach lies in the limited availability of technical capability and infrastructure,[34] it has been argued that the absence of a substantive examination process has the effect of undermining the role of patents in technology transfer and promotion of research and development.[35] This is especially as patents granted in Nigeria may not necessarily reflect the true state of the art.[36]

Patents and genomic research – the Myriad decisions in Australia and the United States of America

For a long time now, the patenting of genetic material and indeed other biological materials has attracted significant controversy globally.[37] This is in part due to ethical objections about the creation of a monopoly over what has been described as our common heritage as humans – the human genome.[38] Other criticisms of gene patenting include concerns about the

29 Patents and Designs Act s 1(4) (a).
30 Patents and Designs Act s 1(4) (b).
31 Patents and Designs Act s 7 (1).
32 Patents and Designs Act s 4(4).
33 Babafemi (n 26) 377–80; Adewopo (n 22) 18, 310.
34 Caroline T Owoseni, 'Recent Developments and Challenges in the Protection of Intellectual Property Rights. New Developments and Challenges in the Protection of Intellectual Property Rights (IPRs) – A Nigerian Perspective' (May 2001) https://www.wipo.int/meetings/en/doc_details.jsp?doc_id=1710 3 [12]; Adewopo (n 22)18.
35 Adewopo (n 22) 18.
36 Ibid.
37 Jacob S Sherkow and Henry T Greely, 'The History of Patenting Genetic Material' (2015) 49 *Annual Review of Genetics* 161.
38 Australian Law Reform Commission, 'Genes and Ingenuity: Gene Patenting and Human Health' (*Australian Law Reform Commission*, 29 June 2004) http://www.alrc.gov.au/publications/report-99 69 [3.39] – [3.40] accessed 28 August 2020; Robert Cook-Deegan, 'Gene Patents' in Mary Crowley (ed), *From Birth to Death and Bench to Clinic: The Hastings Center Bioethics Briefing Book for Journalists, Policymakers, and Campaigns* (The Hastings Center, New York 2008) 69–72.

consequent commodification of life,[39] the potential of patents to increase the cost of healthcare,[40] as well as concerns about the ability of patents to potentially impede research given the resulting monopoly.[41]

Notwithstanding, patents have continued to be an issue for genetic materials. At least, this was the case until recent decisions involving leading molecular diagnostic company – Myriad Genetics in Australia and the United States of America, which appear to have led to a paradigm shift in the assessment of what constitutes an invention/patentable subject matter. As far back as the 1990s, Myriad had received patents in both countries for the BRCA1 and BRCA2 genes, which are crucial in diagnosing early-onset breast and ovarian cancer risk.[42] However, over time, there developed significant public outcry against Myriad's patenting and commercialisation strategy.[43]

In particular, many argued that it was unethical to commercialise the human body and its genetic material by way of patents given the claimed genes were mere 'discoveries' and not 'inventions'.[44] This argument and additional concerns about the impact of Myriad's patents on global biomedical research ultimately led to the validity of Myriad's patents being challenged in both Australia and the United States of America.[45]

In Australia, the claim in dispute was for an isolated nucleic acid that coded for the BRCA1 protein and which contained mutations/polymorphisms indicative of a predisposition to breast and ovarian cancer.[46] Having reviewed the claims, the High Court found that the substance of the claim was genetic information, which was not manmade, but rather discerned.[47] Accordingly, the Court ruled that the claim did not satisfy the 'manner of manufacture' requirement,[48] and was therefore ineligible for patenting. The

39 Australian Law Reform Commission (n 39) 69 [3.41]-[3.46]; Cook-Deegan (n 39).

40 Australian Law Reform Commission (n 39) 69 [3.34]; Cook-Deegan (n 39).

41 Australian Law Reform Commission (n 39) 69 [3.30]; Cook-Deegan (n 39).

42 E R Gold and J Carbone, 'Myriad Genetics: In the Eye of the Policy Storm' (2010) 12 *Genetics in Medicine* S39.

43 Gold and Carbone (n 43).

44 Ibid; Sarah Collerton, 'Legal Fight Over Breast Cancer Gene', (*ABC News*, 8 Jun 2010) https://www.abc.net.au/news/2010-06-08/legal-fight-over-breast-cancer-gene/857620 accessed 28 August 2020.

45 'Myriad Genetics Comes under Legal Fire for Gene Patents' (*Genetic Engineering and Biotechnology News*, 13 May 2009) https://www.genengnews.com/topics/translational-medicine/myriad-genetics-comes-under-legal-fire-for-gene-patents/ accessed 28 August 2020; Gold and Carbone (n 43); Tama Lewin, 'Move to Patent Cancer Gene Is Called Obstacle to Research' (*The New York Times*, 21 May 1996) https://www.nytimes.com/1996/05/21/us/move-to-patent-cancer-gene-is-called-obstacle-to-research.html accessed 28 August 2020; Collerton (n 45).

46 *D'Arcy v Myriad Genetics Inc* (2015) 258 CLR 334.

47 Ibid 339–40 [6].

48 Patents Act 1990 (Cth) s 18(1)(a) provides that an invention is a patentable invention for the purposes of a standard patent if the invention, so far as claimed in any claim is a manner of manufacture within the meaning of section 6 of the *Statute of Monopolies 1623,* 21 Jac 1, c 3.

Court also found that the breadth of the claim was such that, if valid, would have a 'chilling effect upon legitimate innovative activity outside the formal boundaries of the monopoly'.[49]

In the United States of America case, the Supreme Court was requested to resolve the patent eligibility of the isolated BRCA1 and BRCA2 genes under 35 U.S.C. § 101 as well as that of a synthetically created DNA known as complementary deoxyribonucleic acid (cDNA), which had had the introns removed resulting in an exons-only molecule.[50] The Court found that whilst Myriad's principal contribution of discovering the location and genetic sequence of the genes was ground-breaking and took extensive effort to discover, this did not change the fact that it was still a mere discovery.[51] The DNA itself was naturally occurring and isolating it from its surrounding genetic material did not significantly add to the DNA's natural state.[52] Accordingly, it was unanimously held that the isolated DNA was ineligible subject matter. On the other hand, however, the Court held that the cDNA, which was artificially produced was non-naturally occurring and therefore patent-eligible.[53]

The significance of these decisions lies in their representation of the increasing difficulty in distinguishing discoveries from inventions for the purpose of patenting biotechnological inventions in particular. In addition, these decisions also represent an evolving attitude of patent regimes to gene patenting and other emerging technologies, particularly in the biotechnology sector. According to one author, the Myriad decision in the United States of America signals not only the end of the practice of patenting isolated genes or DNA sequences but also possibly the patenting of 'other natural products such as isolated proteins, antibiotics or microRNA sequences'.[54] The author further suggests that while patent laws are territorial in scope, the decision has far-reaching consequences outside of the United States of America such that it could possibly influence the grant of genetic patents in countries such as Canada, Australia and the European Union, which are major commercial partners with the United States of America.[55] This is because of the possibility that these other jurisdictions will likely seek to harmonize their patent laws to some degree 'through different statutory mechanisms (for example, interpretation of the patentability criteria, morality clause) or via judicial interpretation as they have done in the past'.[56]

49 *D'Arcy v Myriad Genetics Inc* (2015) 258 CLR 334, 372 [93]; See also Gordon J's comments at [259]–[264].

50 *Association for Molecular Pathology v Myriad Genetics Inc,* 569 US 576 (2013).

51 Ibid.

52 Ibid.

53 Ibid.

54 Yann Joly and Patricia N Tonin, 'Social, Ethical and Legal Considerations Raised by the Discovery and Patenting of the BRCA1 and BRCA2 Genes' (2014) 33 *New Genetics and Society* 167.

55 Joly and Tonin (n 55).

56 Ibid.

The Myriad decisions and patent practice in Nigeria

It has been suggested that 'the ruling of the Supreme Court of the USA sets an important limit to the commercialization of genomic research in that country, which other jurisdictions are likely to follow'.[57] This would, however, only be possible in countries that provide for substantive examination of patent applications. For countries like Nigeria which only undertake formal examination, it is unclear how the Myriad decisions would immediately influence existing patent practices.

In the absence of substantive examination, it has been remarked that the patent registry in Nigeria mostly rubberstamps foreign patents.[58] Whilst the patent registry does not publish annual statistics on the registration of patents in Nigeria, it has been noted elsewhere that out of a total of 4,048 patents granted between 2009 and 2018, 775 patents were granted to residents and 3,273 to non-residents.[59] Within the same period, out of a total of 2,641 filed patent applications, 461 were filed by residents with the remaining 2,180 filed by non-residents.[60] This indicates a disproportionate number of patent applications filed by local and foreign applicants.

As it stands, it is possible that international biotechnology companies which are unable to patent their inventions in their countries of origin may seek to take advantage of the somewhat lenient patent regime in Nigeria by registering their patents here particularly in light of the developing genomic research landscape. If fundamental research tools are patented, this could be problematic for the continuous development of genomic research in Nigeria. More so as the PDA does not contain specific research/experimental use exemptions. That is not to say the same issues would not arise if the right holders were local. However, it must be understood that with such large biotechnology companies, challenging the validity of such patents or negotiating licences might even be more cumbersome given the inequality in bargaining powers. As has previously been noted, there is evidence of historical exploitation of research participants and African researchers by international health collaborators.[61]

Moreover, irrespective of the country of origin of right holders, it has been noted that perhaps due to the lack of substantive examination, patents are rarely contested in Nigeria.[62] Thus, there has hardly been any case that has truly tested the efficiency of the law especially with regards to patentability.

57 Ibid.

58 Adewopo (n 22) 310.

59 A resident filing refers to an application filed in the country by its own resident; whereas a non-resident filing refers to the one filed by a foreign applicant. 'Statistical country profiles: Nigeria' (World Intellectual Property Organization March 2020) https://www.wipo.int/ipstats/en/statistics/country_profile/profile.jsp?code=NG accessed 28 August 2020.

60 'Statistical country profiles: Nigeria' (n 60).

61 Bentley (n 19), Munung (n 19).

62 Adewopo (n 22) 121.

In the absence of such precedence and up-to-date patent law, it would be difficult for anyone to challenge patents that purportedly encompass principles and discoveries of a scientific nature as is likely to emerge with ongoing genomic research in Nigeria.

Conclusion

For some time now, protecting biotechnology inventions has been identified as an area of concern in Nigeria.[63] Unfortunately, while there is some acknowledgement of the importance of intellectual property in Nigeria, it has been noted that previous attempts to reform patent laws (as exemplified by the Draft Industrial Bill of 1991 and the Nigerian Intellectual Property Commission draft bill of 2007) failed owing to a lack of political will and legislative action.[64]

While some researchers recognise that patentable inventions might emerge from genomic research and biobanking, they seem to dismiss the significance of this by stating that 'these are rare and should not be the focus of benefit sharing discussions'.[65] However, in view of global developments and judicial pronouncements in this field, it is important that researchers reconsider the patent implications of their research.

As local researchers seek to ensure the ethical conduct of genomic research in Nigeria, they must equally consider advocating for a patent law reform that adequately responds to the challenges posed by emerging technologies such as genomics. This is so as to ensure that research is not impeded, and the public can benefit from such research. In any case, as has been noted elsewhere, Nigeria needs new patent law to support the drive towards achieving sustainable economic, industrial and technological development.[66]

63 Owoseni (n 35) 3[9].

64 Adebambo Adewopo, 'According to Intellectual Property: A Pro-Development Vision of the Law and the Nigeria Intellectual Property Law and Policy Reform in the Knowledge Era (5th Inaugural Lecture)' (Nigerian Institute of Advanced Legal Studies, Abuja 2012) 51–3.

65 Yakubu and others (n 20).

66 Adewopo (n 22) 14.

4 Law reform and employee-invention patents in Nigeria

A cue from the United Kingdom

Ayodele A. Adewole

Introduction

Indeed patent law was established to protect the rights of inventors by providing exclusive rights for 20 years.[1] Even though patents are perceived to spur inventive activities, the same might not be said in Nigeria, where the level of technology is low in comparison to other terrains. The focus of this chapter is on employees that are dependent on public or government funds for remuneration. They fall into the category of employees with statutory flavour. The terms and conditions of employment of such employees are regulated by a statute and incorporated into the civil service rules. An employee seeking patent rights in the course of employment is expected to ensure such provision is included in the contract regardless of the fact that such an employee lacks the power or authority to do so.[2]

In a situation where such provision is not included, the court explores the consistency of taking away an invention from the employer with good faith, the obligation of trust and confidence.[3] The imbalance in the position of an employer – employee relationship with regards to inventions is what the Patent and Designs Act (PDA) 1970 tries to balance in these situations.[4]

It is worthy of mention that several scholars have interrogated the relationship between greater incentives and increased inventive activity, some have questioned the generally held notion that inventive activity rises when the monetary benefits for inventing is greater. However, Nigeria has its peculiarities regarding inventions and patent protection. The status of a dependent country due to its consuming rather than producing nature has not helped matters.

1 Catherine Colston, *Principles of Intellectual Property Law* (2nd edn, United Kingdom Cavendish Publishing Ltd 1999) 37.
2 Adejoke O Oyewunmi, *Nigerian Law of Intellectual Property* (University of Lagos Press 2015) 165.
3 Ibid.
4 Cap. P2 Laws of the Federation of Nigeria (LFN) 2004.

DOI: 10.4324/9781003250883-6

This chapter does not seek to repudiate or validate the assertions above; rather it is aimed at highlighting extant provisions of patent law in Nigeria as they relate to employee inventions, in comparison to what is obtainable in the United Kingdom. Reform geared towards providing the required capacity to create incentives for an employee in Nigeria to be inventors for national development is emphasised. The United Kingdom is selected for comparison based on Nigeria's historical past of colonization, the replication of UK laws in Nigeria after independence, and the disparity in the level of technology between both countries.

The patent regime: a perspective from Nigeria

The national framework for patents in Nigeria is comprised in the provisions of the PDA.[5] The Act was enacted in 1970 to make comprehensive provisions for the registration and proprietorship of patents in Nigeria. The PDA makes provisions on inventions that are patentable in Nigeria which include any invention that is either new, results from inventive activity and is capable of industrial application,[6] or constitutes an improvement upon a patented invention and is also new, results from inventive activity and is capable of industrial application.[7] The PDA excludes certain things from the grant of patents. To this end, it stipulates that patents cannot be validly obtained in respect of plant or animal varieties, or essentially biological processes for the production of plants or animals, other than microbiological processes and other products[8]; or inventions whose publication or exploitation would be contrary to public order or morality.[9]

A patent in respect of an invention is a monopoly right that is vested in the statutory inventor[10] and the statutory inventor is the person who is first to file or validly claim a foreign priority for a patent in respect of the invention, irrespective of the fact that he is not the true inventor. Section 2(1) of the PDA provides that the statutory inventor is distinct from the true inventor, though both may be the same. Nonetheless, where the statutory inventor is different from the true inventor, the true inventor is entitled to be named as such in the patent, and this right cannot be modified by contract.[11]

The PDA has provisions on issues when an invention is made in the course of employment or the execution of a contract for the performance of specified work, the right to a patent in the invention is vested either in the employer or in the person who commissioned the work, as the case may be.[12]

5 Ibid.
6 Ibid section 1(1)(a).
7 Ibid section 1(1)(b).
8 Ibid section 1(4)(a).
9 Ibid section 1(4)(b).
10 Ibid section 2(1).
11 Ibid section 2(2).
12 Ibid section 2(4).

The provisions of section 2(4) of the PDA are aimed at ensuring that an inventor who is under a contract of employment is remunerated for bringing about the invention, which is subject to a patent right. The proviso thereto stipulates that an inventor who is an employee is entitled to fair remuneration taking into account his salary and the importance of the invention, and this right to remuneration is not modifiable by contract and is enforceable by civil proceedings. However, is subject to the existence of either of two conditions, which are: (a) the inventor's contract of employment does not require him to exercise any inventive activity but in making the invention, he has used data or means that his employment has put at his disposal; or (b) the invention is of exceptional importance.[13] It is only where either of these two conditions is in existence that the employee may receive any form of remuneration for the invention that he has brought about in the course of his employment.

There are two categories of persons who may be engaged for the purposes of bringing about an invention. They are persons commissioned and persons in employment, and whichever is the case, they are both entitled to be named as the true inventor in relation to a patent application. The rights of employees who are not engaged to bring about inventions are recognised in the Act, even though they do not do so in the course of their employment. Generally, persons in employment are either in private sector or public sector employment. In Nigeria, many research scientists are in the employment of research institutes and universities, most of which are public-funded institutions; and being in such employment makes them public servants. In the case of an employee who is not engaged to bring about an invention but does so, the PDA stipulates that he is entitled to fair compensation, taking into account his salary and the importance of the invention. The key concepts arising from the national framework are discussed below.

The course of employment

The PDA does not define 'the course of employment' in the context of employee inventions. However, according to Gerntholtz, this requirement implies that what occurs before or after the period of employment, cannot create rights for the employer. Consequently, where a contract stipulates that an employee must disclose and assign future inventions in return for a remuneration to be agreed upon, it was held that the clause was void as being a restraint of trade.[14] He added that where an employee invents in the course of his employment so that all rights in the invention belong to the employer, then such rights are not prejudiced by terminating his em-

13 Ibid proviso to section 2(4).

14 R O P Gerntholtz, 'Inventions of Employees' (1968) 1(2) *The Comparative and International Law Journal of Southern Africa* 248, 252 citing the case of *Electric Transmission Ld v Dannenberg* (1949) 66 RPC 183,186.

ployment.[15] It, therefore, means that under Nigerian law the interpretation of the provisions in section 2(4) of the PDA is that all inventions made by an employee during the continuance of his contract of employment belongs to his employer, except the proviso thereto is applicable. The implication is that in any contract of employment where terms are included regarding ownership of inventions, there is no place for restrictive covenants that potentially place ownership of inventions made by the employee after he has left his employment, in the former employer.

Persons in a contract for service

The commissioning of a person to invent means the person is contracted specifically to do so, making the person an independent contractor, rather than having a master/servant relationship with the commissioner. An independent contractor under Nigerian law is not bound generally to obey such orders as his employer may from time to time give. However, the independent contractor is free to act as deemed fit within the terms of the contract.[16] Such a person is described as one who undertakes to produce a given result. The actual execution of the work is under the control of the person who provides the work and the contracted merely uses his discretion in the areas that are not specified.[17]

The relationship between the commissioner and the commissioned is a contract for service. The person commissioned is bound by the terms of the agreement between him and the commissioner. The relationship between the person commissioned to bring about an invention and the commissioner is guided by the terms of the agreement between them, and to a large extent, it is regulated by the doctrine to freedom of contract. Because of the nature of the engagement, it is expected that the agreement would require that the rights in the patent would be vested in the commissioner. To avoid doubt, the PDA stipulates that in such a case, 'the right in the invention is vested in the employer or as the case may be, in the person who commissioned the work'. The statutory inventor is the commissioner; the person commissioned has a right to be named in the application being the true inventor. The right of the person commissioned to be named in the patent application cannot be passed on to another; even though it is doubtful that the person commissioned would do such in the absence of duress. In this regard, the PDA limits the parties' right of freedom of contract.

15 Ibid citing *British Celanese Ld v Moncrieff* (1948) 65 RPC 47,168.

16 *Adewunmi v Plastex Ltd* [1986] 3 NWLR (Pt. 32) 767,790 [paras. D – E] per Karibi-Whyte, JSC.

17 Ibid citing *Performing Right Society Ltd. v Mitchell & Booker Palais de Danse Ltd* [1924] 1 KB 702,765 per McCardie, J, referring to Pollock on Torts 12th edn, 79–80.

Persons in a contract of service

A contract of service is any agreement, whether oral or in writing, express or implied, whereby one person agrees to employ another as a worker and that other person agrees to serve the employer as a worker.[18] A servant is a person subject to the command of his master as to the manner in which he shall do his work.[19] A master-servant relationship, therefore, is characterised by the extent of control that the master has over the way and manner that the servant executes his work. In several cases, the employer gives instructions to the employee regarding the work to be done. In relation to an invention, the idea is actually that of the employer rather than the employee. In other situations, the idea may be that of the employee, nevertheless, the employee works under the direction of the employer. In the context of employee inventions under the PDA, they are categorised as persons who are employed to invent and persons who are not employed to invent.

Persons employed to invent

A person who is employed to invent, whether in private or public service, is in a master/servant relationship with his employer. In this case, the main aim of the employment is for the employee to bring about a particular invention. It is also expected in such a situation that the terms of the employment would require the rights in the patent to be vested in the employer. The law is clear that the right in the patent in the employee's invention shall vest in the employer, who is the statutory inventor. The employee's right to be named in the patent application is sacrosanct under the PDA.[20]

Persons not employed to invent

This category refers to persons who are in employment, whether in private or public service, not for purposes of bringing about an invention, but nonetheless do so in the course of their employment. This is also a contract of service in which the terms of the person's employment do not contemplate bringing about an invention; however, such a person brings about an invention during the course of that employment. The PDA also vests the right in a patent over the invention in the employer, who is the statutory inventor. The employee's right to be named in the patent application as the true inventor is also provided for and cannot be contracted away by the parties.[21]

18 *Shena Security Co. Ltd. v Afropak (Nig.) Ltd. & 2 Others* [2008] 18 NWLR (Pt. 1118) 77, 94 [paras. B – C].

19 Ibid.

20 Section 2(4) Cap. P2 Laws of the Federation of Nigeria (LFN) 2004.

21 Ibid.

Invention of exceptional importance

The PDA does not define what an invention of exceptional importance is. There is also a dearth of case law in this area that may assist in better understanding what it connotes. However, a number of indicators may provide the necessary guidance. It may connote the monetary benefit that the employer derives or is expected to derive from the exploitation or licensing of the patent. Reference could be made to the exceptional novelty of the invention that makes it a significant breakthrough in the relevant field of the art to which it belongs.[22]

Fair remuneration

The PDA provides that where an employee who is not engaged for inventive activity does so using the data and means that his employment has put at his disposal, or where the invention is of exceptional importance, the employee is entitled to fair remuneration. What is fair remuneration is not defined in the statute and there is no Nigerian case law. It is, therefore, unclear whether the remuneration ought to be adequate or simply sufficient. There are no parameters for considering fair remuneration under the PDA. However, in the determination of what is 'fair remuneration', the PDA provides that account shall be taken of the employee's salary and the importance of the invention. These two stipulations of the PDA also deserve some in-depth analysis.[23]

In determining a fair remuneration payable to an employee whose contract of employment does not require him to exercise inventive activity, and whose invention is subject to a patent application, the PDA stipulates that the employee's salary is to be taken into consideration. However, the PDA does not state whether the employee is entitled to a percentage of his salary where his invention is subject to a patent application. In the absence of specific provisions detailing how the employee's salary is to affect the determination of what constitutes fair remuneration to the employee, the amount payable to the employee is entirely left to the discretion of the employer. While the issue of the quantum of the employee's entitlement for the invention may be subject to judicial determination, it is doubtful that the employee would be able to successfully maintain an action against his employer in the event that he is aggrieved by the amount paid out by the employer. In such a case, all that the employer needs to plead in his case is that he took account of the employee's salary, and that would effectively absolve the employer of liability.

Assuming that a court feels compelled to intervene in such cases, there is no benchmark set by the PDA for the court to ascertain what is due and payable to the employee under the circumstances. Consequently, if the court were to intervene then it would do so also applying judicial discretion in the matter. The role of the court in that case would have gone beyond the

22 Ibid.
23 Ibid.

contemplation of the provisions of section 2(4)(b) of the PDA which provides that the right to fair compensation is not modifiable by contract and is enforceable by civil proceedings. What this section envisages is that in any case where the employer either fails or refuses to pay the employee for the invention, then the employee can enforce this right by action.[24]

Another factor that must be considered in arriving at what constitutes fair remuneration to the employee for his invention is the importance of the invention. It is not immediately clear from the statute how to determine the importance of the invention. One of the conditions in which an employee may be entitled to fair remuneration is where the invention is of exceptional importance, that is irrespective of whether the employee was engaged by the employer for inventive activity or not. It is reasonable to conclude that the two are distinct. In the context of the provisions of section 2(4) of the PDA,[25] an invention of exceptional importance refers to the overall utility of the invention to the society as a whole, while in paragraph (a) (ii) of the proviso to section 2(4) of the PDA,[26] the importance of the invention ought to be interpreted to mean the value of the invention to the employer. However, it is not clear how the employer is to determine the importance of the invention, whether the employer is taking into consideration the monetary inflow expected as a result of the invention, or the goodwill and the reputation that accrues to the employer.

The practice in the United Kingdom: the possibility of influence

The law on patents in the United Kingdom is the Patent Act 1977 (as amended) (UKPA). The UKPA allows any person to make an application for a patent either alone or jointly with another person.[27] A patent for an invention may be granted primarily to the inventor[28] or joint inventors[29]; or

24 Ibid.
25 Ibid.
26 Ibid.
27 Section 7(1) United Kingdom Patent Act 1977 (as amended).
28 'Inventor' under the UKPA means the actual deviser of the invention, that is to say the true inventor. Refer to section 7 (3) of the UKPA. In Yeda Research and Development Co. Ltd. v Rhone-Poulenc Rorer International Holdings Inc. (2008) R.P.C. 1 the House of Lords held thus per Lord Hoffman: The inventor is defined in s.7(3) as 'the actual deviser of the invention'. The word 'actual' denotes a contrast with a deemed or pretended deviser of the invention; it means, as Laddie J said in University of Southampton's Application (2005) R.P.C. 11, [39] the natural person who 'came up with the inventive concept'. It is not enough that someone contributed to the claims, because they may include non-patentable integers derived from prior art: see Henry Brothers (Magherafelt) Ltd v Ministry of Defence [1997] R.P.C. 693, 706; [1999] R.P.C. 442. As J Laddie said in the University of Southampton case, the 'contribution must be to the formulation of the inventive concept'. Deciding upon inventorship will therefore involve assessing the evidence adduced by the parties as to the nature of the inventive concept and who contributed to it. In some cases this may be quite complex because the inventive concept is a relationship of discontinuity between the claimed invention and the prior art. Inventors themselves will often not know exactly where it lies.
29 Section 7(2) (a) United Kingdom Patent Act 1977 (as amended).

to any person or persons who is/are entitled to the whole of the property in the invention by reason of any enactment or rule of law, or any foreign law or treaty or international convention, or by virtue of any enforceable term of any agreement entered into with the inventor before the making of the invention.[30]

The inventor or joint inventors have a right to be mentioned as such in any patent granted for the invention, and this right extends to any published application for a patent for the invention, if possible.[31] The applicant for the patent has a duty to file a statement identifying the person or persons whom he believes to be the inventor(s),[32] and where the applicant or applicants is/are not the sole inventor(s) he or they is/are required to file the statement indicating the derivation of his or their right to be granted the patent.[33] Co-ownership of patents, that is where two or more persons are granted a patent, entitles each of them to an equal undivided share in the patent, except otherwise agreed by the co-owners.[34]

An invention that is made by an employee, as between him and his employer, is taken to belong to his employer in any of two circumstances.[35] The first is where the invention is made in the course of the normal duties of the employee or in the course of duties falling outside his normal duties but specifically assigned to him. In either case, the circumstances must be such that an invention is reasonably expected to result from the carrying out of his duties.[36] The second is where the invention is made in the course of the duties of the employee and at the time of making the invention, he had a special obligation to further the interests of the employer's undertaking, by reason of the nature of his duties and the particular responsibilities arising from the nature of his duties.[37] Any other invention is perceived as belonging to the employee[38] and in such cases, nothing is done by the employee or any person acting on his behalf for purposes of pursuing a patent application. Performing or working the invention is to be construed as infringing any copyright or design right to which his employer is entitled in any model or document relating to the invention.[39]

As for inventions made in the course of an employee's duties, it appears that the attitude of the courts is that if an invention is made by an employee during his employer's time and on his employer's premises then it is an indication that it was made in the course of the employee's duties. The fact that

30 Ibid section 7(2)(a).
31 Ibid section 13(1).
32 Ibid section 13(2) (a).
33 Ibid section 13(2) (b).
34 Ibid section 36(1).
35 Ibid section 39(1).
36 Ibid section 39(1) (a).
37 Ibid section 39(1) (b).
38 Ibid section 39(2).
39 Ibid 39(3).

the invention is made during the employee's spare time may not be significant, except that it would depend on what the employee's duties were. In other words, the fact that the invention was made not on the employer's or within the employer's facility does not necessarily render the invention as one made outside the course of the employee's duties.

This principle was stated in *Missing Link Software v Magee*,[40] that if the invention is made in the employer's time and using his materials, the invention is made in the course of the employee's duties. He emphasised that it is generally accepted that if the employee was engaged to make an invention but did some work on it or had some inspiration about it at a time when he was not in the employer's time, for instance, in his own house in the bath, the invention would be deemed to have been made in the course of his employment. In *Greater Glasgow Health Board's Application*,[41]the invention was an optical spacing devise for use with an indirect ophthalmoscope. It was an aid to an ophthalmic examination made by Montgomery, whose duties to his employer as a Registrar in Ophthalmology involved treating patients. He came up with the invention while studying for his examinations at home. In an application at the instance of the employer to be credited with the invention, the Hearing Officer awarded the patent to the employer. However, it was held that Montgomery made the invention in his own time, and not while treating a patient. It was done while he was considering the problem of eye examination generally and he was not acting in the course of his duties as a registrar.[42]

Based on the cases, what is of utmost importance is the nature of the work that the employee was engaged in, juxtaposed with the invention that was made. In a situation where the invention relates to the duties of the employee, then the invention is made in the course of his duties. In *Fireworks Fire Protection Ltd & 1 Other v Andrew Cooke & 1 Other*,[43] the defendant was employed as a senior supervisor, and by his letter of employment his duties were: (a) to carry out works connected with the installation of various fire suppression and detection systems, overall supervision of works both office- and site-based, and liaise with clients; (b) fabrication and installation of bracketry and pipework, pressure vessels and pump units.

The defendant claimed the invention in issue, which relates to a hose reel unit for producing a fine mist or fog of water droplets. The components are located in a cabinet, which could be of the type that is already widely used. After taking evidence, the Comptroller considered the defendant's normal

40 [1989] 1 FSR 361.

41 [1996] RPC 207.

42 Ibid.

43 Intellectual Property Office UK, for the decision of the Comptroller, https://www.ipo.gov.uk accessed on 12 July, 2020. An appeal against the decision was dismissed by the High Court per Arnold J on 3 February, 2014 in 2014 EWHC 125 (Pat). Refer to https://hardwicke.co.uk accessed on 12, July, 2020.

and specially assigned duties and found that the nature of the invention is relevant to the duties being undertaken by the defendant since it relates to a fire suppression system. The Comptroller held, however, that the defendant's duties were not directed to devising new components for fire suppression systems, and as such, the invention was not made in the course of the defendant's duties.

In ascertaining what constitutes the normal duties of the employee, the court considers the contract of employment to determine the exact job schedule that the employee was engaged to perform. The contract of employment, though the most reliable means of proving the employee's normal duties, may not always be conclusive of the fact. Evidence may abound that the employee was engaged in other duties that were not included in his contract of employment, but which duties he performed in the normal course of things, and not necessarily being duties that were specifically assigned to him. English courts had already settled the point that the duties of an employee may evolve over the course of time[44]; and so relying on these principles the United Kingdom Supreme Court (UKSC) overturned a specific finding made by the trial court in *LIFFE Admin v Pinkava* on the normal duties of the employee. In that case, Pinkava was engaged as Manager-Interest Rate and Product Management and about a year thereafter he described his job purpose as being 'jointly responsible for the development of Euronext, LIFFE's interest rate product derivative range'.[45]

On the totality of the evidence, the UKSC found that Pinkava was at all times engaged in seeking to devise a product comparable to a future in respect of credit derivatives such as swaps.[46] The project was ongoing in July 2004 when, as part of it, he attended the 'Futures and Options World' Conference following which he had the creative insight, which led to the inventions.[47] It is, therefore, imperative to consider the employee's progression on the job and the broadening scope of his duties, if any, to properly determine the normal duties that he had at the time of making the invention.

Cases where the invention is made in the course of the duties of the employee and at the time of making the invention, the employee had a special obligation to further the interests of the employer's undertaking, is often applicable to directors of a company who have made inventions while in that capacity. This section was treated in *Harris' Patent*.[48] It was confirmed that section 39(1)(b) of the UKPA imposed a two-stage test noted that the wording of the paragraph, under condition (ii), envisaged that the extent and nature of the 'special obligation to further the interests of the employer's

44 *Armstrong Whitworth Rolls Ltd v Mustard* [1971] All ER 598 and *Carmichael v National Power Plc* [2000] IRLR 43.
45 [2007] 4 All ER 981.
46 Ibid.
47 Ibid.
48 [1985] RPC 2.

undertaking' depends on the status of the employee and the attendant duties and responsibilities of that status. The court concluded that the obligation that Mr. Harris had by reason of the nature of his duties and particular responsibilities was no more than to do the best he could to effect sales of the valves, which the company sold, and to attend to customer's after-sales service of valves supplied. Beyond that he had no special obligation to further the interests of the company's business, and as such Harris' invention did not come within the contemplation of section 39(1)(b) of the UKPA.

In UK law, the employee's entitlement to compensation for an invention that he has made, which belongs to the employer, and for which a patent has been obtained by the employer is preserved. The provisions of the UKPA on compensation for employee inventions relate to two cases, that is where the invention is made by the employee but it belongs to the employer, and where the invention belongs to the employee but has been either assigned to the employer or an exclusive licence under the patent or the application has been granted to the employer.

The question when is an invention of outstanding benefit to the employer was decided in *GEC Avionics Ltd's Patents*.[49] In this case, it was determined that the employee had failed to establish the patent was of outstanding benefit to the employer, who had received substantial orders for equipment not employing the invention well after its merits were known. In *Memco-Med Ltd's Patent*,[50] the word 'outstanding' denoted something special and required the benefit to be more than substantial or good. Even though sales of the products arising from the invention were of great importance to the employer, they were all made for one customer. The claim for compensation failed because the evidence pointed to the fact that the customer's business relationship with the employer would have still been the same whether or not the patents were granted.

Where the conditions in section 40(1) of the UKPA exists, the court or the comptroller may award compensation to the employee for an amount that is determinable under section 41 of the UKPA. However, it is to be noted that sections 40(1) and (2) are inapplicable to the invention of an employee where a relevant collective agreement provides for the payment of compensation in respect of inventions of the same description as that invention to employees.[51] The UKPA has provisions on matters that the court or the comptroller should take into consideration in determining the amount payable to the employee as compensation for the invention. An award of compensation under section 40(1) or (2) shall be such as will secure for the employee a fair share of the benefit which the employer has derived, or may reasonably be expected to derive...[52]

49 [1992] RPC 107, 115.
50 [1992] RPC 403, 414.
51 Section 40(3) United Kingdom Patent Act 1977 (as amended).
52 Section 41(1) United Kingdom Patent Act 1977.

It guarantees the enforcement of any contract relating to inventions made by an employee with the employer, either alone or with another party,[53] or by an employee with some other person at the request of the employer or in pursuance of the employee's contract of employment is guaranteed.[54] Any term in the contract that diminishes the employee's rights in inventions of any description made by him, or the patent for the invention or applications for such patents are unenforceable against the employee to the extent that it diminishes his rights in the invention so made, or the patent for the invention or the application for the patent.[55] However, it does not derogate from any duty of confidentiality owed to his employer by the employee by virtue of any rule of law or otherwise.[56] Significantly, the provisions of the UKPA relating to the enforceability of contracts in respect of employee inventions are applicable to any arrangements made with a Crown employee by or on behalf of the Crown as his employer as it applies to any contract made between an employee and an employer other than the Crown.[57] Persons in the employment of the British Government and its Armed Forces are enabled to equally benefit from the rights that are available under the UKPA, in terms of ownership and compensation for inventions that they generate.

Conclusion: the way forward in Nigeria

Indeed Nigeria can adopt some practices from other jurisdictions on the legal frameworks regulating the treatment of employees and their inventions with a view to reforming the national law. Key areas for reforms in national legislation are proposed: inventor, classification of inventions for purposes of determining ownership rights, remuneration for employee inventions, the scope of the PDA to include inventions made by members of the Armed Forces, and compulsory arbitration in employer-employee disputes on remuneration.

The inventor and the true inventor

The PDA creates a dichotomy between the statutory inventor and the true inventor. The statutory inventor is vested with ownership rights on an invention, even though he may not necessarily be the true inventor. The true inventor, nevertheless, enjoys the moral right of being named in a patent application brought by the statutory inventor in respect of the invention. The natural rights justification for patents emphasises recognition of the true inventor in a way that goes beyond naming him in the patent application,

53 Ibid section 42(1) (a).
54 Ibid section 42(1) (b).
55 Ibid section 42(2).
56 Ibid section 42(3).
57 Ibid section 42(4).

whereas another person described as the statutory inventor is vested with ownership rights in the invention. The patent laws of the other jurisdictions that were examined, notably section 7(3) of the UKPA recognise the individual who invents as the inventor. Patent law in Nigeria requires reform to eliminate the dichotomy between the statutory and true inventor as it perpetuates the common law principles of ownership of employee inventions. The PDA should therefore recognise the true inventor as the inventor, while ownership constitutes another issue altogether.

Joint inventions

The reality of modern inventive activity is that more often than not, inventive activity is undertaken by a team rather than by an individual. Consequently, persons who are employed either with a contract of service or a contract for service usually work in a cluster to bring about an invention. This system brings about a confluence of ideas and efforts and is more likely to result in an invention than where an individual alone is working on an invention. Many jurisdictions recognise joint inventions, and this is evident in the provisions of sections 7(2)(a) and 13(2)(a) of the UKPA. Reform in this direction will encourage collaboration in inventive activity without fear of co-inventors losing any form of moral or economic rights in the invention.

Classification of inventions and ownership

In the classification of inventions in section 2(4) of the PDA for the purposes of making provisions for the ownership of inventions made in different circumstances, the style of legislative drafting adopted in that section is complex. The proviso does not cater for the question on the ownership of inventions made by an employee whose contract of employment does not require him to exercise inventive activity and has not used the data and materials of his employer in bringing about the invention, to necessary implication. Section 2(4) of the PDA further provides that where the inventor is an employee and the invention is of exceptional importance, he is entitled to fair remuneration. The implication of this is that the employer is at liberty to appropriate the ownership of such an invention if he considers it of exceptional importance in consideration of the payment of fair remuneration to the employee.

There is a need through reform to simplify section 2(4) for clarity in expression. The patent laws of some jurisdictions that were examined attempt to classify the different circumstances in which an invention is made by an employee and the ownership rights to such inventions in a much simpler manner as reflected in sections 39(1)(a) and (b) and 39(2) of the UKPA. This type of classification is easier to determine the ownership of the invention. To this end, it is suggested that the PDA be amended to clearly distinguish inventions: (i) devised by persons employed to invent, or specifically assigned to an inventive activity in the course of their duties; (ii) devised by persons not employed to invent, nevertheless do so using the employer's aid, resources and time; and (iii) devised without any connection whatsoever to the inventor's employment duties.

It is suggested respectively that: (i) the invention be wholly and exclusively owned by the employer with the employee named as the inventor; (ii) that the invention be jointly owned by the employer and the employee, except there is an agreement to assign any such invention to the employer on terms agreed in the contract of employment; and (iii) that the invention be wholly and exclusively owned by the employee.

'Course of employment' vs 'course of duties'

In section 2(4) of the PDA, the ownership of an invention made during the course of employment, which has been interpreted in common law to mean during the continuance of a contract of employment belongs to the employer, even though the employee was not engaged to exercise any inventive activity. The scope here is broad regarding inventions that can be brought within the ownership of the employer. Section 39(1) of the UKPA adopts the phrase 'course of the employee's duties', which is narrower in scope and more precise. A consideration of the contract of employment provides clarity as to what exactly constitutes the employee's duties and by extension, whether an invention was made in the course of the employee executing those duties.

There is no evidence to suggest that inventive activity increases where the invention is deemed to belong to the employee but may be assigned to the employer by the contract of employment. The PDA should be amended to make the employer entitled to inventions made by the employee in the course of his normal duties, or duties specifically assigned to him.

Remuneration of employee

The provisions of section 2(4) of the PDA on the remuneration of the employee for his invention stipulate that the employee is entitled to fair remuneration taking into account his salary and the importance of the invention. Where the employee is engaged to exercise inventive activity, he is not entitled to any remuneration over and beyond what he is paid as salary or wages for the employment, even if the invention is of exceptional importance and the employer has derived immense financial benefit from its exploitation. The employee that is not engaged to exercise inventive activity may be entitled to fair remuneration, if the invention is of exceptional importance. The stipulation to determine what is payable to the employee by taking his salary into account has the effect of severely limiting what he may earn as remuneration for the invention. Besides these, another problem with this state of affairs is that there are no parameters set for ascertaining what constitutes an invention of exceptional importance.

The UKPA makes provisions regarding the payment of remuneration to the employee for inventions over and beyond what is paid to the employee as a salary or wage. Significantly, these pieces of legislation stipulate those things that should be considered in ascertaining what is payable to the employee, which generally relates to the financial and other forms of the benefit accruing to the employer from the exploitation of the invention or the patent.

The provisions of the UKPA wherein it is provided that consideration shall be given to the fact it is of outstanding benefit to the employer, and the economic results of the invention to the employer respectively, is suggested for patent law in Nigeria; particularly the provisions of section 41(1) of the UKPA that provides that an award of compensation shall be such to secure a fair share of the benefit which the employer has derived, or reasonably expects to derive from the invention to the employee.

Inventions by persons personnel of the armed forces

The PDA failed to include provisions regulating the treatment of inventions by personnel of the Nigerian Armed Forces, even though the armed forces provide a platform for the exercise of inventive activity. It is imperative to remedy this by amending the law, and it is instructive that all the foreign jurisdiction that is the subject of discussion in this work, make provisions for inventions by members of the military. In Nigeria, provisions can be made in this regard to incentivise military inventors, as a means to share the financial benefits of inventors. The benefits include both moral and economic which are consistent with the rights that abound in relation to patents.

5 Traditional knowledge on the medicinal uses of plants (TKMUP) in Nigeria

Whither the patent system in COVID-19 pandemic

Emeka Polycarp Amechi and Jane Ezirigwe

Introduction: the search for a cure for COVID-19

Coronaviruses are described as a large family of viruses that are known to cause illnesses ranging from the common cold to more severe diseases such as Middle East respiratory syndrome (MERS), severe acute respiratory syndrome (SARS) and now, the coronavirus disease 2019 (COVID-19).[1] COVID-19, which was first identified in Wuhan China, but has now spread throughout the world, has been described as 'the defining global health crisis of our time and the greatest challenge we have faced since World War Two'.[2] Indeed, the novel disease has shown no sign of abatement with confirmed cases worldwide surpassing nine million, as of July, 2020,[3] and continuing to grow. In Africa, where it is not as widespread as other regions, the disease affected 893,365 persons with 18,881 fatalities including Nigeria.[4] However, as aptly pointed out by the United Nations Development Programme (UNDP), the pandemic is much more than a health crisis, but also an unprecedented socio-economic crisis due to the adverse impacts on job security, incomes and tourism.[5] Thus, it is not surprising that the world is racing against time to find a cure for the disease, with scientists pushing forward with efforts to develop treatments to slow the pandemic and lessen the disease's damage.

1 World Health Organisation, 'Coronavirus Disease (COVID-19) Advice for the Public' https://www.who.int/emergencies/diseases/novel-coronavirus-2019/advice-forpublic?gclid=Cj0KCQjwgo_5BR DuARIsADDEntRX3ogXP9CLwdsCvnBu_ycJBYo8rRiN_iBzNY_dp6K72OdcYNbXtjIaAk1tEALw_wcB accessed 28 July 2021.

2 United Nations Development Programme, Covid-19 Pandemic https://www.undp.org/content/undp/en/home/coronavirus.html accessed 28 July 2021.

3 Ibid.

4 African Union, 'Africa CDC: Coronavirus Disease 2019 (COVID-19)' https://africacdc.org/covid-19/ accessed 31 July 2020.

5 It is estimated that 195 million jobs could be lost, with a projection of a US$110 billion decline in remittances this year, which could mean 800 million people will not be able to meet their basic needs. See UNDP 2 above.

DOI: 10.4324/9781003250883-7

Antiviral drugs or vaccines are not available for the treatment. However, more than 150 different drugs are being researched in different countries, with the hope of making a difference for patients both in the near- and mid-term.[6] Three routes are being explored by scientists in this quest vis-à-vis the development of a new vaccine; the development of new drugs by replication of the antibodies that fight the virus and repurposing of existing drugs.[7] The latter involves the use of drugs that are already approved for other conditions or have been tested on other viruses.[8]

The search for the cure is not restricted to the activities occurring in the orthodox medicine field, as practitioners in the traditional medicine field are equally actively involved in the quest. In China, for instance, following the success recorded in the use of traditional Chinese medicine (TCM) in patients during earlier coronavirus outbreaks such as SARS, the government is stimulating the use of TCM herbal formulae in tackling the pandemic, resulting in the use of both conventional medicine and TCM for the treatment of patients with the infection in China.[9] It was reported on 17 February 2020 that 60,107 confirmed COVID-19 patients (85.20% of total confirmed cases) had been treated with TCM.[10] Likewise, clinical trials aiming to evaluate the efficacy and safety of treatments for COVID-19 patients including the exclusive use and joint use of TCM and conventional medicine have been launched in China.[11] This is in addition to the existence of studies identifying anti-novel coronaviral compounds in several TCM herbal extracts or derived compounds.[12]

Nigerian traditional healers and other practitioners in the traditional medicine field albeit without much government support like in China,[13] are

6 James Gallagher, 'Coronavirus Cure: What Progress Are We Making on Treatments?' BBC, 22 July 2020, https://www.bbc.com/news/health-52354520 accessed 31 July 2020

7 Bayer Global, 'How Close Are We to Finding a Treatment for COVID-19?' https://www.magazine.bayer.com/en/how-close-are-we-to-finding-a-treatment-for-covid-19.aspx accessed 31 July 2021.

8 Shawn Radcliffe, 'Here's Exactly Where We Are with Vaccines and Treatments for COVID-19' *Healthline*, 30 July 2020, https://www.healthline.com/health-news/heres-exactly-where-were-at-with-vaccines-and-treatments-for-covid-19 accessed 31 July 2021.

9 Yang Yang, Md Sahidul Islam, Jin Wang, Yuan Li and Xin Chen, 'Traditional Chinese Medicine in the Treatment of Patients Infected with 2019-New Coronavirus (SARS-CoV-2): A Review and Perspective' (2020) 16(10) *International Journal of Biological Sciences* 1708 at 1710 & 17–8.

10 Ibid.

11 Ibid.

12 Ibid. Hussain, Ya-Jia Xie, Dan Li, Shaukat Iqbal Malik, Jin-cai Hou, Elaine Lai-Han Leung & Xing-Xing Fan, 'Current strategies against COVID-19' (2020) 70 *Chinese Medicine* 15.

13 'COVID-19 CURE: FG yet to show interest in our Drug – Iwu' Vanguard, 11 May 2020, https://www.vanguardngr.com/2020/05/covid-19-cure-fg-yet-to-show-interest-in-our-drug-iwu/ accessed 16 August 2020; and News Agency of Nigeria (NAN), 'Oyo Govt, UI Partner with Herbal Practitioners to Find Coronavirus Cure' *Pulse*, 9 May 2020, https://www.pulse.ng/news/local/oyo-govt-ui-partner-with-herbal-practitioners-to-find-coronavirus-cure/2byy5gk.

not left out of the quest to find treatment for the pandemic. There are several claims of the discovery of herbal drugs for the effective management or treatment of the disease by several practitioners within the traditional medicine field.[14] For instance, the Priest-King of Ife, in Osun State has made claims of curing several prominent infected Nigerians using native herbs,[15] and further claimed to have made far-reaching efforts in collaboration with the traditional medicine practitioners in Nigeria, towards finding a cure for COVID-19.[16] Pax Herbal Research and Laboratories, Ewu, Edo State, claimed to have discovered herbal products that can be used for the management of the symptoms of the disease as well as for its treatment.[17] The reported effectiveness of local herbs in the treatment of the disease is further bolstered by the claims of Seyi Makinde, the Governor of Oyo State, that he subjected himself to herbal medicine and was cured after testing positive for the disease.[18] In addition to the activities occurring in the traditional medicine sector, Prof Maurice Iwu, a professor of pharmacognosy, claimed to have invented a drug for the treatment of COVID-19, based on active compounds derived from native medicinal plants.[19] In the midst of these claims, the National Agency for Food and Drug Administration and Control (NAFDAC) has stated that practitioners who claimed to have a

14 Olaronke Alo, 'Coronavirus Treatment: Ooni of Ife, Researchers like Professor Maurice Iwu dey among Nigerians wey claim to get 'Otumokpo' Traditional Herbs to Cure Covid-19 Disease' *BBC Pidgin*, 7 May 2020, accessed https://www.bbc.com/pidgin/tori-52578762 16 August 2021.

15 Alfred Olufemi, 'Ooni of Ife Claims He Has 'Tested' Cure for Coronavirus' *Premium Times*, March 30, 2020, https://www.premiumtimesng.com/news/top-news/384977-ooni-of-ife-claims-he-has-tested-cure-for-coronavirus.html accessed 16 August 2020.

16 Charles Coffie-Gyamfi, 'Traditional Cure for Virus Ready Soon, Says Ooni' *The Guardian* 30 April 2020, https://guardian.ng/news/traditional-cure-for-virus-ready-soon-says-ooni/ accessed 16 August 2020; and Peter Moses, 'Local Cure for COVID-19 at Advanced Stage, Says Ooni' *Daily Trust*, 29 April 2020, https://www.dailytrust.com.ng/local-cure-for-covid-19-at-advanced-stage-says-ooni.html accessed 16 August 2020.

17 Jude Atemanke, 'How a Nigeria-based Catholic Medical Centre Is Responding to COVID-19 Search for Cure' *ACIAfrica*, 2 May 2020, https://www.aciafrica.org/news/1266/how-a-nigeria-based-catholic-medical-centre-is-responding-to-covid-19-search-for-cure accessed 16 August 2020; and Tony Iyare, 'Covid-19: Dusts over NAFDAC Endorsement of Pax Herbal CUGZIN' *National Democratic Report*, 11 July 2020, https://www.ndr.org.ng/covid-19-dusts-over-nafdac-endorsement-of-pax-herbal-cugzin/ accessed 16 August 2020.

18 Chukwuma Muanya, 'Can Carrots, Vitamin C, Black Seed, Honey, Exercise Provide Cure for COVID-19?' *The Guardian*, 9 April 2020, https://guardian.ng/features/can-carrots-vitamin-c-black-seed-honey-exercise-provide-cure-for-covid-19/ accessed 16 August 2020; and Adaku Onyenucheya, 'Seyi Makinde Advocates Local Solutions to COVID-19' *The Guardian*, 15 April 2020, https://guardian.ng/news/seyi-makinde-advocates-local-solutions-to-covid-19/ accessed 16 August 2020.

19 Emmanuel Elebeke, 'We Have Found Cure for Coronavirus — Iwu' *Vanguard*, 2 March 2020, <https://www.vanguardngr.com/2020/03/we-have-found-cure-for-coronavirus-iwu/> accessed 16 August 2020; and Chris Onuoha, 'When We Announced Nigerian Natural Cure 3mths ago, Nobody Listened — Prof Iwu' *Vanguard*, 24 May 2020, https://www.vanguardngr.com/2020/05/when-we-announced-nigerian-natural-cure-3mths-ago-nobody-listened-prof-iwu/ accessed 16 August 2020.

cure for the virus are yet to submit an application to test the efficacy of their drugs.[20] The NAFDAC further stated that the only application received and consequently approved as 'safe to use', was from Pax Herbals for the listing of 'Cugzin capsule 290 mg' as immune boosters and anti-infectives.[21]

Whatever one may make of the claims and counter-claims regarding the efficacy of traditional medicine or medicinal plants to the treatment of COVID-19 in Nigeria, it is apparent from the Chinese examples that traditional medicine has the potential to be utilised for the treatment of the disease. Indeed, after comparing COVID-19 with SARS, MERS and common flu and the effective management practices therefrom, Iqbal *et al.* suggest that medicinal plants could serve as potential ingredients in the development of drug against COVID-19 infection.[22] Similarly, the World Health Organization (WHO) anticipates innovations including traditional medicines and new therapies in the exploration for potential treatments for COVID-19. Medicinal plants such as 'Artemisia annua' are being studied as possible remedies for COVID-19 disease.[23] Such medicinal potential is bound to attract the attention of western biotechnological and pharmaceutical companies who may seek to utilise traditional medicine as a resource for drugs discovery against the virus. This is not surprising as the leads provided by traditional medicines particularly in the form of traditional knowledge on the medicinal uses of plants (TKMUP) serve as a useful source of information for researchers in the pharmaceutical and biotechnological field who seek to identify new chemical and biological elements, as well as new approaches to disease treatment.[24] Most importantly, relying on such

20 Nike Adebowale, 'Nigeria: Claims of COVID-19 Cure Exist Only on Social Media – NAFDAC' *Premium Times*, 14 May 2020, https://allafrica.com/stories/202005140471.html accessed 16 August 2020.

21 NAFDAC also stated that it is currently processing twenty one (21) herbal medicinal products for "Safe to use" or Listing status. See Iyare note 17 above; and Chioma Obinna, 'COVID-19: NAFDAC Processing 21 Herbal Medicinal Products' *Vanguard*, 12 July 2020, https://www.vanguardngr.com/2020/07/covid-19-nafdac-processing-21-herbal-medicinal-products/ accessed 18 August 2020.

22 Rashid Iqbal Khan, Mazhar Abass, Khurram Goraya, Muhammad Zafar-ul-Hye, and Subhan Danish, 'Plant Derived Antiviral Products for Potential Treatment of COVID-19: A Review' (2020) 89 (3) *Phyton-International Journal of Experimental Botany* 438.

23 World Health Organisation Research Office for Africa, 'WHO Supports Scientifically-Proven Traditional Medicine' 4 May 2020, https://www.afro.who.int/news/who-supports-scientifically-proven-traditional-medicine accessed 18 August 2020 ; and World Health Organisation Research Office for Africa, 'WHO, Africa CDC in Joint Push for COVID-19 Traditional Medicine Research in Africa' 22 July 2020, https://www.afro.who.int/news/who-africa-cdc-joint-push-covid-19-traditional-medicine-research-africa accessed 18 August 2020.

24 N P de Carvalho, *'From the Shaman's Hut to the Patent Office: In Search of Effective Protection for Traditional Knowledge'* Paper Presented at the Conference: 'Biodiversity and Biotechnology and the Protection of Traditional Knowledge' April 4–6, 2003, 17, N Roht-Arriaza, 'Of Seeds and Shamans: The Appropriation of the Scientific and Technical Knowledge of Indigenous and Local Communities' (1995–1996) 17 *Michigan Journal of International Law* 919 at 926.

leads usually ensure a higher success ratio in the screening of plants for medicinal purposes.[25]

However, such utilisation has not led to corresponding benefits to indigenous communities either in the form of attribution or compensation.[26] This has made a large number of bio-resources-rich developing countries decry the situation whereby their indigenous communities have been deprived of benefits from the use of their traditional knowledge (TK) which have been monopolised and used by others, mainly multinational corporations without authorisation.[27] Such state of affairs which is mostly manifested in the grant of patents to inventions based on or otherwise derived from indigenous bio-resources and associated TK, has given rise to a phenomenon popularly known as biopiracy.[28] Although the term has been criticised as reflecting more of emotional and rhetorical value,[29] its continuing relevance, as well as juridical significance, lie in the perceived injustice within the global intellectual property (IP) system that it popularly represents – 'the patent claims over biodiversity and [associated] indigenous knowledge that are based on the innovations, creativity and genius of the people of the Third World'.[30]

25 Vandana Shiva, *Patents: Myths and Realities* (Penguin Books, New Delhi, 2001) 52.

26 John Mugabe, *Intellectual Property Protection And Traditional Knowledge: An Exploration in International Policy Discourse* (ACTS Press, Nairobi, 1999) 8, Stephen A Hansen & Justin W Van Fleet, *Traditional Knowledge and Intellectual Property: A Handbook on Issues and Options for Traditional Knowledge Holders in Protecting their Intellectual Property and Maintaining Biological Diversity* (American Association for the Advancement of Science (AAAS) Science and Human Rights Program, Washington DC, July 2003) 5; and Ruth Okediji, 'The International Relations of Intellectual Property: Narratives of Developing Country Participation in the Global Intellectual Property System' (2003) 7 *SJICL* 315, 355.

27 A Chander and M Sunder, 'The Romance of the Public Domain' (2004) 92 *California Law Review* 1331 1350-135.

28 Biopiracy generally refers 'either to the unauthorized commercial use of biological resources and/or associated TK from developing countries or to the patenting of spurious inventions based on such knowledge or resources without compensation'. The term was originally coined as part of a counter-attack strategy on behalf of developing countries, to 'inspire critical perspectives and political activism relating to the role of the IPRs in determining the skewed distribution of benefits from the biotrade…' See Graham Dutfield 'TRIPS-Related Aspects of Traditional Knowledge' (2001) 33 *Case Western Reserve Journal of International Law* 239 at 243–44.

29 Ibid 243–44. Graham Dutfield, 'Disclosure of Origin: Time for a Reality Check?' in Martha Chouchena-Rojas, Manuel Ruiz Muller, David Vivas and Sebastian Winkler (eds.), *Disclosure Requirements: Ensuring mutual Supportiveness between the WTO TRIPS Agreement and the CBD* (IUCN, Gland, Switzerland and Cambridge, UK and ICTSD, Geneva, Switzerland, November 2005) 43 & 44.

30 Vandana Shiva, *Protect or Plunder? Understanding Intellectual Property Rights* (Penguin Books India and Zed Books, 2001) 49. Ikechi Mgbeoji 'Bio-Cultural Knowledge and the Challenges of Intellectual Property Rights Regimes for African Development (2012) 35(2) *Dalhousie Law Journal* 397, 408; Chidi Oguamanam, 'Localizing Intellectual Property in the Globalization Epoch: The Integration of Indigenous Knowledge' (2004) 11(2) *Indiana Journal of Global Legal Studies*135.

The issue of biopiracy would likely increase with the search for a novel treatment for COVID-19. This necessitates that bio-resources-rich developing countries should adopt measures that would strengthen their patent systems to tackle or eliminate biopiracy within their territories. Understandably, biopiracy is global in nature and thus, needs an international approach to be tackled effectively. However, the global patent system as presently structured does not accord recognition to TKMUP and other bio-resources TK, and efforts to change the status quo at multilateral forums such as the World Intellectual Property Organisation (WIPO) and the World Trade Organisation (WTO), have not yielded much result.[31]

This article examines the extent to which the patent system in Nigeria can be used in the protection of its TKMUP against biopiracy in the era of COVID-19. It starts by examining the nature of TKMUP in Nigeria. This is followed by a discussion on the protection that the patent system, as presently structured in Nigeria, can offer to the protection of the knowledge system from biopiracy. It argues that the Nigerian patent system is largely inadequate to protect the knowledge from such misappropriation. This is followed by a discussion on the measures that should be adopted by policymakers towards enhancing the effectiveness of the patent system in preventing the misappropriation of TKMUP in Nigeria. These measures will be based on measures adopted by other biodiversity-rich developing countries in dealing with biopiracy. Finally, the article is concluded with an emphasis on the need for policymakers in Nigeria to muster the adequate political will to adopt appropriate measures for the restructuring of the patent system to protect its TKMUP from biopiracy.

Traditional knowledge on the medicinal uses of plants and the patent system in Nigeria

Patents are granted to protect new inventions or improvements thereon that are considered to have improved the way(s) the earlier inventions were made or used.[32] Granting of patents in Nigeria is regulated by the Patents and Design Act (PDA).[33] The Act which has not undergone much change except

31 Indeed, the role that the IP system can play in the protection of TK has been on the agenda of the World Intellectual Property Organisation (WIPO), and the World Trade Organisation (WTO) for more than 15 years, albeit with little or nothing to show for it. See Surinder Kaur Verma, 'Protecting Traditional Knowledge: Is a Sui Generis System an Answer? (2005) 7/6 *Journal of World Intellectual Property* 765, 778–83; Chidi Oguamanam, 'Patents and Traditional Medicine: Digital Capture, Creative Legal Interventions, and the Dialectics of Knowledge Transformation' (2008) 15(2) *Indiana Journal of Global Legal Studies* 489, 502.

32 F O Babafemi, *Intellectual Property: The Law and Practice of Copyrights, Trade Marks, Patents and Industrial Designs in Nigeria* (Nigeria Justinian Books 2006) 342.

33 Section 4(2) Patents and Designs Act (PDA), Cap P2, Laws of the Federation of Nigeria 2004.

the incorporation of 'few modern nuggets stemming from Nigeria's international treaty obligations',[34] was enacted in 1970 as Decree No 60 of 1970. The Act shares similar provisions which are basic to the nature of a patent with the UK Patents Act of 1949.[35] Similarities between the two legislation are indicative of the fact that the colonial era is reflected still in intellectual property rights regimes in Nigeria and other African countries. This situation might have negative implications on the recognition of TKMUP and other TK dependent on bio-resources as IP in Nigeria. The fact that the Act may not be utilised for the protection of TKMUP as an IP in Nigeria has led to its criticism as a legislation that hardly reflects the industrial needs, cultural attributes and imperatives of Nigeria.[36]

The criteria for patenting inventions is primarily based on western scientific narrative with no regard to other cultural accounts of science thereby leading to the direct exclusion of TKMUP and other non-western scientific narratives.[37] In addition, TKMUP is regarded as not suitable for patent protection as it is usually community property derived from communal effort; is transmitted orally and does not constitute original information as it is generally historical and often incremental information that reside in the public domain.[38] It has been argued based on information in the public domain that the free flow of knowledge from pre-literate to modern societies can be disrupted.

> The public domain may have the unintended effect of congealing TK as "the opposite of property", presenting poor people's knowledge as the raw material of innovation – ancient, static, and natural- rather than as intellectual property – modern, dynamic, scientific, and cultural invention. Under this view, TK holders may receive remuneration for conserving biodiversity and contributing the raw materials of innovation, but they are not recognised as intellectual property holders in their own right.[39]

34 Ikechi Mgbeoji, *Bio-Cultural Knowledge and the Challenges of Intellectual Property Rights Regimes for African Development* 37 (Nigerian Institute of Advanced Legal Studies (NIALS), Lagos, 2011).

35 Gaius Ezejiofor, 'The Law of Patents in Nigeria: A Review' (1973) 9 *African Law Studies* 39, 58.

36 Ibid 36–7.

37 Oguamanam (n 31) 489 at 496; Oguamanam, note 31 above at 146–52; and H A Amankwa, 'Traditional Values and Modern Challenges in Property Law' (2007) 11 (1) *Journal of South Pacific Law* 18 at 18–9.

38 Oguamanam (n 31) 489, 502. M Sunder, 'The Invention of Traditional Knowledge' (spring 2007) 70 *Law and Contemporary Problems* 97 at 104–9. It should be noted that the protection of a subject matter that has fallen into the public is not mandatory under international patent law. See Agreement on Trade-Related Aspects of Intellectual Property Rights (1994), art 70(3).

39 Chika B Onwuekwe, 'The Commons Concept and Intellectual Property Rights Regime: Whither Plant Genetic Resources and Traditional Knowledge?' (2004) 2(1) *Pierce Law Review* 65, 66.

The above conceptions are effectively rebutted by various scholars as based on misconceptions of the nature and dynamism of TKMUP, as well as reflecting the antiquated notion of the inventive process in western societies as solitary work.[40] Despite this, the fact remains that unless progressively construed by the court, the patent system in Nigeria as presently structured under the PDA largely represents an epistemic paradigm that does not augur well for the recognition of TKMUP. However, there is nothing preventing judges in Nigeria from recognising the PDA as a legislation enacted against the background of the country's economic conditions, by construing its provisions in a manner that the Act is protective of TKMUP as vital to the nation's socio-economic development.[41]

The term 'invention' is not defined in the PDA rather it stipulates the circumstances under which an invention could be considered patentable. An invention is patentable if it is new, results from inventive activity and is capable of industrial application; or constitutes an improvement upon a patented invention and also is new, results from inventive activity and is capable of industrial application.[42] It is therefore apparent that the requirement of novelty is a cardinal prerequisite, although the requirements of non-obviousness and utility are equally important in determining inventiveness for the purpose of patent protection in Nigeria.[43] Novelty is usually gauged against the 'state of the art'.[44] The Act defines the state of the art as

> everything concerning that art or field of knowledge which has been made available to the public anywhere and at any time whatever (by means of a written or oral description, by use or in any other way) before the date of the filing of the patent application relating to the invention or the foreign priority date validly claimed in respect thereof.[45]

Consequently, the disclosure of knowledge including TKMUP, whether written or oral is regarded to be in the public domain. Hence, any invention that is simply based on or derived from it does not qualify for patenting in the Act. The absolute novelty requirement adopted by the PDA just like the European Patent Convention,[46] by including oral TKMUP as prior art, is important for the defensive protection of TKMUP in Nigeria, as it will reduce the incidences of fraudulent patenting by individuals and

40 Chidi Oguamanam, 'The Protection of Traditional Knowledge: Towards a Cross-Cultural Dialogue on Intellectual Property Rights' (2004) 15 *Australian Intellectual Property Law Journal* 34 at 38–40.

41 Ibid at 174–5.

42 Section 1(1) PDA

43 Ibid section 1(2) PDA.

44 Ibid section 1(2) (a) PDA.

45 Ibid section 1(3) PDA.

46 Convention on the Grant of European Patents, (October 5, 1973), art 54(4); and Patent Act, 1959, art 29 (Japan).

companies who allegedly 'discovered' such knowledge in the country.[47] This requirement also has extraterritorial application as it effectively precludes from patenting any invention that involves the use of TKMUP disclosed elsewhere other than in Nigeria whether oral or written.

However, as earlier noted, regarding disclosed TKMUP as being in the public domain in Nigeria, may not really advance their recognition in the PDA, as it largely promotes the unintended consequences of congealing disclosed TKMUP as the opposite of property, a raw material of innovation. This is evident from the fact that such knowledge although regarded to be in the public domain by the patent laws of many developed countries, yet when appropriated and represented 'scientifically' by corporate bodies and research institutions, ceases to reside in that domain and becomes entitled to patent protection.[48] The same attitude allows the patenting in the original form of oral TKMUP in countries that do consider unwritten TK as a form of the prior art.[49] For instance, the yellow yam in Nigeria is popularly known amongst traditional healers to be effective in treating diabetes. Yet the U.S. Patent Office granted a patent on a herbal remedy for the treatment of diabetes which is based on the extracts of the same yellow yam to Maurice Iwu, a Professor of Pharmacognosy, and former United Nation's Lead Consultant for the development of Nigeria's National Biodiversity Strategy and Action Plan.[50]

The absolute novelty principle in the Act is only triggered when information about an invention, knowledge or technology has been disclosed to the public in Nigeria.[51] This may raise a peculiar problem as most TKMUP by their nature are usually held confidentially within a community, a smaller group such as amongst traditional healers, or even by individual traditional healers in Nigeria. In such instances of undisclosed confidential TKMUP which are not regarded as prior art under the Act, any invention based on such knowledge is patentable and recognised as IP under the Act. The implication, if such knowledge is inadvertently disclosed to a third party, the knowledge can be the subject matter of a patent provided that other conditions such as non-obviousness and utility are satisfied. It does not imply that biopiracy is the only outcome of the application of the absolute novelty

47 Jay Erstling 'Using Patents to Protect Traditional Knowledge' (2009) 15 *Texas Wesleyan Law Review* 295.
316.

48 Oguamanam (n 40) 34 at 38–40.

49 Laurence R Helfer, 'Regime Shifting: the TRIPS Agreement and New Dynamics of International Intellectual Property Lawmaking' (2004) 29 *Yale Journal of International Law* 1 at 30.

50 Ibid 147.

51 Except in instances where within the period of six months preceding the filing of a patent application in respect of the invention, the inventor or his successor in title has exhibited it in an official or officially recognised international exhibition. Section 1(3) PDA.

principle to undisclosed TKMUP, as it can equally be utilised by holders of such knowledge to patent inventions based on medicinal knowledge.

There is no substantive examination of patent applications as the registrar is charged with the limited duty of examining applications as to formality to determine suitability for a patent grant. Once complied with, the patent shall be granted as applied without further examination of the substantive merits of the inventions claimed under the application.[52] As aptly noted by the WIPO, this system basically 'defers substantive examination on patentability until a patent is actually litigated'.[53] Lack of substantive examination of patent applications may lead to a situation where inventions involving or derived from TKMUP are fraudulently patented by private and corporate bodies in Nigeria.[54] In addition, it leads to the issuance of weak patents which equally does not augur well for traditional healers wishing to patent their innovations as the depository system results in the absence of any guarantee that the patent will be valid.

Indeed, section 4(4) of the PDA expressly states that 'patents are granted at the risk of the patentee and without guarantee of their validity'. Hence, the validity of such inventions is open to challenge in court, and if challenged, the primary onus of proving validity rests on the patentee.[55] As pointed out by Date-Bah, 'Patents issued under a registration [depository] system are, therefore, of lower presumptive validity and usually include a relatively large number of manifestly invalid and "weak" patents'.[56] Particularly where the inventions concern medicinal plants that may have widespread uses in either Nigeria or other African nations,[57] such patent may run the risk of infringing another local innovator's patent or 'be of no substantive value to any… African innovator wishing to commercialize a product abroad'.[58]

The PDA does not provide for the disclosure of origin requirement. Such lacunae when coupled with the simple prior art search and non-substantive examination of patent applications, would surely lead to situations where inventions derived from TKMUP are fraudulently patented by private and

52 Section 4(2) PDA.

53 World Intellectual Property Organisation (WIPO), *Alternatives in Patent Search and Examination* (2014)7 https://www.wipo.int/edocs/pubdocs/en/wipo_pub_guide_patentsearch.pdf accessed 18 August 2020.

54 A Adewopo, *According to Intellectual Property: A Pro-Development Vision of the Law and the Nigerian Intellectual Property Law and Policy Reform in the Knowledge Era*, 5th Inaugural Lecture (2012 Nigerian Institute of Advanced Legal Studies, Lagos) 14.

55 Section 9 PDA.

56 S K Date-Bah, 'Transfer of Technology to Nigeria and the Patents Designs Act of 1970' (1981) 25(2) *Journal of African Law* 82.

57 The transboundary widespread uses of certain TKMUP has necessitated the call under the Nagoya Protocol for a global multilateral benefit-sharing mechanism to address the fair and equitable sharing of benefits derived from such knowledge. See Art 10.

58 D Kaplan, 'Intellectual Property Rights and Innovation in South Africa: A Framework' in World Intellectual Property Organisation (WIPO), *The Economics of Intellectual Property in South Africa* (WIPO, June 2009) 1–17, 3.

corporate bodies in Nigeria. It should be noted that the Access to Benefit Sharing (ABS) Regulations require the evidence of prior informed consent (PIC) from interested persons, local communities and other stakeholders or relevant agencies before an access permit will be granted to a bioprospector.[59] The non-linkage with the PDA has rendered such provision ineffective in preventing fraudulent patenting of inventions derived from TKMUP in Nigeria.

Enhancing the effectiveness of the patent system in protecting TKMUP in Nigeria: recommending a way forward

The patent system can be purposively enhanced to foster the protection of TKMUP in Nigeria. Defensive and affirmative measures can be adopted. Defensive measures make it impossible or difficult for third parties to claim or acquire patent rights on TKMUP or some elements of the knowledge. However, defensive patent measures generally do not prevent third parties from using TKMUP as their impact is restricted to preventing the acquisition of patent rights on such knowledge. On the other hand, affirmative measures seek to prevent undesirable uses of TKMUP by third parties, by encouraging indigenous communities including their traditional healers to actively exploit their plant medicinal knowledge for economic benefits.

Despite the generally acknowledged confidential nature of TKMUP, it still may be prone to outside exploitation.[60] Hence, promoting the commercialisation of third-world traditional products including contemporary innovations by their traditional healers is 'ultimately perhaps the most effective way to protect their traditions'.[61] Due to the peculiar nature of TKMUP in Nigeria, this chapter suggests a combination of defensive and affirmative measures to effectively resort to the patent system.[62] This approach helps in protecting TKMUP by effectively reaping the benefits of these measures while bridging the limitations. The relevant measures in this respect are discussed in a further section.

Perceiving TKMUP as prior art

The perception of TKMUP as prior art serves to defeat any third-party patent application over an invention based on TKMUP, which if granted,

59 Ibid.

60 Y Groenewald, 'Town like Alice Takes on German "Biopirate' *Mail & Guardian*, 22 January 2010; and B Jordan, 'Drug Companies Looting SA's Bounty of Medicinal Plants: State to Protect Shrubs, and Traditional Healers' Rights' *The Times* (Johannesburg), 7 October 2007.

61 M Leibl and T Roy, 'Handmade in India: Traditional Craft Skills in a Changing World' in J M Finger and P Schuler (eds), *Poor People's Knowledge: Promoting Intellectual Property in Developing Countries* (The World Bank and Oxford University Press US 2004) 70.

62 WIPO Intergovernmental Committee on Intellectual Property and Genetic Resources, Traditional Knowledge and Folklore *Practical Mechanisms for the Defensive Protection of Traditional Knowledge and Genetic Resources Within the Patent System*, WIPO/GRTKF/IC/5/6 (14 May 2003) 2, para. 3.

could interfere with the holder's right to use the knowledge. Nigeria recognises disclosed TKMUP as a prior art in the PDA. This position should be strengthened by the creation of an information database or system to make TKMUP searchable by the Nigerian Patents Office and international patent offices in a documented and organised fashion as exemplified by the Indian Traditional Knowledge Digital Library (TKDL).[63] The database can be used in opposing patent applications in countries like the United States where oral disclosure other than within its territory is not recognised as prior art.[64]

The Nigerian Natural Medicine Development Agency (NNMDA) is developing a digital virtual library for Nigeria's traditional medical system, which will be a dedicated focal reference centre for traditional medicine knowledge and practice, as well as for the promotion and safeguarding of intellectual properties arising from such knowledge.[65] The digital library which is modelled after the TKDL, seeks to document and conserve medicinal, aromatic and pesticidal plants (MAPPs).[66] Oral TKMUP will be captured, identified and documented using the scientific and common English names, as well as the local names of the affected plant in the three major Nigerian languages.[67]

Nigeria leans towards the absolute novelty requirement when it comes to determining the novelty of an invention. In essence, any oral or written medicinal knowledge (including TKMUP) once disclosed whether in the country or elsewhere, is regarded to be in the public domain cannot be patented.[68] Surely, it is not the intention of the NNMDA through the virtual library to place undisclosed TK into the public domain, thereby promoting their unauthorised uses. It is therefore envisaged that Nigeria will adopt the same approach used by the South African National Record System (NRS) in safeguarding the confidentiality of the oral TKMUP stored in the system.

63 Ibid at para. 13. Other existing databases similar to the TKDL include the China Traditional Chinese Medicine (TCM) Patent Database, which contains 12,024 deeply indexed records of China TCM patent literature with 31,283 TCM formulas in Chinese and English versions; and the Korean Traditional Knowledge Portal, which is accessible in Korean and English.

64 Section 102(a)-(b) U.S. Patents Act 35 U.S.C. 2006, (a patent will not be granted if the invention was patented or described in a printed publication in the US or a foreign country).

65 WIPO Intergovernmental Committee on Intellectual Property and Genetic Resources, Traditional Knowledge and Folklore, *Policies, Measures and Experiences Regarding Intellectual Property and Genetic Resources: Submission by the Nigeria Natural Medicine Development Agency (NNMDA)*, WIPO/GRTKF/IC/16/INF/7, Annex (19 February 2010) 1.

66 Towards achieving this, the Agency initiated a number of regional projects and programmes across the country. One of the projects, the *identification and documentation* of medicinal plants has so far during the first phase covered two Nigeria World Heritage Sites and six ecological zones of Nigeria. See G E Christian, *Digitization, Intellectual Property Rights and Access to Traditional Medicine Knowledge in Developing states– the Nigerian Experience* (International Development Research Centre (IDRC) Ottawa, Canada) 15–8, https://idl-bnc.idrc.ca/dspace/bitstream/10625/41341/1/129184.pdf. accessed 20 June 2020.

67 Ibid 17–8.

68 Section 1(3) PDA.

The NRS (through the National Indigenous Knowledge Systems Office (NIKSO)) allows limited access to confidential TK to approved scientists, researchers and patent offices as determined by adherence to the requirements of the legal framework between the parties.[69] Such restrictive strategy allows the disclosed information about the confidential TK to be regarded as prior art for the purpose of determining the novelty of an invention, without unduly placing detailed information in the public domain.[70] Adopting such an approach is necessary to prevent unauthorised uses as well as to enhance Nigeria's competitive advantage in the production of herbal drugs and supplements.

Adoption of substantive examination patent system

Nigeria should change to a substantive examination patent system to tackle biopiracy. This system has the advantage of enhancing the speed of the patenting process including inventions involving TKMUP. Studies have shown that as a depository country, it is far easier to obtain patents in South Africa than in any other comparable country including developing countries like India and Brazil.[71] In addition, the depository system places the cost of substantive examination on parties that are directly interested in the patent in the event that the grant of a patent is challenged, thereby allowing the State burdened by manpower and infrastructural challenges to allocate scarce technical skills towards infrastructure development and other key developmental areas.[72] Perhaps this view is the reason why most African countries embraced the system.[73] There are major drawbacks for both the producers and users of the depository system, thus making it crucial to work towards the adoption of the substantive examination system in Nigeria.[74]

Substantive examination of patent applications requires financial and human resources. Qualified examiners in all fields of technology are needed and the technical infrastructure must be upgraded and maintained for

69 This includes prior informed consent and non-disclosure agreements. See the Protection, Promotion, Development and Management of Indigenous Knowledge Systems Bill, GG 39910 of 8 April 2016, ss 20–1; T Suchanandan, 'Explained: South Africa's Recordal System for Indigenous Knowledge' *Afro-IP*, 10 June 2013, http://afro-ip.blogspot.com/2013/06/explained-south-africas-national.html accessed 20 June 2020; and WIPO Intergovernmental Committee on Intellectual Property and Genetic Resources, Traditional Knowledge and Folklore, *Responses to Questions Regarding National-Level Databases and an International Portal: Document submitted by the Delegations of Canada, Japan, Norway, the Republic of Korea and the United States of America*, WIPO/GRTKF/IC/27/INF/11, (27 March 2014) 7, para. 43.

70 Ibid 13, paras. 85 & 91.

71 Department of Trade & Industry (DTI), *Draft Intellectual Property Policy of the Republic of South Africa: Phase I* (International Trade and Economic Development, 2017) 7.

72 Ibid 14.

73 I Mgbeoji, 'African Patent Offices Not Fit for Purpose' in J De Beer, C Armstrong, C Oguamanam and T Schonwetter (eds), *Innovation & Intellectual Property Collaborative Dynamics in Africa* (UCT Press, 2014) 234–47, 238 & 240.

74 Ibid 240–1. See also Robyn-Leigh Merry, 'The Intention to Become a Substantive Search and Examination Office' *Dennemeyer IP Blog*, 16 October 2017, https://blog.dennemeyer.com/intention-become-substantive-search-examination-office accessed 20 June 2020.

appropriate patent searches.[75] In addressing capacity constraints, WIPO suggests that substantive examination in the country concerned should be limited to certain strategic fields of technology; while others could be subject to formality examination only or outsourcing from the same or another terrain.[76] There is another option of the restriction of substantive examination to check compliance with some criteria to be granted a patent.[77]

Disclosure of origins

Some developing countries advocate for disclosure of origin as a defensive measure in patent laws.[78] These countries require as a condition of patentability that inventions based on TK must comply with the disclosure of origins requirement. In addition, evidence of prior informed consent from the relevant national authority to access and use such resources; and evidence of fair and equitable sharing of the benefits derived from such resources with their providers are required. Failure of such disclosure can result in rejection of the patent application or invalidity of the patent.[79] The essence of this requirement TK holders' right to retain control over the use of their knowledge. Implicit in this requirement is the acknowledgement that the invention, at least, must be based on or derived from some elements of TK-MUP. Hence, accountability in the use of TKMUP is ensured. Consequently, the achievement of the objectives of the Convention on Biological Diversity (CBD) and the Nagoya Protocol on Access to Genetic Resources and the Fair and Equitable Sharing of Benefits Arising from their Utilisation.[80]

The compatibility of the disclosure requirement with the provisions of international patent agreements particularly the Trade-Related Aspects of Intellectual Property Rights (TRIPS) agreement has sparked intense debates amongst scholars.[81] A group of WTO members led by Brazil and India proposed the amendment of the agreement to make such disclosure an

75 World Intellectual Property Organisation (WIPO), *Alternatives in Patent Search and Examination* (2014)7 https://www.wipo.int/edocs/pubdocs/en/wipo_pub_guide_patentsearch.pdf accessed 18 August 2020 8.

76 Ibid.

77 Ibid.

78 Ibid.

79 Section 25(1) (j) & 64(1) (p) Indian Patents Act 1970 (as amended) and Decision 486 of the Andean Community (Bolivia, Colombia, Ecuador, Peru and Venezuela), of 14 September 2000, on the Common Intellectual Property Regime, arts 3 & 75(g)-(h).

80 The Nagoya Protocol on Access to Genetic Resources and the Fair and Equitable Sharing of Benefits Arising from their Utilisation to the Convention on Biological Diversity, 29 October 2010, available at http://www.cbd.int/abs/doc/protocol/nagoya-protocol-en.pdf, (hereinafter Nagoya Protocol). It entered into force in October 2014.

81 N P de Carvalho, 'From the Shaman's Hut to the Patent Office: In Search of a TRIPS-Consistent Requirement to Disclose the Origin of Genetic Resources and Prior Informed Consent' (2005) 17 *Washington University Journal of Law &Policy*, 111–86, 112 (hereinafter Carvalho II).

international requirement.[82] The debate has not ended and there are varying positions taken by members of WTO.[83] Pending a common understanding among member states with regard to the TK disclosure or a definite pronouncement by the WTO dispute resolution panel on the non-compatibility of the requirement with the TRIPS agreement, countries are free to formulate and apply their own TRIPS-compliant disclosure measures. Few African nations have provided for the disclosure of origins requirement in patent applications involving inventions based on TK.[84]

Patent opposition proceedings

The opportunity for third parties to present relevant information to patent examiners in an opposition process can augment conducting the substantive examination of patent applications. Thus, the proceedings ensure that only those inventions that meet domestic statutory requirements for patentability are granted patent protection.[85] The proceedings provide some degree of certainty regarding the validity of a patent; and further limit the need to engage in time-consuming and expensive patent revocation proceedings.[86] The latter is very important in view of the fact that revocation proceedings entail prohibitive costs and risks of litigation in the court.

Experience from India has shown that opposition proceedings represent cheaper and easily accessible means for aggrieved parties to oppose the patenting of inventions from fraudulently obtained TKMUP. The inexpensive method of such proceeding is exemplified by the fact that under the Indian Patents Act, pre-grant opposition proceeding is usually handled by the Controller, while for post-grant opposition, the Controller is required to constitute a board to examine the notice and submit its recommendation to the Controller.[87] Some African countries have provided for opposition proceedings although few like Uganda have gone further to provide for pre-grant and post-grant patent proceedings.[88] The Federal High Court has the

82 Council for Trade-Related Aspects of Intellectual Property Rights, *The Relationship Between the TRIPS Agreement and the Convention on Biological Diversity: Summary of Issues Raised and Points Made,* IP/C/W/368/Rev.1 (WTO, Feb. 8, 2006).

83 These vary from those arguing for disclosure as a TRIPS obligation (Brazil and India and including Bolivia, Colombia, Cuba, Dominican Republic, Ecuador, Peru, Thailand, and supported by the African group and some other developing states); disclosure through WIPO by the amendment of the PCT regulations (Switzerland); disclosure, but legal consequences outside patent law (EU); and Use of national legislation, including contracts rather than a disclosure obligation (US).

84 A list of African countries that have provided for the requirement in their patent laws as at May 2020, is available at http://www.wipo.int/export/sites/www/tk/en/documents/pdf/genetic_resources_disclosure.pdf.

85 South Africa's Draft Intellectual Property Policy.

86 Ibid.

87 Section 25 (1) & (3) Indian Patents Act 1970 (as amended).

88 Ibid Section 28 (7)–(12) & 32 (5)–(6), Ugandan Industrial Property Act 2014 (providing for pre and post grant opposition; and section 21(5)–(11)Botswana's Industrial Property Act 2010 Cap. 68:03 (providing for pre-grant opposition).

exclusive jurisdiction under the PDA to hear and dispose of legal proceedings in relation to patents in Nigeria.[89]

Adoption of clear industrial policy on TKMUP

Indeed, Nigeria's wealth of TKMUP, if properly formalised and capitalised through the acquisition of property rights, protects such knowledge from misappropriation. It is an intangible asset that can be used as a driving force for socio-economic growth and comparative advantage in the global economy.[90] Policymakers must adopt a clear and properly funded industrial policy that should prioritise the wealth of the nation which is the cultural knowledge/TK and heritage otherwise adequate recognition for IP protection will not be available. This prioritisation is evident in China where to enhance the patenting of TCM products, the government implemented a clear industrial policy of modernising traditional medicines, including the 'scientification' of TCM like orthodox medicines for easier integration into the later.[91] TCM inventions can easily comply with the substantive conditions of patentability and the technical patent specifications (written description of the invention and how to carry it out).

The latter is described as the core of the patent system, which requires that the technical specifications should incorporate the scientific terminologies that patent examiners or judges are trained to assess. Incorporating scientific terminologies invariably involves employing sophisticated techniques to bioengineer the plants' ingredients to identify the active compounds or substances. Such technologies are usually out of reach for most innovators in the area of traditional medicine.[92] It is therefore not surprising that the establishment of 'scientification' organisations such as the Shanghai Innovative Research Center of Traditional Chinese Medicine (SIRC) further encouraged patent protection for TCM.

The establishment of the NNMDA,[93] and the Nigeria Institute for Pharmaceutical Research and Development (NIPRD),[94] signifies the intention of the government in Nigeria to promote the development and commercialisation of innovative products resulting from bioprospecting activities. The effort of these agencies in promoting the commercialisation of TKMUP should be boosted by the establishment of the National Office for

89 Section 26 PDA.

90 P Basu, 'Trading on Traditional Medicines' (2004) 22(3) *Nature Biotechnology* 263.

91 Towards achieving this, an entire technology park in Houzhou has been devoted to the scientific study of Chinese medicine. See Basu *op cit* note 144.

92 Y Daya and N Vink, 'Protecting Traditional Ethno-Botanical Knowledge in South Africa through the Intellectual Property Regime' (2006) 45(3) *Agrekon* 319 at 328.

93 It is mandated to assist in promoting the development of innovative products from local herbs and medicinal and aromatic plants through appropriate public-private partnership schemes, for further research and commercialization.

94 It was established with the primary objective of developing drugs, biological products and pharmaceutical raw materials from indigenous resources as well as the conservation of Nigeria's medicinal and aromatic plants.

Technology Acquisition and Promotion (NOTAP). NOTAP is mandated to assist in the patenting of all inventions and innovations carried out by government-funded research institutes and others in the private sector.[95] However, poor funding is a critical obstacle to the realisation of the mandates of these organisations. This is despite the fact that the activities of NIPRD led to the development and patenting of Niprisan an anti-sickle cell drug based on a traditional recipe that is known to generations of a Nigerian family as an effective treatment for sickle cell anaemia.[96]

Conclusion

The structure of the patent system in Nigeria offers little or no protection to its rich TKMUP from biopiracy or any other form of misappropriation. It further shows that the issue of biopiracy might be exacerbated by the need to find a cure or vaccine for the COVID-19 pandemic which is ravaging the world. Evidence has shown that traditional medicine has the potential to be utilised for the treatment of this disease. Such potential has attracted the attention of western biotechnology and pharmaceutical companies seeking to utilise traditional medicine or its knowledge system particularly TKMUP as a resource for drug discovery. The perceived value necessitates the restructuring of the patent system in Nigeria to effectively serve as a mechanism for tackling biopiracy and developing TKMUP.

This action of restructuring can encourage inventions based on TK and patenting of these inventions by TK holders, inventors, domestic researchers as well as multinational corporations as already evident in some patents granted on various inventions derived from Nigeria's bio-resources. The measures that should be taken to enable the patent system for effective protection of such knowledge were suggested in the preceding section. There is indeed a need to mobilise political as well as legislative will for effective implementation of policies and laws to enable Nigeria to join other developing nations that have resorted to the adoption of radically different strategies in their approach to IP rights as a protection mechanism for TK based on as bio-resource.

95 National Office for Technology Acquisition and Promotion (NOTAP), 'Patenting Inventions through NOTAP' http://www.notap.gov.ng/content/patenting-inventions-through-notap accessed 30 August 2020; and Senator Ihenyen, 'The National Office for Technology Acquisition and Promotion (NOTAP): Supporting Inventions and Innovations towards Indigenous Technological Advancement in Nigeria (3)' *Nigerian Law Today*, 26 February 2014.

96 For other achievements of these agencies, see the Nigerian Natural Medicine Development Agency (NNMDA), 'NNMDA Collaboration & Linkages' http://www.nnmda.gov.ng/collaborators accessed 30 August 2020; and the Nigeria Institute for Pharmaceutical Research and Development (NIPRD), http://www.niprd.net/ accessed 30 August 2020.

Part II

Trademarks

6 Two strings on a bow

Scope of registrable trademarks from the era of traditional knowledge to digital technology in Nigeria (pre and post 1965)

Ayoyemi Lawal-Arowolo

Introduction

The Trademarks Act of Nigeria 1965 has been in existence for approximately three decades and five years with no fundamental changes since its inception. The change in other jurisdictions in the direction of the use of marks and other significant symbols for distinguishing goods has had a limited effect on the 1965 Trademarks Act. The Federal High Courts (with exclusive jurisdiction on intellectual property issues in Nigeria)[1] have been confronted with and ruled on significant issues concerning trademarks in Nigeria. Nonetheless, the 1965 Trademarks Act remains the same and there are hardly any precedents widening the scope of trademarks registration. Presumably, the archaic nature of the Act has influenced these rulings. Thus, judges do not take into consideration, contemporary ways and practices regarding the scope of registration of trademarks. Cases such as *Ferodo*[2] and *Trebor*[3] show that shapes and packaging are not perceived as marks according to section 67 of the Act.

The perception in this chapter is that the 1965 Trademarks Act remains old law bestowed upon Nigeria as a colony by the colonizers; derived from earlier Ordinances during the colonial era. It is worthy of mention that the territory it was received from has long moved on and no longer perceives the content of some of the provisions of the Act as useful, while the country of reception still holds on to it as valuable law. Moreover, it is common knowledge that intellectual property matters in Nigerian courts do not often tackle

1 Omina Nig. Ltd. v. Dyktrade Ltd. SC. 176/2003. '…I subscribe to the learned counsel for the respondent's argument that the said court has jurisdiction whether or not that claim arises from the infringement of a registered or an unregistered trade mark.'

2 Ferodo Limited and Ferodo Nigeria Limited v. Ibeto Industries Limited [2004] 5 Nigeria Weekly Law Report Part 866 317. In this case the word Ferodo and the word UNION or UNION SUPA was decided as being incapable of infringing FERODO, that the only mark registered for the first appellant is the word FERODO and the coloring outlay and the geometric designs are merely decorative and do not form part of the trademark.

3 It was revealed in Trebor Nigeria Ltd. v. Associated Industries Ltd. (1972) NCLR 471 that the Trademark Act 1965 does not recognize packaging of goods as a trademark.

DOI: 10.4324/9781003250883-9

the substance of intellectual property laws; the procedure is prioritized in the hope that the matter will be thrown out of court or dismissed.

The era of digital technology is not reflected in the Act since there have been no additions to the Act over the years. There are issues that trademark law has struggled with, including the use of a trademark in expressive works, cybersquatting cases related to domains, online counterfeiting and spurious postings online. In addition, technology has made it easy to take online, the logo of a brand that has been registered as a trademark for other forms of commercial activities without appropriate authorization. This scenario creates difficulty for consumers to recognize a genuine post by the company, from a counterfeit post through unapproved use of a trademark by another company.[4]

Since the focus is the scope of registration, an appropriate example to discuss this form of the trademark is the three-dimensional (3D) virtual model trademark infringements of brands like BMW and MARVEL among others. Infringements of trademarks can occur in the marketing of 3D virtual models and logos when used in video games or movies without authorization; since they are likely to confuse consumers about the source of the models, or authorization to sell the models.[5] As earlier mentioned, the 1965 Act is not tolerant of nonconventional trademarks such as those mentioned above and 3D virtual models. Conversely, prior to 1965, there were ordinances that led to the 1965 Act. These ordinances did not take cognizance of traditional forms of marks and symbols for commerce at the communal level.

Traditional or cultural marks or symbols are not often linked to trademarks. They are perceived more like art and craft. Copyright and patent law have been the pivotal themes in discussing cultural expressions or traditional knowledge generally.[6] The use of words or symbols in traditional communities which are adopted as trade or service marks by outsiders are often challenged in other jurisdictions while the atmosphere is silent in Nigeria. In those jurisdictions, there is a perception that 'trade mark law presumes a date-definable point of adoption of a trade mark by the deliberate creation or choosing of a mark for the purposes of actually using it as a trade mark… while a specific form of traditional knowledge may have no definable point of adoption, given its collective nature, let alone that it may be centuries old'.[7]

4 Simon Webster, 'Challenges for Trade Marks in A Digital World: A Review of INTA 2017' 6 June 2017 https://www.ipwatchdog.com/2017/06/06/challenges-trademarks-digital-world-inta-2017/id=84072/ accessed 20 August 2020.

5 Mark P Mckenna and Lucas S Osborne, 'Trademarks and Digital Goods' (2017) 92(4) *Notre Dame Law Review* 1425–6.

6 Ibid.

7 Susy Frankel, 'Trademarks and Traditional Knowledge and Cultural Intellectual Property Rights' (2011) 1(6) Victoria University of Wellington Legal Research Papers Paper No. 36, 2.

While this quotation is acceptable to an extent, majorly the perception that traditional knowledge is collective in all situations is flawed by various literatures showing there are individual as well as communal and spiritual creations which are ongoing, definitely not merely a thing of the past for many communities in Nigeria. In addition, in numerous situations, a mark based on traditional knowledge is intentionally created for identity in order for purchasers to know the region and household the product is from. The use of marks is common in the agricultural and textile sectors of traditional communities in the past and present. Trademark law in Nigeria can provide a means to prevent the unwanted appropriation of marks based on traditional knowledge by those not authorized to engage in it, let alone commercialize it, even if registering traditional knowledge or cultural symbols as a trademark may prove a challenge.

Without a doubt, trademarks are valuable to developing countries and can be valuable to traditional communities. Trademark protection has the potential to develop brand recognition for quality crafts, clothing, music and traditional medicine. Traditional communities seek recognition of traditional brands, signs and symbols. They also 'seek protection and acknowledgement of those systems from the state in which they reside. This may include protection from third parties using such signs and symbols as intellectual property.'[8]

There are many uses of marks or symbols based on traditional knowledge alongside digital technology for trade in Nigeria. The essence of this chapter is to explore these strings comprehensively in alignment with the provisions of the Trademark Act 1965 and propose a way forward to fill in the gap.

Trademarks and customary practices pre 1965 Trademarks Act of Nigeria

There are two eras prior to 1965, the era before colonization and the era of colonization which is significant for the introduction of English laws including ordinances on trademarks. In the precolonial era, even though facial marks were not for commerce, they are symbolic to various regions in Nigeria. In Yoruba land, in the western part of Nigeria, facial marks are used for identification of people regarding their heritage or clan.[9] It is believed that the best way of 'identifying people of same ethnic group is the similarity of their marks…Sango therefore decided that cuts should in future be given,

8 Ibid 6.

9 Canada: Immigration and Refugee Board of Canada, Nigeria: The practice of tribal markings on male children, including groups that engage in the practice; whether the parents of a child can refuse to have the practice carried out, including consequences of such a refusal; state protection available (2012–2013), 30 December 2013, NGA104704.E, https://www.refworld.org/docid/546dc28a4.html accessed 12 July 2020.

not as punishment, but as a sign of royalty...'[10] Facial marks were used for fashion, initiation into age grades and cults, and good health among other uses in later years.

The creation of patterns and symbols as a means of visual communication is not new to the people of Nigeria. Nsibidi is a symbolic system used in the Cross River region of south-eastern Nigeria to decorate gourds, houses, textiles, pottery and other items.

> There are other visual methods of communication...The *àrokò* messaging system was used among Yoruba-speakers in Nigeria to send letters... These letters were made from materials such as cowrie-shells and seeds and their meaning was deduced from factors such as the position of each item...Artists such as Nike Davies-Okundaye use older symbolic systems, such as *adire* cloth patterning, in their paintings.[11]

Adire clothings are significant in the history of trade and fashion in Nigeria, particularly in the western part and some parts of the north. Adire is the tying and dye of pure cotton materials in Indigo plant extract, caustic soda and dye are also used to make Kampala.[12] Some regard Abeokuta in Ogun State, Nigeria as the home of Adire. However, the people of 'Osogbo claim it is theirs in alignment to the story of how Osogbo got its name from the Goddess of the Osun River. "Oso igbo e pele o, gbogbo koko aro mi le ti fo tan" meaning "Hello deity of the forest, you have broken all my dyeing pots." It is this story that has made tie and dye their trade regardless of the claims by Abeokuta people'.[13] Apart from fashion, Adire is also known for health protection against hypertension and diabetes when worn.[14] It is worthy of mention that there is difference in patterns from these regions.

Artworks are branded or symbolic to depict the source or origin. Sculpture from Ile-Ife in Osun state Nigeria, are characterized by the eyeballs 'which are invariably convex without any indication of the pupils and the upper eyelids that overlap the lower ones at the edge'.[15] 'The designs of patterns on

10 Kwekedu, 'Tribal (Facial and Bodily) Marks in African Culture' https://kwekudee-tripdownmemorylane.blogspot.com/2012/09/tribal-facial-and-bodily-marks-in.html accessed 12 July 2020.

11 Marion Wallace and Janet Topp Fargion, 'Language Script and Symbol in West Africa, British Library' https://www.bl.uk/west-africa/articles/language-script-and-symbol-in-west-africa accessed 11 July 2020.

12 Funmi Ajala Adire Tye and Die Process March 16 2018 https://medium.com/@FunmiAjala/adire-the-tie-and-dye-process-c3daa642d128 accessed 20 July 2020; Iyabode Sunmonu, A socialite art of Kampala which is quite different from the art of Indigo. The art of Indigo used in tie and dye is kept by trade secret and its knowledge has not littered the streets like the knowledge of making Kampala which has become common.

13 Funmi Ajala Adire Tye and Die Process (n 12).

14 Ibid.

15 C O Adepegba, *Nigerian Art: Its Traditions and Modern Tendencies* (Ibadan, Nigeria JODAD, 1995) 21–2.

the faces of some of the images are not only antecedent to some present day Yoruba face markings, they also offer some insight into the socio-political background to the sculpture tradition.'[16] Agricultural tools such as hoes are differentiated based the shape. The shape determines the region it is from.[17] 'West Africans are more apt to work bending at the hips and they prefer short-handled hoes.'[18] Apart from the handle the metal plate used in tilling the soil is made in different sizes for particular crops grown in different regions or communities.

These products were communicated to the people using various symbols, shapes or images, hardly were names used. The use of visual communication rather than written could be a result of the literacy level in colonial Nigeria. Indeed, ideas are shared through communication. Culture influences the method of communication. The means of communication depends on the practices the people are conversant with.

> It is a complex process involving several elements; an act of conveying intended meaning from one entity or group to another through the use of mutually understood signs and semiotic rules. But it is this complexity that explains the connection between communication and culture.[19]

Customers of traditional products of trade can identify the product based on symbols or images they are familiar with from the region. A good example is the type of Adire textile made in the western part and the ones made in the northern part of Nigeria. The designs of the textiles and the color are symbols that share meanings of messages used in advertising the product. Adire is perceived by some as mainly different designs based on patterns and the depth of dye. While others are of the view that the sharp contrast in the techniques of the craft is what differentiates Adire from different regions.

Apart from the formal system of protection established by the colonial administration, marks are traditionally used in agriculture, craft and other sectors to indicate ownership of goods including notably, the practice of branding or marking cattle, poultry, tubers, etc.[20] The obvious form of protection of the source of products in trade was keeping the creation of the symbol a secret like the indigo color and images created in dying Adire textiles. Goodwill is another mechanism used. Traders in that era were known for producing the same product for years if not centuries. They used

16 Ibid.

17 Four Nigerian Farming Tools http://www.nationalityrooms.pitt.edu/content/four-nigerian-farming-tools accessed 1 August 2020.

18 Working in the Fields http://departments.fmarion.edu/publicaffairs/hewntimbercabins / hth07/hth/p150.htm accessed 1 August 2020.

19 E Bankole Oladumuye, 'Cultural Symbols and African Symbolism: The Efficacy in Product Advertisement' (2018) 1(2) *Journal of Fine Arts* 16–23, 16.

20 Adejoke O Oyewunmi, *Nigerian Law of Intellectual Property* (University of Lagos Press, 2015) 231–2.

symbols in the course of trade to identify goods and services from a source they are conversant with as being of good quality in similarity but at a different level to what is happening in this era. They also had traditional ways of advertising with songs, sounds and slogans which are still done in rural communities as well as some sections of the urban communities.

Trademark laws during colonization: pre Trademarks Act of 1965

The initial trademark laws in Nigeria were for the southern parts of the country. Even though there were forms of trade and traditional products in existence, the laws introduced were for foreign products and commercial activities. The customary practice continued among the indigenes without the application of the introduced law to traditional trading systems or products. The way the traditional system worked was foreign to the colonizers, the same way the introduced system must have been foreign to the colonies.

Trademarks Proclamation Ordinance (No. 25) of 1900 was culled from the British Trademarks Act of 1883 and introduced to Nigeria. The 1900 Ordinance was followed by the Trademarks Ordinance (No. 18) of 1900. In 1914, the Trademarks Ordinance (No. 20) was for all regions in Nigeria. It is worthy to mention that the amalgamation of Nigeria occurred in 1914 and must have had an impact on the jurisdiction the ordinance covered. There were new ordinances in 1920 (No. 6), 1923 (No. 4) and 1926 (No. 13). The landmark in 1958 was the consolidation and amendments of the ordinances on Trademarks. This consolidation resulted in the Trademarks Act of 1958.[21] There was no significant change until the establishment of the Trademarks Act of 1965. None of the provisions took into consideration the scenario regarding identification, source or branding of goods in Nigeria.

Technology and Trademarks Act 1965: postcolonization and independence

> In particular, the end of the twentieth century introduced significant changes to the market when commerce began shifting towards digital technology and internet services. Six faced with novel issues arising from internet platforms, trademark law adapted to unforeseen characteristics of the internet age…[22]

Developed countries such as the United Kingdom and the United States have witnessed changes over the years regarding trademark laws. Apart from

21 Laws of the Federation and Lagos 1958.

22 James Yang, 'Trademark Law in the Virtual Realism Landscape' (2019) 8(2) *New York University Journal of Intellectual Property and Entertainment Law* 411.

the influence witnessed during colonization, the 1965 Trademarks Act has remained stagnant. In these countries, laws such as what is in existence in Nigeria are old authorities when compared. Even though 'many of the basic concepts appear to be the same or closely similar to those which informed the previous domestic law'.[23] Nevertheless, the streets of Nigeria are engaged with various commercial activities, with various products or brands, some of which have registered trademarks and others unregistered. Traditional forms of branding have remained resilient in the face of contemporary trading systems.

A stagnant protection mechanism for trademarks slowly cripples commercial activities, limiting the potential of various brands that depict products as good quality. There is indeed a need for change for a better trademark system in Nigeria for the importation and exportation of goods. Advertisement of brands and products is an important aspect of commercial activities which involves the use of trademarks for different reasons. Every system of registration of trademarks has to deal with the underlying concepts that form the foundation of such a system: including distinctiveness required for registration and what degree will prevent registration regarding the similarity between a registered mark and an allegedly infringing sign.[24]

> Trade mark means, except in relation to a certification trade mark, a mark used or proposed to be used in relation to goods for the purpose of indicating, or so as to indicate, a connection in the course of trade between the goods and some person having the right either as proprietor or as registered user to use the mark whether with or without any indication of the identity of the person.[25]

The definition in section 67 of this Act appears restrictive and complicated. A simpler and precise update is preferable. The certification mark is better if defined outside the window of trademarks as a concept. The ability of the mark to distinguish goods and services is a vital factor that should be considered in the definition.[26] Service marks are not expressly mentioned and it is not clear if it is implied. The perception in this chapter is that it should be clearly stated that it is goods and services, regardless of the fact that in 2007 the 'Minister by regulation extended the classes of goods from 34 to 45 in accordance with the Nice Classification of Goods and referred to the newly added 11 classes as "intangible goods"—these being services.'[27] The

23 Per Lord Walker of Gestingthrope in R V Johnstone [2003] F.S.R. 748, H.L. at para. 63.

24 David Kitchin et al. Kerly's Law of Trade Marks and Trade Names (14th ed., Sweet & Maxwell, London, 2005) 6.

25 Trademarks Act 1965 CAP T 13 Laws of the Federation of Nigeria (LFN) 2004.

26 Ibid.

27 Olubenga Ajani Olatunji, 'Fundamentals of the Nigerian Trade Marks Act and Implications for Foreign Trade Mark Owners' (2016) 11(2) *Journal of Intellectual Property Law and Practice* 132.

Minister based his actions on the statutory authority provided in sections 42(1) and 45 of the Trademarks.[28] The debate on the actions of the Minister being unconstitutional is not explored in this chapter. However, it is worthy of mention that service marks are protected regardless of the absence of the provision in the Act.

Scope of protection

The scope of marks registrable as trademarks is narrow in the way it is expressed even though there is a possibility of expansion by implication. However, it is preferable to expressly expand the definition of a mark to include 'symbols', 'pseudonyms' shape, form, presentation and packaging, color, smell, sound, taste and virtual models which are in practice in other countries. Symbols have generic nature resulting in the availability of more items as symbols, without the need to resort to verbosity. Pseudonyms are another means to be creative with a brand and should be acceptable since there is no legal objection to carrying on a business by a name other than a person's real name.

The scope of protection of trademarks remains within the conventional. Protecting other forms of trademarks has been a challenge for decades. In other terrains, color, shape (3D shapes and in recent times virtual models), smell and taste are protected by trademarks. A review of the *Ferodo Nigeria Ltd. v. Ibeto Industries Ltd.* reveals that names are prioritized in the protection of trademarks in Nigeria. In the Act, a mark is defined as a device, brand, heading, label, ticket, name, signature, words, letters, numerical or any other combination thereof.[29] The decision on the issue regarding non-conventional marks is imbedded in the quotation below.

> There is nothing distinctive about the colouration and the graphic chequered design to make them part of the registered trade mark… when a word is used to denote a product and when the other features contained are not distinctive, they are merely decorative of the trade mark and not part of it…In summary, I agree with the courts below, that the only mark registered for the first appellant is the word FERODO and the colouring outlay and the geometric designs are merely decorative and do not form part of the trade mark.[30]

The above quotation from the Ferodo case a couple of decades ago shows a territorial lapse in the Act and precedents in case laws. The courts could have set a precedent regarding the scope of marks registrable, rather the courts further confirmed the restrictions. Again in the *Trebor Nigeria Ltd v Associated Industries Ltd* case, the judges interpreted the Act in a similar

28 Ibid.

29 Ibid.

30 Ferodo Nigeria Ltd. v. Ibeto Industries Ltd. [2004] 5 N.W.L.R. Part 866, 320 350–2.

way by not giving recognition to packaging as a trademark device.[31] Even though in the Trebor case the Act was rigidly interpreted and the act was not perceived as an infringement of the rights conferred by the Act, it was concluded that there was an attempt to pass off the product as the plaintiff's product.[32] The claim of passing off in Trebor was the winning strategy for the plaintiff, while the trademark infringement claim in Ferodo was the reason for the loss of the plaintiff. However, it can be strongly argued that the definition of a mark according to the Act is broader than the interpretation bestowed upon it by the courts.

> There is nothing to show that a mark is limited to words only in section 67, particularly because a device is a method with a particular aim or a drawing or design. Device could also be a symbol, logo, motif among others. A further definition of a motif is design, decoration, ornament, shape, emblem and pattern...Logically, a trademark in section 5(2) includes a device which could be the design on the package including the colour as long as the colour can have a secondary meaning to indicate a connection in the course of trade...[33]

Considering nonconventional trademarks is definitely beneficial to the growing commercial activities in Nigeria and technology development.[34] Regardless of the above presumptions regarding the definition of a mark, shapes and appearances of products (3D and every mark digital technology has made available), color,[35] sound,[36] smell[37] and taste[38] should be expressly included in the Act. The reason for these inclusions in jurisdictions like the

31 (1972) NCLR 471.

32 Ibid.

33 Ayoyemi Lawal-Arowolo, 'Ferodo Limited and Ferodo Nigeria Limited v Ibeto Industries Limited: Another Critical Review' (2012) 1(2) *NAILS Journal of Intellectual Property* 118–136, 129–30.

34 Re United States playing card company's application (1908) 1 Cit 197, Trebor Nigeria Ltd V Associated Industries Ltd (1972) HCLR 471 Coca-Cola 7-59 (1986).

35 Lionel Bently and Brad Sherman, Intellectual Property law (4th ed., United Kingdom Oxford University Press, 2014) 894. In the case of LibertelGroep BV. V. Benelux-Merkenbureau Case C-104/01 [2003] ECR 1-3793, the registration of a single colored trade mark was considered and member states were prohibited from operating a per se exclusion of simple colors from registration.

36 Ibid 895. 'A score that comprised a stave with a clef, musical notes and rests, the form of which indicates relative values, and, were necessary accidentals (sharp, flat, etc.) will satisfy the seven Sieckmann requirements...'intelligibility', not 'immediate 'intelligibility'.' Shield Mark BV v. Joost Kist Case C283/01 (2003) ECR 1-14313.

37 Ibid 895. 'A smell will not be adequately graphically represented by a verbal description because it will not be 'sufficiently clear, precise or objective'.' Case C-273/00 [2002] ECRI-11737, [70].

38 Ibid 896. Even though the taste was not distinctive in the Eli Lilly case, it was stated that a verbal description would not be acceptable as a graphic representation of a gustatory sign. Eli Lilly/The taste of artificial strawberry flavourR120/2001-2002 ETMR (4) 59 (OHIM Board of Appeal).

United Kingdom is based on the fact that verbal description will not convey a message on a brand satisfactorily, in comparison to combining it with drawings or photographs, smell, sound, taste and color.[39] Marks should cut across the visual or visible, sound or audio and other aspects of the sensory. Due to the rising level of technology, virtual models are used to an extent by various brands to sell their products in Nigeria. The irony of the situation is that trademark law does not cater for the virtual models directly, rather it is the name, label or device associated with it, that is covered for protection.

Registration of cultural symbols

The restriction in scope affects the use of cultural symbols in advertising. These symbols are not always actual symbols; they can include animals, plants and hand gestures.[40] Cowries, talking drums and horsewhips among other cultural symbols are used in various forms. These symbols are not often used in their crude forms these days 'as they may not readily possess much appeal, especially to the younger generation. In fact, the new generation will only accept culture and cultural symbols which they consider fit and relevant to their lifestyle.'[41] The creativity in cultural symbols to suit products from different eras is not captured by the Act, most especially, due to its rigidity regarding the scope of what is regarded as a trademark.

On one hand, cultural symbols are not protected by trademarks and on the other hand, exploiters use these symbols in modified forms without permission for their brands and seek trademark protection.

> In some circumstances existing trademark regimes may be a means by which to protect their cultural icons, signs and symbols. At the same time third parties have utilized trademark registration as a means of harnessing indigenous peoples culture in pursuit of their own commercial ends.[42]

In Nigeria, it is often the cultural names of the symbols that are exploited, such as cowries to denote banking practices. Even though the symbols are used, it is not often considered a trademark. Indeed, it is not all cultural symbols that are used for trade. Nevertheless, some of these symbols can be protected as artistic work in copyright or industrial designs, such as Adire textiles.

These symbols across traditional communities have their similarities and are still capable of being distinctive enough to fulfill trademark registration requirements. It is worthy of mention that unregistered marks used in connection with trade are protected in common law in Nigeria. Thus, cultural symbols used for trade of the years must have developed enough goodwill to bring an action for passing off. 'Indigenous peoples' use of

39 Ibid 893.
40 Oladumuye (n 19) 18.
41 Ibid.
42 Frankel (n 7) 2.

trademark protection is often dependent on the ability, frequently economic, for them to engage with the system. Most problematically, a number of substantive requirements for trademark protection may be barriers to indigenous people using trademark registration.[43] There are provisions in the Act that appear to be contrary to what traditional communities seek regarding cultural symbols. The peculiarities of cultural symbols as trademarks have to be specifically stated in the Act for precision and clarity regarding protection.

Subsuming the protection of cultural symbols in certification marks is not enough to provide the protection required.[44] A certification mark is dependent on a certification authority rather than a mark of the trader.[45] There is an issue where the cultural symbol is a mark of the trader. Nevertheless, certification marks could be applicable to cultural symbols in a manner that is applicable to other marks, rather than it being the only suitable form of protection. The perception that cultural symbols are often not for trade has to be eradicated, for the major reason that various aspects of traditional knowledge fall into different aspects of intellectual property. Cultural symbols are sometimes categorized as geographical indications. Indeed there are similarities between trademarks and geographical indications; however, there are aspects of traditional knowledge that are more suitable for protection as geographical indications which is a means of identifying the origin of goods with other requirements such as quality and the characteristics of the goods among others. This aspect of protection is yet to be explored in Nigeria.

Registration of trademarks and new technology

> More broadly, a world of increasing digitization implicates important concerns about the boundaries of trademark law vis-a-vis other areas of IP law, and it raises profound questions about the meaning of source indication and the role of trademark law in the digital world…[46]

The alliance between trademark and digital technology has resulted in issues ranging from online brand infringements to the deployment of digital technology in trademark registrations and renewals.[47] There was no known case law or issues in Nigeria regarding this alliance when this chapter was written. Nevertheless, it is crucial to this chapter to lay a foundation on the

43 Ibid 15.

44 Section 43(1) Trademarks Act 1965 LFN 2004.

45 Adewopo, Chuma-Okoro and Oyewunmi, 'A Consideration of Communal Trademarks for Nigerian Leather ad Textile Products' in De Beer, J Armstrong, C Oguamanam, and T Schonwetter (eds) *The Collaborative Dynamics of Innovation and Intellectual Property in Africa* (UCT Press, Cape Town, 2013) 111.

46 Mckenna and Osborne (n 5) 1425.

47 Webster (n 4).

virtual model for clarity on the essence of creating awareness, on the gap in trademark law and the scope of registration in Nigeria. 'In recent years, trademark owners have started to pay closer attention to the symbols presented within games. They have even started to bring lawsuits when they have felt their marks were expressively misappropriated.'[48]

Trademark lawsuits are not limited to the virtual world structured as games. The other categories include social spaces (social platforms) funded by advertising or sales of virtual property and user-generated (such as film) funded by sale and control of virtual property.[49] Out of the three worlds, an example of the game world is briefly explored without suggesting it is not crucial to the film as well as social platforms. The BMW issue with *TurboSquid* though in another jurisdiction is a good example regarding 3D virtual models in games and trademark law. Below is a quotation on the issue of BMW suing online virtual modeling company *TurboSquid* for selling digital models of BMW vehicles with the logo as a means of confusing customers about the source or the presumption of the existence of a license to sell the virtual models.

> BMW alleged that the sale of digital models of BMW cars, complete with BMW logos, was likely to confuse consumers about the source of those digital models, or about whether BMW had licensed TurboSquid to sell models of its vehicles. BMW's case is the latest in a growing number of trademark cases dealing with uses in the digital environment.[50]

Indeed, goods have become digital in a way that they can be transferred in nonphysical form. 'While trademark issues may arise in game worlds and social worlds, they seem no more likely to occur in those worlds than they do in expressive works such as films.'[51] The film industry in Nigeria (Nollywood) is one of the largest and prone to trademark issues. The transfer of digital goods must be considered in all jurisdictions including Nigeria since boundaries across countries have been thinned by digital technology. The Nigerian terrain is indeed not prepared for the contemporary lifestyle in digital trademarks in the 1965 Act. The activities in the environment to an extent are a replica of what is happening in other environments regarding the use of digital goods. The difference in comparing Nigeria to other jurisdictions is that they have a better structure regarding trademark protection even though there are visible challenges. Without a doubt, there are

48 Candidus Dougherty and Greg Lastowka, 'Virtual Trademarks' (2007) 24(4) *Santa Clara High Technology Law Journal* 755 http://digitalcommons.law.scu.edu/chtlj/vol24/iss4/2768 4 accessed August 2020.

49 Dougherty and Lastowka (n 48).

50 Mckenna and Osborne (n 5).

51 Dougherty and Lastowka (n 48).

difficulties in Lanham Act regarding trademarks and digital files that count as goods in the United Kingdom.[52]

In the advertising industry and markets in Nigeria, new forms of technology are adopted in creating digital trademarks. 'In a 3D printing world, design can be done by anyone with access to a CAD program, and production can take place anywhere there is a 3D printer, including an individual's home.'[53] Without a doubt digital technology requires so much of trademark law in every terrain. Nigeria has not been able to achieve what the Lanham Act has achieved even though our laws are fashioned against the United Kingdom law pre- and postcolonization. Nigeria has been stagnant over the years and incapable of conforming to the contemporary lifestyle.

Conclusion

Nigeria is not at the level where actions are brought for issues like those stated in this chapter. Trademark law is obsolete and has not taken into consideration traditional knowledge and digital technology, neither has the judiciary been faced with such issues, even if they are faced with such issues, their reliance on an obsolete law will not lay the required precedent.

Cultural symbols are used to represent some brands for the trade without authorization from traditional communities or persons. Even though names are prioritized regarding protection, cultural symbols are used as part of the packaging of these goods. The rights of the originators of these symbols, whether for trade or not being infringed. The Trademark Act of 1965 should specifically consider cultural symbols as trademarks to reduce the negative impact of infringers. Its existence has to be expressly stated by law, regarding registration by the owner or owners and restriction of use from unauthorized sources.

Conversely, digital technology is on the increase and becoming more sophisticated by the day. Nigeria should no longer avoid the implications attached to the role of technology in trademarks. The space of trademarks continues to expand with technology and overlaps with other areas of intellectual property, such as copyright in expressive works. The issue of source or identification of goods and the role of trademark law in the digital technology era need to be tackled. This scenario can no longer be ignored in Nigeria since it is detrimental to commercial activities regarding nonphysical goods.

52 Mckenna and Osborne (n 5) 1427. 'Digital files should be treated as goods only when consumers' interactions with the files sufficiently resemble their interactions with physical goods that they warrant the same treatment.'

53 Mckenna and Osborne (n 5).

7 Registration of domain name as trademarks in Nigeria

Panacea to cybersquatting

Somto David Ojukwu[1]

Introduction

E-commerce and indeed the use of domain name has become a product of goodwill which like every other intellectual property now requires protection.[2] In recent times, domain names are not only identifiable with businesses, but the goodwill of businesses extend to domain name.[3] While trademark (or service mark) makes a product (or service) prominent in the concerned marketplace, a domain name can also function to deliver the product or service worldwide.

Domain names play a significant role in e-commerce in that technology provides an easy method to access information in cyberspace; it is the world of commerce, social interaction, legal, economic, educational and technological information.[4] Some domain names have attracted great economic value because they are easily recognizable and represent trade names and trademarks.[5]

Domain name has now become much more than merely representing the websites of different companies on the Internet. Today, in this age of well-developed information technology and worldwide businesses through Internet, these domain names have attained the status of being business identifiers and promoters.[6] In valuation of assets of a business, particularly its intellectual asset, value is given to the domain name as an intellectual

1 I wish to express my gratitude to Professor Adebambo Adewopo, SAN for his mentorship.

2 Xuan-Thao Nguyen, 'Shifting the Paradigm in E-Commerce: Move over Inherently Distinctive Trademarks, the E-brand, I-brand and Generic Domain Names Ascending to Power' (2001) 50 *American University Law Review*, 937–78, 939.

3 Marshall Leaffer, 'Domain Names, Globalization, and Internet Governance' (1999) 6(1) *Indiana Journal of Global Legal Studies* 139–65, 143 and 4.

4 Christopher S. Gibson, 'Digital Dispute Resolution: Internet Domain Names and WIPO's Role' (2001) 1 *Computer Law Review International* 23–28, 24.

5 All Answers Ltd, 'The Legal Nature of Domain Names' (Lawteacher.net, February 2020) https://www.lawteacher.net/free-law-essays/copyright-law/the-legal-nature-of-domain-names.php accessed 27 February 2020.

6 David Oturu, 'How to Protect Your Domain Name in Nigeria' https://www.mondaq.com/Nigeria/Intellectual-Property/692414/How-To-Protect-Your-Domain-Name-In-Nigeria accessed 15 February 2020.

DOI: 10.4324/9781003250883-10

asset.[7] For instance, the media online presence of a business adds value to the business as frequent visits to the business site is an income to the business. More so, the company that has established an online presence obviously has created global attention to the business. Invariably in this instance, the business achieves popularity or reputation with the domain name.

Cybersquatting constitutes one of the many thorny issues to domain names. Cybersquatting began after the Internet became commercialized.[8] At the initial stages of the Internet, most companies did not realize the commercial potentials inherent on the Internet and consequently did not envisage the need to register their companies as domain names. Thus cybersquatting at the time was not an illegal offense, as domain names were on a first come first served basis.[9] Industrious companies took advantage of this situation and registered a plethora of trademarks as domain names with the intention to resell to the trademark owner and make profit.[10] This act created commercial problems for trademarks owners, as trademark owners were effectively barred from registering their own marks because only one person is entitled to a domain name.[11] Subsequently, cybersquatting became a problem that had to be contended with because it began to undermine consumer confidence, discouraged Internet use and destroyed the value of established brand names and trademarks.[12] It has spread across different jurisdictions demanding a necessary reaction from all nations. Countries have reacted differently.[13]

Nature of domain name

The Black's Law Dictionary[14] defines a domain as the complete and absolute ownership of land. In the context of the discourse, the definition above gives an actual mental picture of ownership of domain name as property

7 Jacqueline Lipton, *Internet Domain Names, Trademarks and Free Speech* (Edward Elgar Publishing Inc., 2010).

8 Joseph Onele and Emmanuela Onyilofor, 'Domain Name and Cybersquatting: Implications for Trademarks in Nigeria' (2018) 9(4), *The Gravitas Review of Business and Property Law* 115–33, 118.

9 Ibid 118. Proprietors could either institute an action in tort of passing off for wrongful invasion of a right of property or other economic tort such as unlawful interference with economic interests.

10 Leaffer (n 2).

11 Thomas J Curtin, 'The Name Game: Cybersquatting and Trademark Infringement on Social Media Websites' 19 *Journal of Law and Policy* (2010) https://brooklynworks.brooklaw.edu/jlp/vol19/iss1/13 accessed 3 March 2021.

12 Michael Karanicolas, 'The New Cybersquatters: The Evolution of Trademark Enforcement in the Domain Name Space' (2020) 30, 399 *Fordham Intellectual Property, Media & Entertainment Law Journal* 413 https://ir.lawnet.fordham.edu/iplj/vol30/iss2/2 accessed 3 March 2021.

13 The US has enacted the Anti-Cybersquatting consumer Protection Act 1999 to attend to the effects of cybersquatting, and the British courts have responded to the act of cybersquatting through their judicial decisions. Nigeria has enacted Cybercrime (Prohibition, Prevention, ETC) Act 2015.

14 (6th ed. 2004).

in cyberspace. The domain name, unlike other forms of digital property, is unitary, implying that one domain name can only be held by one person or entity at a time.[15] By nature of domain name, largely due to the mode of its application, it exists without limitation to the geographical location provided the user of the domain can access Internet anywhere in the world.

The original scope of domain names was to serve a technical function so as to convert long and complicated numerals into alpha-numeric text which is easier for Internet users to remember and locate. It was intended to perform a technical function in a manner that was convenient to human users of the Internet. In essence, domain names were intended to provide addresses for computers that were easy to remember and identify without the need to resort to the underlying IP numeric address. However, as commercial activities have increased on the Internet, domain names have become part of the standard communication medium by businesses to identify themselves, their products and their activities. It has evolved and is considered to be much more than just a connection between the Internet user and the computer hosting the website[16] as it has come to acquire a supplementary existence as business or personal identifiers. Advertisements appearing in media now routinely include a domain name address, along with other means of identification and communication, such as the corporate name, trademark and phone numbers.

A domain name is a unique name that an individual or organization chooses to identify his/its website. Every website has its own domain name which comprises a registered Internet protocol (IP) address. Example of domain names includes "unizik.edu.ng" and lalegalconsultants.com.

Traffic across the Internet is sent and received using IP addresses. IP addresses are a string of numbers separated by a period, e.g., 192.168.0.2. These numbers are like street addresses or telephone numbers in that they signal to the computer where to look for the information being requested.[17] Because Internet users found it difficult to remember these numerical sequences, domain names developed. So domain names are words or phrases that substitute for and correspond to IP addresses.

A typical website address, or uniform resource locator (URL), has consistent components. The domain name is the part that follows the "http://www." or "http://" part of the URL. For example, in the URL that will land

15 Abdulsalam O Ajetunmobi, *Information and Communications Technology Law in Nigeria: A Comparative Reader* (Princeton Publishing Co. Ltd., 2017).

16 Claudio Caruana, 'The Legal Nature of Domain Names' http://www.elsa.org.mt/wp-content/uploads/2015/02/5.-Caruana-Claudio-The-Legal-Nature-of-Domain-Names.pdf accessed 13 July 2020.

17 Colby B Springer, 'Master of the Domain (Name): A History of Domain Name Litigation and the Emergence of the Anti Cybersquatting Consumer Protection Act and Uniform Dispute Resolution Policy' (2001) 17 *Santa Clara High Technology Journal (HTLJ)* 318–9, https://digitalcommons.law.scu.edu/chtlj/vol17/iss2/5/ accessed 18 February 2020.

a user on Innoson vehicle's website, http://www.innosonvehicle.com, "com" is the top-level domain (TLD) and stands for "commercial." Generic TLDs are the part of the URL that ends in.com for commercial purposes, .org for nonprofit groups, .net for network organizations, .mil for military and .gov for government institutions.[18]

Abusive registration of domain name (cybersquatting)

Cybersquatting is the illegal domain name registration of popular or well-known company names/trademarks with the aim of reselling them to the rightful owners for profit. It is an act of obtaining fraudulent registration with the intent to sell the domain name to the lawful owner of the name at a premium.[19] Cybersquatting entails purchasing domain names that include a trademark in the hope that the trademark owner will purchase the domain from the squatter for a value over the amount that the squatter paid.[20] Anytime a new TLD launches, a "land grab" occurs where domain name speculators register thousands of names hoping to receive a substantially larger sum of money from the trademark owner than what they paid.[21]

A typical case of cybersquatting happened when the Honorable Minister of State for Aviation in Nigeria, Senator Hadi Sirika, made a release on the restoration and unveiling of the new national flag airline carrier. Following the announcement, one Olumayowa Elegbede quickly purchased the following domain names: NigeriaAir.ng and NigeriaAir.com.ng.[22] A search conducted on the NIRA Who is Search database, revealed that the domain names were registered on the 18th of July 2018, the same day the announcement was made by the Federal Government, which immediately raises issue of whether or not the action of Olumayowa Elegbede does not amount to cybersquatting. Another clear case of cybersquatting in Nigeria was between popular bloggers, Linda Ikeji and Emmanuel Efremov who was the cybersquatter in the instant case. Emmanuel Efremov knowing Linda Ikeji's blogs on Lindaikejisblog.com went ahead and registered Lindaikeji.net and

18 Sara D Sunderland, 'Domain Name Speculation: Are We Playing Whac-a-Mole' (2010) 25(1), Article 18, *Berkeley Technology Law Journal* 465–92, 467 https://www.jstor.org/stable/24118643?seq=1 accessed 3 May 2021.

19 Abiodun Ashiru, 'Criminalisation of Cybersquatting in Nigeria, England and The United States: An Unusual Coexistence of Criminal Law and Intellectual Property Right' (2021) 7(1) *Journal of Legal Studies and research* 161–80, 163.

20 Christopher G Clark, 'The Truth in Domain Names Act of 2003 and a Preventative Measure to Combat Typosquatting (2004) 89(6) *Cornell Law Review* https://ssrn.com/abstract=754524 accessed 10 January 2020.

21 Steve DelBianco and Braden Cox, 'ICANN Internet Governance: Is It Working?' (2008) 21(1) PAC. *McGEORGE Global Business and Development Law Journal*, https://scholarlycommons.pacific.edu/globe/vol21/iss1/3/ accessed 15 June 2020.

22 Toba Obaniyi, 'Nigeria Air Domain Registration Saga. Who Wins?' (28 July 2018) https://blog.whogohost.com/nigeria-air-domain-name-saga/ accessed 3 March 2021.

used the reputation of the blogger to earn advertising revenue. Upon the exposing of his cybersquatting activity, he redirected the infringing site to Linda Ikeji's blog to erase evidence of the cybersquatting. There was no evidence of action brought against him.[23]

ICANN[24] defines cybersquatting as the bad faith registration of the trademark of another entity in a domain name. Cybersquatting has been aptly explained as follows: "When you settle on another person's land or property without authority, you are a squatter. On cyberspace, you are a cybersquatter. Cybersquatting is settling on someone's domain on the Internet in bad faith."[25]

The Cybercrime Act[26] made an elaborate definition of cybersquatting as the acquisition of a domain name over the Internet in bad faith to profit, mislead, destroy reputation and deprive others of registering the same, if such a domain name is:

i Similar, identical or confusingly similar to an existing trademark registered with the appropriate government agency at the time of the domain name registration;
ii Identical or in any way similar to the name of a person other than the registrant, in case of a personal name; and
iii Acquired without right to or with intellectual property interests in it.

In popular terms, cybersquatting is the term most frequently used to describe the deliberate, bad faith and abusive registration of a domain name in violation of rights in trademarks and service marks. However, precisely because of its popular occurrence, the term has different meanings to different people and authors have given an elastic meaning to the term.[27] Some authors, for example, include "warehousing"[28] or the practice of register-

23 News Rescue, 'Man Who Got Linda Ikeji Suspended Admits his Director, Cybersquatter Owner of LindaIkeji.net' (9 October 2014) https://newsrescue.com/man-got-linda-ikeji-suspended-admits-director-cybersquatter-owner-lindaikeji-net/ accessed 2 May 2021 2018.

24 ICANN means Internet Corporation for Assigned Names and Numbers. ICANN was established to oversee and regulate the domain name industry. The tasks of ICANN includes the responsibility for IP address allocation, protocol identifier assignment, TLDs system management and root server system management functions

25 Nidhi Sethi, 'A Review on Recent Computer Crimes' (2016) 7(06) *International Journal of Computer Science and Engineering Technology (IJCSET)* 244–6, 245, Nigerian Law Today, 'Squashing the Squatter on Cyberspace Today' (13 October 2015) http://nigerianlawtoday.com/squashing-the-squatter-on-cyberspace/ accessed 14 June 2020.

26 Cybercrimes Act (Prohibition, Prevention, ETC) 2015, S. 58.

27 Jennifer Golinveaux, 'What's in a Domain Name: Is Cybersquatting Trademark Dilution' (1998–1999) 33 *University of San Francisco Law Review* 641. In the publication, cybersquatters were called cyber pirates.

28 Bernadette Dino, 'Passive Warehousing under ICANN's Uniform Dispute Resolution Policy: A Utilitarian Perspective' (2002) 10 *CommLaw Conspectus: Journal of Communications Law and Technology Policy* 301–14, 301.

ing a collection of domain names corresponding to trademarks with the intention of selling the registrations to the owners of the trademarks, within the notion of cybersquatting, while others distinguish between the two terms. Similarly, some consider "cyberpiracy" to be interchangeable with "cybersquatting."[29] Cyberpiracy apparently relates more to violation of the copyright in the content of websites, rather than abusive domain name registration.

Essentially, all that the cybersquatter has to do to make quick money is to register a domain name that contains the name of someone's trademark, trade name and business name or even registers an email identity that contains the name of a person or his business which only he alone had the exclusive right to use.[30]

Cybersquatting and other related domain malpractices

a **Domain name speculation:** Domain name speculation is the practice of registering or acquiring Internet domain names bearing nonexisting identities, with the intent of selling them later for a profit at a time any person or business wishes to use the identity. Domain name speculation is different from cybersquatting, which is the identification and registration of domain names to an existing entity with the intention to resell the same to the entity at a profit. While the first is a legal business endeavor, the other is a crime and is illegal. For instance, a person could register animal.com and resell at a higher price to whoever wishes to buy the domain on the agreed terms. With cybersquatting, the converse is the same – there is a deliberate step taken to register popular/well-known marks, for example, innosonvehicle.com, with the intention of reselling it to the rightful owners.

b **Typosquatting:** Typosquatting is speculative and was developed shortly after cybersquatting.[31] Typosquatters register domain names that are intentional misspellings of distinctive or famous names[32] with the hope that the domains will generate traffic when an Internet user makes a typographical error when typing a URL directly into the browser's URL bar. Typosquatting can be accomplished in several ways. A typosquatter might register a common misspelling of a trademarked

29 John G White, 'ICANN's Uniform Domain Name Dispute Resolution Policy in Action' (2001), 16 *Berkeley Technology Law Journal* 229, 230 stating that other cybersquatting activity involves "cyberpiracy" by luring Internet traffic from the trademark owner's site by incorporating a variation of the trademark term and "typo-squatting" by luring Internet traffic by misspellings or missing characters.

30 Deepanjan Dutta Roy, 'Cybersquatting: A New Form of IP Extortion – Position in India & US and Its Remedies' *Law Mantra*. http://journal.lawmantra.co.in/wp-content/uploads/2016/06/2.pdf accessed 27 February 2020.

31 Sunderland (n 17).

32 Shields v. Zuccarini, 254 F.3d 476, 483 (3d Cir. 2001).

word, a foreign spelling, a common typographical error ("unifik.edu.ng" instead of "unizik.edu.ng"), different formations of a word (the trademarked word with the addition of an -s or - ed), or a different TLD version of the trademarked word (".org" instead of ".com").[33] Some typosquatters have even purchased domain names with the period after "www" removed, e.g., "wwwunizik.edu.ng."[34]

Domain name as trademark

The relationship between domain name rights and intellectual property rights deserves deep and comprehensive analysis. The question is whether domain names are a kind of intellectual property or not. The answer to this question depends on the answer to a more basic question: are intellectual property rights limited to those stated and guaranteed by legislation or not? A positive response is correct because where a law is passed to protect some special rights under the title of intellectual property, it means that the legislator does not intend to protect other rights.[35] Nigerian laws have not categorized domain names as intellectual property rights and unlike trademarks, there are no international treaties regulating domain names. Even the Agreement on Trade-Related Aspects of Intellectual Property Rights (TRIPS Agreement)[36] did not mention domain names which indicate that domain names are not intellectual property rights. Yet, they may be registered as trademark if they meet its requirements and consequently enjoy trademark law protections (intellectual property protections).[37]

Domain name qualifies as a trademark when it is used in connection with a website that offers services to the public.[38] This includes all sites conducting

33 Reshika Dhir, 'Typosquatting: A Civil Conspiracy?' (2008), IP Osgoode Intellectual Property Law and Technology Program, https://www.iposgoode.ca/2008/11/typosquatting-a-civil-conspiracy/ accessed 20 February 2020.

34 Dara B. Gilwit, ''The Latest Cybersquatting Trend: Typosquatters, Their Changing Tactics, and How to Prevent Public Deception and Trademark Infringement', (Vol. 11, 2003), *Washington University Journal of Law and Policy*, <https://openscholarship.wustl.edu/cgi/viewcontent.cgi?article=1326&context=law_journal_law_policy>. accessed 20th February 2020

35 This maxim of interpretation is known as *Expressio Unius Est Exclusio Alterius,* meaning that the mention of one (thing) is the exclusion of others; Buhari vs. Yusuf (2003) 14 NWLR (Pt. 841) 446 at 499; Agbareh vs. Mimra (2008) NWLR (Pt. 1071) 378.

36 Although Nigeria is a party/signatory to the TRIPS Agreement, TRIPS Agreement is yet to be domesticated as required by S. 12 CFRN (1999) as amended.

37 Mostafa Bakhtiarvand, 'Legal Nature and Protection of Domain Names with Emphasis on Iranian Law' (2016) 21 *Journal of Intellectual Property Rights* 166–74.

38 Mohammad S Al Ramahi, 'Internet Domain Names & Trademark Law: Does the Current Legal Scheme Provide an Adequate Protection to Domain Names under the US & the UK Jurisdictions?' (April 2016) 21st BILETA Conference: Globalization and Harmonization in Technology Law at p. 5 https://www.bileta.org.uk/wp-content/uploads/

e-commerce and sites such as google.com that provide web-related services. Section 67 of the Trademarks Act[39] defines a trademark to mean

> A mark used or proposed to be used in relation to goods for the purpose of indicating, or so as to indicate, a connection in the course of trade between the goods and some person having the right either as proprietor or as registered user to use the mark, whether with or without any indication of the identity of that person, and means, in relation to a certification trade mark, a mark registered or deemed to have been registered under section 43 of this Act.

Furthermore, s. 67 of the Trademarks Act also defines a mark to "*include a device, brand, heading, label, ticket, name, signature, word, letter, numeral, or any combination thereof.*"

In the light of the statutory definition of a mark, it may be safely argued that the definition of mark is broad enough to cover the use of domain names which may consist of name, word, letter and numeral. In fact, the use of the word "include" indicates that the mentioned words are not exhaustive. Therefore, even if domain names consists of character not specifically mentioned in the definition of mark, the domain name may still be accommodated within the meaning of the mark as defined by the Trademarks Act, provided the character is similar to the characters itemized by the Act. This principle is known as *ejusdem generis* rule in the interpretation of statute.[40] In addition, taking into consideration the use of the following words in the definition, "any combination thereof" it may be rightly submitted that a domain name will qualify as a mark under the Trademarks Act.

Similarly, Article 15(1) of the TRIPS Agreement contains a definition of Trademark thus: "any sign, or any combination of signs, capable of distinguishing the goods or services of one undertaking from those of other undertakings."

Following the above definitions, it may rightly be mentioned that determinants of what qualifies as a trademark include that it must consist of a mark, the registration may be based on prior use or it may be futuristic, the trademark is to be used in relation to goods and services[41] and the use of the

---

Internet-domain-names-and-trademark-law-does-the-current-legal-scheme-provide-an-adequate-protection-to-domain-names.pdf accessed 4 August 2021.

39 Cap T13 LFN 2004.

40 P S Langan and P B Maxwell, *Maxwell on the Interpretation of Statutes* (12th ed., Sweet & Maxwell, London, 1969) 297; In Okewu v Federal Republic of Nigeria (2012) All FWLR (Pt. 625) 205 at 223, the Supreme Court of Nigeria in applying *ejusdem generis* rule held that Indian hemp, otherwise known as Cannabis Sativa falls with the phrase, "any other similar drug" used in the NDLEA Act even though it is not expressly mentioned in the Act.

41 The Trademarks Act provided for goods only. However, in 2007, the Minister of Commerce, Trade and Industry in exercise of the powers conferred on him by sections 42 and 45

trademark must be in the course of a trade.[42] As earlier mentioned, domain names have attained the status of being business identifiers and is therefore qualified to be regarded as trademark.

It is worth noting that the court had considered whether domain name registered by cybersquatters could be considered an infringement on trademark in view of the fact that there is neither a prior use of the name by the cybersquatter nor there an intention to use same in future in the course of trade. This was an issue in the English case of *British Telecommunications Plc. v. One in a Million*[43] which undoubtedly brought a major breakthrough for trademark owners. In that case, the cybersquatter registered several domain names that were trademarks of various companies with the aim of selling to the trademark owners subsequently. The English Court was faced with the daunting task of determining the case through the prism of trademark infringement, as the cybersquatter merely registered the names and did not use them in the course of trade in connection with the goods and services. The English Court held that "passing off" action could be established and that a remedy in passing off was better available as the cybersquatter's actions merely profited from the goodwill of the registered domain names and did not use them in the course of trade similar to the goods and services. The English Court stretched the classical trademark infringement elements to cover the claim, based on policy considerations of not letting cybersquatters go unpunished against trademark owners.

Furthermore, the eligibility for trademark registration is provided in s. 9 of the Trademarks Act which provides that for a trademark to be registrable, it must contain at least one or more of the following essential particulars:

- a The name of a company, individual or firm represented in a special or particular way
- b The signature of the applicant for registration or some predecessor in his business
- c An invented word or invented words
- d A word or words having no direct reference to the character or quality of the goods, and not being according to its ordinary signification a geographical name or a surname
- e Any other distinctive mark

A carefully combined interpretation of the definition of trademarks as provided by s. 9 and 67 Trademarks Act brings to clarity that only some types of commercial domain names qualify for trademark protection. For instance,

of the Act undertook an amendment of the First and Fourth Schedules of the Trademarks Regulations and made new schedules which incorporate service marks.

42 Adejoke O Oyewunmi, *Nigerian Law of Intellectual Property* (University of Lagos Press and Bookshop Ltd., 2015).

43 1998 FSR 26.

while domain names that use common or descriptive terms, such as jobfinder.com or scholarship-opportunities.com, may work very well to bring users to a website, they usually do not qualify for much trademark protection. This means that owners of such domain names generally won't have much luck stopping the use of these words and phrases as domain names. In other words, by using common terms that are the generic name for the service or by using words that are merely descriptive of the service or some aspect of it, the owner of the name will have fewer trademark rights against the users of similar domain names than he would if her domain name was distinctive.

Domain names can also be registered and protected as trademarks or service marks, provided that the domain names do satisfy all conditions to be duly registered and protected like the trademark and service marks.[44]

Any unique Internet domain name which is capable of identifying and distinguishing goods or services of a company from that of other companies, and can also act as a reliable source identifier for the concerned goods or services on the Internet, maybe registered and thus protected as trademark, if it satisfies all other rules and requirements for registration which are commonly applicable to the trademarks and service marks. Again, for proper registration of a domain name as a trademark or service mark, this must be unambiguously unique from all other domain names and well-known trademarks on the Internet, so that it does not mislead, confuse or deceive customers of other companies engaged in the same or different fields, or violate public order or morality. Such cases may give rise to instances of trademark infringement litigation. There have been so many decisions of both courts and administrative tribunals in other jurisdictions, taking a clear position that domain names are much like trademarks and should enjoy trademark protection.

Case laws

The first case decided by any Indian court which accorded trademark protection to domain names is the case of *Titan Industries Limited v. Prashanth Koorapati and Ors.*[45] In this case, the plaintiff had registered "Tanishq" as a trademark since 1994 for the production and marketing of jewelry and watches in 23 countries. The defendant registered "tanishq.com" as its domain name and the plaintiff objected to the use of its trademark as a domain name by the defendant on the ground that the domain name is based on the plaintiff's registered trade name. It was argued that consumers would likely believe that the defendant is an affiliate of the plaintiff. This would likely cause confusion and deceive the public, ultimately diverting business traffic

44 Onele and Onyilofor (n 7) 115–33, 123–7.

45 Delhi High Court Suit No. 179 of 1998, Decision dated 28 January 1998.

to the defendant. The Delhi High Court found in favor of the plaintiff and granted an ex-parte ad-interim injunction restraining the defendant from using the trade name "Tanishq" or any other name that is deceptively similar and would likely lead to passing off of the business and goods of the plaintiff.

In *Satyam Infoway Ltd v. Sifynet Solutions*,[46] the Honorable Supreme Court of India held that as far as India is concerned, there is no legislation that explicitly refers to dispute resolution in connection with domain names. Although the operation of the Trademarks Act may not allow for adequate protection of domain names, this does not mean that domain names are not to be legally protected to the extent possible under the laws relating to passing-off.

In *Tata Sons Ltd v. Manu Kosuri & Ors*,[47] the defendant registered a series of domain names incorporating the well-known trademark "TATA." The Court held that Internet domain names are not merely Internet addresses but are in fact corporate assets that are extremely important and valuable and as such, are entitled to protection equivalent to that afforded to registered trademarks.

Administrative resolutions of cases of cybersquatting as trademarks infringements

The administrative bodies for the resolution of disputes on intellectual property have in so many instances recognized domain name as registrable and capable of protection as trademark.

Particularly, ICANN using Uniform Domain Name Dispute Resolution Policy (UDRP) has recognized the protection of domain name as trademarks.[48] The UDRP is basically an international arbitration process for the resolution of domain name disputes. It is designed to solve disputes between a trademark owner and a domain name registrant and they have approved dispute resolution service providers that accept complaints.[49] These providers follow the UDRP as well as its own supplemental.

In *Volkswagen v. Emmanuel Efremov*,[50] WIPO[51] as approved administrative dispute resolution service provider considered domain name complaint, where the Respondent, a Nigerian, registered domain names bearing "Volkswagen" in different countries.[52] In this case, the disputed domain

46 2004(3) AWC 2366 SC.

47 III AD Delhi 545, 90 (2001).

48 All Answers Ltd (n 5).

49 World Intellectual Property Organization (WIPO) is one of the approved dispute resolution service providers.

50 WIPO Case No. D2014-0191.

51 WIPO means World Intellectual Property Organization.

52 The Complainant is the parent company of the Volkswagen Audi Group which, amongst other things, through various subsidiaries produces Volkswagen, Audi, Bentley, Bugatti, Lamborghini, MAN, Porsche, Scania, Seat and Skoda vehicles.

name was "my-volkswagen.com" registered with GoDaddy.com, LLC (the "Registrar"). The effect being that the disputed domain name is identical or confusingly similar to the complainant's own in the case. The emphasis of WIPO in the case was on the protection of existing trademark of Volkswagen. Thus the panel stated thus:

> Further, it is plain from the renown of the VOLKSWAGEN trademark and the number of other well-known trademarks which the Respondent has used as the basis of his domain names that the Respondent was well aware of the trademark significance of VOLKSWAGEN when he registered or acquired the disputed domain name...

Accordingly, the panel finds that the complainant has established that the disputed domain name is confusingly similar to the complainant's trademark and the requirements under UDRP are satisfied. The Panel eventually made an order that the disputed domain name "my-volkswagen.com" be transferred to the complainant.

In another administrative panel decision of WIPO in the case of *Konga Online Shopping Limited v. Rocket Internet GmbH, Arnt Jeschke*,[53] the consideration of WIPO in the proceeding was whether or not the complainant has a trademark right to the use of the word "Konga." This formed the fulcrum of the decision dismissing the complaint as it was the position of the panel that although the registration has commenced, the complainant having not been granted the trademark, cannot seek to restrain the use of the mark by a third party. The complainant in the case asserted that the use of the word "Konga" by the Respondent in the disputed domain name is so similar to the complainant's name and the trademark applications is likely to cause confusion by leading people to believe that the disputed domain name belongs to the complainant. The Panel found that the complainant has commenced trademark registration of the name "Konga" but had not gotten a grant. It consequently dismissed the complaint on that sole ground without considering other issues raised in the matter.

Conclusion

Generally, domain name performs the same functions online, which a trademark serves in the offline business dealings and transactions. While trademark is a striking graphic signifier of brand or business, domain name

53 Case No. DSC2014-000, https://www.wipo.int/amc/en/domains/search/text.jsp?case=-DSC2014-0001. Rocket is the owner/investor of Jumia which is Konga's biggest competitor in Nigeria. Rocket registered 11 domain names related to Konga outside Nigeria and they are konga.cd (Cote d'Ivoire), konga.cm (Cameroun), konga.ly (Libya), konga.ma (Mauritius), konga.mu (Morocco), konga.mw (Malawi), konga.sc (Seychelles), konga.sh (Saint Helena), konga.co.ke (Kenya) and konga.co.za (South Africa).

is a magnificent navigator to a company on the Internet, and an indication of its virtual presence. Owing to the importance of domain name as identifier of brands on the Internet, there is a need for legal protection of same against the activities of cybersquatters. Hence, proper statutory and regulatory protection of domain name against cybersquatting is imperative.

Cybersquatting constitutes one of the challenges of domain names and has been on increase following the advancement of e-commerce. It has become a thorny commercial issue for trademark owners and is heightened and made possible by the present system for domain names registration which does not require proof of commercial use. Cybersquatting has spread across different jurisdictions demanding a necessary reaction from all nations. Countries have reacted differently with courts in some jurisdictions proactively holding that domain name is protectable as trademark.

There is the challenge on domain name being regarded as trademark or any other intellectual property right because the prevailing opinion is that intellectual property rights are those specified and regulated by statute and since domain name has not been declared to be intellectual property rights in any law, it will be inappropriate to assume so. Notwithstanding the above, there has been in addition to legislative intervention by many nations, an international response in this respect through ICANN and WIPO which have set-up administrative processes for cases of domain name abuse. These administrative tribunals have in many cases as discussed in this work, given trademark owners relief against cybersquatting, including making order that domain name registered by cybersquatters be transferred to the trademark owners. The basis of many decisions of these administrative tribunals and courts in different jurisdictions is the acceptance that domain name is protected as trademark being an identifier of business brand in the cyberspace.

8 Trademark in the digital age in Nigeria

Ifeoma Anne Oluwasemilore

Introduction

A trademark in modern times has assumed greater significance as a branch of intellectual property law.[1] The world has become a global village, and the advent of the Internet has created incredible opportunities for global business. Consumers in Nigeria can buy from a business in America via the Internet and businesses can advertise to a much wider market for a fraction of the cost of traditional media in their localities.[2] However, these benefits have introduced the dilemma of what to do about trademark infringement on the Internet, which is a virtual world with no borders and universal laws.[3] Trademark protection in the digital age has become increasingly difficult during the past couple of years because of rapidly evolving technology in the area of Internet usage that makes protecting a company's marks more challenging. The Internet is indeed disrupting the delicate balance struck by pre-digital trademark laws.[4] The number of online companies today has made the possibility of trademarks confusion and infringement a concern. Due to the broadening use of the Internet and its platforms, protecting a company's trademark has become more important due to the ease in which infringement may occur.

The expansion of the Internet has created an enormous consumers market where many businesses now advertise their products or services and

1 M M Aminu, 'Trademarks in Nigeria: An Overview' (2016) 4(4) *International Journal of Innovative Legal & Political Studies* 11–8.

2 Y Simonyuk, 'Unauthorised Use of Another's Trademark on the Internet' http://scholarship.law.duke.edu/cgi/viewcontent.cgi?article=1050&context=dltr&sei-redir=1&referer=http%3A%2F%2Fwww.google.com.ng%2Furl%3Fsa%3Dt%26rct%3Dj%26q%3Dhow%2520is%2520trademark%2520is%2520infringed%2520in%2520the%2520internet%26source%3Dweb%26cd%3D2%26ved%3D0CCcQFjAB%26url%3Dhttp%253A%252F%252Fscholarship.law.duke.edu%252Fcgi%252Fviewcontent.cgi%253Farticle%253D1050%2526context%253Ddltr%26ei%3DztGRU7zxKMim0AWCnIA4%26usg%3DAFQjCNHX8p7gxC9WfHPVaZkBxE8xnrXd-w#search=%22how%20trademark%-20infringed%20internet%22 Accessed on 20th July, 2020.

3 Ibid.

4 Ibid.

DOI: 10.4324/9781003250883-11

communicate directly with consumers. Trademark rights are effectively regional or territorial in nature. Traditionally, consumer confusion resulted from more than one company using similar marks within the same territory, geographical area, or region.[5] Thus, where two companies sold competing products in the same country or territory, usage of similar marks would likely lead to confusion; however, confusion would not result where the companies are thousands of miles apart. Before the Internet and the World Wide Web, identical or nearly identical trademarks could exist in different geographic areas at the same time without the issue of trademark infringement ever arising. This is no longer the case. In recent years, the Internet has served to diminish the divide between regions and territories.[6] Although consumers have traditionally been exposed to products only within their own market, the Internet has bridged the gap between local and urban as well as between national and international. As a result, trademark law has had an exceedingly difficult time keeping up with the problems associated with the digital age.

In addition to contributing to erasing the geographic boundaries of trademarks, the Internet has also created new possibilities for the unauthorised use of trademarks. Apart from the Internet-specific means of infringement still based on traditional types of trademark infringement, for instance, where a trademark is simply displayed on a website as it would on more traditional forms of advertising, like television or magazine adverts, trademark uses specific to the Internet, such as in domain names, cybersquatters, meta-tags, hyperlinks, and framing, have also introduced new means of infringement and new laws.

According to Adewopo, "It is significant to note that the need for the reform of IP laws should not merely be informed by a stereotyped introduction of new IP rules but more by a nuanced and strategic revision of IP law consistent with the socio-economic conditions and defined development objectives, in an environment that is desirous of transiting into a competitive knowledge economy. IP law reform is justified by the paramount need to birth a knowledge economy that supports or contributes to the overall economic growth. The rationale for law reform is not to further a blanket or strong IPR standard that is now largely discredited in contemporary IP studies. It requires a careful understanding and analysis of the present state of the law in relation to the prevailing realities requiring policy consideration that will promote investment in innovation and creativity and the emergence and sustenance of a viable local knowledge economy."[7]

5 Nnenna Ajufo, et al. 'Protecting Trade Marks in the Digital Era' (2014) 2(1) *Nasarawa State University Law Commentaries* 21–35.

6 Ibid.

7 Adebambo Adewopo Ademola, 'According To Intellectual Property: A Pro-Development Vision of the Law and The Nigerian Intellectual Property Law And Policy Reform In

Against this backdrop, the chapter demystifies trademarks and makes some conceptual clarifications. The chapter examines the infringement of trademarks in the digital environment with reference to international best practices. It concludes that these diverse issues give rise to a need for legal responses to protect trademark owners and unsuspecting members of the public from the fraudulent antics of tricksters, and recommends that to achieve this objective, the 1965 Trademarks Act (TMA) needs to be reinvigorated to respond to the emergence of the Internet, to safeguard businesses from the unauthorised exploitation of their names and goodwill in the online digital environment.

Demystifying trademarks

The TMA[8] regulates trademarks in Nigeria. According to the Act, "trademark" means: except, in relation to a certification mark, a mark used or proposed to be used in relation to goods for the purpose of indicating, so as to indicate, a connection in the course of trade between the goods and some person having the right either as proprietor or as a registered user to use the mark, whether with or without any indication of the identity of that person, and means, in relation to a certification trademark, a mark registered or deemed to have been registered under section 43 of this Act.[9]

In the case of *Ferodo Ltd. v. Ibeto Ind. Ltd*,[10] the Supreme Court, in distinguishing a mark from a trademark held inter alia:

> The essence of a trade mark is that it indicates a connection in the course of trade between the goods and some person having the right to use the name. A trade mark can also be defined as a distinctive picture which would indicate to a purchaser of an article bearing it, the means of getting the same article in future by getting an article with the same mark on it; A mark, in this connection, includes a device, brand, heading, label, ticket, name, signature, word, letter, numeral or any combination thereof. A trade mark, on the other hand is a mark used or proposed to be used in relation to goods for the purpose of indicating, or so as to indicate a connection in the course of trade between the goods and some person having the right either as a proprietor or a registered user to use the mark.

Furthermore, section 67 of the TMA defines a mark to include "a device, brand, heading, label, ticket, name, signature, word, letter, numeral, or any

---

The Knowledge Era' 5th Inaugural Lecture Nigerian Institute of Advanced Legal Studies, Lagos (2012) 45.

8 Cap. T13 Laws of the Federation of Nigeria, (LFN) 2004.

9 Section 67 Trademarks Act.

10 (2004) 5 NWLR (Pt.866)317; (2004) 2 S.C. (Pt I) 1.

combination thereof."[11] In the light of the statutory definition of a mark, it may be safely argued that the definition of mark is broad enough to cover the use of domain names. In addition, taking into consideration the use of the following words in the definition "any combination thereof," it may be rightly submitted that a domain name will qualify as a mark under the TMA.[12]

Similarly, Article 15(1) of the Agreement on Trade-Related Aspects of Intellectual Property Rights ("TRIPS Agreement") contains a definition of trademark thus: "any sign, or any combination of signs, capable of distinguishing the goods or services of one undertaking from those of other undertakings."[13] Interestingly, although Nigeria is a party/signatory to the TRIPS Agreement, the TRIPS Agreement is yet to be domesticated.

In a simplistic form, the Black's Law Dictionary defines trademark as

> a word, phrase, logo, or other graphic symbol used by a manufacturer or seller to distinguish its product or products from those of others. The main purpose of a trademark is to designate the source of goods or services. In effect, the trademark is the commercial substitute for one's signature.[14]

To compartmentalise the above definitions, trademarks could be said to be any sign that individualises the goods of a given enterprise and distinguishes them from the goods of its competitors. A trademark is registrable under the TMA and the essence of a trademark is that it indicates a connection in the course of trade between the goods and some person having the right to use the name.

The registration of a trademark grants a monopoly right and once registered it can be protected both under the statute and under the common law of passing off.[15]

Value of trademark

Some reasons can be adduced as to why trademarks are protected: The essence of trademarks is to distinguish one proprietor's goods from those of his competitors' belonging to the same class. Thus registration of trademarks that are identical or closely resembling each other in respect of the same class of goods is prohibited, this is to avoid likelihood of deceit or confusion in the minds of the consumers. The protection of trademarks also encourages the manufacture of quality goods. Long usage of trademark may associate the goods upon which it is used with either high quality

11 Section 67 Trademark Act.

12 Trademarks Act Cap. T13, Laws of the Federation of Nigeria, 2004.

13 Article 15(1) of Trade- Related Aspect of Intellectual Property (TRIPS) 1995.

14 Bryan Garner (ed.) *Black's Law Dictionary* (9th ed., Thomson Reuters, St. Paul, MN, 2009) 1630.

15 See *Patkun Ind. Ltd. v. Niger Shoes Manufacturing Co. Ltd.* [1988] 5 NWLR (Pt. 93) 138.

or low quality. Thus, a proprietor known by a particular trademark that has been associated with high quality will be encouraged to maintain the high-quality standard and maintain his goodwill. Competitors will also be forced to produce high standard goods to match the goodwill of their counterparts. Trademark protection is also granted to avoid imitation. Unscrupulous businesspersons who are aware that a particular trademark has been associated with high quality may want to imitate the trademark and use the same on their product without a correspondingly high-quality product like that of the trademark proprietor. This will in effect bring down the goodwill of the trademark proprietor, hence the trademark protection.

Trademark can be used as a secret weapon in domain name disputes. It is a valuable adjunct to a particular business technology. The man who thinks up a distinctive and original name, device, or get-up to market his goods to make the goods easily recognisable or even more attractive to the average purchaser, and had over a period of time procured through the quality of his goods substantial goodwill for the name, device, or get up, deserves some protection for such name, device, or get up, and he is indeed protected by the law of trademarks. Like some other intellectual property rights, the registration of trademark confers protection on the proprietor for a limited period subject to renewal from time to time and payment of prescribed fees, which may then give the trademark a perpetual protection.[16]

By section 2(1) of the TMA, there shall continue to be kept the record called the Register of Trademarks, in which shall be entered all registered trademarks with the names and addresses of their proprietors, the date on which applications were made for their registration, notifications of assignments and transmissions, the names and addresses of all registered users, and such other matters relating to registered trademarks.[17] Section 2(3) provides that the register shall continue to be divided into two parts, Part A and Part B, respectively.[18] Generally, the effect of registration is the grant of monopoly right to use to mark and exclude others from using the mark; and in the event that another person uses the mark, the registered proprietor has the right to sue for infringement of his trademark. However, a proprietor of an unregistered trademark has a right of action in passing off against infringers. Most specifically, the part of the register wherein a trademark is registered determines the extent of the rights and protections granted to the proprietor of the registered trademark. Registration under Part A of the Register confers on the proprietor more rights and protection than those registered under Part B. For instance, a registration in Part A is valid in all respects after seven years and can no longer be removed from the register

16 Section 23(3) TMA.
17 Section 2(1) TMA.
18 Section 2(3) TMA.

unless where the registration was obtained ab initio by fraud or where the mark is scandalous or deceptive.[19]

Trademarks are regulated by each country independently; but because goods travel beyond country borderlines and bear trademarks, trademark law has international implications. The 1883 Paris Convention for the protection of industrial property was the first major international treaty designed to help the people of one country obtain protection in other countries for their intellectual creations, in the form of industrial property rights.[20] The Madrid Agreement concerning the international registration of marks (1891) offers trademarks owners the possibility to protect a trademark internationally.[21] The World Intellectual Property Organization (WIPO) administers both treaties. Established in 1970, WIPO is an international organisation dedicated to helping ensure that the rights of creators and owners of intellectual property are protected worldwide and that inventors and authors are therefore recognised and rewarded for their ingenuity.[22] The object of most trademark laws, therefore, is to permit an enterprise by registering its mark to obtain an exclusive right to use its license and assigned mark. It thereby prevents fraudulent practice where non-owners of a registered trademark copy and use such a trademark without the consent and authority of the owner of the trademark or its registered proprietor or licensor of the registered trademark.

Broadly speaking, trademarks have several functions, from the perspective of an owner, a trademark is the right to put a product for which a trademark is registered or on which the trademark is attached by the mark into circulation for the first time. From the viewpoint of the customer, a trademark serves the following functions: – designates the origin of a product or service – indicates a particular standard of quality – represents the goodwill of the manufacturer – protects the consumer from confusion – identification with a particular trade and for distinguishing or differentiation.[23]

Unlike other jurisdictions like the United Kingdom, Ghana, and South Africa, the Nigerian TMA does not cover service marks in its definition of what constitutes a trademark for registration purposes.[24] Likewise, the Federal High Court has an exclusive jurisdiction in matters relating to registered trademarks, while a cause of action in tort only lies for persons with unregistered trademarks under the legal head of passing off, actionable at the State High Courts.

19 Part A TMA.
20 Paris Convention for the Protection of Industrial Property 1883.
21 The Madrid Agreement concerning the international registration of marks (1891)
22 World Intellectual Property Organization (WIPO), 1970.
23 World Intellectual Property Organization, background Reading Material on Intellectual Property, 145.
24 See section 67(1) of the Trademarks Act.

Clarification of terms

Domain name

"A domain name is an address that people use on the Internet, whether for websites or for e-mail. It is a string of characters which usually spells out a word, a company name or person's name."[25] In addition to the foregoing, a domain name can also be said to be an Internet site identifier: it is often used to identify an Internet Protocol (IP) address.[26] Consequent upon this, most corporate entities employ the use of domain names to establish online addresses.[27] Thus, it is not uncommon for trademark owners to employ such trademarks as domain names, because it is common practice to guess domain names, an ascertained domain name is an invaluable business asset.[28] The process for registering domain names is a separate one from trademark registration, many countries have reached the conclusion that there is a strong need to take precautionary measures to prevent conflicts between trademarks and use of domain names.

Cybersquatting

Cybersquatting has been defined as registering or using a domain name with the intent to profit from the goodwill of a trademark belonging to another.[29] In essence, the cybersquatter uses the domain name as leverage against a trademark holder to induce them to buy the domain name. This act thus created problems for trademarks owners, as trademark owners were effectively barred from registering their own marks because only one person is entitled to a domain name.

Metatags

A metatag is a special HTML[30] tag that provides information about a Web page. Metatags or other forms of buried or hidden code are not normally visible to the average Internet surfer. Metatags have been used to direct traffic

25 What is a domain name & what can I do with a domain, available at http://getdotted.com/what - is - a - domain - name.php and accessed 3 July 2020.

26 Domain name, http://www.webopedia.com/TERM/D/domain_name.html accessed 3 July 2020.

27 Quite ironically, someone allegedly registered www.wipo.com to sell it back to WIPO. See 'Cybersquatting" http://www.webopedia.com/TERM/C/cybersquatting.html accessed 18 July 2020.

28 Domain Names, http://cyber.law.harvard.edu/property99/domain/ accessed 5 July 2020.

29 "Cybersquatting" available at http://www.webopedia.com/TERM/C/cybersquatting.html accessed 18 July 2020.

30 Short form for HyperText Markup Language, the authoring language used to create documents on the World Wide Web. HTML defines the structure and layout of a Web document by using a variety of tags and attributes.

to unrelated sites and keying has given competing firms the opportunity to advertise on the same web pages as their competitors. Therefore, website operators realise that metatags can be used to lure or deceive search engines by making unauthorised use of a famous trademark to attract attention to their website. In describing the unauthorized use of another's trademark in one's metatag, The Ninth Circuit stated that "Using another's trademark in one's metatags is much like posting a sign with another's trademark in front of one's store."

Protecting trademarks in a digital age

The rise of this electronic medium that disregards geographical boundaries has thrown the law into disarray by creating an entirely new phenomenon that needs to become the subject of clear legal rules.[31] The digital age brings both promise and peril to content creators and content consumers alike. Putting information online makes it available to an unlimited audience, from anywhere there is a telephone or network connection.[32] On the Internet, an infringement can actually take place all over the world, across borders, and in every jurisdiction. Trademark protection in the digital age has become a 24/7, 365-day a year fight for intellectual property rights holders.[33] Due to new electronic platforms and increased usage of the Internet, it is becoming more difficult to protect a company's brand, thus, in the past few years, trademark protection has advanced to the forefront of conversations, litigation and legislation, as governments, businesses and consumers daily strive to protect trademarks.[34]

Trademark protection ensures that the owners of marks have the exclusive right to use them in identifying goods or services or to authorise others to use them in return for payment. Trademark protection is legally enforced by courts in most jurisdictions and thus has the authority to stop trademark infringement. There is substantial case law relating to the application of the trademark infringement test in general, and the number of cases involving trademark infringement in cyberspace is growing.[35]

31 D R Johnson and D Post 'Law and Borders: The Rise of Law in Cyberspace' (1996) 48(5) *Stanford Law Review* 1367–402, 1375.

32 B T Muragendra 'Copyright and Trademark in Cyberspace' (2012) 3(6) *International Journal of Scientific &Engineering Research*, 1.

33 Nnenna Ajufo, et al. 'Protecting Trade Marks in the Digital Era' (2014) 2(1) *Nasarawa State University Law Commentaries* 21–35.

34 B Dalling (2001) 'Protecting against International Infringements in the Digital Age Using United States Copyright Law: A Critical Analysis of the Current State of the Law' (2001) *Brigham Young University Law Review* 1279–312.

35 The Nigeria Trademarks Registry of the Commercial Law Department (CLD) confirmed the release of its first-ever compendium of trademark opposition rulings derived from published applications.

As registered trademarks can only be protected within the Jurisdiction, within which they thrive, extending such protection to the Internet, which has no territorial restrictions or a uniform body of regulations has proved problematic, at best, this has spurred the need that traditional trademark concepts be reviewed to recognise this new phenomenon.[36] This need has given rise to the emergence of international agreements governing issues of trademarks on the Internet. These treaties include the TRIPS. TRIPS is a multinational agreement under the aegis of the World Trade Organisation (WTO), establishing rights and duties in trans-national transactions between citizens of different countries that are signatories to the treaty relative to property rights. Another is the WIPO administered Treaties. These treaties include the Paris Convention for the Protection of Industrial Property,[37] the Trademark Law Treaty,[38] Singapore Treaty on the Law of Trademarks,[39] and the Madrid Agreement,[40] which is a one-stop solution for registering and managing marks worldwide.[41]

The Internet poses a fundamental challenge for the regulation of trademarks and the situation is likened to an approach of governance without government. One obvious problem that has grossly been an impediment to the regulation of trademarks in the contemporary digital age is that of jurisdiction, applicable law, and enforcement.

"The effects of online activities are not tied to geographically proximate locations.[42]" As regards jurisdiction, trademark protection is territorial, while the Internet cannot be limited to any territory and jurisdiction. The problem of jurisdiction arises because it is only in the real world that there exists a mechanism to confer rights, immunities, privileges, etc. with no corresponding equivalent in the Internet world. Cyberspace is not and cannot be likened to the real world. By its nature, it has no territorial boundaries as it has no physical location. Hence, the difficulty in conferring rights and protecting trademarks.

36 It is extremely expedient for the Nigeria Trademark Act, 1965 to be reviewed to adapt to technological advancement.

37 These treaties include the Paris Convention for the Protection of Industrial Property of 1883, amended September 28, 1979.

38 Trademark Law Treaty adopted in Geneva in 1994.

39 Singapore Treaty on the Law of Trademarks adopted in Singapore in 2006.

40 Madrid System for the International Registration of Marks. The Madrid Protocol was adopted in June 1989 and entered into force in 1995. The protocol is one of two treaties comprising the Madrid System for international Registration of Trademarks. The first treaty, the 1891 Madrid Agreement provides for the registration of trademarks in several countries through the filing of one international trademark registration with WIPO. There is also a Protocol Relating to the Madrid Agreement

41 Nigeria has not adopted the Madrid Protocol. Madrid Agreement which provides for the registration of trademarks in several countries through the filing of one international trademark registration with WIPO.

42 Johnson and Post (n 31) 1375.

In almost every jurisdiction, trademark is governed by statute and local legislation. The difference in laws also creates a problem and there is no one international trademark law that governs trademark infringement in the cyberspace. What might constitute trademark infringement in Nigeria might not be the same in Singapore. In places like Europe, trademark law is governed individually by each country that is part of the European Union. However with recourse to the prevalent issues related to the infringement of trademarks in cyberspace, the European Union has passed directives that require member states to achieve certain intellectual property protection results.[43] Yet, numerous countries are still left out and there does not appear to be a legal framework available for trademark owners for infringements like user-name cybersquatting.

According to MacQueen,[44] laws can be written in the most draconian terms, but the critical question is whether they can be enforced. The enforcement of trademark law, rights, and privileges in the present digital age seems impossible. Attention is not presently being given to enforcing liability for infringement on the Internet or in cyberspace. In many jurisdictions, such awareness does not exist for lawmakers and law enforcement agents, albeit the enforcement of liability.

The problem of knowledge in this area is extremely problematic. In many cases, users are unaware of trademark restrictions in the use of the Internet and the fact that they can be held liable for trademark infringements. Information available on the World Wide Web is available simultaneously to anyone with a connection to the global network of cyberspace and individuals seem unaware of this issue as they move through the virtual space of cyberspace. In fact, trademark holders are at the mercy of websites when claiming a user name infringes upon its trademarks because many websites have specific user name policies in place when a trademark holder claims that a user name infringes upon its intellectual property rights. The only remedy available seems to be trademark owners being proactive in obtaining user names for Internet platforms.

Another problem that has long been acknowledged is that the use of the Internet has long outstripped the development of legislation. It seems issues that emerge every day from the use of the Internet are ahead of the legislation. Technology is moving faster than the Law. The volume of electronic communication and transaction crossing territorial boundaries through cyberspace is insurmountable when compared with the resources available to government authorities and their law enforcement mechanism. While they can assert jurisdiction over physical issues in the geographical borders they control, they cannot exercise such rights over issues in cyberspace.[45]

43 See for example the European Union Directive 2008/95/EC of 22 October 2008.

44 H MacQueen, 'Copyright and the Internet' in L Edwards and C Waelde, *Law and the Internet Regulating Cyberspace* (Oxford: Hart Publishing, 1997) 93.

45 For instance, even Local Governments in the United States have expressed concerns about their loss of control over information and transactions flowing across their borders. A

However, in many jurisdictions, efforts have been geared towards protecting trademark in this Internet age, to remove territorial and jurisdictional barriers to protecting trademark infringement. The WIPO, which is an agency of the United Nations that promotes intellectual property protection throughout the world administers the Madrid System for the International Registration of Marks. The Madrid System enables a trademark holder to protect his marks in multiple countries by filling only one trademark application. Thus, intellectual property protection is afforded to trademark holders in countries that are part of the Madrid System. The Internet Corporation for Assigned Names and Numbers (ICANN), Uniform Domain-Name Dispute-Resolution Policy (UDRP) which enables trademark owners to obtain through arbitration, domain names that parties are utilising that infringe upon their marks is a powerful tool that intellectual property right holders may utilise to acquire infringing domain names. A group of Countries have also negotiated the Anti-Counterfeiting Trade Agreement (ACTA). The agreement is proposed to increase intellectual property protection and the aim of the agreement is to establish international standards for enforcing intellectual property rights to fight more efficiently the growing problems associated with intellectual property infringement. The agreement, which is still being negotiated, is expected to be binding on those countries that ratify it and it is too early to determine how the agreement may affect trademark owners.

Nigeria is not left out. With the recent enactment of the Cybercrime (Prohibition, Prevention, etc.) Act 2015, the days of cybersquatters seems to be numbered. A cursory look at section 25(1) of the Act reveals that:

> Any person who, intentionally takes or makes use of a name, business name, trademark, domain name or other word or phrase registered, owned or in use by any individual, body corporate or belonging to either the Federal, State, or Local Governments in Nigeria, on the internet or any other computer network, without authority or right, and for the purpose of interfering with their use by the owner, registrant or legitimate prior user, commits an offence under this Act and shall be liable on conviction to imprisonment for a term of not more than two years or a fine of not more than N5,000,000 or to both fine and imprisonment.[46]

Jared Silverman, former chief of the New Jersey Bureau of Securities, expressed concern about the ability of the State to protect its residents against fraudulent schemes if it does not assert the right to regulate every online securities offering accessible, via the net, from within the State. A. Jared Silverman, Online Offerings: Is cyberspace a medium for capital formation, or a jurisdiction unto itself? 2–3 (Jan. 1996) (unpublished manuscript, on file with the Standford Law Review); in Johnson and Post (n 31) 1372.

46 Section 25(1) Cybercrime (Prohibition, Prevention, etc.) Act 2015.

In addition to the penalty stipulated in the provision reproduced above, the Federal High Court is empowered to make an order directing the offender to relinquish such registered name, mark, trademark, domain name, or other word or phrase to the rightful owner.[47]

A further reading of section 25(2) of the Cybercrimes (Prohibition, Prevention, etc.) Act 2015 also reveals that the Federal High Court, in awarding a penalty against an offender found guilty of cybersquatting, shall have regard to the following factors: 37.1 a refusal by the offender to relinquish, upon formal request by the rightful owner of the name, business name, trademark, domain name, or other word or phrase registered, owned or in use by any individual, body corporate or belonging to either the Federal, State or Local Governments in Nigeria[48]; or 37.2 an attempt by the offender to obtain compensation in any form for the release to the rightful owner for use of the name, business name, trademark, domain name or other word or phrase registered, owned or in use by any individual, body corporate or belonging to either the Federal, State or Local Government of Nigeria.[49]

Infringement of trademark in the digital environment

Cybersquatting

The TMA,[50] makes provisions for instance where individuals can bring actions for infringement of trademark, by establishing that the mark was used in the course of trade. The Act provides that a person uses a sign if, he affixes it to goods or the packaging thereof; offers or exposes goods for sale, puts them on the market or stocks them for those purposes under the sign, or offers or supplies services under the sign; imports or exports goods under the sign; or uses the sign on business papers or in advertising.[51] However, such use should be in the context of commercial activity with a view to economic advantage and not as a private matter.[52]

New technologies create novel issues and inform our understanding of existing laws. The statutes that form the basis of the Nigeria intellectual property regime are decades old and, as such, could not have contemplated how technology (and technology-assisted infringement) would evolve. As a result, traditional methods of intellectual property enforcement often lag behind the rapidly changing online environment. Cybersquatting is an example of the infringement of trademark in the digital environment.

47 Section 25(3) Cybercrime (Prohibition, Prevention, etc.) Act 2015.
48 Section 25(2)(a) Cybercrime (Prohibition, Prevention, etc.) Act 2015.
49 Section 25(2)(b) Cybercrime (Prohibition, Prevention, etc.) Act 2015.
50 Trade Marks Act, Cap T13 LFN.
51 Section 10(4) TMA.
52 L Bently and B Sherman, *Intellectual Property Law* (3rd ed., Oxford, New York, 2009) 922.

Generally, cybersquatting is the practice of registering names (popular Internet addresses), especially well-known company or brand names, as Internet domains, in the hope of selling them to their rightful owners.[53] Cybersquatting began after the Internet became commercialized. At the initial stages of the Internet, most companies did not realise the commercial potentials inherent to the Internet and consequently did not envisage the need to register their companies as domain names. Thus, cybersquatting at the time was not an illegal offence, as domain names were on first come first serve basis.[54] "Industrious companies" took advantage of this situation and registered a plethora of trademarks as domain names with the intention to resell to the trademark owner and make profit. This act thus created problems for trademarks owners, as trademark owners were effectively barred from registering their own marks, because only one person is entitled to a domain name. Subsequently, cybersquatting became a problem that had to be contended with because it began to undermine consumer confidence, discouraged Internet use and destroyed the value of established brand names and trademarks.[55]

Cybersquatting constitutes one of the many thorny issues between trademarks and domain names. It has spread across different jurisdictions demanding a necessary reaction from all nations. Countries have reacted differently. The US has enacted the Anti-Cybersquatting Consumer Protection Act 1999,[56] to attend to the effects of cybersquatting, and the British courts have responded to the act of cybersquatting through their judicial decisions.[57]

It is worth noting that the earliest stab by the English courts on cybersquatting was in the case of *British telecommunications Plc. v. One in a Million.*[58] In that case, the cybersquatter registered several domain names that were trademarks of various companies with the aim of selling to the trademark owners subsequently. The English Court was faced with the daunting task of determining the case through the prism of trademark infringement, as the cybersquatter merely registered the names and did not use them in the course of trade in connection with the goods and services.

Whilst the English Court held that a "passing off" action can well be established and that a remedy in passing off was better available as the cybersquatters' actions merely profited from the goodwill of the registered domain names and did not use them in the course of trade similar to the goods

53 "Cybersquatting" http://www.webopedia.com/TERM/C/cybersquatting.html accessed 18 July 2020.

54 Dunn Adam, the relationship between trademarks and domain names, Central European university collection, March 2014.

55 Dunn Adam, ibid.

56 The ACPA defines cybersquatting as the registration or use of a trademark as a domain name in bad faith with an intention to profit from the mark (15 usc, s1125(d)).

57 Nigeria also enacted the Cybercrime (Prohibition, Prevention, etc.) Act 2015.

58 1998 FSR 265

and services, the English Court stretched the classical trademark infringement elements to cover the claim, based on policy considerations of letting cybersquatters go unpunished against trademark owners. There is no doubt that this case can be said to be a major breakthrough for trademark owners.

Similarly, it is worth noting that the US courts, in a bid to protect trademark owners, sometimes stretch the law to meet the formal requirements of trademark law. However, it should be noted that the US has cybersquatting legislation to cater for the frustrating actions of the cybersquatters in its jurisdiction. Generally, there are certain theories, which have permeated the decisions given on disputes that have arisen between domain name owners and trademark owners. First is the traditional trademark infringement theory which requires that the infringing use causes a likelihood of confusion[59]; second theory is the dilution theory which seeks to protect the owner of a famous trademark standing to forbid others from using that mark in a way that would lessen its uniqueness,[60] and; third theory is the unfair competition, which is quite similar to the traditional trademark infringement but only applies to unregistered marks.[61]

Both sections 2 and 32 and section 43 of the Lanham Act can serve as the statutory basis for a trademark infringement claim. Sections 2 and 32 may only be invoked for registered marks whereas section 43 may be invoked for any marks. Despite significant differences in statutory language; Supreme Court precedent, lower court case law, and current scholarly criticism all indicate that the standards for protectability of a mark under sections 2 and 43 do not differ.[62]

The position in the US is best highlighted with the case of *Panavision v. Toeppen*,[63] and the case of *Intermatic v. Toeppen*.[64] In that case, the plaintiff (Panavision) had sued the defendant (*Toeppen)* for registration of the domain names panavision.com and panaflex.com. When Panavision asked *Toeppen* to relinquish the name, he demanded money, which Panavision refused to pay. *Toeppen* then retaliated by registering panaflex.com for a website that contained only the word hello. Therefore, the owners of the registered Panavision and *Panaflex* trademarks brought a lawsuit against Dennis Toeppen. The court granted injunctive relief against *Toeppen,* forcing him to relinquish the domain names panavision.com and panaflex.com. In

59 In this respect the courts traditionally protect the exclusive rights to use a trademark only within a particular field of trade and as against direct competitors. It is worth noting that trademark law was traditionally intended only to prevent competitors from dishonestly diverting customers who otherwise would have gone to the senior user of a mark.

60 *Ty Inc. v. Perryman, 306 F.3d 509.*

61 Intellectual Property in Cyberspace, 'Domain Names' http://cyber.law.harvard.edu/property99/domain/ accessed 25 August, 2020.

62 James C Bartholomew, The Scope of Protection Under §§ 2 & 43 of the Lanham Act. BARTHOLOMEW+LANHAM+ACT&ie=utf-8&oe=utf-8&client=firefox-b-ab accessed 15 September 2020.

63 141 F.3d 1316 (1998).

64 947 F. Supp.1227, 1230 (N.D. Ill. 1996).

granting the reliefs sought by the plaintiff, the Court held that unauthorised domain-name registration of a famous mark (such as Panavision) is actionable under trademark law.[65] The above-stated US decision was hinged on the trademark dilution theory.

Similarly, *in Hasbro, Inc. v. Internet Entertainment Group, Ltd. et al.*,[66] the defendants utilised "*Candyland*" in its domain name for a sexually explicit site. However, Hasbro, owner of a federal trademark in the name Candy Land, utilized principally in connection with a children's game, claimed that defendants' conduct violated federal and Washington trademark anti-dilution statutes. On Hasbro's application, the court issued a preliminary injunction, enjoining the defendants from continuing to use the name *Candyland* in their site's domain name.[67] However, in the case of *Lockheed Martin Corp. v. Network Solutions, Inc.*[68] The registration of similar trademarks to multiple parties was in dispute. The court found that the defendants were not liable for trademark infringement as the commercial use element was missing in the domain name dispute.[69] In addition, in the case of *Brookfield Communications, Inc. v. West Coast Entertainment Corp,*[70] the Court of Appeal for the Ninth Circuit granted a preliminary injunction in favour of the plaintiff against the defendant for use of domain name – "*moviebuff.com.*" This was based on the rationale that there was a likelihood of consumer confusion as regards the plaintiff's trademark "*moviebuff.*" Finally, in the case of *Planned Parenthood Federation of America. v. Bucci,*[71] the Court granted an injunction restraining the defendant from continuing to utilize the plaintiff's service mark Planned Parenthood in its domain name and further held that the conduct of the defendant is likely to cause confusion among the users of the Internet.

An action for trademark infringement or passing off in Nigeria

It is beyond cavil that the registered proprietor of trademark can bring an action to prevent the infringement of trademark similar to or resembling his own registered trade by another. He can also institute the action even if the

65 See further David V Radack, Understanding Some Ground Rules in Internet Domain Names Disputes" available at http://www.tms.org/pubs/journals/jom/matters/matters - 9801.html accessed 6 July 2020.

66 1996 WL 84853 (W.D. Wash. 1996); 1996 U.S. Dist. LEXIS 11626 (W.D. Wa. 1996); 1996 U.S. Dist. LEXIS 11626 (W.D. Wa. 1996).

67 Internet Library of Law and Court Decisions available at http://www.internetlibrary.com/cases/lib_case96.cfm and accessed 6 July 2020, see also University of Louisville "Hasbros Internet Entertainment Group "CANDY LAND Case" https://louisville.edu/faculty/ddking01/cecs311/cases/ Hasbro.htm and accessed on 6 July 2020

68 *Lockheed Martin Corp. v. Network Solutions, Inc., 985 F. Supp. 949 (C.D. Cal (1997)*

69 Trademarks infringement is provided for in section 43 of the U.S Lanham Act, 15 USC1125.

70 174 F.3d 1036 (9th Cir. 1999).

71 *Parenthood Federation of America v. Bucci, 42 U.S.P.Q.2d 1430, 1437 (S.D.N.Y).*

trademark infringing his own mark has already been registered.[72] Basically, the Supreme Court has held in *Ferodo Ltd. v. Ibeto Ind. Ltd.*[73] that an action for infringement will usually lie where a competitor uses a registered trademark in connection with proprietor's goods for the purpose of confusing them with his own goods in the same class.[74]

Under the Nigerian law, a trademark can be said to have been infringed when there has been an unauthorised use of a trademark or service mark on or in connection with goods and/or services in a manner that is likely to cause confusion, deception, or mistake about the source of the goods and/or services. Section 5(2) of the TMA describes what amounts to an infringement. It provides thus:

> Without prejudice to the generality of the right to the use of a trade mark given by such registration as aforesaid, that right shall be deemed to be infringed by any person who, not being the proprietor of the trademark or a registered user thereof using it by way of the permitted use, uses a mark identical with it or so nearly resembling it as to be likely to deceive or cause confusion, in the course of trade, in relation to any goods in respect of which it is registered, and in such manner as to render the use of the mark likely to be taken either as being used as a trade mark; or in a case in which the use is use upon the goods with which such a person as aforesaid is connected in the course of trade.[75]

The apex Court, while breathing life to the provision of section 5(2) of the TMA, established when an action for infringement of trademark can be maintained in the case *Ferodo Ltd. v. Ibeto Ind. Ltd,*[76] as follows:

> Following the provisions of section 5(2) of the Trade Marks Act, an infringement of a registered trade mark cannot be maintained unless the court finds that the defendant is engaged in the use of a mark identical with the registered trade mark or uses a mark so nearly resembling the registered trade mark, as to be likely to deceive or cause confusion in

72 *Bell Sons & Co V Godwin Aka 1972 UILR VOL 3 (PART 1) 42; Savage V Allen 13 N.L.R 34; The Procter And Gamble Company V. Global Soap And Detergent Industries Ltd & Anor (2012) LPELR - 8014(CA).*

73 (2004) 5 NWLR (Pt.866)317; (2004) 2 S.C. (Pt I) 1.

74 The apex Court further held that in deciding whether two marks are confusingly similar, the marks alone must be considered, divorced from associated features or get up and the like: Evidence is admissible to show which of the features shown in the register, in this case, are essential and which are inessential so as to be unimportant in deciding questions of infringement. It was also held that not all the features contained in the mark are important for the purpose of the infringement of the trademark and not all the components are to be considered as forming part of the trademark. Finally, the apex Court held that the resemblance-giving rise to infringement must lie in the basic idea of the mark.

75 Section 5(2) Trademarks Act Cap. T13 LFN 2004.

76 (2004) 5 NWLR (Pt.866)317; (2004) 2 S.C. (Pt I) 1; (2004) 17 NSCQR 560.

> the course of trade; or uses in relation to any goods in respect of which it is registered, or uses in such a manner as to render the use of the mark to be taken as importing a reference to the goods which the plaintiff's trade mark is connected.[77]

Furthermore, in *Ayman Enterprises Ltd v. Akuma Industries,* the Supreme Court stipulated what a plaintiff needs to prove to be successful in an action for infringement of a trademark when it held thus:

> The Plaintiff must establish his title either as proprietor or as a registered user entitled to sue. He must then prove that the defendant has acted or threatens to act in a way as to infringe the right conferred upon him by the registration of the trade mark under the Act.[78]

In the light of the foregoing, the requirements for an action hinged on trademark infringement are as follows: (i) the trademark must have been used by a person who is neither a proprietor nor has obtained permission to use same; (ii) the mark used must have been identical with the trademark or so nearly resembles it; (iii) the mark used must be likely to deceive or cause confusion in the course of trade and in relation to any goods or services in respect of which it is registered; and (iv) the mark must have been used as a trademark or used upon the goods or services in the course of trade.

Nonetheless, it is worth noting the distinction between infringement of trademark and passing off. While an action for infringement of trademark is a statutory remedy conferred on the registered proprietor of a registered trademark for the enforcement of his right to use the trademark in relation to the goods for which the mark has been, an action for passing-off is common law remedy and the plaintiff need not establish a title for the same. Putting the distinction more clearly, the Court of Appeal in *Virgin Ent. Ltd.* v *Mohammed,*[79] held thus:

> An action for infringement of trademark is a statutory remedy conferred on the registered proprietor of a registered trademark for the enforcement of his right to use the trademark in relation to the goods for which the mark has been. An action for passing-off is an action for deceit for colourable imitation of a mark adopted by a person in relation to his goods which has acquired distinctive reputation in the market as referring to the goods belonging to or produced by that person only. An action for passing-off is common law remedy and the plaintiff need not establish title for the same. What he is required to show is that his goods have distinctive features.[80]

77 Ibid.
78 (2003) 6 SCNJ 307.
79 (2009) 12 NWLR (Pt. 1151) 136.
80 Ibid.

Conclusion

The criminalisation of cybersquatting in Nigeria is quite commendable. There is much to be desired with respect to the civil remedies available to registered trademark owners as it is. Nigerian courts have not really been seized of the opportunity to pronounce on the infringement of trademarks by domain names. However, it is suggested whenever such an opportunity avails itself, it is hoped that the courts would be able to situate such claims within the tenets of the provisions of trademarks law or its common law cousin – passing off. While some have argued that the only remedy to cybersquatting in Nigeria for now in Nigeria is to take benefit of the provision of section 25 of the Cybercrime (Prohibition Prevention) Act 2015, it is humbly suggested that the judiciary can still expound the provision of section 67 of the existing TMA to accommodate actions arising from domain name disputes and cybersquatting.[81] A mixture of national and international legislation could bring about some solution; however, legislation alone cannot bring total change. Perhaps, education, self-imposed regulation, creation of awareness, and cooperation by Internet service providers and online users could be immensely positive. With education, awareness, and self-imposed regulation, individuals will begin to conduct searches before the registration of domain names to avoid registering names that have already been registered thus, infringing trademarks. This will greatly avert the number of trademark disputes.

The mere display by a business of her trademark online does not establish when used, that the mark is distinctive. While registering trademarks is not mandatory due to the availability of common law protection, in this present digital age, registering trademarks is highly recommended because it seems, it is only registration that would enable a mark owner to take full advantage of the protection the law may provide (if any) for trademark infringement in cyberspace. This chapter concludes that these diverse issues give rise to a need for legal responses to protect trademark owners and unsuspecting members of the public from the fraudulent antics of tricksters, and recommends that to achieve this objective, the 1965 TMA needs to be re-invigorated to respond to the emergence of the Internet, to safeguard businesses from the unauthorised exploitation of their names and goodwill in the online digital environment.

81 If indeed the definition of our s.67 covers domain names, then once the unlawful identical or nearly resembling domain name is being used as a site for goods or services that the lawful trademark proprietor trades in, even if the type of goods or services are branded with various other marks, one should be able to expound the TMA and succeed in a claim for infringement. This is primarily on account of the inclusion of the phrase "importing a reference to the goods..." in section 5 TMA. If however, it is for unrelated goods or services, or the domain name is not in use but merely registered, then no trademark infringement.

Part III

Copyright

9 The quagmire of open access

Availability, accessibility, and impact

Kunle Ola

Introduction

The creation of a scholarly work makes it available but due to institutionalized and systemic legal, financial, and technical restrictions, accessibility to works is limited thereby stalling impact. This chapter explores the concepts of availability, accessibility, and impact, against the background of scholarly works and how they affect the current access to knowledge movement. It examines how the structures and mechanisms around these concepts have constituted barriers to authors and users globally, but particularly to those within developing countries. Academic scholars in developing countries are no different from their counterparts in the North when it comes to the "publish or perish" culture.[1] The difference is clearly seen when considering accessibility to, and impact on their scholarly works. Academics in developing countries are particularly caught in the dilemma of whether to publish locally or publish abroad.

Perhaps publishing locally is great for the local market. However, it seems inadequate for the international market and for purposes of review, tenure, and promotion. Publishing abroad depicts reputation because such works are connected to the international publishing system. Whatever option the developing country scholar chooses, they have something to lose and are caught in a quagmire. In exploring the concepts of availability, accessibility, and impact of works by authors in developing countries on the current access to knowledge movement, a social contract and utilitarian prism has been adopted. It explains that publishing a work is a statement by an author of a readiness to make expressions of ideas available, accessible, and impactful.

From a social contract prism, it sees the process as an agreement between authors, government, publishers, and the general public. Authors create works; governments grant intellectual property (IP) rights, publishers produce and fund the publication of such works thereby making them available,

1 Seema Rawat and Sanjay Meena, 'Publish or Perish: Where Are We Heading?' (2014) 19(2) *Journal of Research in Medical Sciences* 87–9.

DOI: 10.4324/9781003250883-13

accessible, and impactful to the general public for purposes of seeking the greatest good for the greatest number of people. It also examines the structures and mechanisms around these three concepts and demystifies the open access to knowledge quagmire around works from developing countries. It puts forward suggestions on how to navigate through the access/impact barriers and break the walls to enable not just availability but also accessibility and impact on scholarly works originating from developing countries.

Africa and the publishing trade

Developing countries have been involved in the trade of publishing for a long time.[2] Way back in the seventeenth century, Sudan was known to be involved in publishing, while at about the mid-eighteenth century, Nigeria and South Africa were at the forefront of mission run printing presses.[3] Today, publishing is still a trade in most developing countries.[4] The Nigerian Publishers Associations has 77 members,[5] and South Africa has 117 members.[6] Oxford University Press, Longman, and Macmillan came to Nigeria in 1949, 1962, and 1965 respectively.[7] In the 1960s they expanded into Southern Africa.[8] At about the 1970s when Indigenization policies where on the front burners of most developing nations, these companies evolved into locally run organizations and at the same time there was the establishment of University presses in Nigeria such as "University of Nigeria and University of Lagos press."[9]

Today publication still goes on in Nigeria and in other developing countries, but the global network platform that supports the production and dissemination of printed materials is evidently lacking in most developing countries.[10] For purposes of emphasis and brevity, this research will focus on one developing country, Nigeria. The choice of Nigeria is predicated on

2 Elizabeth le Roux, 'Book History in the African World: The State of the Discipline' (2012) 15 *Book History* 248–300, 248.

3 Stanley Gazemba, 'African Publishing Minefield and the Woes of the African Writer' *Elephant* https://www.theelephant.info/culture/2019/12/13/african-publishing-minefields-and-the-woes-of-the-african-writer/?print=print

4 WIPO & IPA, 'The Global Publishing Industry in 2018' https://www.wipo.int/publications/en/details.jsp?id=4251

5 Nigerian Publishers Association (NPA), 'List of Members' https://nigerianpublishers.com/list-of-members/

6 Publishers Association of South Africa, 'PASA Members' https://www.publishsa.co.za/members/category?all=all

7 Gazemba (n 3).

8 Ibid.

9 Ibid.

10 Susan Murray, *The Current State of Scholarly Journal Publishing in Africa. Findings & Analysis* (African Journals Online, 2014) 7, https://www.ajol.info/public/Scholarly-Journal-Publishing-in-Africa-Report-Final-v04c.pdf

the facts that Nigeria is the most populous nation in Africa,[11] that several multinational publishers have operated in Nigeria and that a high number of publishers are still actively in operation.[12] As a result, Nigeria will provide a reasonable representation for other developing countries.

Nigerian authors are active contributors to the global library.[13] Many Nigerians are doing exploits in their different fields of learning and are writing in the academic and scholarly space about these exploits.[14] The intellectual creations of any of the aforementioned authors expressed in a tangible medium can be categorized as "available works." As a result of this availability, there is the potential for the work to be accessed, used, and reused and for it to positively affect individuals, communities, and nations, thereby making an impact. Unfortunately, access to created works (available works) is often stalled by institutionalized restrictions, thereby curtailing the potential impact of such works.

Exploring the concepts and the barriers

Publishing a work in any format makes it available.[15] The ability to retrieve, read, use, and reuse a work as at when required refers to its accessibility,[16] and the ability of such a work to address and help redress a problem or to facilitate development through contributions to scholarship, research, juristic, legislative, or executive/administrative analysis implies impact.[17] Publication in any format brings the work from the realm of abstraction to the realm of reality, thereby making the work a tangible product that is readily

11 Statista, 'African Countries with the Largest Population as of 2021' https://www.statista.com/statistics/1121246/population-in-africa-by-country/, Nigeria's population is almost double that of the Ethiopia which is number 2 in the African continent. As of February 2021, Nigeria had an estimated population of 206,140 million, Ethiopia had 114,964 million, Egypt, 102, 334 million, DR Congo had 89, 561 million.

12 NPA (n 5).

13 Rebecca Jagoe, 'From Achebe to Adichie. Top Ten Nigerian Authors' 11 January 2018, https://theculturetrip.com/africa/nigeria/articles/from-achebe-to-adichie-top-ten-nigerian-authors/. It contains names of popular Nigerian fiction authors like Chinua Achebe, Wole Soyinka, Femi Osofisan, Ben Okri, Buchi Emecheta, Sefi Atta, Helon Habila, Teju Cole, Adaobi Nwaubani and Chimamanda Ngozi Adichie.

14 Oluwadamilare Akinpelu, '7 Nigerian Innovators Emerge Finalist in WHO Africa Innovation Challenge' 11 March 2019, https://technext.ng/2019/03/11/7-nigerian-innovators-emerge-finalists-in-who-africa-innovation-challenge/

15 Section 1(2)b, *Nigerian Copyright Act2004*, where it requires that works be fixed in definite medium of expression where it can be perceived, reproduced or otherwise communicated directly or indirectly. See also s. 29 of Australia's *Copyright Act 1968* (Cth) which explains that literary, dramatic, music and artistic works are deemed published when they have been supplied to the public.

16 Budapest Open Access Initiative, https://www.budapestopenaccessinitiative.org/read

17 Brian Fitzgerald, 'Copyright in the Age of Access' (2017) 39 *European Intellectual Property Review* 131.

available.[18] The fact that a work is available does not, however, mean that the work is accessible. It, therefore, means that the availability of a work does not guarantee accessibility to such a work. It also means that the availability of a work is not synonymous with impact by the work.

The Barriers

Structures have been built within and around the publishing industry that determines accessibility, that is, who, how, and when a work can be accessed.[19] These structures are gates that serve as barriers to those wishing to access the content. Lessig identifies overregulation as one of such barriers and notes that "overregulation stifles creativity. It smothers innovation."[20] Access barriers were identified in the Budapest Open Access Initiative as financial, legal, and technical.[21] Ola explaining these barriers noted that

1 Financial barriers include price barriers in the form of subscription fees.
2 Legal barriers refer to IP rights that grant exclusive rights to owners, restrict access to works, and require intending users to seek and obtain permission to use such works.
3 Technical barriers refer to technologies deployed by right-owners to restrict and control access to copyrighted digital contents. They are referred to as technological protection measures (TPM) and digital rights management (DRM).

Suber identified copyright as a legal barrier and explained that

> Copyright can also be a significant access barrier. If you have access to a work for reading but want to translate it into another language, distribute copies to colleagues, copy the text for mining with sophisticated software, or reformat it for reading with new technology, then you generally need the permission of the copyright holder. That makes sense when the author wants to sell the work and when the use you have in mind could undermine sales. But for research articles we're generally talking about authors from the special tribe who want to share their work as widely as possible. Even these authors, however, tend to transfer their copyrights to intermediaries—publishers—who want to sell their work. As a result, users may be hampered in their research by

18 *Cummins V Bond* [1927]1 Ch 169 involving a spirit or ghost, a medium and Mr Bond. The courts decided amongst other things that it had no jurisdiction over the afterlife.
19 Peter Suber, *Open Access* (MIT Press, 2012) 4–5.
20 Lawrence Lessig, *Free Culture: How Big Media Uses Technology and the Law to Lock Down Culture and Control Creativity* (Penguin Press, 2004) 199.
21 Budapest Open Access Initiative, https://www.budapestopenaccessinitiative.org/read

> barriers erected to serve intermediaries rather than authors. In addition, replacing user freedom with permission-seeking harms research authors by limiting the usefulness of their work, harms research readers by limiting the uses they may make of works even when they have access, and thereby harms research from both directions.[22]

The fact that these barriers enjoy legitimacy through the current copyright system makes it illegal to work around the barriers outside the purview of accepted rules.[23] This can be really frustrating and has been so noted in one of Litman's classical works, "Copyright Noncompliance, (or why we can't 'Just say yes' to licensing)" where she noted a growing gravitation by citizens to non-compliance to copyright rules.[24] Lessig, in "Free Culture" notes that this frustration is gradually turning our children into criminals. He stated that "When forty to sixty million Americans are considered 'criminals' under the law, and when the law could achieve the same objective—securing rights to authors—without these millions being considered 'criminals,' who is the villain?".[25]

The copyright structure protecting creative works has existed for over 300 years and provided the legal platform for related structures that have evolved into a complex mechanism, which are all engrained in the system.[26] They have played and continue to play a critical role in determining how impactful works turn out to be.[27] The impact of a work is a factor of multiple things but based on the current global publishing structure, availability, accessibility, and impact of a work is influenced by the identity and location of the publisher.[28] Works emanating and published in the North, appear to enjoy certain advantages in comparison to works emanating and published in developing countries.[29]

22 Suber (n 19).

23 See, The WIPO Internet Treaties: (*WIPO Copyright Treaty 2002* Articles 11 & 12 and *WIPO Performance and Phonograms Treaty 2002* Articles 18 & 19).

24 Jessica Litman, 'Copyright Noncompliance (or Why We Can't "Just Say Yes" to Licensing)' (1997) 29 *New York University Journal of International Law and Politics* 237.

25 Lessig (n 20) 202.

26 Michael L Voight and Barbara J Hoogenboom. 'Publishing Your Work in a Journal: Understanding the Peer Review Process' (2012) 7(5) *International Journal of Sports Physical Therapy* 452–60, 452.

27 H Marcovitch, 'Editors, Publishers, Impact Factors, and Reprint Income' (2010) 7(10) *PLoS Medicine* e1000355. https://doi.org/10.1371/journal.pmed.1000355. See also, Jill O'Neill, 'The Significance of an Impact Factor: Implications for the Publishing Community' (2000) 13 *Learned Publishing* 105–9, 105.

28 Joanna Adcock and Edward Fottrell, 'The North-South Information Highway: Case Studies of Publication Access among Health Researchers in Resource-Poor Countries' (2018) 1 *Global Health Action* doi:10.3402/gha.v1i0.1865.

29 M. Blicharska, R Smithers, M Kuchler *et al.* 'Steps to Overcome the North–South Divide in Research Relevant to Climate Change Policy and Practice' (2017) 7 *Nature Climate Change* 21–7, 21. https://doi.org/10.1038/nclimate3163

Peter Lor describes the above-referred situation as the North-South divide in scholarly communication and notes that "it is a complex problem that has to be tackled holistically."[30] Litman captures it aptly as the divide between the "haves and have not."[31] Works by authors in developed and developing countries easily tick the availability box. The accessibility and impact boxes have however shown a different indication. The structures and mechanisms that control the operation of these concepts have constituted and continue to constitute barriers to authors and users in developing countries.[32]

Access and development

The United Nations has identified "knowledge" as a pivotal element for development.[33] It is therefore not surprising that everyone has been granted the right to education.[34] The United Nations Declaration of Human Rights further provides that "everybody has the right freely to participate in the cultural life of the community, to enjoy the arts and to share in scientific advancement and its benefit."[35] The millennium development goals (MDGs) and the sustainable development goals (SDGs) identified knowledge in MDG 2 and in SDG 4 as imperatives tools for development.[36] Whereas MDG 2 set the goal of achieving universal primary education, SDG 4 set out to ensure inclusive and equitable quality education and promote lifelong learning opportunities for all.[37]

Ban Ki Moon acknowledged that these policies have enabled remarkable improvements in the lives of people around the world. He noted that

> Sub-Saharan Africa has had the best record of improvement in primary education of any region since the MDGs were established. The region achieved a 20-percentage point increase in the net enrolment rate from 2000 to 2015, compared to a gain of 8 percentage points between 1990 and 2000.[38]

30 Peter Johan Lor, 'Bridging the North-South Divide in Scholarly communication in Africa-a Library and Information Systems Perspective' (2007) 33(4) *IFLA Journal* 303–12, 303.

31 Jessica Litman, 'Revising Copyright Law for the Information Age' (1996) 75 *Oregon Law Review* 19, 22.

32 Kunle Ola, *Open Access to Knowledge in Nigeria: A framework for Developing countries* (Routledge, 2019) 3.

33 United Nations, 'We Can End Poverty, Millennium Development Goals' https://www.un.org/millenniumgoals/

34 Article 26(1), United Nations, 'United Nations Declaration of Human Rights' https://www.un.org/en/universal-declaration-human-rights/

35 Article 27(1), United Nations, 'United Nations Declaration of Human Rights' https://www.un.org/en/universal-declaration-human-rights/

36 United Nations, (n 33).

37 Ibid.

38 United Nations, 'Millennium Development Goals Report 2015' https://www.un.org/millenniumgoals/2015_MDG_Report/pdf/MDG%202015%20rev%20(July%201).pdf

Knowledge is an indispensable ingredient for development and without access to this critical element called knowledge, development becomes a mirage. It is, therefore, accurate to say that "acquiring knowledge is therefore imperative for development, and the currency for acquiring knowledge is 'access'."[39]

Dewey postulates through his theory of experience that knowledge emanates from experience and that experience is the best teacher.[40] Others ponder and ask, is experience really the best teacher?[41] Knowledge can be acquired in many ways. Jenkins noted that, "It seems to me that the traditional six ways of knowing, identified by philosophers-appeal to authority, intuition, formal logic, empiricism, pragmatism, and skepticism."[42] Evidently, some of these methods have gained dominance due to their prevalent use in the educational sector and due to the gravitation toward evidence-based analysis.[43] The concern with the dominance of evidence-based enquiry based on empiricism is the resulting effect of subjugating other methods and compelling the use of this method over others in the educational sector.

Scholars are however speaking up against this dominance in favor of other methods and noting the need to adopt methods based on individual circumstances.[44] Regardless of the philosophical method used in acquiring knowledge, knowledge is often captured in a medium covered and protected by IP rights. The process of investigation could lead to the making of an invention, which are protected as patents.[45] The outcome of these investigations is often published as either journal articles, book chapters, books, or in some written form and these are all protected as literary works under copyright.[46] It is, therefore, appropriate to say that works covered by IP

39 Ola (n 32) 8.

40 Schmidt, Margaret, 'Learning from Teaching Experience: Dewey's Theory and Preservice Teachers' Learning.' (2010) 58(2) *Journal of Research in Music Education* 131–46.

41 Tom R Karl and Jeffrey P Jacobs, 'Is Experience the Best Teacher?' (2017) 51(2) *European Journal of Cardio-Thoracic Surgery* 299–300. https://doi.org/10.1093/ejcts/ezw287

42 M D Jenkinson, 'Sources of Knowledge for Theories of Reading' (1969) 1(1) *Journal of Reading Behavior* 11–29, 12. doi: 10.1080/10862969609546837

43 William M Webb, 'Rationalism, Empiricism, and Evidence-Based Medicine: A Call for a New Galenic Synthesis' (2018) 5(2) *Medicines* 40. doi:10.3390/medicines5020040

44 George Bealer and P F Strawson, 'The Incoherence of Empiricism' (1992) 66 *Proceedings of the Aristotelian Society* 99–143. See also, Peter Markie, 'Rationalism vs. Empiricism' (2017) *The Stanford Encyclopedia of Philosophy*, https://plato.stanford.edu/entries/rationalism-empiricism/.

45 Jennifer Davis, *Intellectual Property Law* (Oxford University Press, USA 2008) 261.

46 See for example, s3(2) *Copyright Design and Patent Act (CDPA) 1988* UK which provides that Copyright does not subsist in a literary, dramatic or musical work unless or until it is recorded, in writing or otherwise. See also s.178 *Copyright Design and Patent Act1988* which provides that, writing includes any form of notation or code, whether by hand or otherwise, and regardless of the method by which, or medium in or on which it is recorded.

rights, particularly patent and copyright, are a major source of knowledge.[47] Sources of knowledge also includes traditional knowledge, indigenous knowledge, folklore, and knowledge from indigenous cultural expressions.[48]

Knowledge and access to knowledge

The goal of IP is explicitly stated in legislative instruments providing these rights. The long title to the Statute of Anne captures it succinctly as "An act for the encouragement of learning, by vesting the copies of printed books in the authors or purchasers of such copies, during the times therein mentioned."[49] A similar goal is mentioned in the US constitution. It states that the goal of copyright is "to promote the progress of science and useful arts, by securing for limited times to authors and inventors the exclusive right to their respective writings and discoveries."[50] To encourage learning and promote the progress of science and useful arts are the stated goals. These are public interest goals.

Conversely, by vesting authors with the copies of printed books, and granting them exclusive rights to their writing and discoveries for limited times, the instruments provide an economic interest-based mechanism for achieving the public interest goal. Striking and maintaining the balance between the public interest goals and the economic interests have been an abysmal failure and the albatross of the IP system.[51] One could ask that if the goal was to encourage learning and to promote the progress of science and useful arts, why has copyright become a restrictive tool rather than an enabling tool for accessing knowledge? Why are there so many restrictive structures built around IP and that are now barriers to accessing knowledge? Could Ginsburg's one-word answer "greed" be correct?[52]

47 Sirlei de Almeida Pereira, Luc Quoniam, 'Intellectual Property and Patent Prospecting as a Basis for Knowledge and Innovation – A Study on Mobile Information Technologies and Virtual Processes of Communication and Management' (2017) 14(4) *RAI Revista de Administração e Inovação* 301–10. https://doi.org/10.1016/j.rai.2017.07.006.

48 Adebambo Adewopo, *Nigerian Copyright System* (Odade Publishers, Lagos 2012) 64–5.

49 *Statute of Anne*, 8 Ann. c. 21.

50 *Constitution of the United States of America*, Article 1 section 8.

51 See Jessica Litman, 'Real Copyright Reform' (2010) 96 (1) *Iowa Law Review* 1.

> A copyright system is designed to produce an ecology that nurtures the creation, dissemination, and enjoyment of works of authorship. When it works well, it encourages creators to generate new works, assists intermediaries in disseminating them widely, and supports readers, listeners, and viewers in enjoying them. If the system poses difficult entry barriers to creators, imposes demanding impediments on intermediaries, or inflicts burdensome conditions and hurdles on readers, then the system fails to achieve at least some of its purposes. The current U.S. copyright statute is flawed in all three respects.

52 Jane C Ginsburg, Essay 'How Copyright Got a Bad Name for Itself' (2002) 6(1) *Columbia Journal of Law & the Arts* 61–2.

The IP-based industry is a multifaceted industry serving different interest groups and striking a balance between these interests, appears to be an age-long challenge.[53] Whereas propublic interest groups like Creative Common, Wikipedia, Internet archive, and Public domain review, seek to focus on the aspect of the goal that speaks to the encouragement of learning and the promotion of the progress of science and useful arts, other groups made of entities such as Elsevier, Taylor & Francis, Springer, Routledge, Penguin, Macmillan, Harper Collins, Simon and Schuster, and Hachette Book Group are focused on the aspect that vests copies of printed books in the author for a specified period and that secures for limited times to authors and inventors, exclusive rights. The problem is that both sides of the divide are legally protected and use the same legislative instruments to further their different agendas.

From the tenor of the goal set by the IP legislations mentioned above, IP rights are structured as a social contract between government, creators, and users. The government provides creators with an exclusive right in exchange for access to the created work by users.[54] This social contract aligns with Bentham's utilitarian theory of the greatest good for the greatest number of persons.[55] It achieves this by providing access to the widest audience, therefore, working in the broadest interest to provide the greatest happiness to all.[56] The social contract fulfills both a public interest and an economic interest objective. The commercialization of IP rights enables content to be available to those who need it, when they need it, thereby creating commerce and strengthening the economy and incentivizing creativity in line with the incentivization theory.[57] In the words of Chun,

> Intellectual property (IP) is well recognized as an important economic asset. Many companies rely heavily on their IP to contribute value to their enterprise: Apple has built an empire on its trademarked logo and branding, Coca-Cola on its secret soft drink formula, and Pfizer on its pharmaceutical patents (to name just a few). The economic value of IP and its strong relationship to business is even reflected in IP legislation. For example, trademark statutes in various jurisdictions share an underlying policy of promoting free and fair competition in trade.[58]

53 Ruth Okediji (ed), *Development Policy in Copyright Law in an Age of Limitations and Exceptions* (Cambridge University Press, 2017) Preface, xi–xii.

54 Anne Monjar, 'Social Contract: The Distributive Significance of a Native Nation's Patent agreement with Allergan' (2018) 16 *Northwestern Journal of Technology and Intellectual Property* 107.

55 See generally, Rosenblum Nancy, *Bentham's Theory of the Modern State* (Cambridge University Press, 1978).

56 J Janewa Osei Tutu, 'Humanizing Intellectual Property: Moving beyond the Natural Rights Property Focus' (2017) 20 *Vanderbilt Journal of Entertainment and Technology Law* 244.

57 See generally Nicola Searle and Martin Brassell, *Economic Approaches to Intellectual Property* (Oxford University Press, Great Britain 2016).

58 Alexandria Chun, 'Economic Approaches to Intellectual Property by Nicola Searle and Martin Brassell' (2017) 54(4) *Osgoode Hall Law Journal* 1389–94, 1389. http://digitalcommons.osgoode.yorku.ca/ohlj/vol54/iss4/18

IP rights are numerous, and the interests are divergent. The tussle between the economic, social, and political interests involved in IP has caused an increased imbalance in the copyright pendulum.[59] The conundrum to finding a balance between economic interests and providing access for social purposes based on the incentive and open access theories continue to fill up pages of scholarly literatures.[60] The next section will explore the structures that have enabled these barriers and how they are largely disproportionate between developed and developing countries. It will explore suggestions on how these gaps can be bridged.

Structure and mechanism

Most writers (academic and fiction) in developing countries prefer to publish abroad.[61] This is not unconnected to the fact that review, tenure, and promotion in most of the higher educational institutions, is largely assessed based on the ability of academics to publish in foreign journals.[62] This simply means that the yardstick for measuring the quality of a researcher's work is dependent on where such researcher publishes. The ability of a work to make the required impact expected in the academic and research community is largely dependent on the global reach of the work, which in turn depends on the type of journal/publisher publishing the work.[63]

The major publishers (Penguin, Hachette Book Group, Harper Collins, Simon and Schuster, and Macmillan) are all in the North and they control the publication industry by determining style, arrangement, and more importantly, distribution of scholarly works.[64] It is therefore not surprising

59 Kunle Ola, 'Open Access- A Disruptive Initiative: A Stopgap, Substitute and Challenge' (2021) 43(1) *Egyptian Initiative for Personal Rights* 42–52, 43.

60 See David Bollier, *Viral Spiral, How the Commoners Built a Digital Republic of Their Own* (New Press, 2008) 4. See also, Lessig (n 20). See also, Brian Fitzgerald, 'Open Content Licensing (OCL) for Open Educational Resources' (Paper commissioned by the OECD's Centre for Educational Research and Innovation (CERI) for the project on Open Educational Resources) available at: *httpl/www.oecd.orgleduloer.*

61 Enowbeyang Tarkang et al. 'The Bane of Publishing a Research Article in International Journals by African Researchers, the Peer-Review Process and the Contentious Issue of Predatory Journals: A Commentary' (2019) 32(119) *Pan African Medical Journal* doi: 10.11604/pamj.2019.32.119.18351.

62 Lesley A Schimanski and Juan Pablo Alperin, 'The evaluation of scholarship in academic promotion and tenure processes: Past, present, and future' (2018) 7 (1605) F1000Research, doi:10.12688/f1000research.16493.1.

63 Tarkang et al (n 61).

64 Glenn McGuigan and Robert Russell, 'The Business of Academic Publishing: A Strategic Analysis of the Academic Journal Publishing Industry and its Impact on the Future of Scholarly Publishing' (2008) 9(3) *Electronic Journal of Academic and Special Librarianship* https://southernlibrarianship.icaap.org/content/v09n03/mcguigan_g01.html See also, Valerie Bence and Charles Oppenheim, 'The Role of Academic Journal publications in the UK Research Assessment Exercise' (2004) 17 *Learned Publishing* 53–68, 53.

that publications in the North are generally regarded of higher quality than local publications.[65] This perception is quite problematic for many scholars in developing countries because journals are generally based on specific issues, and interests are mostly focused on national issues but sometimes they could be international. Some journals represent themselves as international in approach, but in reality, the editors of such journals are influenced by an unconscious bias which makes them consider submissions from some countries as substandard and therefore places submissions from such countries at a disadvantage.[66]

Another issue is that publishing in an international journal by a local scholar raises the issue of access to such works considering the financial, technical, and legal barriers to accessing journal articles in most developing countries.[67] Scholars in developing countries are in a quagmire. They are in an impossible situation where they need to publish or perish.[68] It is true that this is a general problem for all academics globally, but scholars in developing countries like Nigeria are in a peculiar situation. If they publish locally, the work has the likelihood of spreading within their locality and those who need it the most are likely to access it. However, for purposes of review, tenure, and promotion, such publications are not highly regarded and would therefore not enhance their careers.[69] They are therefore faced with the dilemma of publishing locally and gaining stronger impact from those who may need it the most and then face the challenge of poor review, no promotion and possibly losing their tenured position. On the other hand, they have the option to pursue publishing abroad but when scholars from developing countries attempt to publish abroad, they are at an immediate disadvantage because of the subconscious bias that works from scholars in developing countries are substandard.[70]

Assuming the work is published, authors in developing countries are faced with the problem of accessing their own works due to the financial, technical, and legal barriers placed on the work by the system. Even worse is the fact that those who need the work the most (those from the developing countries) face the same trio barriers. The work is therefore available, that is, it has been published and we know it is available, but it is inaccessible to those who need it the most and that automatically limits its potential impact. Ola captured it aptly when he noted that "If there is no knowledge,

65 Fernanda Beigel, 'Introduction: Current tensions and Trends in the World Scientific System' (2014) 62 (5) *Current Sociology* 617–25, 619.

66 Tarkang et al. (n 61).

67 Kunle Ola, 'Fundamentals of Open Access' (2014) 36 (2) *Egyptian Initiative for Personal Rights* 112–23, 113.

68 Rawat and Meena (n 1).

69 Tarkang et al. (n 61).

70 Selmi Michael, 'The Paradox of Implicit Bias and a Plea for a New Narrative' (2018) 50 *Arizona State Law Journal* 173.

there is no development; if there is no access, there is no knowledge."[71] As there is no access to the required knowledge, development is stifled, and this is unfortunate because it is stifled for those who are in dire need of development.

Availability

If the goal is development and it is acknowledged that this is a knowledge-driven economy, knowledge is invariably an indispensable tool to attain the goal of development and access to knowledge is therefore imperative.[72] The access to knowledge and development process requires availability, accessibility, and impact. Availability is the easy part in this process. Once the work is published in any format, it brings the work into the realm of availability. Asein notes that a "genuine offer to the public whether through sale or otherwise would qualify as publication so long as there is readiness on the part of the publisher to fulfill demand."[73]

As noted in Nigeria's Copyright Act, the work must have been fixed in a definite medium of expression where it can be perceived, reproduced, or otherwise communicated directly or indirectly.[74] It further states regarding publication in section 51(2) that "a work shall be deemed to have been published if copies of it have been made available in a manner sufficient to render the work accessible to the public."[75] The Australian Copyright Act provides a similar provision and states that,

> a literary, dramatic, musical or artistic work, or an edition of such a work, shall be deemed to have been published if, but only if, reproductions of the work or edition have been supplied (whether by sale or otherwise) to the public.[76]

The concept of availability can be understood from the prism of the idea/expression dichotomy which connotes the existence of a work in a tangible medium and that it no more resides in the realm of ideas.[77] It depicts information that is no more locked up in the creator's head but which is now clearly expressed and fixed into a definite medium and made available (supplied to the public) in a manner sufficient to render the work accessible

71 See, Ola, *Open Access to Knowledge* (n 32) 1.
72 Ibid.
73 John Asein, *Nigerian Copyright Law and Practice* (Books and Gavel Publishing, Abuja, 2012) 63.
74 Section 1(2)b, *Nigerian Copyright Act 2004.*
75 *Nigerian Copyright Act 2004.*
76 s29 *Copyright Act 1968* (Cth).
77 Edward Samuels, 'The Idea-Expression Dichotomy in Copyright Law' (1989) 56 *Tennessee Law Review* 321–77, 322.

to the public.[78] The responsibility of making a work available rests on the author(s), as this is one of the exclusive rights of an author.[79] This is the first process in a series of processes leading to development via knowledge. De Beer describing this process explains that the "framework for studying IP, innovation and economic outcomes, maps roughly onto the linear model of innovation itself, which depicts a process moving from basic research, to applied research, to development, to diffusion."[80]

Basic research requires the availability of works. Once the work is available, the linear model is easily activated moving from the basic to the applied research stage which necessarily entails the ability to use and reuse works thereby enabling an environment for development and diffusion. It is the ability to apply (use and reuse) knowledge, that leads to development.[81] Online availability of scholarly works enables easier visibility of such works. To be able to use a scholarly work, it must first be discoverable and visible to anyone searching for it. Some journals in developing countries are still locked to the old tradition of hard copy publications and are skeptical about online publication options. To be clear, I am not against hard copy publications, they are good.

The issue with publishing exclusively in hard copies is that it must be physically sent and retrieved by those needing it. Hard copies are rivalrous in nature and therefore, use by one person implies the inability of others to use it at the same time. The cost and time associated with sending hard copies are other challenges counterposing the actual availability of the work. Online availability in addition to the physical copy, enables immediate visibility to anyone with an Internet connection.[82] In this digitized and electronic age, adopting an online publication strategy is crucial for the visibility of scholarly works in developing countries.[83] The next phase in the knowledge-development process is accessibility. It is in the accessibility section that the

78 Ed Barker and Iona Harding, 'Copyright, the Ideas/Expression Dichotomy and Harmonization: Digging Deeper into SAS' (2012) 7(9) *Journal of Intellectual Property Law & Practice* 673–9.

79 See generally L R Patterson, 'Copyright and "The Exclusive Right" of Authors' (1993) 1 *Journal of Intellectual Property Law*. See also Jane C Ginsburg, 'The (New?) Right of Making Available to the Public' in David Vaver and Lionel Bently (eds), *Intellectual Property in the New Millennium: Essays in Honor of William R. Cornish*' (Cambridge University Press, Cambridge, 2004).

80 J De Beer 'Evidence-Based Intellectual Property Policymaking: An Integrated Review of Methods and Conclusions' (2016) 19 (5–6) *Journal of World Intellectual Property* 150–77, 161.

81 Ann Majchrzak, Lynne P Cooper, and Olivia E Neece. 'Knowledge Reuse for Innovation' (2004) 50 (2) *Management Science* 174–88. 174. http://www.jstor.org/stable/30046057 accessed 3 January 2021.

82 Eben Moglen, 'View of Anarchism Triumphant: The Free Software and the Death of Copyright' (1999) *First Monday*, https://firstmonday.org/ojs/index.php/fm/article/view/684/594

83 Elizabeth Le Roux and Peter Ogum Nwosu, 'Indexing Africa: Revisiting the Issue of Knowledge Production and Distribution' (2006) 16 (1–2) *Africa Media Review*, 1.

application of research becomes relevant and activated, but as noted earlier, availability of a work is not tantamount to accessibility to such works.

Accessibility

Accessibility in the context of scholarly works refers to the right to use and reuse a work. This right is governed by IP rules particularly copyright as most works fall within the published terrains which in turn are literary works. The concept of accessibility as it relates to use and reuse could be understood from the analogy below. B is working on a research that requires collation of data. The proposal for collating this data entails amongst others, a time frame of 12 months, four personnel, and a budget of $500,000. During the literature review, B realizes that A has successfully conducted a similar research which entailed collating the exact data but for a different purpose. B's research will be greatly helped by free, immediate, unrestricted access to A's data. A however has the right, based on copyright rules to deny B access to the data. On the other hand, A could authorize B to use the data under certain conditions such as payment of a certain sum. If B can afford the amount, the situation is resolved in favor of both parties.

The problem arises where B cannot afford the amount but still needs the data. Accessibility then becomes not just an issue of removing the legal barrier to authorization, but it also entails removing the price/financial barrier associated with authorization to accessibility. If these barriers are removed, accessibility becomes a key to development, but without it, development is stifled. The question may be asked, why is accessibility stifling development? Ginsburg suggests that it is due to both corporate and consumer greed.[84] She noted that

> Copyright owners, generally perceived to be large, impersonal and unlovable corporations… have eyed enhanced prospects for global earnings in an increasingly international copyright market. Accordingly, they have urged and obtained ever more protective legislation that extends the term of copyright and interferes with the development and dissemination of consumer-friendly copying technologies.[85]

The resultant effect of this greed is the inability to access available content. Development is enabled when accessibility is enabled, that is, people can interact with the ideas of others and build upon such ideas.[86] Ginsburg explains it in terms of the public interest and notes that a balanced copyright system should provide meaningful incentives to first authors, but also

84 Ginsburg (n 52).

85 Ibid.

86 *Sega v Accolade*, 977 F.2d 1510, 1525 (9th Cir, 1992). See also Sony v Connectix, 203 F.3d 596 (9th Cir. 2000).

provide second authors the room to build on the endeavors of their predecessors.[87] Isaac Newton's letter where he noted "if I have seen further it is by standing on the shoulders of giants" captures the essence of development based on the works of others.[88]

Lessig explains the importance of accessibility from a "free culture" prism and notes that

> A free culture supports and protects creators and innovators. It does this directly by granting intellectual property rights. But it does so indirectly by limiting the reach of those rights, to guarantee that follow-on creators and innovators remain *as free as possible* from the control of the past.[89]

Boyle pointed out in his book, that the current IP system has enabled an environment where inaccessibility restrains the next generation of creators instead of encouraging them.[90] IP owners have been able to ride on the wings of the current IP system to restrict access.

Litman decries the heightened access restrictions and notes that the access restriction strategy championed by some right owners is excessive and "would give copyright holders the means to prohibit access to or use of the contents of their works for any reason whatsoever."[91] She further noted that "as sympathetic as we may find creators' interest in preserving their work from distortion, that interest is not so weighty that it impels us to sacrifice long-standing principles ensuring public access."[92] Okediji approaches accessibility from a balancing paradigm and bases it on the human right claim which seeks to consider the interests on the two sides of the divide. She notes that "Each claim-the public and the individual-exerts its own force within the system, thus forcing a balancing act that provides room for the exercise of limitations and exceptions to promote public access."[93]

The problem of access to scholarly works is particularly grim in developing countries like Nigeria due to the high cost associated with accessing scholarly works. When Ivy League universities like Harvard decries the high cost of journal subscriptions, what is the hope of the higher educational

87 Ginsburg (n 52).

88 Isaac Newton, 'From a Letter Written by Isaac Newton to Robert Hooke' 5 February (1676).

89 Lessig (n 20) xiv preface.

90 James Boyle, *The Public Domain, Enclosing the Commons of the Mind* (Yale University Press, USA, 2008) 8–9.

91 Litman, J., *Digital Copyright: Protecting Intellectual Property on the Internet* (Prometheus Books, Amherst, New York 2006) 184.

92 Ibid.

93 R L Okediji, 'The International Relations of Intellectual Property: Narratives of Developing Country Participation in the Global Intellectual Property System' (2003) 7 *Singapore Journal of International & Comparative Law* 345–6.

institutions in developing countries who can hardly afford basic infrastructures.[94] For developing countries to have a foot in the door, they would need to explore accessibility options such as green open access (using preprint versions) and online e-resource initiatives made available by publishers and other organizations.

The green open access option works as a double-edged sword, allowing for both availability and accessibility to works. Members from developing countries can upload their preprint version on a personal, institutional, or independent repository thereby making the work both available and accessible. In the same vein, works uploaded to such repositories are also available and accessible for free, immediate, and unrestricted use depending on the type of license.

A number of online e-resource initiatives have been developed to enable free access to scholarly works for developing countries. Research4Life is an in-country and online e-resource initiative that provides free or low-cost access to peer-reviewed research in low-middle income countries.[95] The initiative covers areas such as Health, Agriculture, Environment, Development, and Law.[96] In "Scholarly Publication in Nigeria: Implications of Open Access," the author identified some of the organizations that support the goal of free, immediate, unrestricted, and online access to all peer-reviewed literature.[97] The organizations include HINARI, INASP, AJOL, AGORA, OARE, ARDI, Siyavula, African LII, and SSRN.[98] Where scholars in Nigeria and other developing countries want a foot in the door and truly desire a way out of the publication quagmire, exploring the option of publishing preprint versions (green open access strategy) and drawing from established online e-resource initiatives provide a useful door.

Impact

Let us assume that scholars in developing countries can leverage the access provided through the online e-resource initiatives and are therefore able to develop their thoughts and come up with a draft for a publication. They

94 Justine Norrie, 'Harvard: Journal Subscription Is Prohibitive' *The Conversation* (24 April, 2012), https://theconversation.com/harvard-journal-subscription-fees-are-prohibitive-6659.

95 Taylor & Francis Group, Accessing Research in Developing Countries, https://taylorandfrancis.com/about/corporate-responsibility/development-initiatives/#

96 Ibid.

97 Kunle Ola, 'Scholarly Publication in Nigeria: Implication of Open Access' (2015) 2(2) *World Intellectual Property Organization Journal* 122.

98 Ibid 122–5. Health InterNetwork Access to Research Initiative (HINARI), The International Network for the Availability of Scientific Publication (INASP), African Journal Online (AJOL), Access to Global Online Research in Agriculture (AGORA), Online Access to Research in the Environment (OARE), Access to Research for Development and Innovation (ARDI), African Legal Information Institute (African LII), Social Science Research Network (SSRN).

are still left with the challenge of where to publish and the eventual impact of that publication. The impact is measured using different variants. It often deals with how scholarly works by academics, researchers, and scientists are assessed for purposes of promotion and funding.[99] Universities, research institutions, and funding organizations often set yardsticks for promotions and for obtaining grants. At a time, the mere publication of a work in any outlet was praised as a remarkable impact. Today, if publication is not within specified types or classes of journals, it is not regarded as credible.[100] In some places, publishing in a lower-ranked journal could attract penalties such as reduced research allocation, warning letters, and in some extreme cases, loss of employment.[101] Impact is a combination of several factors including publication, citation, and reference to works by the executive, judicial, and legislative arms of government.

Publishing in the academic world requires strategy. It is not enough to work hard; you must work smart and this is where the impact comes in. The online availability and accessibility of a work are not enough to bring the work into the realm of works making an impact. It is crucial that when making the choice of where to upload your work, you upload it to a site that curates your data as well as that of many others and one that is recognized and respected in the academic environment. International Scientific Indexing (ISI) is recognized as the first indexing service for the sciences, but to some extent, it is regarded as exclusive to the North.[102]

There are other services that are nonexclusive and open to everyone such as Google Scholar, SSRN, and Orchid. It is possible that some employers will regard the exclusive indexing services (ISI and SCOPUS) as higher quality than the nonexclusive indexes (Google Scholar, SSRN, Orchid). It is therefore preferential for one's work to be listed in the exclusive indexes, but my point is that it is better for one's work to be listed in the nonexclusive index than to not be listed at all. One's foot is in the academic metric door once your work is listed in any of the respected indexes.

The problem with impact can be compartmentalized into two, indexing and corporate interest. A major measuring factor for impact is determined by indexing which is in turn determined by whether a journal is listed in reputable indexes. It has been observed that "authors have started searching for

99 Beigel (n 65) 617.

100 Ann Martin-Sardesai, Helen Irvine, Stuart Tooley and James Guthrie, 'Government Research Evaluations and Academic Freedom: A UK and Australian Comparison' (2017) 36(2) *Higher Education Research & Development* 372–85. Doi: 10.1080/07294360.2016.1208156

101 *Zhao v University of Technology Sydney*, [2020] FWC 416, 11 March 2020. See also, Nick Bonyhady & Natassia Chrysanthos, 'Industrial Umpire Lashes Universities Obsessed with Rankings and Reputation' *The Sydney Morning Herald*, March 11, 2020, https://www.smh.com.au/national/nsw/industrial-umpire-lashes-universities-obsessed-with-rankings-and-reputation-20200311-p5495e.html

102 O'Neill(n 27). See also, Beigel (n 65).

indexed journals to publish their articles."[103] Indexing is a tracking, searching, and measuring mechanism. It refers to the action or process of compiling an index. In the scholarly world, journal indexing facilitates the easy identification of information. This type of tool is indispensable in this age of infomania and infobesity.[104] The challenges that have come with indexing are that it has created a class system in the journal world such that journals that are not indexed are not in the league of highly regarded journals.

A high number of journals in developing countries are not captured within the major indexing services.[105] This situation is not unconnected with the fact that the first science indexing service, ISI started in the North and is managed there. Most of the journals published in developing countries are often categorized as predatory journals and are therefore excluded from the indexes.[106] The problem with this situation is that scholars from developing countries who publish with these local journals which are regarded as predatory journals are automatically locked out of the global indexing services.[107] When searches are conducted, their works cannot be discovered because it has not been indexed. The implication is that such a work cannot be found, tracked, or measured for impact, and therefore when an assessment is made, the impact on the work will be zero.

The other challenge is corporate interest. It refers to the ever-widening and changing yardstick by research institutions, universities, and funding organizations for research outputs and impact.[108] It is encapsulated in the question "whether the career interest of academics or researchers is of any concern when considering the research intensification strategy of research institutions." The current institutional attitude with regards to output of research and impact appears to be one that puts the interest of the organization as the sole interest and relegates the interest of academics and researchers. A situation where academics are told to publish in only certain categories of journals even where the researchers' field is very low on such categories is self-centered, and totally oblivious of the interest of academics and researchers. Institutional change is required in this regard and it has been suggested that employers should reframe their questions from not "what impact has this research had," but "what have you done about your

103 Dhammi, Ish Kumar, and Rehan Ul Haq, 'What Is Indexing' (2016) 50(2) *Indian Journal of Orthopaedics* 115–6.

104 Rogers Paul et al., 'Infobesity: The Enemy of Good Decisions' *Insight*, www.bain.com/publications/articles/infobesity-the-enemy-of-good-decisions.aspx. See also, Nat Eliason, 'Fighting Infomania: Why 80% of Your Reading Is a Waste of Time' (2016) *Productivity*, https://www.nateliason.com/blog/infomania

105 Murray (n 10) 81, where it was noted that "Several journals remain obscure because they are not indexed on major indexing platforms. This hinders patronage by researchers desiring to publish scholarly and impactful articles."

106 Tarkang et al. (n 61). doi: 10.11604/pamj.2019.32.119.18351.

107 Murray (n 10) 83.

108 See generally, Martin-Sardesai, Irvine, Tooley and Guthrie (n 100).

discovery?"; not "what is your evidence of research leadership," but "what have you done to enable the research and careers of others?."[109]

Conclusion

The scholarly publishing industry has created a divide between what transpires in the North and the South. It would have been great if we had Aarons's rod to part the red sea of publication challenges facing the academic community and particularly the quagmire in which Nigerian scholars and those from other developing countries find themselves. The desire in scholars to publish with local publishers and share their works with those who can easily access them is juxtaposed against the need to comply with their employer's expectation to publish abroad for purpose of review, tenure, and promotion. At the same time, they are faced with the bias from publishers abroad that works from developing countries are substandard and are therefore confronted with multiple rejections.

The concepts of availability, accessibility, and impact have been explored in this research as concepts that influence the academic publishing industry. Nigeria and other developing countries can begin a process of addressing the divide between the North and South in the academic publishing industry by adopting an open access online publication strategy that addresses the availability, accessibility, and impact problem. This strategy would entail publishing works online, thereby ensuring the works are available and globally visible. It would also include providing preprint versions of their work as well as exploring the preprint version of the works of others and online e-resource initiatives that are available. For purposes of impact, scholars in developing countries should not just work hard but work smart and ensure that their works are indexed in a recognized indexing service.

109 Kimberlee Gai Weatherall and Rebecca Giblin, 'Inoculating Law Schools Against Bad Metrics' in K Bowrey (ed), *Feminist Perspectives on Law, Law Schools and Law Reform Intellectual Property & Beyond* (Forthcoming), SSRN: https://ssrn.com/abstract=3772437

10 Evolution of digital performance

Leveraging rights in performances

Dorcas A. Odunaike and Oluwatobiloba O. Olanrewaju

Introduction

The emergence of new media performances borne out of technological advancements dates back two decades with the introduction of robotic dance in stage and the integration of visual media in live performances.[1] Digital performance in its current form[2] resulted from the creative production of musical, dramatic, sound recordings (SRs) and cinematograph films in the twentieth Century. The emergence of digital streaming platforms such as Spotify, iTunes, Apple music, Napster, Google music, Deezer, Audiomack among others changed the narratives about sale and distribution of SRs and audio-visual performances.

Streaming is the continuous transmission and distribution of online content, an ingenuity that has greatly impacted the creation of SRs, musical and dramatic performances. For instance, with applications such as YouTube Music, Instagram or Facebook that offer live streaming services, a performer can do a live stream of his musical or dramatic performance on a mobile device and distribute it to the whole world within a few seconds. In the same vein, a bootlegger can with the same software application make an unauthorized recording of a live performance and distribute it to the whole world within seconds—an act which contravenes performers' right to prevent the fixation of their unfixed performances.[3]

With the COVID-19 Pandemic, the use of digital tools to create new digital content in a manner not envisaged by the law became rampant. Restriction of artistes to the confines of their homes further enhanced ingenuity

1 In contra-distinction with digital performance in sound recording, a form of public performance right. See Drama, Performance and Digital Multimedia available online at https://noemalab.eu/specials/drama-performance-and-digital-multimedia/ accessed 6 August 2020.

2 Simulation of musical and theatrical performances in a form that has never been imagined, a form of novelty worthy of legal protection.

3 Article 7, Rome Convention, 1961.

DOI: 10.4324/9781003250883-14

in recording and streaming non-embodied live performances, an ingenuity worthy of legal protection.[4] The word 'digital' originated from a Latin word *digitus* which means 'fingers used for discrete counting'.[5] Simply put, it is 'data in binary form'.[6] Performance has been defined as 'an act of presenting a play, musical concert or other forms of entertainment'[7] while right in performances is "a copyright holders exclusive right to recite, play, act show or otherwise render protected copyright work publicly, whether directly or by technological means (such as broadcasting the work on television)".[8]

Digital performance can therefore be defined in three ways: (i) live musical or dramatic performance streamed as digital content, (ii) public performance of SRs and (iii) performance facilitated through technology which connotes a form of interactivity between humans and machines and between humans.[9] According to Anthonio Pizzo,[10] the ability of digital technology to generate an object and give its interpretation to it is on all fours with theatrical performances. Hence, Brenda Laurel viewed digital performances as simulations beyond what happens in the real world and not just mere innovation in SRs, musical or theatrical performances.[11] She is of the view that this simulation results in new sounds, new dance, new media, simulation of space and time in virtual representations—an ingenuity worthy of legal protection.

Performance in public within the meaning of the Copyright Act, connote a broadcast of an opera by wireless telephony. Thus, every public performance of a copyrighted work requires the authorization of the copyright owner else there is an infringement. The regulation of copyright works vests on the Nigerian Copyright Commission, the question is whether new communication technology made possible by mobile online platforms will now necessitate that this role is played in conjunction with agencies that regulate

4 Theatre Companies are Pushing Storytelling Boundaries with Online Audiences amidst COVID 19, available online at https://theconversation.com/theatre-companies-are-pushing-storytelling-boundaries-with-online-audiences-amid-covid-19-141583 accessed 11 September 2020. See also, Nigerian artistes now surviving on digital shows after losing gig money to coronavirus, available online at https://nairametrics.com/2020/04/14/nigerian-artistes-now-surviving-on-digital-shows-after-losing-gig-money-to-coronavirus/ accessed 11 September 2020.

5 'Digital, Origin and Meaning' https://www.etymonline.com/word/digital accessed 31 August 2020.

6 Ibid.

7 Oxford English and Spanish Dictionary, https://www.lexico.com/definition/performance> accessed 31 August 2020.

8 Bryan A Garner, *Black's Law Dictionary* (Thomas West Publishing Coy USA) 1174.

9 Nadja Masura, PhD, Digital Theatre, http://www.nadjaart.com/teach/Digital%20Theatre%20Dissertation%20Exerpt.pdf accessed 16 August 2020.

10 Ibid.

11 'Computers as Theatre' https://www.researchgate.net/publication/273947125_Computers_as_theatre_Brenda_Laurel accessed 16 August 2020.

online content such as the National Information Technology Development Agency?

This chapter is divided into five parts. After this first introductory part, the second part highlights international protection of SRs and rights in performances, followed by Part 3 on the historical developments of digital performances in the United States of America (US)and its legal protection. Part 4 undertakes an overview of rights in performances under the Nigerian law and juxtaposes it with best practices garnered from some developed countries. Part 5 concludes the work and proffer recommendations for legal reform.

International protection of sound recordings and rights in performances

The international protection of SRs, musical and dramatic performance is traceable to the Berne Convention of 1886 when by Article 11[12] the authors of dramatic and dramatico-musical works were conferred with the right of public performance and the communication of their performance to the public. The Berne Convention did not expressly protect producers of SRs but under Article 9, any sound or visual recording is considered as a reproduction. Under Article 11bis on broadcasting and related rights, permission granted for the broadcasting of literary and artistic works does not extend to license to record the broadcast. The Convention further provides that ephemeral recordings of broadcast shall be regulated by legislation in each contracting State.[13]

The International Convention for the Protection of Performers, Producers of Phonograms and Broadcasting Organisations, 1961 (hereinafter referred to as Rome Convention, 1961) expressly protects the 'aural fixation of sounds of a performance or other sounds'. Article 4 offered legal protection to 'performances incorporated in a phonogram or carried by a broadcast'. Article 3 defines performer to include actors who perform literary and artistic works while Article 7 conferred minimum protection on performers, by granting performers' the "possibility of preventing the fixation of their unfixed performances". Article 12 of the Rome Convention of 1961[14] established public performance right in SRs when it conferred economic rights on the performer or producers of the phonogram whenever a "phonogram is published for commercial purposes or reproduction of such phonogram is used directly for broadcasting or for any communication to the public".[15]

12 Berne Convention of 1886 available online at WIPO Administered Treaties https://www.wipo.int/treaties/en/index.html accessed 6 August 2020.

13 Ibid.

14 Nigeria is a signatory to Rome Convention of 1961, accession took place in 1993.

15 See WIPO Performance and Phonogram Treaty (WPPT), 1996 available online at. https://www.wipo.int/treaties/en/ip/wppt/

The WIPO Copyright Treaty and WIPO Performance and Phonogram Treaty 1996 enhanced copyright protection in a digital environment when they expressly filled the gaps created by the non-existence of applicable norms relevant to the demands of a digital economy. Article 11 and 12 of the WIPO Copyright Treaty protects digital right technologies, which make it impossible to share or steal online content. Though the WIPO Copyright Treaty did not expressly protect public performance right in SRs, it mandates contracting states to provide adequate legal and effective remedies in the light of evolving technology.[16]

The adoption of the WIPO Performance and Phonogram Treaty 1996 aimed at proffering solutions to questions raised by 'technological developments and convergence of communication technologies on the production and use of performances' (among others).[17] Hence, Articles 18 and 19 expressly protects technological measures and rights management information while Articles 5–10 headed Chapter 2 expand legal protection of performers to be at par with authors' rights, it provides for moral and economic rights, rights of reproduction, distribution and rental, among others. Article 6 expressly confers on performers the exclusive right to fix unfixed performances and to authorize such fixation.

The evolving nature of digital technology brought to limelight the lacuna on audio-visual performances, therefore, the Beijing Treaty on Audiovisual Performances, 2012 came into existence to balance public interest and the right of performers in their audiovisual performances. Article 2, defined audiovisual fixation as "the embodiment of moving images, whether or not accompanied by sounds or the representations thereof from which they can be perceived, reproduced or communicated through a device". It is worthy of note that, since digital performance covers both the aural and visual elements of a performance, the 2012 Beijing Treaty bears more semblance to digital performance than all the other aforementioned treaties. Although Nigeria is a signatory to the WIPO Copyright Treaty, 1996, WIPO Phonogram and Performance Treaty, 1996 and the Beijing Treaty on Audio-visual Performances, 2012, the country still needs to do more by domesticating these treaties.[18]

Historical developments and protection of digital performance in the United States

Right in the public performance of SRs using digital audio transmission changed the narrative for the legal protection of SRs in the United States in the nineteenth century with the enactment of the Digital Performance

16 See Article 11, WIPO Copyright Treaty, 1996.

17 See Preamble to WPPT.

18 See, We have signed the WIPO Treaties, now What? *Punch*, https://punchng.com/we-have-signed-the-wipo-treaties-now-what/ accessed 31 August 2020.

Rights in Sound Recordings Act in 1995. In the United States, the chronicling of the creation of Digital Performance Rights (DPRs) can be traced to the lacuna in the Copyright Act and the ever-evolving nature of technology. As technology advanced so also did copyright holders' rights increase. Not until 1971 with the enactment of the Sound Recordings Act of 1971 was Section 102 Copyright Act amended to include Sound Recordings (SR) as an area protected by copyright.[19] The bundle of rights, however, that was given to a copyright holder of a SR included reproduction, distribution and adaptation rights with the exclusion of performance rights.

The exemption of performance rights by the amendment created a limitation in the rights and steered many controversies leading to the necessity to clarify the rights in SRs protected by copyright in relation to internet usage. This was in consideration of the fact that advancement in technology had graduated from digital dissemination to the era of music proliferation via the internet that involved downloading SRs. Consequently, there arose confusion as to whether downloading SRs was a reproduction, distribution or performance right.[20] However, considering the analysis that transmission of SRs involves the public (higher percentage of audience), it was successfully argued to be a performance.[21]

Congress, therefore, figured out that if greater protection was not conferred on creative works, there could be a plunge in the rate of creation which ultimately will rob the public of the advantages accruing from this novel 'digital transmission technologies'.[22] This, therefore, called for the need for a legislation expressly providing for performance right as a right in SR protected under copyright, as it was not one of the rights conferred on the copyright holder of a SR by the Copyright Act or the Sound recording Act, 1971.

Ultimately in 1995, the Digital Performance Rights in Sound Recordings Act (DPRA) was birthed to tackle the long-standing controversy that plagued SRs before its enactment in1995. The DPRA amended the Copyright Act not just to tackle the present digital technologies but also in a futuristic manner that effectively covers *any form of digital technologies that could be created in the future which may affect copyright.*[23] It also vests two major exclusive rights on copyright holders; the 'Digital Performance Right and the Digital Distribution Right'. The former focuses on protection in

19 Lynne B Lubash, 'How the Digital Performance Rights in Sound Recordings Act of 1995 Protect Copyright Owners on the Internet' (1998) 14 *Santa Clara High Tech Law Journal* 497 http://digitalcommons.law.scu.edu chtlj/vol14/iss2/7 accessed 7 August 2020.

20 Ibid.

21 Ibid.

22 Derek M Kroeger, 'Applicability of the Digital Performance Right in Sound Recordings Act of 1995' (1998) 6(1) *UCLA Entertainment Law Review* https://escholarship.org/uc/item/5c82t9zk accessed 8 August 2020.

23 Ibid.

relation to current digital technologies while the latter right is the futuristic element that focuses on future digital technological innovations.

DPR, which is the focus of this chapter, vests the exclusive right on copyright holders in SRs to perform their creations in public via digital audio transmission.[24] This connotes that upon the public performance of an SR, the copyright holder is entitled to compensation. It is, however, imperative to state that DPR is not without exceptions to its exclusive use by copyright holders.

This exempts some digital audio transmissions such as non-subscription transmissions from licensing. It is worthy of note that while some (such as subscription transmissions) requires obtaining statutory licenses, an interactive transmission requires voluntary licenses.[25] Exempted digital audio transmissions include non-subscription television[26] and radio broadcasts; their retransmissions[27] and transmission within business premises and environs in the normal course of business activities.[28] The retransmission of a television or radio broadcast must not be intentionally retransmitted beyond a 150 mile radius of the original broadcast.[29]

Subscription transmissions that require a statutory license are usually organised and are target specific, that is, the transmission is limited to the paying subscribers to its services.[30] Other forms of subscription transmissions and interactive services are required to obtain a voluntary license. This means that the license is subject to be granted or withheld by the copyright holder. Further, the terms and conditions of a license to be granted will be negotiated with the copyright holders of an SR. This particularly affects interactive services because it allows its users access at any time to the SR as desired that could adversely affect the sales of the record. It is noteworthy that DPRA limits the timeframe within which the exclusive right can be granted. This limitation is however dependent on the purpose for which the license was granted[31] and if the same was also granted to other interactive services.

Finally, it is worthy of note, with regard to Online Copyright Infringement Liability Limitation, that Section 402 of the Digital Millennium Copyright Act of 1998 modified Section 112 of the DPRA on exemptions of ephemeral recordings to include recordings made to facilitate digital transmission of SRs.

24 See U.S.C. 106(6).

25 See U.S.C. 114(d)(1); U.S.C. 1 14(d)(1)(A)(i).

26 See S. REP. NO. 104–28, at 18(1995).

27 Note that even if the retransmission of a radio broadcast is a subscription retransmission it is still exempted. See e S. REP. No. 104–28, at 19.

28 See U.S.C. 114(d)(1)(C)(ii).

29 See U.S.C. 114(d)(1)(B)(i)–(iv).

30 See U.S.C. (1140) (8).

31 For instance, if the exclusive license granted is to promote the sound recording the limitation period of DPRSRA will not apply.

Sound recordings and rights in performances under the Nigerian Law

In Nigeria, data and online content is legally protected by the Nigeria Data Protection Regulation 2019 and the Cybercrime (Prohibition, Prevention, etc.) Act, 2015. However, SRs, musical and dramatic performances have been legally protected by copyright as far back as the nineteenth century. Whereas, Section 25(1) of the 1911 Copyright Act extended the provisions of the Act to the British colonies and the protectorates, the publication of a work does not include public performance.[32]

However, the 1970 Copyright Act, expressly offered legal protection to SRs as copyrightable work.[33] Section 19 of the 1970 Copyright Act defines SR as the "first fixation of a sequence of sound capable of being perceived aurally and of being reproduced but does not include a soundtrack associated with a cinematograph film".

It is worthy of note that the definition of SR under the Nigerian law is of general application, hence 'fixation of sequence of sound capable of being perceived aurally and of being reproduced' can be extended to cover SRs in digital or other forms of new media format.[34]

Producers of SRs have the right to control the direct and indirect reproduction, broadcasting or communication of the whole or substantial part of the recording in original 'or any other format recognisably derived from the original'. It is the submission of the writers of this chapter, that in the absence of an express provision of law on digital performance, this phrase 'or any other format recognizably derived from the original' can be extended to cover digitalisation of SRs.

In the same vein Section 7(1)(b) prohibits distribution to the public for commercial purposes. Public performance of SRs has been held to constitute unlawful communication to the public especially where it is unauthorised. The Court in the United States held in *Herbert v Shanley Co*[35] that public performances of music contribute to the profit-making ability of an establishment and constitutes a performance for profit that must be licensed even if no special admission was charged.

However, right in performances under the Nigerian law does not, strictly speaking, cover digital performance, whereas evidence of digital performance in theatre and other live performative arts abound in the country.[36]

32 See Section 1(3), Copyright Act, 2011.

33 Section 1 and Section 7 Copyright Act of 1970.

34 The legal protection of sound recordings under the 1988 Copyright Act is in pari-material with the 1970 Copyright Act. See Section 7 of the Copyright Act, Cap. C28 Laws of the Federation of Nigeria, 2004.

35 242 U.S 591(1917).

36 For instance, BAP Productions has been at the forefront of promoting digital dramatico-musical performances in Nigeria, see MOREMI the Musical and Saro the Musical on YouTube. See also, Joe Akan, 'The Rise of Music Streaming in Nigeria and its Role in

The need to leverage right in performances under the Nigerian law necessitates this study.

The Nigerian Copyright Act defines performance to include "live performances of dramatic performance, a musical performance, a reading or a recitation of literary act or any similar presentation".[37] It is worthy of note that the word 'include' under Section 26(2) and 'any similar presentation' under Section 26(2)(c) may be interpreted to mean that the acts that constitute performances are not closed but will accommodate acts similar to those enumerated under Section 26(2).

Going by that interpretation, a stand-up comedy show qualifies as a performance and the category of dramatic work is confined to those elements peculiar to dramatic performance.[38] However, whether this phrase 'or any similar interpretation' can be extended to cover digital performance is a question of fact depending on each case. It is recommended that this ambiguity be clarified through a concise definition of the term.

While Section 6 (1)(a)(iii) of the Copyright Act[39] vests the exclusive right to control the public performance of a literary or musical work on the author of the work, Section 7 gives the owner of the SR the exclusive right to control in Nigeria the communication to the public of the whole or any substantial part of the recording either in its original form or a derivative form. The right vested in the author of an SR to control the direct or indirect communication of the work to the public is certainly different from the right to control the performance of the work. This is clear when compared with Section 6, which provides for both the right to perform the work in public and the right to control its communication to the public.[40]

Generally, music can be protected as both a musical work and an SR. Johannes observes that musical work is a combination of notes and instrumentation, which the author combines to form melodies and harmonies, together with any accompanying lyrics, while SR is the 'actual aggregate of vocal and instrument sounds that one hears'—a derivative of the author's musical work.[41] Sometimes, ownership of the copyright in a musical work, which is converted into an SR may be vested in different persons.

---

the Development of the Entertainment Industry; 'The Guardian', available online at https://guardian.ng/life/music/the-rise-of-music-streaming-in-nigeria-and-its-role-in-the-development-of-the-entertainment-industry/ accessed 11 September 2020.

37 See Section 26(2) of the Act.

38 Catherine Colston and Jonathan Galloway et al., *Modern Intellectual Property Law* (3rd ed., Routledge, New York, 2010) 300.

39 Cap. C28 Laws of the Federation of Nigeria 2004.

40 Section 6(1) iii & vii.

41 Laura E Johannes, 'Hitting the Right Notes: The Need for a General Public Performance Right in Sound Recordings to Create Harmony in American Copyright Law' (2011) 35 *Washington University Journal of Law and Policy* 445.

Musical work is usually comprised of the lyrics and musical notes, while the SR is an audio recording of the performance of the musical work.[42] Generally, copyright in the musical work is vested in the person who created or wrote the music. Whereas, copyright in the SR of a musical work may be vested in the person by whom arrangements for the making of the recording were made.[43] When an artiste is signed to a record label, arrangements for the recording or production of an SR are usually made by the record label, since the artiste may not have the resources to bear the cost of producing the song. The Nigerian Copyright Act has dual provisions on the ownership of the copyright in SR. Section 51 of the Copyright Act states that:

> "Author" in the case of sound recording, means the person by whom the arrangements for the making of the sound recording were made, except that in the case of a sound recording of a musical work, "author" means the artist in whose name the recording was made, unless in either case the parties to the making of the sound recording, provide otherwise by contract.[44]

Copyright is vested in the author of the SR. So, in the first instance, copyright in an SR is vested in the person who made the arrangement for the recording. However, where the SR is a recording of a musical work, it will be vested in the author in whose name the recording was made, and not in the person by whom the arrangements were made. The provision of the law on the ownership of the copyright in an SR may be modified by contract. In the Nigerian music industry, it is often the case that by virtue of a contractual agreement, copyright in both the musical work and the SR are assigned to the record label, to enable it recoup its money expended in the production, marketing and promotion of both the artiste and his music.[45]

The provision of the Nigerian Copyright Act on the rights of performance in an SR can be contrasted with the provisions of the Canadian Copyright Act which is on all fours with the US Act. The Canadian Copyright Act has clear provisions for the right of performers in SRs. It makes specific provisions for Canadian citizens and permanent residents, Rome Convention countries and the WIPO Performance and Phonogram Treaty (WPPT) countries. Section 19(1) of the Canadian Copyright Act provides that: "If a sound recording has been published, the performer and maker are entitled, subject to subsection 20(1), to be paid equitable remuneration for its performance in public or its communication to the public by telecommunication..."

42 Jennifer L Pridgeon, 'The Performance Rights Act and American Participation in International Copyright Protection' (2010) 17(2) *Journal of Intellectual Property Law* 417, 420.

43 Section 51, Nigerian Copyright Act.

44 Cap C 28 Laws of the Federation of Nigeria 2004.

45 Ese Atakpu, Understanding Nigerian Copyright Law for Music and Musicians, https://kurating.com/nigerian-copyright-law-music-musicians/ accessed 12 September 2020.

Telecommunication is defined in the Act as "any transmission of signs, signals, writing, images or sounds or intelligence of any nature by wire, radio, visual, optical or other electromagnetic systems".[46] This definition is extensive and accommodates digital communication of an SR to the public by means of any form of technology.

Section 19(2) of the Canadian Copyright Act goes further to provide that a person that performs a published SR or who communicates it to the public by telecommunication is required to pay royalties. The same protection given to the Canadian citizens and residents is also extended to citizens and residents of countries that are parties to either the Rome Convention or the WPPT. However, the Minister may limit the scope and duration of the protection conferred on a Rome Convention country or a WPPT country, if he is of the opinion that the country does not grant a right to remuneration that is similar in scope and duration to Canadian nationals and permanent residents.

While the Nigerian Copyright Act vests the author of an SR with the right to control the direct or indirect broadcasting or communication to the public, it does not expressly capture its communication to the public by means of new forms of digital technology in existence today, whether or not the 'right to control broadcast of sound recordings and performances' can be extended to cover broadcast through any form of digital technology will be a question of fact depending on the circumstances of each case. Law reform in this regard, which spells out the exact scope of the rights of copyright owners is essential, in view of the constantly evolving technology that permits the rights of copyright owners to be effortlessly infringed. Performance rights in SR is one of the critical sources of revenue for makers of music and is worthy of effective protection through all-encompassing legislation.[47]

Unlike the United States DPRA 1995, which grants rights of performance only in digital public performances and broadcasts on digital platforms, the Nigerian Copyright Act affords a copyright owner the right to control the broadcast or communication to the public of his SR.[48] The Nigerian Act does not specify the scope or extent of this right in the light of digital technology, nor does it provide for a right of digital performance.

In the United States, the DPRA has been critiqued for its disparate treatment of copyright in SR, based on whether the broadcast or communication to the public is done through a digital or analogue platform and its refusal to extend performance rights to SRs.[49] In this regard, the Nigerian law on

46 Section 2 of the Canadian Copyright Act.

47 James A Hayes, 'Copyright and Related Rights in Canada and Abroad: A View towards a More Globally Unified System of Neighbouring Rights (2017) 12(43) *Journal, Copyright Society of the USA* 411, 416.

48 See Section 7, Copyright Act, Cap. C28, Laws of the Federation of Nigeria, 2004.

49 See Jennifer L Pridgeon, 'The Performance Rights Act and American Participation in International Copyright Protection' (2010) 17(2) *Journal of Intellectual Property Law* 417,

copyright in SR has fared better than the US law, however, its failure to expressly provide for DPRs, broadcast rights and public communication rights on digital platforms is a gaping lacuna in the Nigeria's copyright law.

The desirability of legislative clarity in the Nigeria's laws on the rights of digital performance in SR and the rights of copyright owners generally in a digital age through law reform is underscored by Nigeria's judicial history and the technicalities that often besiege its justice administration system. This is illustrated by Nigeria's tortuous experience on the admissibility of computer-generated evidence/electronic evidence, before the advent of the Evidence Act of 2011 that expressly provided for the admissibility of electronic evidence.

Prior to the Evidence Act 2011, it was uncertain if electronic evidence could be admitted in judicial proceedings by relying on the old Evidence Act. This uncertainty was compounded by two Supreme Court decisions that appeared to sanction two different views. One decision- *Esso West Africa Inc V T Oyegbola*[50] adopted a forward-looking, contemporary, problem-solving, purposive approach to the interpretation of the provisions of the old Evidence Act.[51] To this end, the court held that:

> Law cannot be and is not ignorant of the modern business methods and must not shut its eyes to the mysteries of a computer. In modern times reproduction and inscriptions on ledgers or other documents by mechanical process are commonplace and Section 37 cannot therefore only apply to books of accounts.[52]

The other decision—*Yesufu v ACB*—adopted a strict, positivist interpretation, despite acknowledging the impact of technological advancements.[53] It, therefore, held that:

> While we agree that for the purpose of Sections 96 (1) (h) and 37 of the Act, "bankers books" and "books of account" could include "ledgers cards", it would have been much better, particularly with respect to a statement of account contained in document produced by a computer, if the position is clarified beyond doubt by legislation as had been done in England in the Civil Evidence Act.[54]

In 2009, Marybeth Peters, the Register of Copyrights from 1994 to 2010, wrote to the United States Senate urging that the Proposed Performances Right Act be passed, which would extend the scope of the public performance right granted in sound recordings under the DPRA. Marybeth Peters, 'The Performance Rights Act and Parity among Music Delivery Platforms' https://www.copyright.gov/docs/regstat070509.html accessed 4 August 2009.

50 (1969) NMLR 198.

51 Ibid.

52 (1969) NMLR 216–7.

53 (1976) LPELR-3525(SC).

54 (1976) LPELR-3525(SC).

Legislative clarity is therefore desirable to ensure that copyright is adequately and comprehensively protected in the light of modern digital technology that may permit effortless copyright infringement. This will also obliterate any uncertainty as to the scope and extent of the rights conferred under the copyright system.

Conclusively, it is also important to amend Section 26 (2) of the Copyright Act[55] to include digital performance in theatre, since digital theatre is a type of digital theatrical performance that accommodates computer media, live performers and a limited level of interactivity.[56]

Conclusion and recommendations

In conclusion, this chapter has established that public performance right otherwise protected in the United States of America as DPR in SRs is otherwise protected as public performance right under the Nigerian law. Evidence of royalties collected by COSON on behalf of right owners includes digital royalties and performance royalties (among others) in the event of public performance of musical works.[57] However, to avoid ambiguity it is important to amend the Nigerian Copyright Act to cover digital performance made possible by present technologies as well as any form of digital technologies that could be created in the future.

The emergence of digital performance also made it imperative to re-define the scope and application of copyright protection to live performances in the twenty-first century, especially in light of new possibilities made possible by new software 'apps'[58] whose usage became evident during the COVID-19 pandemic. As stated above, it is also imperative to amend Section 26 (2) of the Copyright Act[59] to include digital performance in theatre, since digital theatre accommodates live performances through computer media.

While there is ample evidence that public performance of SRs is legally protected under the Nigerian law, the subject matter of protection does not include performance facilitated by new media especially in light of the creative production and sharing of musical and dramatic works made possible by simulation of space and time as virtual representation.

55 Cap. C28 Laws of the Federation of Nigeria, 2004.

56 See Nadja Masura PhD, f.n 10.

57 Part of the function of COSON is to collect royalties from public and commercial users of musical works or sound recordings. There is ample evidence of collection of royalties on behalf of right owners from Hotels, Telecommunication companies, Clubs (among others). See https://www.cosonng.com/. See also COSON takes MTN to Court, The Nation, available online at https://thenationonlineng.net/coson-takes-mtn-court/ accessed 12 September 2020.

58 Abbreviation of the word 'application'. Note that software application is usually referred to as an 'app'.

59 Cap. C28 Laws of the Federation of Nigeria, 2004.

Although the United States DPRA exempts non-audio digital transmission from licensing, the emergence of software application that permits the recording and re-posting of live performances and streaming of digital content further necessitates the legal protection of all forms of digital streaming and transmission of live performances as well as a digital performance of SRs in whatever form.

The operation of the doctrine of national treatment that governs the extension of the same copyright protection to nationals of member countries, further necessitates the need to leverage rights in performances under Nigerian laws. With the amendment of laws in developed countries to cover future technological devices, an amendment of the Copyright Act to cover new forms of technology-enabled performances will go a long way in filling the hitherto existing gaps, such that right owners will also be able to enjoy reciprocal protection of works as citizens of member countries of such treaties or international agreements.

11 Non-consensual pornography in Nigeria and the copyright law

Ifeoluwa A. Olubiyi and Faith K. Bamidele

Introduction

Technological development has immensely contributed to the recording of people's personal lives for posterity. It has also led to a widespread practice of recording intimate and personal moments (digital intimacy) including sexually explicit images and videos for the purpose of sharing with partners who are physically distant or the mere desire to keep such memories alive.[1] Unfortunately, this has also led to an increase in the non-consensual sharing of sexually explicit images and videos on the internet which is becoming a worrisome trend in the Nigerian society.[2] The increasing access to the internet and smartphones have contributed greatly to the challenge of non-consensual pornography, which is popularly referred to as revenge porn and is now conceived as an image-based sexual violence.

While there are quite a number of instances of the non-consensual distribution of nude pictures or videos in Nigeria, recent ones are stated here. In 2019, the social media space in Nigeria was dominated by the sex video of a female student of a private faith-based university who was allegedly expelled from school for this unfortunate incident (which according to the school amounted to the breaking of school regulations).[3] The female folk

1 S Chisala-Tempelhoff and M T Kirya, 'Gender, Law and Revenge Porn in Sub-Saharan Africa: A Review of Malawi and Uganda' (2016) 2 *Palgrave Communications*, 2. https://doi.org.10.1057/palcomms.2016.69.

2 L Akor, 'The Social Media, Deviance and Youths in Nigeria' in P N Ndubueze (ed) *Cyber Criminology and Technology-Assisted Crime Control: A Reader* (Nigeria ABU Press, 2017) 47–64; J O Ayodele, 'Perception of Online Deviance and Social Media Censorship among Undergraduates' in P N Ndubueze (ed) *Cyber Criminology and Technology-Assisted Crime Control: A Reader* (ABU Press, 2017) 65–88; C O Okafor, O E Efetobor and A C Apeh, 'An Evaluation of the Correlation between Internet Pornography and the Sexual Behaviour of the Nigerian Undergraduates' (2015) 1(1) *African and Global Perspectives* 1–14.; H B Adebayo and U A Ojedokun, 'Trajectories of University of Ibadan Undergraduates ' Exposure to Cyber Pornography' (2018) 12(1) *Journal of Social, Behavioral and Health Sciences* 140.

3 M Adekanye, 'Babcock Lady : A Victim Of Revenge Porn Or Decadence ?' *The Guardian* (20 November 2019) https://guardian.ng/life/babcock-lady-a-victim-of-revenge-porn-or-decadence/ accessed 16 June 2020.

DOI: 10.4324/9781003250883-15

has not been the only victim of this menace. In December 2019, the sex video of an Enugu-based man, Nevo Mike Obiayo, who usually recorded sex with his girlfriend was uploaded online allegedly by either someone repairing his girlfriend's phone or his wife.[4]

In February 2020, the naked video of MB, a popular Hausa actress in Kannywood, trended showing her as she was about to dress up.[5] Although the video indicated that she tried to stop whoever was filming her, it was unclear who released the same online. She alleged that the video was released by her ex-boyfriend, who had threatened to release the video to extort her of money. The ex-boyfriend has since denied doing so.

In April 2020, Salawa Abeni, a popular female singer, had to release semi-nude pictures of herself on her Instagram page because someone had attempted to blackmail her with these pictures taken over 20 years ago to extort her of money.[6] After disclosing this on her social media, the Nigerian Police was able to track down the perpetrator who confessed to have seen the pictures on a memory card he saw on the floor of his school.[7] Although the case of SA was a consensual distribution of her pictures, she would not have done so voluntarily but for the abuse and extortion sought to be perpetuated by the young man. Many such videos and pictures have grazed the online environment in Nigeria. Many are released on social media sites and other websites.

While many developed countries, particularly, those in the Northern hemisphere, have earlier dealt with this challenge and have worked at developing their legal framework to combat this menace, the legal framework in Nigeria has not adequately risen to the challenge of curbing the menace of non-consensual pornography. This paper provides a perspective of the use of laws to address the problem from a Nigerian perspective. While there are existing criminal and civil laws that can contribute to curbing this menace, its uniqueness requires specially crafted legislations to address the problem. Many times, such laws are used to punish the perpetrator or compensate the victim and at most order the perpetrator to remove the nude image or video. Yet, with the nature of the online environment, in a few minutes such a video

4 A G Gsong, 'Popular Enugu Based Man , Nevo Mike Obiayo In Trouble After Video of His Extra Marital Escapades Leaked Online' 1 https://www.withinnigeria.com/2019/12/11/popular-enugu-based-man-nevo-mike-obiayo-in-trouble-after-video-of-his-extra-marital-escapades-leak accessed 15 June 2020.

5 O Ganiu, 'Hausa Actress Threatens Legal Action over Nude Video' *The Nation* (February 12, 2020), https://thenationonlineng.net/hausa-actress-threatens-legal-action-over-nude-video/ accessed 15 June 2020.

6 T Ige and S Abeni, 'ICYMI : Insider Could Have Leaked My Nude Photos – Salawa Abeni' *The Punch* (April 4, 2020) https://punchng.com/insider-could-have-leaked-my-nude-photos-salawa-abeni/ accessed 15 June 2020.

7 J Augoye, 'How I Obtained Nude Photos of Popular Musician, Salawa Abeni — Suspect' https://www.premiumtimesng.com/entertainment/music/395493-how-i-obtained-nude-photos-of-popular-musician-salawa-abeni-suspect.html accessed 15 June 2020.

could have been watched, downloaded, shared, reposted and uploaded by many others. This is where copyright law plays a significant role by preventing the distribution of the offending material online. Unfortunately, the Nigerian copyright law does not provide adequate protection to copyright owners in the online environment that makes victims of non-consensual porn handicapped.

Part 2 of this chapter therefore attempts a conceptual clarification of revenge porn. It identifies the impact of revenge porn on its victims and particularly why it is considered an image-based sexual abuse that mostly affects the women folk. Part 3 examines some existing laws that are useful in combating revenge porn in the Nigerian society. Part 4 focuses on the use of copyright laws in combating this menace. The chapter is concluded in Part 5.

Non-consensual pornography: an image-based sexual abuse

Non-consensual pornography, popularly referred to as revenge porn, refers to the distribution of sexually explicit images or videos of a person without the authorisation of the subject of the image or video. The video or image could have been created with the consent of the person and the person could have even shared or sent it to a partner in a trusting relationship. However, the distribution of the video or image beyond that partner is usually without the consent of the person involved. In this case, the non-consensual nature focuses on the distribution of such images or videos and not its creation. For instance, in early 2020, a video showing about 30 women in Jos having sex on camera was shared online.[8] Although the women knew that they were being recorded and were paid for participating, the person who procured them assured them that the video was not to be marketed in Nigeria. Unfortunately, it was secretly released online for everyone to see beyond the scope of the audience they agreed to. The video was downloaded by many and went viral in their communities leading to many losing their relationships and families, relocating and one of them committed suicide. Some victims stated that the act took place some years before the video was released and although the video was later removed online; the harm had been done. This does not, however, deny the fact that sometimes such images or videos are taken without consent such as while the person is sleeping, secretly or under the influence of drugs. The term pornography also suggests that the image or video is sexually explicit or for sexual pleasure.

Revenge porn is not the only form of non-consensual pornography. Revenge porn refers to when such images or videos are shared by an ex-partner

8 D S Adama, 'Married Women, 'Nigeria : For ₦30,000 , Married Women , Girls Engage in ' Immoral Act ' in Jos' *Daily Trust* 23 January 2020 https://allafrica.com/stories/202001230148.html accessed 15 June 2020.

to punish or humiliate the person involved for leaving the relationship or something they have done.[9] Other instances of when there can be non-consensual pornography include when the victim's accounts or phones and other storage devices are hacked, stolen or missing or where such images or videos are secretly obtained. In these instances, the perpetrator may be unknown to the victim as seen in the case of SA, the popular Nigerian singer. Deep fakes and photoshopped images are another example of non-consensual pornography where the image of a person's face is grafted into a video or image of another person in a sexually explicit video or image.[10] In such instances, it is difficult to tell that the image or video has been manipulated and unfortunately the innocent victim suffers all the same. In addition, revenge is not the only reason for this act, other reasons include humiliation, extortion or blackmail, to make money such as where such videos are sold to porn sites, notoriety or even sheer entertainment.[11] Hence, although the term revenge porn is usually used interchangeably with non-consensual pornography, the latter entails much more. Suzoe *et al* condemn the use of the term 'revenge' on the basis that revenge is not the only motivation for such despicable actions, and more importantly, the term 'revenge' entails victim blaming, presupposing that the victim must have done something wrong for which the perpetrator is avenging.[12]

However, the term 'non-consensual pornography' has recently been criticised by some writers.[13] One is that the term 'pornography' suggests that the victim intended to give sexual pleasure in the creation of the image or video and this is not always the case. For example, MB, who was simply dressing up while a short video clip of her nakedness was made, had no interest in giving sexual pleasure. Upskirting[14] and some forms of vouyeristic acts[15] are done while the victim is oblivious or where the victim is under the influence of drugs or forced to be recorded or raped, such victim has no intention of giving sexual pleasure hence the term 'pornography' may be inappropriate. Also, by tagging it 'pornography', there seems to be a presumed sense of choice and legitimacy in the creation and/or distribution of

9 C McGlynn and E Rackley, 'Image-Based Sexual Abuse' (2017) 37 *Oxford Journal of Legal Studies* 534, 537.

10 Ibid 539.

11 Ibid 536.

12 N Suzor, B Seignior and J Singleton, 'Non-Consensual Porn and the Responsibilities of Online Intermediaries' (2017) 40 *Melbourne University Law Review* 1057, 1059; V N Griffith, 'Smartphones, Nude Snaps, and Legal Loopholes: Why Pennsylvania Needs to Amend Its Revenge Porn Statute' (2016) 56 *Journal of Technology Law & Policy*, 135–136. doi: 10.5195/tlp.2016.19.

13 Chisala-Tempelhoff and Kirya (n 1) 2; McGlynn and Rackley (n 9) 536.

14 Unauthorised image or video of a person's pubic area underneath their outer clothing.

15 Making a video or taking a picture of a person in a place where they averagely expect privacy such as in bathrooms.

it.[16] There is already some connotations of victim blaming by calling such acts 'porn'. Franks argues that making and sharing explicit images or videos with a partner in an intimate or trusting relationship is not pornography.[17] It is the sharing of the image or video that has rather turned an intimate and private moment to public sexual entertainment.[18] It has rather been referred to as an image-based sexual abuse particularly as advanced by McGlynn and Rackley.[19] We shall return to this concept shortly.

The impact of non-consensual pornography on the victim is grave and enormous.[20] Victims suffer emotionally and psychologically. They can lose their self-worth or dignity and relationships such as marriages and friendships.[21] They may lose employment or their studentship as allegedly suffered by the student of the faith-based university in Nigeria. They could also find it difficult to gain another employment as a search of their names online reveals such sordid details about them. Many victims become depressed and may even commit suicide.[22] Because the names, social media handles, work or home details and phone numbers of the victims usually accompany such online posts, victims can suffer harassment and unsolicited calls for sex, slut-shaming, 'dragging' among others.[23] Some have to change their names, addresses, phone numbers and other details.[24] Their family and close associates also suffer humiliation.

The online distribution of non-consensual pornography is made worse by the fact that within a few seconds, billions of people all over the world have access to the image or video which could have been downloaded or shared on other platforms even when it has been removed from the original website on which it was posted. Years or months later, someone who had earlier downloaded it could upload it again online and make it trend again. The image or video can hardly every actually go away forever.

Although the victims of non-consensual pornography can be both male and female; evidence shows that it is the females that are usually mostly

16 McGlynn and Rackley (n 9) 536.

17 M A Franks, 'Drafting an Effective "Revenge Porn" Law: A Guide for Legislators (2014) https://www.cybercivilrights.org/wp-content/uploads/2016/09/Guide-for-Legislators-9.16.pdf accessed 20 June 2020.

18 Franks (n 17); S Lichter, 'Unwanted Exposure: Civil and Criminal Liability for Revenge Porn Hosts and Posters' (2013) *Harvard Journal of Law and Technology* 1.

19 McGlynn and Rackley (n 9) 534–61.

20 D K Citron and M A Franks, 'Criminalizing Revenge Porn' (2014) 49 *Wake Forest Law Review* 345, 350–4.

21 Z Franklin, 'Justice for Revenge Porn Victims: Legal Theories to Overcome Claims of Civil Immunity by Operators of Revenge Porn Websites' (2014) 102 *California Law Review* 1303, 1309.

22 Suzor, Seignior and Singleton (n 12) 1061.

23 L Fielder, 'Public Shaming in The Digital Age: Are Criminal Laws The Most Effective Means To Regulate Revenge Porn?' (2013) 34 *Loyola of Los Angeles Entertainment Law Review* 155.

24 Ibid 159.

affected.[25] Where a sex video shows both male and female, the female is usually slut-shamed while the male is subtly chided or even praised for his sexual prowess because of the chauvinistic nature of the society and the double standards that exist in the society with this regard.[26] Females are upbraided for having sex and are expected to make it a covert affair, not to be seen or talked about. While men in the society can boast publicly of their sexual conquests, talk and jest about it. The exposure of a female's body or sex life is met with strong opposition, denigration and opprobrium while it is not considered so bad for a man to have a sexually explicit image or video in the public.

Furthermore, non-consensual pornography can sometimes be used to control women, in particular, with threats. This could occur where a partner threatens to release such images or videos if the partner leaves the relationship, reports an abuse, fails to pay the perpetrator or do his or her bidding. It can also be used as a tool for sex traffickers to prevent unwilling persons from continuing, for rapists to further humiliate or punish a victim, and prevent victims from reporting or speaking out against abuse.[27] McGlynn and Rackley summarise the harm done to victims as the violation of personal and bodily integrity, infringement of dignity and privacy, inhibition of sexual autonomy and expression, and a cumulative adverse cultural or societal harm.[28] Dekeseredy and Schwarz have also argued that male peer support exacerbates the incidents of image based sexual abuse because the perpetrators are mostly male, the audience is predominantly male and this provides them the needed support and approval.[29] All these has validated the perception that non-consensual pornography is a form of sexual abuse, particularly, an image-based sexual abuse.

Non-consensual release of these videos is a way of victimising women. For instance, after the August 2007 release of a video of popular Hausa actress MH, having an intimate relationship with her boyfriend surfaced online, the Kano State Censorship Board (KSCB) pledged to sanitise the Hausa film industry. The alleged sanitation was the announcement of stricter guidelines, such as the banning of married women from acting,

25 P J Patella-Rey, 'Beyond Privacy: Bodily Integrity as an Alternative Framework for Understanding Non-Consensual Pornography' (2018) 21 *Information Communication and Society* 786, 788–9; Chisala-Tempelhoff and Kirya (n 1) 2; McGlynn and Rackley (n 9) 536; Citron and Franks (n 20) 353; J Halliday, 'Revenge Porn: 175 Cases Reported to Police in Six Months' *The Guardian* (Manchester, 11 October 2015). Similarly, figures from the UK's Revenge Porn Helpline show that 75% of 1800 calls over six months were from women [Government Equalities Office Press Release, 'Hundreds of Victim-Survivors of Revenge Porn Seek Support from Helpline' (20 August 2015)].

26 Chisala-Tempelhoff and Kirya (n 1) 2. Fielder (n 23) 155, 159.

27 Chisala-Tempelhoff and Kirya (n 1) 2.

28 McGlynn and Rackley (n 9) 545–51.

29 W S DeKeseredy and M D Schwartz, 'Thinking Sociologically About Image-Based Sexual Abuse' (2016) 2 *Sexualization, Media, & Society*, 1. DOI: 10.1177/2374623816684692.

while also requiring women in the industry to have a male guardian who would be legally responsible if their ward broke the rules.[30] The alleged sanitation amounts to public shaming of females, as anyone wishing to tarnish the image of a woman with nude images can easily post such nude pictures online. The expectation is that any form of sanitisation of the system should entail a legal response to image-based sexual abuse that protects all victims irrespective of their gender.

Existing legal framework for combating revenge porn

Non-consensual pornography can be addressed using both the criminal and civil laws.[31] The advantage of criminal law in curbing revenge porn is that it sends a strong message that the act is not condoned but is punished by the society and serves as a deterrence to others.[32] Also, the state prosecutes crimes and victims do not have to bear the expensive cost of investigation and litigation of the crime. However, taking legal action depends on the police and such similar agencies understanding the seriousness of the case. The prosecutors must also know how to gather evidence and investigate these cases as the perpetrator is not always known to the victim. Knowledge, skills and resources are needed in this regard. Non-consensual pornography could also be cross-jurisdictional hence it may go beyond the scope of authority of the Nigerian police. Many perpetrators post anonymously and the website operators may be unwilling to disclose identities.[33] In such instances, there is a need to obtain an injunction to mandate disclosure. All these can make prosecution slow and difficult.

Some relevant criminal provisions that can be used to curb non-consensual porn are hereby examined. Chapter 21 of the Criminal Code Act criminalises obscene publications in the interest of the public.[34] By section 233D, 'any person who, whether for gain or not, distributes or projects any article deemed to be obscene for the purposes of this Chapter, commits an offence'. By subsection 2:

> A person shall not be convicted of an offence … if he proves that he had not examined the article in respect of which he is charged and had no reasonable cause to suspect that it was such that his publication of it would make him liable to be convicted of an offence against this section.

30 Ganiu (n 5).

31 Suzor, Seignior and Singleton (n 12) 1061–5.

32 Citron and Franks (n 20) 349.

33 A Dickson, '"Revenge Porn": A Victim Focused Response' (2016) 2 *UniSA Student Law Review* 42, 51.

34 Cap C38, Laws of the Federation of Nigeria (LFN) 2004.

The test for what is obscene is as contained on section 233C (2) which applies to:

> any article of two or more distinct items the effect of any one of which is such as to tend to deprave and corrupt, but nothing in this section shall apply to exhibitions in private houses to which the public are not admitted or to anything done in the course of television or sound broadcasting." This test of obscenity is one of the major pitfalls of any attempt to use obscenity laws to curb revenge porn. First is the idea of 'article of two or more distinct items.

Does this mean there must at least be two nude pictures involved before there can be an action? Would a video satisfy this requirement? The provision also excludes exhibition in private houses. It is possible for a person's nudity to be made accessible in an alleged private house which is not open to members of the public and yet such is made without consent or beyond the scope the subject of the image or video intended it for. More so, obscenity laws are intended for the protection of the members of the public and not the victims of the obscene publication.[35]

The Cybercrimes (Prohibition, Prevention, etc.) Act of 2015 is probably the most apt criminal provision that can be used to combat non-consensual pornography in Nigeria. Section 24 of the Act provides that:

> any person who knowingly or intentionally sends a message or other matter by means of computer systems or network that is grossly offensive, pornographic or of an indecent, obscene or menacing character or causes any such message or matter to be so sent.

commits an offence and is liable upon conviction to a maximum of ₦seven million fine or a term of imprisonment not exceeding three years or both such fine and imprisonment. By section 24(2), to:

> knowingly or intentionally transmit or cause the transmission of any communication through a computer system or network to bully, threaten or harass another person, where such communication places another person in fear of death, violence or bodily harm or to another person.

is also an offence under the Act. Non-consensual pornography harasses the victim and is a form of sexual abuse, exposes the victims to sexual violence and depressive thoughts of suicide and bodily harm; hence, this provision is also useful in combating it. Child pornography is also expressly prohibited under section 23 of the Act.

35 N G Ikpeze and O Apara 'The Rise of Non-Consensual Pornography in Nigerian Cyberspace: Imperatives for Statutory Criminalisation' (2019) 3 *AJLHR* 79, 84.

Civil actions that can be taken by the victim include a breach of his or her fundamental rights. Non-consensual pornography contravenes the right to the human dignity of the victims that is guaranteed under section 34 of the Constitution of the Federal Republic of Nigeria 1999.[36] Every individual is entitled to respect for the dignity of his person and as such no person shall be subject to degrading treatment. The slut shaming and banters that go on about the bodies of victims amounts to degrading treatment; it violates their bodily integrity.[37] More so, the fact that an essentially private act or at least a picture or video shared in a trusting relationship in which privacy was expected becomes public entertainment is a gross violation of the right to privacy of the victims as enshrined in section 37 of the Constitution which protects the privacy of citizens and their correspondence. Therefore, even when such information was obtained unscrupulously such as by hacking, the victim's right to privacy is still violated.

Civil actions put the victim in control and taking legal action does not depend on persuading others, such as the police, of the seriousness or strength of the case.[38] The remedy of (punitive) damages and an injunctive relief can also be beneficial to a claimant while attempting to rebuild his or her life.[39] The challenge of civil litigation is that the litigant may not be able to afford the cost of litigation which usually entails using technology to investigate and prove the liability of the defendant, it could also involve multiple defendants and who are across multiple jurisdictions.[40] Also, where the real names of the victim are used in litigation which is usually the case for litigants above 18 years, the name of the litigant will continue to be mentioned and the bad publicity would never end. The trial is in public, hence, the image or video can be viewed again and again and the facts can be rehearsed over and over again. Also, sometimes the defendant may not be judgement worthy in that he or she may lack the financial ability required to pay the damages hence eluding the plaintiff of any remedy.[41]

The distribution of non-consensual pornography also amounts to a breach of confidence or breach of confidential obligations.[42] The victim could have shared the image or video with a partner in a trusting relationship. Where such information now becomes public cynosure by the act of the partner or with the knowledge or consent or even negligence of the ex-partner, it may be possible to sue for breach of confidence. This is an equitable remedy and

36 Cap C20, Laws of the Federation of Nigeria.

37 Patella-Rey (n 25).

38 McGlynn and Rackley (n 9) 556.

39 Ibid.

40 Ibid 559; Franklin (n 21) 1315.

41 McGlynn and Rackley (n 9) 559.

42 L Fiedler, 'Public Shaming in the Digital Age: Are Criminal Laws the Most Effective Means to Regulate Revenge Porn' (2013) 34 *Loyola of Los Angeles Entertainment Law Review* 155, 179; Suzor, Seignior and Singleton (n 12) 1062; Dickson (n 33), 52–55.

to succeed, the claimant has to prove that (a) the information is confidential; (b) the information was imparted in circumstances importing an obligation of confidence and (c) there has been an unauthorised use or threatened use of the information. Breach of confidential obligations may however not be able to cover instances where the information was obtained scrupulously such as by hacking.[43] Sometimes, the information becomes public due to the negligence of the partner, it may also be argued that such an ex-partner may be liable for negligence.

The challenge of litigation generally is that investigations and gathering of evidence are daunting. Also, the perpetrator may even be unknown to the victim such as in instances of hacking or where missing phones or storage devices are found. The victim has to share the nude image or video with lawyers, judges, prosecutors and so on, thereby increasing the shame and humiliation and by the time the victim has succeeded in court, the harm would have been amplified.[44] The long period it takes to conclude a court action also reduces the impact of remedies for the victim and in fact allows for more harm to be done as the information keeps going viral. Also, with the nature of the internet, even where the perpetrator is sued, the image or video would usually have been shared, downloaded and reposted, which means that the perpetrators can be uncountable. Also, that a perpetrator is sued does not mean that the image or video is no longer on the internet. The video can continue to be distributed on social media and other websites. This is where copyright law comes in to forestall the distribution and redistribution of the content on the internet and to assist the victim to remove the image or video from these websites.

Copyright as a mechanism for combating non-consensual pornography

While many other laws aim at punishing or getting compensated from the person who posted the video or picture, copyright law also focuses on the distributors of these images. This is because without the secondary or hosting distributors (internet service providers, website owners and so on) non-consensual pornography loses its mighty power and its significance.[45] Where the defendant is injuncted but the distribution of the nude images online is left untackled, the victory obtained by a victim of non-consensual pornography would only be pyrrhic.

Copyright grants exclusive rights to the owner of a literary and artistic work to the exclusion of others. The rights granted include the right to reproduce the work in any material form; publish the work; perform the work in public; produce, reproduce, perform or publish any translation of the work; make any cinematograph film or record in respect of the work; distribute the

43 Dickson (n 33) 53.

44 Ibid 51.

45 McGlynn and Rackley (n 9) 539.

work to the public for commercial purposes; broadcast or communicate the work to the public; and make an adaptation of the work.[46]

Without the consent of the copyright owner, any person who deals in the copyright work in any of these specified ways would have infringed the copyright vested in such work.[47] In the case of non-consensual pornography, the relevant work is an artistic work for photographs and a cinematograph film for a video.[48]

To be protected, registration is not required for a work to be protected by copyright. This means that there is no fear or concerns of having to register the nude image or video with a government agency or depositing the same for public access that usually worsens the publicity and shame of the victim. All that is required for copyright protection is for the work to be original and fixed in a definite medium of expression.[49] Originality means that sufficient effort has been expended on the work to give it an original character.[50] The standard of originality in Nigeria, like in many common law jurisdictions, is a low threshold which means that the author has invested time, skill, effort, labour and even money in the creation of the work.[51] For photographs, originality lies in the exercise of the photographer's judgement as to what to photograph, the arrangement of the scene including positioning, lighting, skill and labour in taking a photograph among others.[52] The picture or video, therefore, has copyright protection and on this basis, the victim can sue the perpetrator for copyright infringement.

The ownership of copyright works is initially vested in the author.[53] The author of a photograph is the person who took the photograph and the author of a cinematograph film is the person who made arrangements for the making of the film unless the parties to the making of the film provide otherwise by contract.[54] Where the victim of non-consensual pornography took his or her own picture (selfie) or made a video and sent same to a partner or stored it on a device, such a victim would own the copyright in the work and on this basis can sue a perpetrator for copyright infringement. In the case of a sex video made by the two parties involved, they could be considered as joint authors, and copyright law may not be so helpful in this regard as a license, for instance, granted by one of the owners of a copyright work is

46 Copyright Act 1988, Cap C28, Laws of the Federation of Nigeria (LFN) 2004, s 61).

47 Copyright Act 1988, s 15(1)(a).

48 Copyright Act 1988, s 51 (1).

49 Copyright Act 1988, s 1(2).

50 Copyright Act 1988, s 1(2)(a).

51 *Masterpiece Investments Ltd v. Worldwide Business Media Ltd & Ors* (1997) FHCLR 496; *University of London Press v. University Tutorial Press* (1916) 2 Ch 601; *Ladbroke (Football) Ltd v. Willian Hill (Football) Ltd* (1964) 1 WLR 273; A Oyewunmi, *Nigerian Law of Intellectual Property* (Unilag Press, 2015) 33.

52 *Peter Obe v. Grapevine Communications Ltd* [2003–2007] 5 I.P.L.R; Oyewunmi (n 40) 39.

53 Copyright Act 1988, s 10(1).

54 Copyright Act 1988, s 51(1).

deemed granted by the co-owners.[55] Unfortunately, the Nigerian Copyright Act is not equipped to handle infringement in the online environment. The definition of communication to the public for instance is restricted to communication 'by loudspeaker or any other similar device'.[56]

With respect to deep fakes (where a person's face is implanted on a porn image or video even though the person is not involved actually), where the image or posture was obtained from another copyright work by the victim, the victim can sue for an infringement of his or her moral rights on the ground that this amounted to a distortion, mutilation or other modification of the work which is prejudicial to the victim's honour or reputation.[57]

Another area where copyright law can help is through the provision of taking down notices. Service providers and online platforms for user-generated content such as social media sites are protected by the 'safe harbour principle' which emanated from the United States under the Digital Millennium Copyright Act.[58] The rationale is to safeguard secondary distributors from copyright infringement litigation in order not to stifle the development of information and communication technology. However, such service providers have a duty to take down any content which is flagged or they have been notified infringes copyright, after following the stipulated procedure, otherwise they may be liable for copyright infringement.

While it is agreed that many social media sites already have these policies and procedures especially the popular ones such as Facebook and YouTube domiciled in developed countries such as the United States, non-consensual images and videos are also uploaded or shared on other websites and blogs that may not already have such procedures or obligation. Granted that many service providers especially the popular social media sites are located outside Nigeria but with the advancement of IT in Nigeria, the country is having increasing service providers and website owners; hence, there is a need to have such similar provisions in Nigerian laws to cover such service providers and website operators or owners.

The 2015 Copyright Draft Bill seeks to ensure better copyright protection in the online environment.[59] Para 47(1) of the Bill stipulates that the owner of copyright in a work in respect of which copyright has been infringed, may issue notice of such infringement to the relevant service provider requesting the service provider to take down or disable access to any infringing content or link to such content, hosted on its systems or networks. Service provider are defined under the draft bill as:

> provider of online services or network access, or the operator of facilities therefor, and includes an entity offering the transmission, routing,

55 Copyright Act 1988, s 11(5).
56 Copyright Act 1988, s 6(1)(vii).
57 Copyright Act, section 12(1)(b).
58 Digital Millennium Copyright Act 1998, section 512.
59 The bill has been forwarded to the National Assembly for passage into law.

> or providing of connections for digital online communications, between or among points specified by a user, of material of the user's choosing, without modification to the content of the material as sent or received.

The right of communication to the public is also intended to expressly include 'making available the work or copies thereof to the public, including by digital transmission over computer networks',[60] thereby providing better protection for copyright works in the online environment.

Another effective remedy is the right to be forgotten that emanated from the European court.[61] The European Court of Justice ('ECJ') held that individuals could ask internet search engines to remove links of their personal information that is inaccurate, inadequate, irrelevant or excessive.[62] This means that a person has the right not to have his or her name come up in searches made on online search engines. This remedy is also important for victims of non-consensual pornography. Otherwise, a simple search of their names on the internet through any of the search engines will pop up those images or videos which as stated earlier are usually posted with their names on it. By filing the necessary forms and taking up this procedure with the search engines, their names may not show up or at least pop up in prominent positions in web searches, therefore, reducing the likelihood of such images or videos being shared or denting their reputation further.

Conclusion

It must be stated that the attempt is not to present copyright as the perfect solution to the challenge of non-consensual pornography since it is mostly useful where the victim owns the image or video such as where it was made by the victim. Nevertheless, the copyright law complements other civil or criminal remedies available to victims. Its effectiveness in particular, is that it can be used to forestall the distribution of the image and to remove the image or video in question from websites or platforms where they have been shared. This would go a long way in curbing the continued harassment and shaming of the victim that would have been continuous due to the nature of the internet despite obtaining a judgement against the perpetrator. Copyright, therefore, presents a very effective tool in mitigating the harm non-consensual pornography inflicts on its victim.

60 Copyright Draft Bill, para 85(1).

61 Suzor (n12) 1073–6; Fiedler (n 42) 181–5; M L Ambrose, 'A Digital Dark Age and the Right to Be Forgotten' (2012) 17 (3) *Journal of Internet Law* 1, 9; M L Ambrose, 'It's About Time: Privacy, Information Life Cycles, and the Right to be Forgotten' (2013) 16 *Stanford Technology Law Review* 369, 397.

62 *Google Spain SL v Agencia Espaiiola de Protecci6n de Datos* (C-131/12) [2014] ECJ 317 ('Google Spain').

12 Intellectual property law and the protection of creative MSMEs in the digital economy of Nigeria

Leveraging AfCFTA

Helen Chuma-Okoro and Omolara 'bisi Olabanji

Introduction

The digital economy has emerged as a global phenomenon creating opportunities for both big and small enterprises. Nigeria, like other African countries, is not left out of these developments.[1] By definition, the digital economy is "that part of economic output derived solely or primarily from digital technologies with a business model based on digital goods or services."[2] The digital economy comprises both formal and informal digital enterprises, and small and large enterprises.[3] Among these are creative enterprises, described as "entities that have their origin in individual creativity, skill and talent, and which have a potential for wealth and job creation through the generation and exploitation of intellectual property."[4] The important linkage between digital creative enterprises and the protection afforded by intellectual property rights (IPRs) is what MSMEs must fully and effectively utilise. Yet, it has been established that small business entities find it difficult to effectively utilise the advantages of IPRs as a tool for achieving competitiveness and growth.

1 Richard Boateng, et al., 2017, 'Digital Enterprises in Africa: A Synthesis of Current Evidence' 1, https://diodeweb.files.wordpress.com/2017/04/diode-paper-2-digital-enterprises-in-africa.pdf accessed 27 May 2021; World Bank Group, *Nigeria Digital Economy Diagnostic Report* (World Bank, Washington DC, 2019) https://documents1.worldbank.org/curated/en/387871574812599817/pdf/Nigeria-Digital-Economy-Diagnostic-Report.pdf accessed 27 May 2021. In the World Bank Report, the World Bank noted, however, that Nigeria is currently capturing only a fraction of this growth and needs to strategically invest in the foundational elements of its digital economy to keep pace, such as, improving digital skills and literacy, coverage of digital identity schemes, and access to digital payments and other financial services.

2 Ibid 2.

3 Ibid 1.

4 Xavier Greffe, *Managing Creative Enterprises: Creative Industries* Booklet No. 3, 2006 https://www.wipo.int/edocs/pubdocs/en/copyright/938/wipo_pub_938.pdf accessed 27 May 2021.

DOI: 10.4324/9781003250883-16

Intellectual property (IP) and its value are often not adequately appreciated due to lack of awareness on the part of small businesses regarding the protection it can provide for their IP assets, such as inventions, brands and designs.[5]

Apart from lack of awareness, the inadequacy of the legal protection framework for the digital economy is also an inhibiting factor for some small businesses particularly in countries like Nigeria with outdated IPRs legislation.[6]

Entering the arena of continental development, the African Union's agreement establishing the African Continental Free Trade Area (AfCFTA) has been designed to enhance the competitiveness of the economies of State Parties in the global market. Phase two negotiations focuses on providing a conducive environment for recognising African IPRs, facilitating intra-African investment, and addressing anti-competitive challenges.[7] Given the trajectories of Nigeria's creative enterprises, the Agreement presents an opportune framework, which if effectively deployed, can spur the sector as a key player on the continent. With focus on the creative industry, this chapter gauges Nigeria's readiness to draw the benefits of the Agreement by examining existing IP legislation, and policy, to highlight gaps that must be addressed in the digital economy in order for Nigeria to be in a position to benefit by the time phase two negotiations become fully operational. A facilitative environment for e-commerce is also being mooted as a possible additional phase two topic.[8]

No doubt, all businesses, MSMEs inclusive, can have more than a single kind of IPRs in their portfolio, such as trademark protection for their logos, patents for protecting their inventions and designs for their two or three-dimensional materials, such as packages.[9] While other types of IPRs are also useful to MSMEs albeit not equally, this chapter focuses on copyright

5 WIPO, *Intellectual Property, Innovation and New Product Development* (2005) 6–10 https://www.wipo.int/wipo_magazine/en/2005/04/article_0002.html accessed 27 May 2021; Sati-Salmah Sukarmijan and Olivia de Vega Sapong, "The Importance of Intellectual Property for SMEs; Challenges and Moving Forward" (2014) 1 *UMK Procedia* 74–81 (75); Eric M K Osiakwan, "The Kings of Africa's Digital Economy", in B Ndemo and T Weiss (eds) *Digital Kenya* 58–83.

6 WIPO Magazine (n 5) 6–10. The core intellectual property statutes were enacted over four decades ago and have not been amended.

7 Africa Continental Free Trade Area Questions and Answers, compiled by the African Trade Policy Centre (ATPC) of the Economic Commission for Africa (ECA) in association with the African Union Commission, available at https://au.int/sites/default/files/documents/36085-doc-qa_cfta_en_rev15march.pdf, accessed on 27 May 2021.

8 Ibid.

9 Rahul Bagga, "Why MSMEs Should Treat Intellectual Property Rights as Assets *The Economic Times*, May 13, 2019, available at https://www.google.com/amp/s/m.economictimes.com/small-biz/sme-sector/why-msmes-should-treat-intellectual -property-rights-as-assets/amp_articleshow/69304077.cms, accessed on 27 May 2021.

which unarguably is the most relevant to creative enterprises as the primary IP mechanism for deriving measurable values from their works.[10]

Intellectual property rights and MSME competitiveness

Defining MSMEs

While the meaning of "enterprise" as "a unit engaged in the production of goods or services for sale or barter – be it corporations, non-profit institutions, government-owned unincorporated enterprises, or private unincorporated enterprises" –[11] is straight forward, there is a lack of uniform definition of MSMEs. Basically, what qualifies as an MSMEs depends on the country that is defining it, and who is defining it; and it could be based on one or more of the following variables: employment, turnover, assets and paid up capital in quantitative terms.[12] Largely, MSMEs covers enterprises with up to 250 employees.[13] In the specific context of Nigeria, the Small and Medium Scale Enterprises Development Agency (SMEDAN) endorses a dual criteria classification based on the employment and assets different from the model of the Bank of Industry which is based on additional variables such as turnover and loan eligibility.[14] Following SMEDAN's classification, MSMEs refers to enterprises with up to 199 employees.[15]

Intellectual property rights and competitive advantage

Generally, competition is basic for market players, both large and small. As Paul Kegame, observed, competition is good for everybody. It helps bring

10 UNCTAD-ICTSD, *Resource Book on TRIPS and Development* (Cambridge University Press, New York, 2005) 136.

11 ILO, *Sustainable Enterprises and Jobs: Formal Enterprises and Decent Work* (International Labour Office – Geneva, 2017) 7 https://www.ilo.org/wcmsp5/groups/public/---dgreports/---dcomm/---publ/documents/publication/wcms_579893.pdf accessed 27 May 2021.

12 Small and Medium Scale Enterprises Development Agency (SMEDAN), *National Policy on Micro, Small and Medium Enterprises*, (2007) 12, available at https://www.smedan.gov.ng/images/PDF/MSME-National-Policy.pdf accessed May 27 2021. Berisha, Gentrit and Pula, Justina, "Defining Small and Medium Enterprises: A Critical Review (2015) 1, 17–28; Invoice, 'Micro, Small and Medium Enterprises in Nigeria: An Overview' https://invoice.ng/blog/msmes-in-nigeria-overview/#:~:text=The%20definitions%20of%20small%20and,between%2050%20and%20249%20employees, accessed 27 May 2021.

13 ILO (n 11) 13.

14 See Table 2.

15 See tables one and two. Note that following the SMEDAN standard. But the employment-based classification takes precedence where there is a conflict in classification between employment and assets criteria. For instance, an enterprise that has assets worth seven million naira but employs seven persons will be classified as a micro enterprise. The employment-based classification is seen as relatively more stable than asset-based definition which may be easily distorted by inflationary tendencies. SMEDAN, (n 12) 13.

Classification of MSMEs in Nigeria

Size Category	*Employment*	*Asset N Million (Excluding Land and Building)*
Micro enterprises	Less than 10	Less than 5
Small enterprises	10–49	5–less than 50
Medium enterprises	50–199	50–less than 500

Source: Small and Medium Enterprises Development Agency of Nigeria (SMEDAN), Abuja, 2007, 12.

Enterprise Category	*Number of Employees*	*Total Asset (N' Million)*	*Annual Turnover (N' Million)*	*Loans (N' Million)*
Micro	≤10	≤5	≤20	≤10
Small	>11≤50	>5≤100	≤100	>10≤100
Medium	>51≤200	>100≤500	≤500	>100≤500

Source: Bank of Industry https://www.boi.ng/smedefinition/

out everybody's potential. And it does not matter what level of society. Even the poor people have that energy, and deserve that freedom where they can be able to compete with the rest and do the best they can.[16] The ability to penetrate the market depends on competitive advantage, which in turn entails providing products or services that capture consumer preferences over alternatives in the market. In its technical market context, competition has been defined as "the rivalry between companies selling similar products and services with the goal of achieving revenue, profit, and market share growth," and that "market competition motivates companies to increase sales volume by utilising the four components of the marketing mix," namely, product, place, promotion and price.[17] In another context, market competition is a "business environment where different firms, located within and out of a country, have to compete with one another solely on the merits of their goods and services."[18] In both instances, IPRs protection serves as the basic tool for managing and valorising intellectual resources generated along the

16 Povertycure, 'Market Competition' https://www.povertycure.org/learn/issues/market-competition, https://www.facebook.com/watch/?v=1619329858091067 accessed 27 May 2021.

17 James Camrite, 'Principles of Marketing: Help and Review' https://www.google.com/search?q=market+competition&oq=market+competition+&aqs=chrome.69i57.19209j0j15&sourceid=chrome&ie=UTF-8 accessed 27 May 2021.

18 Povertycure (n 16).

process from production to marketing,[19] and MSMEs are implicated. Invariably, competitiveness invariably involves the generation and/or use of IPRs in any of its forms, in addition to other concepts within competition law.[20]

IPRs protect outputs arising from intellectual activities. They refer to the exclusive legal but temporary rights granted to owners of creative works and inventions to control the use of their works for profit through licensing, sale or other means of commercialisation. These rights could be in the form of patents, trademarks, copyrights, industrial designs and geographical indications.[21]

The strong recognition of IPRs as a source of competitive advantage for enterprises arises from their major role in an economic environment. IPRs protect firms from the competition by granting them temporary monopoly rights to exploit the economic value of their IP assets in several ways.[22] Enterprises could obtain a temporary technological lead (incumbency advantages) with patents,[23] protect strong brands as trademarks[24] or geographical indications,[25] and protect promotional resources like brochures or other works of expression under copyright. Such guarantees of returns from innovation and creativity incentivises further innovation and creative endeavours. Conversely, absence of such encouraging safeguards would result to decrease in these activities and endeavours.[26]

Protecting IP is relevant for every company, in particular MSMEs, primarily to avoid the misappropriation or theft of one's IP at their infancy stage. A well-managed IP portfolio could help generate wealth for the enterprise.[27] Adequate protection of a company's IP is a crucial step in deterring potential infringement and in turning ideas into business assets with a real market value. Taking full advantage of the IP system enables enterprises to profit from their innovative capacity and creativity, which encourages and helps fund further innovation.[28] IP can become a valuable asset if it is legally

19 WIPO, *Guide on Surveying the Economic Contribution of the Copyright-Based Industries* (2013) 18.

20 WTO/UNCTAD/International Trade Centre, *Secrets of Intellectual Property: A Guide for small and Medium-sized Exporters* (ITC/WIPO, Geneva, 2003; WIPO, *Intellectual Property Handbook: Policy, Law and Use* (WIPO, Geneva, 2004) 3.

21 Ibid.

22 WIPO, 'Intellectual Property for Business' https://www.wipo.int/sme/en/S accessed 27 May 2021.

23 WIPO, *Inventing the Future: An Introduction to Patents for Small and Medium Sized Enterprises* (2006). WIPO Publication No. 917.1 4.

24 WIPO, *Making a Mark: An Introduction to Trademarks and Brands for Small and Medium-sized Enterprises,* 2017, WIPO publication No. 900.1 2.; WIPO, "Looking Good: an Introduction to Industrial Designs for Small and Medium-Sized Enterprises, WIPO Publication No. 498.1 3.

25 Aurora A C Teixeira and Catia Ferreiria, 'Intellectual Property Rights and the Competitiveness of Academic Spin-Off' (2019) 4 *Journal of Information and Knowledge* 151–61.

26 WIPO 2004, (n 24).

27 WTO/UNCTAD, (n 20).

28 Ibid.

protected and well managed, and there is a demand for the IP-related products or services in the marketplace.[29] Effective appropriation of IP assets entails enterprises' ability to commercialise their inventions, knowhow and creativity through a multiplicity of options offered by the legal system of IPRS for managing innovation, knowledge and creativity. IPRs enable companies to differentiate their products and maintain exclusivity over their IP such as trade secrets, trademarks, designs, patents (inventions) literary and artistic creations, thereby decreasing the likelihood of copying and "deal more effectively with the violations of their IP rights."[30]

Value of intellectual property rights to MSMEs

Experts are not entirely unanimous on the value or relevance of IPRs to the success of MSMEs in the market environment. On the contrary, there seems to be a consensus that a lot more is involved beyond IPRs. For instance, Amir Kanaan, Managing Director of Kaspersky – Middle East, Turkey and Africa – notes as follows:

> Intellectual property is the life blood of any organization, and for small businesses, even more so! A strategic handling of a company's intangible assets (e.g. trademarks, copyrights, trade secrets, and patents) can catapult small, local businesses toward greater global recognition. By developing and protecting their best-in-class technologies and products, they can establish themselves as market leaders and industry experts, thereby attracting a sizeable clientele. This is especially the case for small businesses that rely predominantly on the fruits of their intellectual labor. However, innovation forms only half the equation in the success and growth of a business.[31]

Experts have indeed expressed doubts as to whether MSMEs heavily rely on IPRs to appropriate returns from their business. Studies have stablished that owners of small companies rely on alternative (informal) protection mechanisms such as lead time, secrecy, product quality maintenance, customised services and continued innovation. One of the reasons for the lack of major interest in IPRs is attributed to lack of awareness of their existing IPRs and/or their benefits, lack of expertise and cost considerations in managing and enforcing the rights.[32] It has been established that small business owners placed more emphasis on informal methods to protect IP as they

29 WIPO Magazine (n 5).

30 WTO/UNCTAD, (n 20) 180.

31 Amir Kanaan, 'The How – To: Protecting your Intellectual Property as a Small Business". *Entrepreneur*, August 24, 2020, https://www.entrepreneur.com/article/355187

32 Teixeira and Ferreiria (n 25) 155–6.

consider these methods more familiar, cheaper, less time-consuming and usually more effective than the more formal rights like patents.[33]

Thus, we agree that IPR protection is only relevant for MSMEs in boosting competition if it is contemplated as an integrated approach that takes into account several factors, such as knowledge of the benefits of appropriate IPR protection, access to the proper IPR protection frameworks and services ensuring effective IPR enforcement alongside other supporting strategies like quality improvement.[34] Nevertheless, to the extent that IPRs are relevant MSMEs, the existence of an enabling framework for them to effectively appropriate their IPRs is imperative. As someone noted, "adopting appropriation strategies that results from combination of different formal and informal protection mechanisms may be advantageous" for MSMEs.[35]

It cannot therefore be gainsaid that proper utilisation of IPRs could help an MSME in several ways. Indeed, the strategic utilisation of IP assets can substantially enhance the competitiveness of SMEs.[36] IPR may support MSMEs in every part of business development and competitive strategy from product development and design to marketing, including marketing abroad through IP assignments, i.e., through franchising[37] and licensing.[38] IPRs, combined with other marketing tools (such as advertisements and other sales promotion activities) are crucial for product differentiating and differential marketing objectives as important market boosting strategies.[39] They may also generate income for MSMEs and improve market share and profit margin through sale or commercialisation of the IP products or services. Furthermore, they may significantly enhance the value or worth of MSMEs in the eyes or financing institutions (in obtaining credit facilities) and investors, including joint ventures and collaboration schemes.[40] [41] For example, a unique trademark and brand name could help MSMEs create a

33 John Kitching and Robert Blackburn, "Intellectual Property Management in the Small and Medium Enterprise (SME)", (1998) 5(4) *Journal of Small Business and Enterprise Development* 327–35. This consideration however does not apply to copyright which are automatic, the only been usually ignorance and cost consideration with regards to enforcement against infringements.

34 Ibid.

35 Ibid.

36 WIPO, 2005 (n 5).

37 WIPO, *In Good Company: Managing Intellectual Property Issues in Franchising*, WIPO Publication No. 1035, 2019.

38 WIPO, 2005 (n 5).

39 WIPO Magazine (n 5), citing P K Urwin, *Valuing Brands in the UK Economy* (Westminster Business School University of Westminster, London, 2008). WIPO Magazine 2005, Kamel Idris, *Marketing Crafts and Visual Arts: The Role of Intellectual Property* (2003).

40 WIPO Magazine (n 5).

41 Suparji, 'Implementation of Intellectual Property Right to Strengthen Small and Medium-Sized Enterprise Business Capacity in Global Competition' (2020) 9(6) *Academic Journal of Interdisciplinary Studies*, 139. https://doi.org/10.36941/ajis-2020-0118 accessed 27 May 2020

strong recall value and strong position for their products and/or services in the market making the trademark a valuable asset.[42]

Nevertheless, MSMEs usually lack the requisite knowledge to apply these market boosting strategies. And even where there is knowledge, the adequacy of the relevant legal and policy frameworks still has to be considered.[43] Nevertheless, for creative MSMEs, IPR protection assumes particular strategic importance because success depends largely on creativity.[44] For them, copyright is easily the most relevant and important form of IPR.[45]

MSMEs and copyright

The scope of copyright protectable works is wide. It includes publications, music, films, computer programs, databases and architectural works, and lots more.[46] Copyright is essential to MSMEs in several ways regardless of whether their core business deals with creativity. Any literary, artistic, musical or cinematographic material produced in the course of business, such as brochures, pamphlets, reports, products manuals, promo jingles or visual content falls under the subject matter of copyright law. Others are computer programs or software; content on websites; and artwork.[47] The increasing integration of digitalised content into some of these collections of expressive assets brings them within the scope of the digital economy.

Apart from the positive protection it provides to protected works against misappropriation or unauthorised uses, copyright constitutes part of the profit yielding income from content. Adequate copyright protection transforms a company's creative content into valuable business assets which makes the company credit worthy and more attractive to investors.[48]

Copyright grants to their owners a monopoly right to control some uses of the protected material which in itself constitutes an enviable market advantage.[49] But copyright could pose serious challenges for MSMEs: weak

42 Aayush Sharma Mondaq, 'India: Intellectual Property and Small and Medium-Sized Enterprises' 05 December 2012 by Aayush Sharm (2012), *Mondaq* https://www.mondaq.com/india/trademark/209194/intellectual-property-and-small-and-medium-sized-enterprises) accessed 27 May 2021.

43 WTO/WIPO.

44 Creative Expression: An Introduction to Copyright and Related Rights for Small and Medium-sized Enterprises. WIPO publication No. 918 5.

45 WIPO refers to creative industries alternatively as copyright-based industries. See WIPO, 'The Economic Performance of Copyright-based Industries' https://www.wipo.int/copyright/en/performance/

46 Ibid. (*The challenge of change: Perspectives on the future for content providers'*)

47 WIPO, *Creative Expressions: An Introduction to Copyright and Related Rights for Small and Medium Scale Enterprises* (Intellectual Property for Business Series No. 4, 2006).

48 Sukarmijan and de Vega Sapong, (n 5) 74.

49 The right of control over works which copyright guarantees to the work owner is not absolute, rather, it is subject to exceptions and limitations. See Ruth Okediji, *Copyright Law in an Age of Exceptions and Limitation* (Cambridge University Press, Cambridge, 2017).

domestic laws may not provide the necessary framework and MSMEs could lack the ability to successfully manage their copyrights. Monitoring and enforcement of copyright infringements across borders, which is a constant and increasing battle for copyright enterprises in the digital economy, involves access to information, expertise, resources and mechanisms that may be hard for MSMEs to mobilise. Underestimation and lack of appreciation of the real value of their IP is a common weakness among MSMEs.[50]

To derive satisfactory benefits from their copyright assets, MSMEs must first be able to earn monetary rewards by assigning ownership of their copyright assets to third parties permanently or licensing use temporarily and earning royalties or similar remuneration. In the digital economy, managing transactions and or monitoring uses could be challenging given the diverse, sometimes anonymous, users globally. Copyright, like other forms of IPRs, are largely territorial in nature and governed by domestic laws. But just as market is broader given globalisation, infringements also occur globally given the ubiquitous and borderless nature of the Internet, and the fluidity of digital content or data.[51] Therefore, an MSME must be able to effectively manage their copyright.

Overview of the creative industry in Nigeria

The Nigerian creative industry is vast and of great importance.[52] It comprises several players across diverse sectors like film, theatre, music, dance, literature, fashion, television, radio, arts, sports, information technology, media, advertising and gaming.[53] These activities are connected by their affiliation with IPRs as the primary product of all activities across the different sectors.

50 Ibid 77.

51 David Allweiss, "Copyright Infringement on the Internet: Can the Wild, Wild West Be Tamed?" (1999) 15(3) Article 9 https://www.lawallianz.com/publications/the-nigerian-creative-industry-and-intellectual-property-rights-in-a-digital-environment/accessed 27 May 2021

52 British Council, *Mapping of Nigeria Creative Industries: Report of Lagos Pilot Study* (Music, Fashion and Film), November 2013. Yemi Kale, "Measuring Better: Preliminary Results of the Rebased Nominal Gross Domestic Product (GDP) Estimates for Nigeria 2010 to 2013" (2014) https://scirp.org/reference/ReferencesPapers.aspx?ReferenceID=1823553 accessed 27 May 2021.

53 Olusola Mesele, 'The Nigerian Creative Industry and Intellectual Property Rights in a Digital Environment' https://www.lawallianz.com/publications/the-nigerian-creative-industry-and-intellectual-property-rights-in-a-digital-environment/ accessed 27 May 2021 (d,n,a). The Nigerian Creative Industry comprises several players across diverse sectors like film, theatre, music, dance, literature, fashion, television, radio, arts, sports, information technology, media, advertising and gaming. The common tie that binds the entire industry is Intellectual Property (IP), as it is the primary product of all activities across the different sectors.

It is undeniable that comparatively, Nigeria enjoys greater advantage than most other African countries in the creative industry. The nascent success of Nigeria's creative economy is gaining recognition among global partners.[54] The fast-growing copyright-dependent audio-visual, technology, literary, music and fashion sectors are imprinting themselves as strong exporters of culture, education, arts and entertainment; competing closely with America and India for the global market share.[55] For instance, *IrokoTv,* dubbed as "Netflix of Africa" is the world's largest online platform for African entertainment and is one of the most respected technology brands at the heart of Africa's exciting tech space.[56] Since start-up in 2010, it has closed several funding rounds in excess of US$30m.

There is no doubt that Nigeria's movie industry *"Nollywood"*[57] has emerged as an industry to reckon with given its significant contribution to the growth of the creative economy. Nigeria's film industry employs more than one million people – making it the second largest employer after Agriculture.[58] *Nollywood* is rated second largest in the world second to Hollywood.[59] In 2016, *Nollywood*'s annual revenue was valued in the region of US$3.6 billion and will increase at a 12.2% compound annual growth rate (CAGR) till 2021, reaching up to US$6.4 billion.[60] It contributed 2.3% to Nigeria's gross domestic product (GDP), and is considered a priority sector within the Federal Government's Economic Recovery and Growth Plan.[61] This is for their impact on economic development as key drivers of

54 Tom Fleming, 'Developing Creative Economies in ODA Countries' (2019) https://www.britishcouncil.org/sites/default/files/british_council_creative_economy_development_in_four_countries_summary_report_tfcc.docxx_.pdf

55 UNDP Press Release, (2020) 'Nigerian Creative Sector Steps Out for UNDP Create to Develop Connect in Lagos' https://www.ng.undp.org/content/nigeria/en/home/presscenter/pressreleases/2020/nigerian-creative-sector-players-including-don-jazzy--sola-sobow.html accessed 27 May 2021.

56 Olumide Obasemo, 'Why Lagos (in Nigeria) Is Africa's Silicon Valley' https://www.startupgrind.com/blog/why-lagos-in-nigeria-is-africas-silicon-valley/

57 https://en.wikipedia.org/wiki/Nollywood; Connor Ryan, '*New Nollywood*, accessed 27 May 2021; C Ryan, 'A Sketch of Nollywood's Metropolitan New Style' (2015) 58(3) *African Studies Review* 55; Uchenna Onuzulike 'Nollywood: The Birth of Nollywood: The Nigerian Movie Industry' (2008) 22(1) *Black Camera* 25–6 (25).

58 Mayowa Tijani, 'IMF: Nollywood is Nigeria's Second Biggest Employer' *The Cable*, May 26, 2016, https://www.thecable.ng/imf-nollywood-nigerias-second-biggest-employment, accessed 27 May 2021.

59 Charles Igwe, 'How Nollywood Became the Second Largest Film Industry' https://www.britishcouncil.org/voices-magazine/nollywood-second-largest-film-industry accessed March 22 2021.

60 PwC Entertainment and Media Outlook: 2017–2021, An African Perspective, 20, www.pwc.co.za/outlook, accessed 27 May 2021; Ijeoma Onyeator, 'Glocalizing the Creative Industries Concept: Identifying the Characteristics of the Nigerian Creative Industries' (2019) 7(3) *European Journal of Research in Social Sciences* 52.

61 UNDP (n 5).

job creation, foreign trade and income generation[62] within the context of MSMEs.[63] According to Pierre Barrot, *Nollywood* is a cultural, economic, business and technological phenomenon without precedence.[64]

While smaller firms within the vibrant tech sector are providing budding e-commerce platforms and retail-related services, large firms are delivering services in healthcare, agriculture and finance.[65] In a survey of tech firms conducted in 2018, it was reported that most firms start small but grow quickly; more than doubling their size in the few years after the start of operations, despite poor infrastructure.[66] Example is *Okada Books,* a digital book publishing firm aiming to be the largest distributor of literary works in Sub-Saharan Africa.[67]

The functions of some businesses depend largely on the production, aggregation and use of copyright-protected materials (books, newspapers, periodicals; motion pictures; music and sound recordings; radio and television broadcasting and computer software, including both business applications and entertainment software). Others by virtue of the nature of their business are ancillary to copyright[68] (manufacturers, wholesalers and retailers of CD/DVD/Blu-Ray players, TV sets, VCRs, personal computers and usage-dependent products including blank recording material and USB thumb drives and certain categories of paper). There are also people, organisations and investors that add substantial creative, technical or organisational skill in the process of bringing a protected work to the public. These are altogether described as the total copyright industries.[69] Generally, they have

62 See generally "Economic Contribution of Copyright-based Industries" of various nations including Australia, Lebanon, South Africa, Trinidad and Tobago, Tanzania, Kenya, Canada, China, USA, www.wipo.int/copyright/en/performance accessed 27 May 2021.

63 Nigeria's Bank of Industry defines MSMEs as enterprises with less than 200 employees and less than N500,000,000 total assets or annual turnover. See Bank of Industry at http://www.boi.ng/msmedefinition/ accessed 27 May 2021.

64 Pierre Barrot et al. (eds), 'Nollywood: The Video Phenomenon in Nigeria' (2008) xi, xi; Jeremy Nathan '*No-Budget Nigeria*' filmmaker mag. (2002) Available at www.filmmaker-magazine.com

65 Vijaya Ramachandran, et al., "The New Economy of Africa: Opportunities for Nigeria's Emerging Technology Sector" (November 2019), https://www.cgdev.org/sites/default/files/new-economy-africa-opportunities-nigerias-emerging-technology-sector.pdf accessed 27 May 2021.

66 Ibid.

67 Hadassah Egbedi "Okadabooks – The Innovative Platform Revolutionizing Book Publishing in Nigeria". September 2017, http://venturesafrica.com/blog/2017/09/20/okadabooks-the-innovative-platform-revolutionising-book-publishing-in-nigeria/ accessed 27 May 2021.

68 Vanus James, 'The Economic Contribution of Copyright-based Industries in Trinidad and Tobago' (2012) 7 *WIPO's Creative Industries Series* 8.

69 WIPO, Guide on Copyright-Based Industries, (2013) 18, https://www.wipo.int/export/sites/www/copyright/en/performance/pdf/econ_contribution_cr_mw.pdf. Stephen E Siwek '*Copyright Industries in the U.S. Economy: The Report of International Intellectual*

had to metamorphose and adapt their operations to electronically compliant platforms to catch up with emerging realities brought by digitalisation and globalisation,[70] to retain market influence or risk extinction.[71] For all these activities (sectors), the terms of the IP protocol and its operation within the AfCFTA regional framework would likely have significant implications.

The combined reports of Organisation for Economic Co-operation and Development (OECD)[72] and United Nations Conference on Trade and Development (UNCTAD)[73] identified information and communication technology as powerful business tools that help MSMEs increase their market visibility, improve access to clients, reduce transaction and administrative costs and contribute to their overall competitiveness.[74]

With the rise of mobile telephony and broadband Internet access (*Internet World Stats* rates Nigeria as Africa's biggest technology market) accounts for 23% of Internet users with 122 million people online in December 2019),[75] it is no longer sustainable for copyright enterprises to operate solely within the traditional mediums of production and dissemination of copyright works, i.e., cinematic exhibition of movies, broadcasting of terrestrial and cable television, hard copy publication of texts, production of CDs and DVDs containing music, movies and computer programs, but rather through contemporary channels now enabled by the Internet.[76]

Following an increased appetite for digital content, the medium for developing, producing, transmitting and distributing copyright works have dramatically changed.[77] As technology now enables the ubiquitous availability of media,[78] the audience have shifted their consumption habits, thereby making it inevitable for content creators and distributors to adapt

---

Property Alliance (IIPA) (2014) 5; Ike Janita Dewi, 'A Study on the Economic Contribution of Copyright and Related Right Industries in Indonesia' (2014) 115 *Procedia – Social and Behavioural Sciences* 207–20 by Elsevier L. See also World Intellectual Property Organization, '*National Studies on Assessing the Economic Contribution of the Copyright*' (2005) Copyright Industries No. 1 Report Available at www.wipo.int

70 Lund Susan and James Manyika '*How Digital Trade Is Transforming Globalisation*' ICTSD and World Economic Forum (2016) www.e15initiative.org/

71 Accenture Global Content Study Report, '*The Challenge of Change: Perspectives on the Future for Content Providers*' (2008) 3.

72 Graham Vickery et al. '*ICT, E-Business and SMEs*' (2004) OECD https://www.oecd.org/sti/34228733.pdf.

73 UNCTAD Commission on Enterprise and Expert Meetings '*Improving the Competitiveness of SME's through Enhancing Productive Capacity*' UNCTAD/ITE/TEB/2005/1 www.unctad.org

74 Graham et al. (2004).

75 Chinecherem Umezuruike, Awodele Oludele, Kuyoro, Izang Aaron, '*Broadband Internet Penetration in Nigeria*: A Review' (2015) *International Journal of Research Studies in Computer Science and Engineering (IJRSSE)* 4 Available at www.arcjournals.org

76 Lund and Manyika (2016).

77 Jeremy West, '*Enquiries into Intellectual Property Economic Impact*' (2015) 221 www.oecd.org KBC2-IP. final pdf

78 Accenture (2008).

to making digital content available to consumers whenever and wherever they want it.[79] This has necessitated copyright enterprises to break out of their siloed offerings by re-strategising content distribution to be across multiple channels like on the television, online (webcasting, downloading and streaming) and mobile platforms through the abstraction of content from the device so that it can be leveraged across channels.[80] Doing this requires having strong content and rights management capabilities, as well as the ability to properly control content distribution and deploy effective enforcement mechanisms beyond national boundaries for the desired benefits.

The national legal framework in perspective

The shift in global trade to more knowledge-based products made it imperative to incorporate protection of IPRs in the World Trade Organization (WTO) instrument negotiated within the Uruguay Rounds in 1994.[81] Innovation, creativity and branding represent a large amount of the value that changes hands in international trade. How to enhance this value and how to facilitate the flow of knowledge-rich goods and services across borders have become integral considerations in development and trade policy.[82] Consequently, the Agreement on the Trade Related Aspects of Intellectual Property Rights (TRIPS) became part of the WTO's multilateral trading system. Countries were obligated to grant certain defined standards of protection to IPRs. The TRIPS Agreement requires member states, among others, to comply with the Paris text of the Berne Convention for Literary and Artistic Works, 1886, which Convention adds some further obligations in the field of copyright.[83]

Twenty-six years after onboarding TRIPS globally, Nigeria has not had a tangible holistic review of its policy and legal framework despite significant developments both in the international and domestic copyright community despite several past efforts.[84] Success has been recorded in some specific

79 Ibid.

80 Ibid.

81 The Uruguay Round, https://www.wto.org/english/thewto_e/whatis_e/tif_e/fact5_e.htm

82 Understanding the WTO: The Agreement 'Intellectual Property Protection and Enforcement' https://www.wto.org/english/thewto_e/whatis_e/tif_e/agrm7_e.htm

83 Introductory Notes of Circulation Copy of the Draft Copyright Bill 2016 by Nigerian Copyright Commission Technical Working Group. http://graduatedresponse.org/new/wp-content/uploads/2016/02/DRAFT_COPYRIGHT_BILL_NOVEMBER-_2015.pdf

84 Ibid. One of such efforts to comprehensively amend the country's intellectual property law is Industrial Property Commission Bill which started since 1991 with the main aim of providing a unified system of industrial property regulation but is yet to be passed. See John C Onyido, Yetunde Okojie, Oluwasolape Owoyemi, 'The Industrial Property Commission Bill (IPCOM) and the New Trademarks Bill: Highlights, Issues and Recommendations' (2019) *Mondaq* https://www.mondaq.com/nigeria/trademark/764946/the-industrial-property-commission-bill-ipcom-and-the-new-trade-marks-bill-highlights-issues-and-recommendations?login=true

areas such as the passing of the Cybercrime legislation in 2015,[85] while efforts are ongoing to bring the country's seed protection and copyright legislations up to standard.[86] The emergence of digital technologies revolutionised the creative economy as production and dissemination of creative works became more accessible and lent themselves to global exploitation beyond national boundaries. Responding to these challenges, the global IP community adopted a number of unique solutions, including international treaties like the WIPO Copyright Treaty and WIPO Performances and Phonograms Treaty of 1996[87]; the WIPO Beijing Treaty for Protection of Audiovisual Performances of 2012 and the Marrakesh Treaty for the Blind and Visually Impaired Persons of 2013.

The Nigerian Copyright Act[88] is the principal legislation governing the protection of copyrights in the country. To some extent, it serves the digital economy. It protects literary, musical and artistic; as well as cinematograph films, sound recordings and broadcasts.[89] It defines literary works broadly to include compute programs[90] and recognises digital works and online platforms for information production, storage, use and dissemination by conceptualising fixation broadly to include transient copies. These works are only protected if they qualify as original works and have been fixed in a definite form whether permanent or transient.[91] The principle of territoriality is firmly stated by extending eligibility for protection based on Nigerian nationality or domicile,[92] place of publication[93] or treaty obligation.[94] Thus it grants protection only to works whose makers are Nigerians or non-Nigerians domiciled in Nigeria, and to entities established under Nigerian laws if owned by a company.[95] These conditions and terms of protection allow for the management of the digital rights of materials or works belonging to MSMEs if desired. However, for a law enacted long before the WIPO Internet Treaties and last amended in 1988, Nigeria's principal legislation governing copyright protection is indisputably deficient especially

85 Cybercrime (Prohibition, Prevention, etc.) Act, 2015. See also, John Odumesi, 'Nigeria's Cybercrimes (Prohibition, Prevention, etc.) Act 2015 and Critical National Infrastructure'. doi: 10.13140/RG.2.1.4778'6726.

86 Agency Report, 'Plant Variety Protection Law Will Boost Food Security-DG Seeds Council' *Independent*, November 6, 2019, https://www.independent.ng/plant-variety-protection-law-will-boost-food-security-dg-seeds-council/ Food Farm News, Tuesday 12 Nov. 2019; Nov. 6 2019 Independent); Bob Aroture, 'Nigeria: Federal Executive Council Approves Copyright Bill' January 10, 2012, *NLIP Watch*.

87 Sometimes referred to as the WIPO Internet Treaties.

88 Cap C28 LFN 2004.

89 Section 1(1).

90 Section 51.

91 Section 1(2).

92 Section 2(i).

93 Section 3(1).

94 Section 5.

95 Section 2(ii).

in relation to the digital economy and the effective management of digital rights. The core provisions of the WIPO Internet Treaties safeguarding digital content, such as the anti-circumvention provisions safeguarding technological safeguards of copyright against unauthorised uses, on-demand availability rights and provisions regulating the liability of Internet service providers are conspicuously absent.

Taking cognizance of these new treaties and the gaps in the national frameworks, in 2012, the Nigerian Copyright Commission launched the Reform of the Copyright System which effort included the preparation of the Draft Copyright Bill.[96] The key objective of the reform was to reposition Nigeria's creative MSMEs for greater growth; strengthen their capacity to compete more effectively in the marketplace, and also enable Nigeria to fully satisfy its obligations under the various International Copyright Instruments, particularly in the digital environment. The Draft Bill established the protection of copyright works in the digital environment by delineating certain exclusive rights. They are the right of reproduction, the right of making available and the right of communication to the public for both core copyright owners and related rights stakeholders. For the purpose of rights management and enforcement, the Bill criminalises the circumvention of technical protection measures and right management information.[97]

Unfortunately, since the supervising Ministry[98] approved this laudable Draft Bill for transmission to the Federal Executive Council (FEC) in 2017, progress has been very slow.

There were several stakeholder interventions to push the passage of the Bill, including by the United States Mission in Nigeria when it converged Government and Industry for the National Intellectual Property (IP) Symposium in September 2019 as a vehicle to motivate political and legislative interest.[99] Following these efforts, the Presidency communicated to NCC to provide written submissions on some aspects of the Bill that were raised as concerns during the FEC meeting. NCC treated the concerns (which did not affect the substance of the Bill) and resubmitted to the Presidency in October 2020. In a commendable development in July 2021, FEC has transmitted the approved Bill to the National Assembly to commence the legislative process and enactment into law.[100]

Whereas, stakeholders continue to express displeasure at how poorly subsisting laws leave them vulnerable to unauthorised users and infringers of their works. For example, when information is represented digitally for music, book or a film file, having access inevitably means making a copy,

96 Ibid.

97 See generally Article 8 WCT; Articles 7, 10, 11 and 14 WPPT; Articles 7, 10 and 11 Beijing Treaty.

98 Federal Ministry of Justice and Office of the Attorney General.

99 U.S. Embassy Outcome Statement- *IP Symposium on Piracy and Counterfeiting*, September 16–17, 2019, transmitted to State House, Abuja.

100 July 6, 2021, FG sends Bill on Copyright to NASS, newdawnngr.com.

even if it is only an ephemeral (temporary) copy. On the Internet, multiple copies are being made and the potential of even bypassing any access control illegally is high. Although the Internet network provides a vibrant market for digital products, however, once stolen, digital products can be quickly broadcasted to the corners of the earth.[101] That is why Digital Rights Management (DRM) is set to achieve:

a Identification of digital rights,
b Description of associated usage rules and
c Enforcement of usage rules using DRM Software.

Should these structures be circumvented, an action in law can be brought against the infringer on the strength of the provision of copyright law.[102] But in the absence of a legal framework, managing and enforcing rights in the digital environment becomes tough for small businesses that are made to grapple with the challenges.

The utility of DRM can further be explained with reference to the United States Digital Millennium Copyright Act (DMCA) in 1998.[103] The DMCA extended copyright law to include two very different kinds of legal protection for digital media: traditional infringement protections[104] and new, distinct anti-circumvention and anti-trafficking protections unrelated to infringement.[105] According to Stephen Kramasky, "traditional infringement protection is something of a blunt instrument." Similar to Nigeria's copyright protection regime,[106] a copyright holder enjoys the following exclusive rights:

a to reproduce the copyrighted works in copies or phonorecords;
b to prepare derivative works based upon the copyrighted works;
c to distribute copies or phonorecords of the copyrighted works to the public by sale or other transfer of ownership, or by rental, lease, or lending;
d in the case of literary, musical, dramatic, and choreographic works, pantomimes, and motion picture and other audiovisual works, to perform the copyrighted work publicly;
e in the case of literary, musical, dramatic, and choreographic works, pantomimes and pictorial, graphic or sculptural works, including the

101 Longe Babatope, '*Intellectual Property Protection in the Age of Open Access and Digital Rights Management- Balancing the Odds* "University of Ibadan; See also: A Van Moffaert, O Paridaens and J Carrr '*Digital Rights Management*' (2003) https://www.researchgate.net/publication/296740827_Digital_rights_management.

102 Stephen M Kramasky, '*Copyright Enforcement in the Internet Age: The Law and Technology of Digital Rights Management*' (2001) 11 *DePaul Journal of Art, Technology & Intellectual Property Law* 1 https://via.library.depaul.edu/jatip/vol11/iss1/2.

103 PL. 105–304—OCT. 28, 1998, https://www.govinfo.gov/content/pkg/PLAW-105publ304/pdf/PLAW-105publ304.pd.

104 17 U.S.C. § 106.

105 17 U.S.C. §§1201.

106 Sections 6 and 7 of the Nigerian Copyright Act Cap C20 LFN 2004.

individual images of a motion picture or other audiovisual work, to display the copyrighted work publicly and

f in the case of sound recordings, to perform the copyrighted work publicly by means of digital audio transmission.[107]

This statutory protection is broad, although it does not provide much in the way of fine control over copyrighted materials of the kind contemplated by most DRM schemes. Nonetheless, since circumvention and infringement are provided as distinct offenses, traditional infringement continues to keep its role in the digital world. It is thus the combination of encryption technology and anti-circumvention protection that will dominate the digital copyright landscape.[108]

The AfCFTA opportunity for African creative MSMEs

Africa Union's Agenda 2063 aspires for a continental market that enables free movement of persons, capital, goods and services. These are crucial factors that deepen economic integration, promote development and structural economic transformation.[109] Under the auspices of the AfCFTA, this aspiration will be achieved by creating an expanded and secure market for goods and services through adequate infrastructure, reduction or progressive elimination of tariffs and the elimination of non-tariff barriers to trade and investment.[110]

In the current context of globalised trade, African economies must improve their competitiveness and diversify their economic base. Although trade in commodities is still the major generator of foreign exchange earnings and employment, by itself, it can no longer power Africa's development.[111] Export preferences for traditional products such as crude oil and sugar are eroding. It is time for the African economies to focus on new, sustainable sources of employment, exports and growth, and the creative sector is proving to be a viable path that should be keenly explored. Through the progressive liberalisation of services, service suppliers will have access to the markets of all African countries on terms no less favourable than domestic suppliers, and more so the digital movement of works.[112]

The AfCFTA will cover a market of 1.2 billion people and a GDP of $2.5 trillion, across all 55 member States of the African Union.[113] The AU main-

107 17 U.S.C. § 106. See generally Sections 5–8 Nigerian Copyright Act.

108 Stephen M Kramasky (supra) at 17.

109 Agreement Establishing the African Continental Free Trade Area, Preamble.

110 Ibid.

111 Sherry Stephenson and Carolyne Tumuhimbise '*Overview of Services Exports for Growth and Development: Case Studies from Africa*' December 2015, page 1.

112 Charles Rapulu on Afrikan Heroes '*Key Things Startups Should Know as the African Free Continental Free Trade Agreement (AfCFTA) Comes into Operation July 7*'.

113 Ibid.

tains that the AfCFTA will offer Africa an opportunity to reconfigure its supply chains, reduce reliance on others and speed up the establishment of regional value chains that will invariably boost intra-Africa trade and services.[114] In tandem with that objective, Paragraph 4 of the AfCFTA Preamble identifies the need:

> ... to establish clear, transparent, predictable and ***mutually-advantageous* rules** to govern Trade in Goods and Services, Competition Policy, Investment and ***Intellectual Property among State Parties***, by resolving the challenges of multiple and overlapping trade regimes to achieve policy coherence, including relations with third parties (Emphasis added).

At the policy level, the mutually advantageous rules that will govern the protection of copyright enterprises is the long-awaited expansion that the sector must key into to boost its competitiveness within the African market. African countries, including Nigeria, could leverage the opportunities that would be provided by AfCTA in surmounting the challenges of territoriality and enforcement, and in establishing a single digital market for rights management for MSMEs. Given the strength of her creative industries, Nigeria should push for cooperation with other African countries in the fight against the production of and the trade in counterfeit and pirated goods in Africa.

Territoriality and enforcement

Effect of territoriality

The effect of the continental cooperation, among other things is that, the territorial nature for the protection of IPRs will be expanded beyond national boundaries. It portends a collapse of borders that would have normally restricted movement of services. This situation will require a protocol that will harmonise and standardise the scale of protection across markets. However, the issue of enforcement mechanisms will still remain the responsibility of individual governments regardless of the existence of any multilateral arrangements. Considering the digital economy, and the borderless nature of the Internet, both the AfCFTA and local legislation must be in alignment to resolve the challenges of a common market.

A single digital market for rights management

Regarding the use of musical works in the digital economy, it is imperative for Africa to consider the European Union's approach to rights management. Under the auspices of its Copyright Directive, the key goal of the

114 David Ochieng Mbewa, 'AfCFTA Targeting First Trade Deal in 2021' https://africa.cgtn.com/2020/08/16/afcfta-targeting-first-trade-deal-in-2021-african-union-says/

European Copyright Directive is to reduce the value gap between the profits made by Internet platforms and by content creators.[115]

The objectives of the European Directive on Copyright in the Digital Single Market and the Directive on television and radio programmes are to provide more cross-border access to content online, to ensure wider opportunities to use copyrighted materials in education, research and cultural heritage and an overall better functioning copyright marketplace.[116]

By ensuring a good balance between copyright and relevant public policy objectives such as education, research, innovation and the needs of persons with disabilities, the Directives help European copyright industries flourish in a Digital Single Market by enabling European authors to reach new audiences and works widely accessible to European citizens and across borders.

Specifically, Article 24 was negotiated to assess capacity of collective management organisation (CMO) to process multi-territorial licenses to wit:

> *Member States shall ensure that a collective management organization which grants multi-territorial licenses for online rights in musical works has sufficient capacity to process electronically, in an efficient and transparent manner, data needed for the administration of such licenses, including for the purposes of identifying the repertoire and monitoring its use, invoicing users, collecting rights revenue and distributing amounts due to right holders.*

To adopt best practices in facilitating seamless multi-territory licenses of protected work, it would be important to meet the conditions hereunder:

a to have the ability to *identify accurately* the musical works, wholly or in part, which the collective management organisation is authorised to represent;

b to have the ability to identify accurately, wholly or in part, with respect to each *relevant territory, the rights and their corresponding right holders for each musical work* or share therein which the collective management organisation is authorised to represent;

c to make use of *unique identifiers in order to identify right holders and musical works*, taking into account, as far as possible, voluntary industry standards and practices developed at international or Union level and

d to make use of *adequate means to identify and resolve in a timely and effective manner inconsistencies in data* held by other collective management organisations granting multi-territorial licenses for online rights in musical works.[117]

115 European Commission, *'Shaping Europe's Digital Future: Modernisation of the EU Copyright Rules'* https://ec.europa.eu/digital-single-market/en/modernisation-eu-copyright-rules

116 *Supra.*

117 Directive 2014/26/EU of the European Parliament and the Council of 26 February 2014 on collective management of copyright and related rights and multi-territorial licensing of rights in musical works for online use in the internal market.

South Africa's *CAPASSO* (a mechanical rights licensing agency based in Johannesburg, South Africa is a rights management organisation that collects and distributes royalties to its members made up of music publishers and composers) is spearheading the trend regarding cross-border licensing models as a rights management mechanism in the digital environment. It is running a one-stop-shop joint licensing scheme for mechanical rights among collective management organisation across Africa. iTunes, Google/YouTube, Deezer's among others have successfully been issued licenses and royalties have been recovered and remitted to respective CMO in the region on behalf of their respective members.

Conclusion

No doubt, digital economy presents increased opportunities for market growth not only by tapping into new areas or strategies but also by consolidating and improving on old models. Although copyright is a useful strategy for MSMEs in achieving growth, the successful management of copyright remains challenging for small businesses who may not be able to effectively manage their copyright in a largely borderless ecosystem with worldwide, and sometimes anonymous players, that the MSMEs may not easily identify. AfCTA provides many layers and dimensions of not only surmounting these challenges but also in benefitting from the opportunities it provides for new markets and the consolidation of old markets.

A harmonised system can ease the difficulties of enforcing copyright by MSMEs in all the member states. The harmonised system, if carefully constructed, can also guarantee support for the management of digital rights to generate substantial benefits. However, this does not take away the responsibility of establishing a workable up-to-date national copyright framework from the states. Thus, it is still necessary for Nigeria to complete the process of reforming her copyright legislation to meet global standards without however deviating from the parameters established by AfCTA's IP protocol.

Indeed, the need to align with the standards of AfCTA's regional framework would provide a good opportunity to revisit the Copyright Bill and address some of the weaknesses that may have been left unresolved. There is, therefore, a fundamental responsibility on both the AfCTA and African countries to ensure a framework that is properly and inherently synchronised and not antithetical or conflicting.

13 Registration of copyright works in Nigeria from the prism of *TV XTRA Productions Ltd v National University Commission and Zain Nigeria*

Ridwan 'Lanre Ajetunmobi

Introduction

The concept of copyright registration is dynamic and territorial, as a requirement for registration of copyright differs depending on the jurisdiction or copyright laws of a state. Copyright is conferred by statute, and in line with the international and global norm, copyright protection is automatic, and requires no registration or formality.[1] Once a work meets the minimum standard for copyright protection set by the Berne Convention, the work automatically enjoys protection.[2] Also, as a fundamental rule of copyright law, ideas are not protected, but only the expression of ideas,[3] therefore, once an idea or concept is original and fixed in a tangible form, it enjoys protection, save for broadcast in Nigeria. In simple term, Originality and fixation are the determining factors for copyright protection in Nigeria without any registration or formality.[4] Copyright laws of some nations such as the US and Canada require registration by owners of copyright works as a requisite for bringing an action for infringement.[5] These works still enjoy protection once the work is created. The effect of the failure to register a work in those states only prevents enforcement of any action in an event of infringement until such registration is done.[6] In Nigeria, however, failure to register or notify the Nigerian Copyright Commission (NCC) of the existence of a work

1 Kunle Ola, 'Evolution and Future Trends of Copyright in Nigeria' 2014 (2)1 *Journal of Open Access to Law*. 5.

2 Section 5(2) Berne Convention for the Protection of Literary and Artistic Works, September 9, 1886.

3 Adebambo Adewopo, *Nigerian Copyright System: Principles and Perspectives* (Odade Publishers, 2012) 183.

4 Ibid 18.

5 F O Babafemi, 'Intellectual Property: The Law and Practice of Copyright, Trademarks, Patents and Industrial Designs in Nigeria (1st ed., Justinian Books Limited, 2007) 20.

6 Especially in the United States, see generally Sections 411 & 412 of the Copyright Act of 1976 Title 17 of United States Code (1976).

DOI: 10.4324/9781003250883-17

does not affect the right of a copyright owner to commence an action in respect of an infringement suit requiring enforcement.

The case of **TV XTRA PRODUCTIONS LTD v NATIONAL UNIVERSITY COMMISSION AND ZAIN NIGERIA**[7] provided an opportunity for the Federal High Court constitutionally saddled to hear IP matters to adjudicate and interpret basic copyright principle of eligibility of copyright. The main query is whether a work requires registration for copyright protection. The court failed in that respect in the opinion of this chapter, and the failure of the court to correctly respond to this query made it crucial to explore the position of registration of copyright works in Nigeria. The case is instructive on the ground that the damage awarded is unprecedented as such a sum of 703 million naira has never been awarded in any copyright case in Nigeria. The case is beyond infringement of basic copyright principles as it also touched on the regulatory scheme of the NCC, most especially its copyright notification scheme. The review shows a gap in the context of the regulatory role of the NCC in maintaining a data bank of works to avoid registering of already existing protected work as obtainable in other jurisdictions such as the US.

Eligibility criteria for copyright protection

Copyright unlike other aspects of IP deals with creations of the mind and offers direct protection to the owners of creation or works.[8] Hence, copyright is a bundle of rights that the right holder enjoys for a limited time over artistic creations or expressive content, such as poems, books, music, art, cinematographic works and broadcast. It is important to note here that the right holder may not necessarily be the work creator but one that has acquired such right from the right owner or creator. Copyright is different from the patent, as patent is granted to persons over their inventions, which confer on them the exclusive right to exploit or utilise the invention. Patents are generally granted over ideas, unlike copyright which does not protect ideas, but only protects the manner in which the idea is expressed.

Eligible works for copyright protection

Although the Copyright Act ('the Act')[9] does not define the term copyright, section 1 of the Act; however, generally provides for the scope of copyright protection by listing the kind of works eligible for protection as well as

7 Suit No: FHC/ABJ/CS/680/2008 (unreported).

8 Copyright also protects what is called 'related or neighbouring rights' which include the right of performing artists in their performance; the rights of phonograms producers in their phonograms; and the rights of broadcasting organisations in their radio and television broadcasts; and more recently right of making available.

9 Copyright Act 1988 Cap C28 LFN 2004.

criteria for protecting them. Such works include: literary works, musical works, artistic works, cinematograph films, sound recording and broadcast. The Act[10] further clarifies the kind of works envisaged under each broad category. It should therefore be noted that no work shall enjoy copyright protection unless it falls within the classification as mentioned above.[11]

Criterion/prerequisite for copyright protection

The basic idea of preventing people from unauthorised copying or use of copyright work without permission is the main idea underlying and still driving the force of copyright protection. The criterion of originality, fixation and connection are the prerequisite that qualifies a work for copyright protection in addition to the broad classification of eligible works.[12] Section 1(2) of the Act provides that work shall not be eligible for copyright unless: (a) sufficient effort has been expended in the making of the work to give it an original character; and (b) the work has been fixed in any definite medium of expression now known or later to be developed, from which it can be perceived, reproduced or otherwise communicated either directly or with the aid of any machine or device.

The Act does not provide a definition or guideline as to when sufficient effort will be deemed to have been expended to give a work an original character, but the general guiding principles as provided by case law are that the work must originate from the skill, labour and judgement of the author, and not copied from another source.[13] In other words, the general view seems to be that, it is compulsory that the work must be the expression of original or inventive thoughts of the author or creator.[14] All that is needed is sufficient effort of the author as to give the work an original character.[15] In the case of **Cramp & Sons v. Frank Smythson Ltd**,[16] the work was a pocket diary with a number of pages containing information such as is usually found in diaries. Viscount Simon, L.C. in approving the judgement of Lord Atkinson in **Macmillan & Co. v. Cooper**[17] to the effect that the precise amount of knowledge, labour, judgement or literary skill or taste which the author must bestow to acquire copyright must in each case be very much a question of degree, and the court opined that:

10 See generally sections 39 and 51 of the Act.

11 Babafemi (n 5)10. Please note that copyright has now been extended to public performances, folklore, traditional knowledge and computer programs (under literary works).

12 Section 1(2) of the Act.

13 See *Masterpiece Investments Ltd v Worldwide Business Media &Ors.* (1977) F.H.C.R. 496. See also ICIC (Directory Publishers) v. EkkoDelta (1977) FH. CLR 346.

14 Adewopo (n 3) 19.

15 Ibid.

16 (1944) A.C. 329.

17 (1923) 40 T.L.R. 186.

> There was no evidence that any of these tables were composed specially for the respondents diary: there was no feature of them which could be pointed out as novel or specially meritorious or ingenious from the point of view of the judgment or skill of the compiler; it was not suggested that there was any element of originality or skill in the order in which the tables were arranged...[18]

The concept of copyright only espouses the negative right of preventing the copying of physical material. Thus, if it can be shown that two precisely similar works were in fact produced wholly independently of each other, there can be no infringement of copyright by the author of either of the works so long they can prove independent labour, judgement and skill in their respective works.[19] It is also important to note that copyright does not prohibit copying completely. It only prohibits substantial copying in quantitative and/or qualitative terms.[20] In order words, what must be copied must be enough to qualify as an infringement of copyright. Therefore, the applicable standard or test for determining originality is the 'sweat and brow doctrine'[21] as the test for sufficient effort, as applicable in the UK[22]; and/or with reference to the US that has a different standard of judging originality based on 'independent creation' and 'minimum of creativity'. The question has always been 'how do you determine 'sufficiency of the effort?' Under the 'sweat and brow doctrine', the creator of a work, even if it is completely unoriginal, is entitled to have their effort and expense or 'labour and skill' protected.

The requirement of fixation requires that the work must be reduced to a physical form before it can be granted copyright protection.[23] In other words, for a work to qualify for protection, it must be fixed in any tangible medium of expression now known or yet to be developed in a form from which it can be perceived, reproduced or otherwise communicated to the public, either directly or with the aid of mechanical device.[24] It is important to note at this juncture that as a fundamental rule of copyright law, ideas are not protected, but only the expression of ideas.[25] In other words, unlike

18 See also *OladipoYemitan v Daily Times of Nigeria* (1980) FHCLR 186; *Offrey v. Chief S. O. Ola &Ors.* (Unreported) suit No: HOS/23/68; Babafemi (n 7) 11–3.

19 *OladipoYemitan v Daily Times of Nigeria* (1980) FHCLR 186.

20 Adewopo (n 3) 16–7.

21 Shuchi Mehta, 'Analysis of Doctrines: 'Sweat of the Brow' & 'Modicum of Creativity' vis-à-vis Originality in Copyright Law https://www.indialaw.in/blog/blog/law/analysis-of-doctrines-sweat-of-brow-modicum-of-creativity-originality-in-copyright/ Accessed 10 August 2021.

22 Ibid.

23 Adewopo (n 3) 20.

24 Section 1(2)(b) of the Act.

25 Kunle Ola, 'Evolution and Future Trends of Copyright in Nigeria' 2014 (2)1 *Journal of Open Access to Law* 6. See also *University of London Press Ltd. v. University Tutorial Press Ltd* (1916) 2 Ch. 601.

Patents that are generally granted over ideas, copyright does not protect an idea, but only the manner in which the idea is expressed. It is also instructive to note that copyright is conferred by statute,[26] and in line with the international and global norms, copyright protection is automatic, and requires no registration or formality.[27] In other words, it is not necessary to apply any authority to enjoy copyright protection.[28] Therefore, an idea, concept or format once expressed in writing by any means either mechanical or otherwise, it is the *expression* that is protected. On a final note, it is important to note that the requirement of fixation does not affect broadcast, as broadcast may be protected even in an unfixed form.[29]

Copyright notification scheme

By virtue of section 34(3)(e) of the Act, the NCC is enjoined as part of its mandate to maintain an effective data bank on authors and their works. In compliance with the Act, the NCC introduced the Copyright Notification Scheme in 2005.[30] The notification scheme is voluntary, and different from 'registration' as it grants no copyright protection whatsoever other than the one granted by the Act.[31] The scheme only permits a right owner to notify the NCC that he is the owner of copyright in a particular work. This is done by paying the prescribed fees to the commission, and obtaining, filling and returning the appropriate form. It is also mandatory for the right owner to swear or declare before a Commissioner of Oaths that the information provided in the form is true.[32]

One of the advantages of the notification scheme is that the database created will provide necessary rights management information to the public for purposes of securing licenses.[33] Although copyright in a work exists automatically when an original work is created, subsequent notification of the work under the NCC notification scheme is evidence that a creation is protected by copyright; facilitates recording and proof of the possible date of creation of the work and other facts stated in the application form.[34]

26 Adewopo 2(n 3) 6.
27 Kunle Ola (n 1) 5. Once it conforms with the minimum standard for protection as stipulated by the Berne Convention and other relevant treaties on copyright.
28 Copinger and Skones, James *on Copyright* (vol 1, 14th ed., Sweet & Maxwell, 1999) 26.
29 John Asein, *Nigerian Copyright Law and Practice* (2nd ed., Books and Gavel Limited, 2012) 21.
30 Kunle Ola (n 1) 22.
31 Ibid.
32 This is imperative to curb fraudulent applications.
33 Adebambo Adewopo, 'Intellectual Property Crime: An Overview of Control and Challenges of Modern Trends' Paper presented at the 26th Cambridge International Symposium on Economic Crimes, Cambridge University, UK, in September 2008.
34 See About NCeRS – Nigerian Copyright eRegistration System http://www.eregistration.copyright.gov.ng/ncc/about Accessed 3 August 2020.

Fact of the case

The plaintiff alleged that he submitted a proposal/format of a quiz programme to be aired on the Nigerian television titled 'University Challenge' to the first defendant for approval, after the said proposal has been registered with the NCC for copyright protection. After about four weeks of the submission of the proposal to first defendant for approval, the plaintiff was informed that a similar proposal had earlier been approved by the first defendant in favour of the second defendant. The case of the plaintiff against the defendants is that the first defendant maliciously connived with the second defendant to plagiarize and broadcast a programme (Zain African Challenge) which they had no right to do on the Nigeria's broadcast space based on the notification certificate issued by the NCC, which the plaintiff believed gave him the sole right in a television quiz programme titled 'University Challenge' amongst Nigeria Universities and so registered with the NCC and certificate issued to that effect, thereby infringing on his right in the said proposal. It is also the averment of the plaintiff that the defendants aired a programme titled 'ZAIN African Challenge' on AIT and NTA which is the same programme that copyright was granted to the plaintiff by the NCC registration.

The defendants merely changed the name, thus, an infringement on the copyright of the plaintiff in the said work. This averment was backed by the evidence of PW1 during cross examination by the second defendant that the defendants aired and broadcasted a programme which they had no right to have done on the Nigeria's terrestrial broadcast space based on the certificate by the NCC which gave him a sole right in the programme. The plaintiff acknowledged the programme (ZAIN African Challenge) had started in other African countries in 2006 before the plaintiff conceived and submitted its own proposal/concept (Universities Challenge) in 2007, and certification of the concept by the NCC in 2008 but his case is about Nigeria broadcast space.

The case of the second defendant is that it is not the plaintiff that developed the concept but copied a fraction of the format of the concept from the production of either 'ZAIN African Challenge' or the original owners of 'University Challenge' without the plaintiff obtaining license or permission from either ZAIN or British University. The format being utilized by the second defendant in its 'Zain African Challenge' was fashioned after the 'University Challenge' concept and had commenced since 2006 in other African Countries, hence, it is completely and entirely different and larger in scope and focus from the plaintiff's alleged 'University Challenge' format. It is also averred that the concept of 'University Challenge' which is a Quiz Programme to be aired on the Nigerian television is not the intellectual property (IP) of the plaintiff because the concept of 'University Challenge' as a Quiz Programme was first published in Britain and it is the IP of the British University (from whom the second defendant got permission to air 'ZAIN African Challenge') and by extension is protected in Nigeria.

Consequently, one of the questions formulated for determination that directly influenced the basis for decision in the case was: whether the plaintiff has sufficiently proved the infringement of its copyright in 'Nigeria Universities Challenge' in this suit to entitle it to the orders of the Court? The court found in favour of the plaintiff and grants all its prayers. In reaching its decision, the court held that:

> I have studied the content of Exh. 2 which is the certificate of copyright ownership given to the Plaintiff by the NCC upon registration of the said Copyright. It can be safely said going by Exh. 2 that the Plaintiff's copyright ownership belongs to the category of work stated in S, 1 (1) (a) of the Copyright Act as literary work eligible for copyright protection. Going by Exh. 1, I can see that sufficient effort has been expended on making the work to give it an original character in Nigeria. It must be stated that it is registration by the NCC that qualifies a person to the exercise of copyright ownership in Nigeria as stated in S. 2(1)(i) of the Copyrights Act of the category of work which the copyright is granted. It is a person who has registered ownership of copyright in Nigeria that can exercise all the rights that accrue to that registration exclusively. It is in that regard that it must be stated that any other person seeking to use any work to which there is copyright ownership can only do so by express permission of the owner of the copyright.

Flowing from the above, it may be said with respect that the court erred in its pronouncement in the case under review. The case was a window for the court to change the narrative of having insufficient knowledge of IP on the Bench by exhibiting their understanding and expertise of IP in general and copyright in specific through pragmatic reasoning and application of the extant laws in the field.[35] However, that opportunity was wasted again in the case under review. So, many questions could be raised from the case:

35 There are several decisions from both the Federal High Court and the Court of Appeal showing lack of sufficient knowledge of IP on the bench. One of such decisions that is of considerable importance is the Court of Appeal decision in MICROSOFT CORPORATION v FRANIKE (Suit No FHC/L/CS/610/05. The case basically dealt with the issue of reciprocal extension of foreign works in Nigeria. Microsoft's case was that the respondent infringed on its 'Windows' operating system and product (software). The Court of Appeal declined reciprocal extension of protection to Microsoft under the Nigerian Law on the basis of ineligibility as a foreigner. The Court went further to request a certificate from the Copyright Commission conferring copyright protection on Microsoft; and a proof of an Order under the Copyright Act evidencing the reciprocal extension of protection. The decision clearly shows lack of understanding of basic copyright principle or IP Law on the Bench, as copyright does not require any formality, registration or condition for eligibility for a work to enjoy protection. Furthermore, the Copyright (Reciprocal Extension) Order of 1972 which was made pursuant to the Copyright Act specifically provided for reciprocal protection of foreign works in Nigeria, in which United States was named as one of the countries listed to enjoy reciprocal protection under the Nigerian Copyright Act. This

what was infringed? Is it an idea or format/concept? Was the infringement sufficiently proved? Would adaptation of a proposal avail the plaintiff in the instant case? Does broadcast need to satisfy the criteria of fixation before it enjoys protection, amongst other questions? However, the main question that strikes the heart of the case under review is whether a foreign work need be registered with the NCC before it enjoys copyright protection in Nigeria?

Appraisal of the case

For proper appraisal of the case under review, two key questions arise or needed to be addressed: first is the issue of the idea/expression dichotomy, i.e., the basic principle that copyright does not protect ideas (whether original or not); copyright only protects the manner in which the idea has been expressed; (may be called the style of the person expressing the idea). The protection of the idea itself is a matter for patent law. The classic example of this principle is a cook book which describes recipes. The author may only claim copyright with regards to the manner in which she describes the recipes but not for the recipes themselves. But sometimes it is difficult to separate the idea from the expression, and there are several examples: for instance, when there is only one way in which such an idea can be expressed or when there is only one set of words that accurately conveys the idea. This is the case in *computer programs*. In that case anyone can copy the set of words.

For the case under review, the question arises as to whether the plaintiff's claim of copyright is over the work as an original expression or over the concept or idea of a University quiz TV program. The pertinence of this question is obvious from the confusion of both the plaintiff and the Court referring to patent, copyright and IP in the same breath as if these concepts or terms are interchangeable, whereas they are not. Copyright and patents are totally and absolutely distinct and governed by distinct criteria.[36] So, a pertinent question for the court would have been the issue of whether what the plaintiff is complaining about is the copying of its idea of a University Quiz television program for Nigeria that forms the basis of the proposal (and which is not a subject for copyright); or whether it is complaining about the copying or reproduction of the proposal itself, i.e., the manner in which the idea has been expressed or the program designed.

The second question would naturally flow from the finding on the above, i.e., if the plaintiff's complaint is about the manner in which the defendant's program has been written or designed as amounting to a reproduction of the plaintiff's proposal, the court would then have to decide the

---

Order is a subsidiary legislation as it was made pursuant to the Act and need not be specifically proven before any Court.

36 See generally Adebambo Adewopo, *Intellectual Property Rights in Nigeria: Law and Development* (Nigerian Institute of Advanced Legal Studies (NIALS) Press, 2015) 16–33.

originality question and whether the plaintiff's work was actually copied; or whether the defendant actually infringed on the plaintiff's copyright. The question usually is whether what was copied is sufficient to amount to an infringement. This question arises because copyright does not prohibit copying completely. It only prohibits substantial copying in quantitative and/or qualitative terms.[37] What is copied by the defendant must be enough to qualify as an infringement of the plaintiff's copyright. So, all the court needed to decide was whether the defendant's work was sufficiently original even though it is based on the same idea of a University Quiz TV program as the plaintiff's work; or whether the defendant's work was indeed a reproduction of the plaintiff's.

This review believed that on this question, the Court itself concluded that the two works are not the same, though the ideas are similar. This was as posited in page 24 of the judgement to wit: '... For the avoidance of doubt, Exhs D2B, D3 and D4 do not establish copyright ownership of 'Zain Africa Challenge' in Nigeria or dispel the fact that the concept of 'Zain African Challenge' is not similar to that of the plaintiff's Universities Challenge' which ownership of copyright belongs to the plaintiff'". And indeed, the facts of the case call for an interrogation of this issue because there is evidence before the court that the programme (ZAIN African Challenge) which the plaintiff claimed is an infringement of its copyright over the work, the University Challenge, had started in other African countries in 2006 even before the plaintiff's proposal was conceived and submitted to the first defendant for adoption in Nigeria in 2007, and before the certification of the concept by the NCC in 2008.

On this basis alone, it was enough to hold that there was no infringement of copyright as such. This review would imagine that, on the contrary, the plaintiff's submission of the proposal to the NCC for notification was pre-emptive and an attempt to take undue advantage of the law erroneously. But what makes this judgement really significant for IP jurisprudence in Nigeria is not the correctness/soundness of the judge's conclusion that the plaintiff's work was infringed, but the basis of such conclusion which is really shaky. For the sake of emphasis, once again, it is elementary knowledge that copyright is automatic and does not require any formality beyond fixation. It is also axiomatic that the NCC notification scheme is purely for administrative purposes and does not confer any legal right. It could be useful for evidential purposes to prove first in time; for instance, if the plaintiff and defendant are claiming copyright over an identical work and the question is who first created. But in this case, both the parties concede, perhaps inadvertently on the part of the plaintiff, that the content of the two works are not the same even if the concept or idea is.

37 Adewopo (n 3) 16–7.

Summarily, for the avoidance of doubt, there is no contention as to what work is eligible for protection under the Act. In the same vein, the bedrock of eligibility for copyright protection is the requisite of originality, fixation and connection.[38] In other words, for a work to be eligible for copyright protection, sufficient effort must be shown to have been expended in making the work to give it an original character; and the work is fixed in a definite medium of expression now known or later to be developed, from which it can be perceived, reproduced or otherwise communicated either directly or with the aid of any device. Therefore, copyright notice or registration does not confer copyright protection in a work.

Contrary to the reasoning in the case under review, notice and registration of copyright are not required for copyright protection in Nigeria. In Nigeria, and in fact, globally, once a work meets the minimum standard for copyright protection set by the Berne Convention, the work automatically enjoys protection.[39] In other words, as soon as an original work is reduced to a fixed and tangible form, the work is automatically protected by copyright laws in Nigeria.[40] Although, copyright laws of some states[41] require registration by the owners of copyright works as a requisite for bringing an action for infringement,[42] this does not take away or invalidate the automatic conferment of protection granted, once the work is created. The effect of the failure to register a work in those states only prevents enforcement of any action in an event of infringement until such registration is done.[43]

In Nigeria however, unlike the registration system in the United States, for instance, failure by a copyright owner to notify the NCC through the notification scheme on the existence of a work does not affect the right of a copyright owner to commence an action in respect of an infringement suit requiring enforcement.[44] Therefore, as mentioned earlier, except for broadcast, once an idea or concept is fixed in a tangible medium it enjoys protection. In other words, once a work is broadcasted, such work is automatically protected.

The Copyright Notification Scheme of the NCC only provides copyright owners option to register their work and deposit a copy of the work in a database maintained by the NCC as enjoined by the provision of section 34(3)(e) of the Act.[45] Such registration and issuance of notification certificate

38 Ibid Adewopo. 27 See also Section 1(2) of the Act.

39 Ibid (n 2).

40 Ufuoma Akpotaire, 'Embracing "The Option": Nigerian Copyright Commission's Copyright Notification Scheme https://nlipw.com/embracing-the-option-nigerian-copyright-commissions-copyright-notification-scheme/ 25 August 2020.

41 USA, Canada, Australia among others.

42 Babafemi (n 5) 20.

43 Ibid 21.

44 Kunle Ola (n 17) 6.

45 Adebambo Adewopo and R Ajetunmobi, 'Microsoft Corporation v Franike Associates Ltd: A Critical Analysis' (2013) 2(1) *NJIP* 210.

do not in any way confer protection on such work. However, notice and registration of copyright provides some advantages to wit: it serves as public notification of the existence of the work and that it is protected by copyright.[46] Registration of work in a public record even gives a stronger notice of ownership claim, as notice is given to the entire world and not limited to those who see the work with the copyright notice attached.[47] Notice allows anyone who wishes to use a work of another, to contact the owner for permission to use his work. Notice also limits the ability of someone who infringes your work to claim they did not know of the copyright's existence.[48] Indeed, it is interesting to note that it is written at the bottom end of the notification certificate that the certificate does not confer protection.

Therefore, owing to the above analysis, it could be safely said that the court erred by pronouncing that the plaintiff has sufficiently proved his case by the provision of 'notification of copyright certificate from the NCC'. The reasoning/decision of the court in the case under review that ZAIN does not have the right to broadcast their 'ZAIN African Challenge' within the Nigeria's broadcast space without permission from the plaintiff who is the first to register its work with the NCC would have been different if the foregoing analysis was taken into consideration.

Conclusion

The case reviewed emphasises the crucial status of the eligibility requirement for the copyright protection. The query, whether a work should be registered before it enjoys copyright protection arose. The perception of this chapter based on its findings is that the opinion of the court has not resolved the matter regarding registration as it relates to eligibility. This opinion highlights the increased need for the improved advocacy and adjudication of copyright cases and the enhancement of IP knowledge at the bench for quality adjudication and development of IP laws in Nigeria.

This chapter has shown that there is no duty placed on right owners to register their works in Nigeria. However, a duty is placed on the NCC as part of its mandate for regulating and administering copyright in Nigeria, to maintain an effective data bank of authors and their works.

NCC initiated the copyright notification scheme where records of the authors and their works are kept. Obviously, there is a big gap in how the NCC has fared in operating and maintaining the notification scheme. Much is left to be done by the regulatory body as there are reports of multiple notification/recordation by right owners; fraudulent activities of depositing of works by persons who are not the original owners of a work; and poor

46 Ufuoma Akpotaire (n 25).

47 See Digital Media Law Project – Copyright Registration and Notice https://www.dmlp.org/legal-guide/copyright-registration-and-notice Accessed 25 August 2020.

48 Ibid.

number of works deposited so far with the NCC. These challenges could be overcome through pragmatic and proactive actions on the part of the commission. It is suggested that the commission initiate requests from the publishers, producers and record labels to notify the commission by depositing the list of works with their attendants' details created, published or produced by them. In the same vein, more enlightenment by way of jingles and symposium is desirable to avoid cases of copyright infringement, even though it seems to be capital intensive.

Overall, it can be safely submitted that the case under review was decided per incuriam. Clearly, the court failed to understand the basic principle of copyright that a work does not require any registration or formality to enjoy copyright. Similarly, a broadcast is exempted from eligible works that require to undergo the criteria of originality and fixation, as broadcast enjoys protection even in an unfixed form. The decision of the case would have been different if the court averted its mind to the aforesaid. Hopefully, the decision might be different and reversed at the Appeal Court, if either of the defendants is desirous of appealing against the decision on those grounds enumerated.

14 Inequality of bargaining power between artists and recording companies

A critical review of the case of *African Songs Ltd.* V. *Sunny Ade*

A.A. Adedeji and O. Durotolu

Introduction

The music scene in Nigeria is booming and contracts have become crucial to its existence. There is a boom comparable to the oil boom era in Nigeria. Various genres of music have transcended the borders of Nigeria. There are quite a number of relationships in the music industry that require contractual tools to enter into a business relationship to outline the roles and responsibilities of both parties.[1] These relationships include record deals,[2] publishing deals,[3] distribution deals,[4] 360 deals[5] among many others. The concern of this chapter is to record deals. One of the most widely known types of music industry connected disputes seen in the media consists of the 'artist record label relationship' despite the fact that there are many types of other disputes occurring from the relationships between managers, agents, record companies, band members…[6] Indeed music contracts are an aspect of copyright law linked to some provisions in the copyright Act on licences and assignments. The obsolete nature of the Act makes it more important to have contracts that cater to the present rather than the past, when the Act was established, which was prior to the music industry boom. These contracts must have the essential elements of forming a contract which includes offer, acceptance, consideration and intention to enter into a legal relation.

1 Ernest Francis, Music Industry Contract Law, 2020 ResearchGate, doi:10.13140/RG.2.2.33419.31525.
2 Ownership of copyright is assigned by the artist to the recording company for advancement and further returns in the form of royalty. The assignee (recording company) agrees to promote, market and licence the music recording to users.
3 This relationship is between the songwriter and the music publisher. Ownership is transferred by assignment.
4 This deal is linked to permission to distribute sound recording.
5 This contract is between the recording label and the recording artist, where the former earns from all rights related to the artist.
6 Ernest Francis, Music Industry Contract Law, 2020 ResearchGate. doi:10.13140/RG.2.2.33419.31525.

DOI: 10.4324/9781003250883-18

A valid contract generally and specifically in the area of copyright is intended by the contracting parties to have legal consequences for enforcement. In the late nineteenth century case of *Carlill v Carbolic Smoke Ball Co,*[7] the test applied by the court to determine the intention of parties to a contract was objective rather than subjective. The question for determination was, would a reasonable person not regard the offer made to him as one which was intended to create a legal relationship?

In essence, where parties to a contract are of unequal bargaining strength as found in the music industry in Nigeria, the weaker party is unduly influenced into entering the contract. The type of contract that emerges from such a bargain is a contract of adhesion. Contracts of adhesion are usually contracts where the parties are not equal. They are usually contained in standard forms of contract, "Take it or Tear it" sort of transaction. These contracts are concentrated in relatively few hands and the terms are usually not negotiated between the parties thereto.

The party with strong bargaining power dictates the terms of the contract. This scenario is peculiar in Nigeria. The weaker party is presented with a form and asked to "sign here". He does, of course, and nothing happens until trouble arises. It is at this point that the court would now look at the contract to see whether truly there is an intention by the parties to enter into a legal relation. Though the contracting parties might be *ad idem prima facie*, there could be no intention where the weaker party was coerced into entering the contract by circumstances far beyond his control as at the time of contracting. It is in that regard the one could presume that consent is absent based on undue influence.

Music contracts: case law to the rescue of the weaker parties or not?

There are two conflicting judicial views as to whether one could say consent is absent in a contract where a weaker party is induced by undue influence or duress. It was at one time common to treat the legal rules relating to undue influence as resting on the absence of consent. A party who is subjected to undue influence is claimed to have his will over borne, thus, limiting his freedom to choose or take decisions.

Law relating to undue influence requires reconsideration given the House of Lords decision in *Lyncy v D.P.P. of Northern Ireland*,[8] where the court rejected the contention that undue influence or duress deprives a person of his free choice or makes his acts non-voluntary. In the opinion of the Lords, undue influence or duress does not "overbear" the will nor destroy it; it "deflects" it. It does not deprive between evils. In essence, a person acting under

7 (1893). 1 Q.B. 256.
8 (1975) A.C. 693.

duress or undue influence intends to do what he does but does so unwillingly. According to this view, undue influence deflects without destroying the will of the contracting parties.

There is still an intention on his part to contract in the consensual terms but there is *consent under compulsion* on his side, the contract is not the party's deed. The contract is mistakenly signed, and the weaker party is allowed to deny the validity of the contract by pleading it is not his deed in any action brought against him to enforce the contract. According to Byles J. in *Foster v Mackinnon*[9] such a contract is invalid

> ...not merely on the ground of fraud, where fraud exists, but on the ground that the mind of the signer did not accompany the signature; in other words, that he never intended to sign, and therefore in the contemplation of the law never did sign the contract to which his name is appended[10].

Despite this clear principle, there are decisions where the judges made statements on undue influence or duress as negating the true consent and rendering the action of the coerced party non-voluntary. In *Universe Tankships of Monrovia v I.T.F.*[11] Lord Diplock stated that 'the rationale was that the party's consent was induced by pressure which the law does not regard as legitimate with the consequence that the consent is treated in law as revocable.'[12]:

> Conversely, it could be inferred from these judicial attitudes that, no matter what, whether "deflection" or "overbear" one thing is sure and this is the fact that the contract was procured by fraud and the stronger party has taken advantage of the weaker party. The situation, no doubt, is inequitable, and consequently, make the behaviour of the stronger party unconscionable.

Lord Denning demonstrated in his judgment in *Lloyds Bank v Bundy* that there are various categories of the contract having striking similarities with contracts in the category of undue influence.[13] According to the Master of the Rolls.

> No bargain will be upset which is the result of the ordinary interplay of forces. There are many hard cases which are caught by this rule ... When the parties have not met on equal terms when one is so strong in bargaining power and the other so weak that as a matter of common

9 (1869) L.R. 4 C.P. 704.
10 Ibid.
11 (1983) A.C. 366.
12 Ibid 384.
13 (1974) 3 ALL E.R. 757; (1957) 1 Q.B. 326 C.A.

> fairness it is not right that the strong should be allowed to push the weak to the wall. Hitherto, those exceptional cases have been treated each as a separate category in itself. But I think the time has come when we should seek to find a principle to write them...I go only to those where there has been inequality of bargaining power...[14]

Lord Denning laid down the general principles based on inequality and bargaining power.

> By virtue of it, the English law gives relief to one who without independent advice enters into a contract on terms which are very unfair or transfers property for a consideration which is grossly inadequate, when his bargaining power is grievously impaired by reason of his own needs or desire, or by his own ignorance or infirmity, coupled with undue influences or pressures brought to bear on him by or for the benefit of other. When I use the word "undue" I do not mean to suggest that the principle depends on proof of any wrongdoing...[15]

This general principle drives special consideration for the contract between artists on the one hand and their managers, recording and publishing companies on the other hand. English Courts have extended the principles of restraint of trade cum the doctrine of unequal bargaining power to contract between artists, i.e., composers and musicians, on the one hand, and recording companies or publishing houses on the other hand. In all cases involving the two, Courts have refused to enforce the strict terms of the contracts involved on the ground that they were contrary to public policy and involved unconscionable conduct on the part of the recording companies or the publishing house.

The manager in each case appeared skilled in business and was an expert in matters relating to finance, while the artist or composer or musicians were only skilled in their art. There was in essence, a presumption of undue influence in the relationships and the absence of independent advice for the artists was fatal to the agreement in each case. Cases where the English Courts enunciated the above principles includes *Instone v Schroeder (A) Music Publishing Co.,*[16] *Schroeder Music Publishing Co. Ltd v Macaulay,*[17] *Clifford Davies Management v W.E.A. Record*[18] *and O'Sullivan v Management Agency & Music Ltd. IV*[19] among other cases. They are perceived as worthy of mentioning to emphasis the principles.

14 Ibid.
15 Ibid.
16 (1974) 1 All ER.
17 (1974) 1 W.L.R. 1308, which is an appeal from *Instone v Schroeder ibid.*
18 (1975) 1 W.L.R. 61.
19 (1985) Q.B. 428.

African songs Ltd v Sunday Adeniyi

The decisions analysed in the prior subsection lay the foundation for a critical analysis of the case of *African Songs Ltd v Sunny Ade*.[20] This case is one of a kind on the issue of restraint of trade and inequality of bargaining power concerning the artist that came before the court in Nigeria.[21] The plaintiff in this case was a limited liability company whose main business was the making of record tapes and the publication of music for sale by the name African Songs Ltd. The first and other defendants were a group of musicians performing with the name 'Green Sports Band' later changed to 'Sunny Ade And His New African Beats'. The first defendant was a performing musician and his music was in great demand in Nigeria and the other jurisdictions.

On October 6, 1970, the first defendant, Sunny Ade (acting on behalf of other seven defendants who were members of his musical group) entered into a contract of service with the plaintiff. The agreement contained many onerous and harsh terms concerning the defendants which included the following:

The defendant was tied to the service of the plaintiff exclusively for five years.

The plaintiff was given the right to dictate where and when the defendant was to make music recordings.

The remuneration of the defendant for his services was grossly inadequate, compared to what the plaintiff was to get out of the contract. For example, for the sale of a 12-inch double-sided L.P which costs about N6.00 (at that time), the defendant was to get only 15kobo while the plaintiff would get the remaining N5.85k.

The plaintiff was assigned the full copyright of all the compositions and recordings of the defendants.

The plaintiff was entitled to the sole right of production, reproduction, use and performance (including broadcasting) of the defendants work throughout the world.

The defendant was during the currency of the agreement prohibited from rendering any performance whatever to himself, any company or group of persons.

The plaintiff had the exclusive right to decide whether and when to commence or discontinue or recommence the production or sale of records, and the fixing or alternation of their prices.

20 (Unreported) High Court of Lagos State, Dosunmu J. Suit No. LD/1300/74 delivered on February 14, 1975.

21 It is instructive to note that the eventual settlement out of court of a similar case of *OmoAje Sound Studio v Wasiu Ayinde Anifowos* has deprived this chapter of analyzing a judgement from a Nigerian court in relation to the subject matter again.

The plaintiff had the option to renew the contract at its expiration for a further two years or "for any longer period". The defendant had no such right.

The plaintiff reserved the right to terminate the contract in the event of the defendant's illness or involvement in an accident, which rendered the defendant incapable of performing.

The plaintiffs claimed that in breach of the above agreement, the defendant in 1974 proceeded to form a recording company, and recorded a music album for this company, which they distributed for sale to the public. The plaintiff therefore sought:

a declaration that the agreement between them and the defendant was still subsisting,

an injunction restraining the defendants or their agents, assignees etc. from distributing or selling the records and

an account of all sales of the record, and damages of one million nairas for breach of the contract.

In the above agreement, it is apparent that the plaintiff is in total control of the artists and their creative works. There was hardly any room for the defendants to maneuver or make decisions regarding music recordings. However, the court held that:[22]

This was not a case of restraint of trade.

Furthermore, although some of the terms of the contract were stringent, that was not a ground for holding the contract invalid. The court, therefore, granted the first two claims of the plaintiffs but dismissed the third one.

Based on the perception of this chapter, the decision of the judge is unacceptable and perceived as erroneous. The proposition by the judge that 'this was not a case of restraint of trade' was not established. A party forfeits his future liberty in a contract in restraint of trade for his business with who he chooses.[23] Stating that the plaintiff had assigned the future liberty of the defendant to practice his profession to himself based on the clauses of the agreement. The purpose of the last part of the agreement listed above is to release the defendant when he is no longer useful to himself, which is contrary to the principle that "an unwilling servant cannot serve a willing master". Therefore, it is apt to assert that contrary to the view expressed

22 (Unreported) High Court of Lagos State, Dosunmu J. Suit No. LD/1300/74 delivered on February 14, 1975.

23 Lord Diplock in *Petrofina (Great Britain) Ltd.* v. *Martin* [1966] Ch. 146, 180.

by the judge, it is a contract in restraint of trade. The party with superior knowledge and much stronger bargaining power used these factors in drafting an extremely unconscionable agreement. It is instructive to note that the opinion of the learned Professor was occasioned by the decisions of the English courts which we would endeavour to examine in turns hereunder.

In *Schroeder Music Publishing Co. Ltd. v Macaulay*,[24] the respondent, then a young and unknown songwriter, entered into a contract with the appellant whereby the latter engaged his exclusive services for five years. The agreement that was in the appellant's standard form provided that "the respondents assigned to the appellant's full copyright for the whole-world, in each original composition and lyrics for which he either solely or in collaboration, with others, was responsible at any time before it in so far as the respondents, still owned and controlled them". The appellant agreed to pay the respondent 50 pounds as an advance royalty payable under the contract and to recoup it from the future earnings of the respondents.[25]

Perhaps, if during the five years of the contract, the total earnings of the respondent from royalties reached the sum of 5,000 pounds, the agreement would automatically be renewed for another five years. The appellant could at any time terminate the agreement by one month's written notice, but the respondent had no such rights. The appellant had a right to assert their rights under the agreement, but the respondent could not without the appellant's consent. Furthermore, the appellants were under no obligation to publish any of the respondent's work.[26]

The respondent brought an action for a declaration that the agreement was contrary to public policy. He was successful both at the High Court and in the Court of Appeal. The defendant appealed to the House of Lords which held that:

The contract was void for being contrary to public policy. Public policy required in the interest of the public and the parties that everyone should as far as practicable be free to earn a living and give the public the fruit of his abilities and talents. The terms of the contract conflicted with these principles.

Contractual restrictions which appear to be unnecessary or to be reasonably capable of being enforced oppressively must be justified before they could be enforced.

The refusal to enforce the provisions of a contract where a party has agreed to exploit or refrain from exploiting power for the benefit of another, the public policy which the court based on public policy will attempt to implement

24 *(1974)*1 W.L.R. 1308.
25 Ibid.
26 Ibid.

the prevention of the party with stronger bargaining power from entering into unconscionable bargains.

Two songwriters, members of the 'Fleetwork Mac' band, entered into a copyright agreement with their manager, who was also a music publisher in the case of *Clifford David Management v W.E.A. Records.*[27] They assigned to him the copyright in all their compositions in all jurisdictions for five years. There was the possibility of an extension for another five years. One of the writers promised to deliver at least one complete composition to the manager every month. However, there was no corresponding undertaking on his part to publish it. The group broke away and tried to publish an album independently. The manager brought an action for an injunction to restrain the defendants from infringing his copyright in the songs.

The Court of Appeal held that the terms of the contract were manifestly detrimental to the defendants and it was capable of enforcement in an oppressive manner. The court noted that each defendant was tied to the manager for ten years at the latter's option, he had the sole right to all their compositions, which he could simply put in a drawer and forget all about it. They could not exploit their talents on their initiative. In addition, the bargaining power of each of the composers was gravely impaired by the position in which he or she was placed *vis-à-vis* the manager. They were fully dependent on the manager to get their work published.

> Their needs and desires were dependent on his will. He could say, Ayes or No. He is skilled in business and finance. They were composers... that was why they needed a manager...undue influences or pressure were brought to bear on the composers for the benefit of the manager. It seems to me that if that publisher wishes to exact such onerous terms or to drive such an unconscionable bargain, he ought to have seen that the composer had independent advice.[28]

The court held that there was such inequality of bargaining power that the agreement should not be enforced and the assignment of copyright was invalid and should be set aside. Unfortunately, these cases, most especially the case of *Schroeder Music Publishing Co. Limited v Macaulay* was not cited before the court in *Sunny Ade's* case and the judgment therefore was delivered without the benefit of the House of Lord's persuasive authority on an almost identical point.

The contract in *Sunny Ade's Case* is *ex-facie* lawful (lawful *perse*) however, it was performed illegally. In this situation, the issue of guilty intention and innocence is crucial. The innocent party can exercise his right under the contract. The most authoritative and lucid statement of the law on this point

27 (1975) 1 W.L.R. 61.
28 Ibid 65.

was stated by Lord Mansfield in *Holman v Johnson,* that 'the principle of the public policy is *ex dolomalo non oritur action* – No court will lend its aid to a man who found his cause of action upon an immoral or an illegal act ...'[29]

The plaintiff in *Sunny Ade's Case* found his cause of action on a contract whose terms were morally reprehensible and offensive of the rule of morality. The court should have declared the contract illegal; the defendant resisting the performance of his obligation in the contract is permitted to also raise the plea of illegality. The parties are not in *pari delicto* (equally guilty). Contracts dealing with the restriction imposed on artistes by their employers such as a film company, music publishers or managers are subject to the rules of restraint to trade. Unless the contracts are proved to be reasonable in the interest of the parties and in particular, of the artistes, such contracts are void. In *Schroeder Music, Publishing Co. Ltd v Macaulay*[30] and *Clifford Davis Management v W.A.E. Records Ltd,*[31] it was held that, where the terms of the contracts with the artistes are restrictive of trade and are capable of being enforced oppressively, they are void.

The issue of the adequacy of the consideration in this case is reasonably questioned. The law on this issue is *prima facie,* in the absence of fraud, duress or misrepresentation, the court will not question the adequacy of consideration. It is not the business of the court to measure the comparative values of the consideration furnished by the plaintiffs and the defendants, respectively, nor will they declare a contract to be invalid simply because one party has a better bargain than the other since there are reciprocities of detriments and benefits on both the sides. Lord Sommerwell stated in *Chappel v Nestle,*[32] that 'a contracting party can stipulate for what consideration he chooses. A peppercorn does not cease to be a good consideration if it is established that the promisee does not like the pepper and will throw away the corn'.

In principle, therefore, no consideration is too small or too much or unfair. When two parties of full capacity agree based on their free will, the courts will only interfere for compelling reasons. However, the fact that consideration is too small or too much may show evidence of fraud, duress, undue influence, mistake, or misrepresentation; and it may alert the court to consider these possibilities. Thus, whilst consideration should be adequate, it must be valuable before the law, comprising some elements regarded as the price of the defendant's promise. Where consideration appears tedious, vague, unascertainable, or insignificant, it is perceived as insufficient and constitutes no consideration.

There have been discussions about what ought to be the component of this elusive term. According to Ames; 'with obvious reservations in the

29 (1975) 1 Cowp. 341, 343.
30 *(1974) 1 W.L.R. 1308.*
31 (1975) 1 W.L.R. 61.
32 (1960) A.C. 87; 1957 A E. R. 701 HL.

interest of morality and public policy, any act or any promise, accepted by one party to a contract as the price for his act or promise, constitutes a valid consideration.'[33] Where the behaviour of the plaintiff as a party to a contract is morally reprehensible, then the court can question the adequacy of consideration.

In *African Songs Ltd. v Sunny Adeniyi*, the term of the contract is to the effect that the remuneration (consideration) of the defendant for his services was grossly inadequate, compared to what the plaintiff was to get out of the contract. Regarding the sale of 12-inch double-sided L.P. which cost about N6.00 (at that time), the defendant was to receive 15kobo while the plaintiff would receive the remaining N5.85k. Emphasis is laid on the fact that the contract of service persists for five years and was subject to renewal by the plaintiff for another two years without a review of the remuneration to the defendant even though the remuneration as at the time of contract was very low. Consequently, it is safe to conclude that the consideration was inadequate.

At common law, the requirement of intention is essential. The question is always whether there had been an intention to enter into a legal relationship between a contracting party. However, where a party with stronger bargaining power used his influence to coerce the other to enter into a morally reprehensible contract, the intention of the weak party could be said to have been overborne.

The beauty of the Judicature Act of 1873 is that it created a court of law and equity in Nigeria. In essence, where a contract discloses an element of undue influence and the contract is morally reprehensible on the ground of inequality of bargaining power between the stronger party and the weaker party, as in *African Songs Ltd. v Sunny Adeniyi*, equity will impeach the transaction. This is likely to occur when the victim is in a very weak bargaining position in comparison with the other party.[34] The following requirements must be satisfied without equity: (a) The influencer, i.e., the stronger party must use an unfair advantage, (b) He must put the victim in a manifestly disadvantageous position and (c) The victim must have entered into a hard and inequitable agreement.

These features in *African Songs Ltd. v Sunny Adeniyi* show the inequality of bargaining power, though a relevant factor, is not enough to attract equitable intervention, even where the victim did not have independent legal advice.[35] The elements above must be present. The presumption is likely to be rebutted, if independent legal advice is given, so long as it is given in full knowledge of the relevant facts. Perhaps, if the influencer is equally strong, it is also necessary that the adviser approves the transaction. This is

33 J B Ames, *Lecture on Legal History and Miscellaneous Legal Essays* (Wentworth Press, USA 2016) 223.

34 Ibid.

35 (1975) 1 Cowp. 341, 343.

the basis of the decision of the English Court of Appeal in the very recent case of *O'Sullivan v Management Agency And Music Ltd,*[36] where a management agency, which was in a fiduciary relationship with a composer of music (Gilbert O'Sullivan), persuaded him to enter into various contracts without independent professional advice. The contracts were set aside by the court based on undue influence.

Another argument is that the plaintiff has done something inequitable. He has entered into a contract that ought to affect his conscience. A contract that is morally reprehensible. Unconscionable bargaining of the highest order. It is, therefore, according to this line of reasoning that one is apt to express the view that the plaintiff has not done equity in the bargain involving him and *Sunny Ade*. This same plaintiff that had done something inequitable now comes before a court of equity to seek equitable relief. The court should not have granted his request based on the equitable maxim that 'he who comes before equity must come with clean hands'. This maxim means that a plaintiff who seeks an equitable remedy or any other equitable relief must show that his past conduct in the transaction has been fair, honest and above board. This maxim refers to behaviour before the suit, as opposed to future conduct.

Moreover, this is supposedly a case involving a contract of service wherein some of the terms of the agreement are to that effect. First, the defendants were tied to the service of the plaintiffs exclusively for five years. And, apart from all other harsh terms of the contract, the plaintiff had the option to renew the contract at its expiration for a further two years or any longer period. The defendant had no such right. The combined effect of this term is to attach the service of the defendant to the plaintiff perpetually. This makes it look like a contract of slavery if the defendants were not allowed to opt out of the contractual arrangement. The courts are bound to be zealous less they should turn contracts of service into a contract of slavery.

From the foregoing, it is apparent that a contract will not be set aside merely because the aggrieved party did not have independent advice or based on the inadequacy of consideration. Also, therefore, it must be shown that:

The other party engaged in unconscionable conduct or an unconscionable use of power.[37]

The other party had behaved in a morally reprehensible manner that ought to affect his conscience. In this respect, the classic example of an unconscionable bargain is where advantages have been taken of a young, inexperienced or ignorant person to introduce terms which no sensible,

36 (1985) Q.B. 428.

37 *Alec Lobb (Garager) Ltd.* v *Total Oil (Great Britain) Ltd.(1985) 1W.L.R. 173.*

> well-advised person would have accepted.[38] In the words of Lord Brightman: 'There must be procedural unfairness as well as contractual imbalance, though contractual imbalance may be so extreme as to raise a presumption of procedural unfairness, such as undue influence or some other forms of victimization.'[39]

The above factors were the issues that ought to have been raised and considered by the court in the case of *African Songs Ltd v Sunny Adeniyi.*[40] It is a pity that there was no appeal against the decision of the Court in this case, but the fact remains that as it stood, the case represents a bad law. The decision was contrary to what abounds in a contract of such a nature the world over as the survey of the commonwealth and American developments reveals. Commonwealth Courts appear to be more in favour of a possible general doctrine of unconscionability.

There is a good deal of Canadian authorities which were on all fours with the decisions of the English courts cited above. Examples in this regard include *Black* v *Wilcox*[41] and *Paris v Coast Finance.*[42] In Australia, the Courts seem to prepare to give relief in a wide range of circumstances provided that advantage has been taken as could be seen in. *Boomley v Ryan*[43] and *Common-Wealth Bank of Australian v Amadio.*[44] And in America by contrast, "unconscionability" is now a well-established principle of the law-entitling courts to refuse to endorse contracts or contractual clauses, which are harsh, exorbitant or unconscionable. The principle is partly statutory, deriving from the Uniform Commercial Code. A distinction is generally drawn in the American Law between procedural unconscionability and substantive unconscionability.[45]

Procedural unconscionability can be invoked where some elements of oppression or wrongdoing have occurred in the process of making the contract. This enables the courts to use doctrines such as duress and undue influence as a mere illustration of broader principle requiring that undue advantage should not be taken of a party. Thus, the general inability to comprehend the purport of a complicated document may be treated as a matter of procedural unconscionability. However, substantive unconscionability goes to the actual substances of the contract and its terms. See Chitty on contract.

38 *Multiservice Binding Ltd. v Marden* (1979), CH34, 110.
39 *Harts v O'connor*(1985) AC. 1018.
40 (1975) 1 Cowp. 341, 343.
41 (1976) 30 D.L.R. (3D) 192.
42 (1972) 30 D.L.R. (3D) 710.
43 (1956) 99. C.L.R. 362.
44 (1983) 57 A.L.J.R. 358.
45 A A Left, 'Unconscionability and the Code-The Emperor New Clause' (1967) *Pennsylvania Law Review* 115.

Based on the above points of law, the judgement of the court in *African Songs Ltd v Sunny Adeniyi* should be regarded as delivered *per in curiam.*

Conclusion

From the above analysis, taken into consideration case law development, the case under review ought to be decided differently particularly against the background of many vitiating factors that coalesced in the contract. Therefore, one ought to advise musicians or artists that they should always have their lawyers by their side anytime they wish to enter into a contract with a recording company. This is necessary to ensure that they do not enter into any inequitable agreement. As we have noted above, the agreement in *African Songs Ltd v Sunny Ade*[46] is inequitable. An equitable agreement is the one that would favour the musicians and at the same time favour the recording company. It ought not to be an agreement to enslave a contracting partner, which is contrary to public policy and at the same time illegal in law.

It is, however, interesting to note that the age-long disputes resurrected as King Sunny Ade dragged African Songs Limited and its sister company, Take Your Choice to the Federal High Court of Lagos, alleging a breach of copyright in his work, as the defendants continued the mass-production of his works without compensation even though he owns the copyright in his work. He claimed further, that the copyright subsists in him after the expiration of the five years agreement he and his band entered with the defendants. In a judgment delivered by the Lagos Federal High Court by Justice Tsoho, the court awarded 500 million Nairas as general damages in favour of King Sunny Ade as the plaintiff, ordered the return of his works and made an order of perpetual injunction against the defendants/appellants, restraining them from further infringement of the copyrights in the works of the Plaintiff/Respondent. It is of interest to the academic world that the defendants/appellants had proceeded to the Supreme Court claiming that they were the perpetual owners of the copyright of the intellectual properties of the plaintiff/respondent, as we await the decision of the apex court in this matter.

46 (1975) 1 Cowp. 341, 343.

15 Seeking protection for use of images in commercial practices in Nigeria

A pathway to intellectual property reform and development

Nkem Itanyi and Christian Aniukwu

Introduction

Image can be an expression of an individual's personality in the public domain.[1] The right associated with the use of images reflects the control or the powers of a person over the use of the image. The unique features or characteristics of an individual is often what is explored for a particular purpose. A person is entitled to maintain privacy regarding their image or to use the same for business, either for commercialising goods and services of self or of others. A brand could be attached to a specific image or personality for commercial reasons to influence potential customers. Therefore, unauthorised use of a person's image for purposes unknown to the person or not permitted by the person amounts to an actionable wrong. Based on the principle of *ubi jus ibi remedium*, when a person is wronged, the law should provide a remedy.

It is acknowledged in this chapter that the body of Nigerian laws has not set out any specific procedure or head of law for the enforcement of the breach of image right of a person. Inferences and analogies are drawn from other jurisdictions, including the United Kingdom, since it is the foundation of most Nigerian laws. This chapter recommends, amongst other things, the provision of a specific procedure for the enforcement of rights over unauthorised use of image.

The possibility of copyright protection of images in Nigeria

The Copyright Act of Nigeria[2] finds its origin in the earlier UK laws.[3] Most of the provisions were similar until the last amendment of 1999 when Nigeria

1 Intellectual Property Office of Guernsey "What Are Image Rights' http://ipo.guernseyregistry.com/article/103037/What-are-Image-Rights accessed 25 September 2020.

2 Cap C28, Law of the Federation of Nigeria, 2004.

3 Caroline B Ncube and Desmond O Oriakhogba, 'Monkey Selfie and Authorship in Copyright Law: The Nigerian and South African Perspectives' (2018) 21 *Potchefstroom Electronic Law Journal* 1, 2.

DOI: 10.4324/9781003250883-19

failed to further reform and develop the Copyright Act, such that the digital era is not reflected.[4] The nature and scope of copyright protection and duration in Nigeria is identical to the UK Act.[5] Both jurisdiction bestow copyright ownership of a photograph on the photographer. Any reproduction of that picture must be with the photographer's express permission; otherwise, it is an infringement of his copyright. Copyright in this regard belongs to the creative human being as envisaged by the law and no other.[6]

Artistic and cinematograph works are eligible for copyright protection.[7] Artistic work is eligible for copyright protection only when sufficient effort has been expended on making the work to give it an original character, and the work has been fixed in any definite medium of expression.[8] Additionally, artistic work includes 'paintings, drawings, etchings, lithographs, woodcuts, engravings and prints; maps, plans and diagrams; works of sculpture; photographs not comprised in a cinematographic film; works of architecture in the form of building models; and works of artistic craftsmanship...'[9] Thus, a person's image can be subject of copyright protection as an artistic work if it falls under any of the listed types of work or similar works. The list appears not to be exhaustive.

However, when a person's image is subject of copyright protection, the question then is who owns the copyright? The law created a difference between the author of a work eligible for copyright and the owner of the work,[10] with both having different legal significances.[11] The Copyright Act confers first ownership of the copyright on the author of the work[12] and not the subject of the work. 'The author of the work may be described as the person who created the work or made the production of the work possible'.[13]

The United States Supreme Court defined an author as 'the party who actually creates the work, that is, the person who translates an idea into

4 Adebambo Adewopo, *Nigerian Copyright System – Principles and Perspectives*, Vol 1 (Odade Publishers 2012).

5 The Act in Section 1 clearly states those works which would be eligible for protection. The works eligible for copyright protection are as follows: Literary works: novels, stories, choreographic works, computer programmes, amongst others; Musical works: works composed for accompaniment; Artistic works: paintings, drawings, woodcuttings, maps, amongst others; Cinematograph works: the fixation of a sequence of visual images that can be seen and associated soundtracks that can be heard; Sound recordings: the fixation of a sequence of sounds capable of being held but does not include soundtracks associated with cinematographic films; and Broadcasts. See also the First Schedule to the Act which provides for duration of copyright.

6 Ncube and Oriakhogba (n 3) 1, 25.

7 Section 1 (c) and (d) Copyright Act Cap C28, Law of the Federation of Nigeria, 2004.

8 Ibid Section 1 (2).

9 Ibid Section 51.

10 Ibid Section 10.

11 John Asein, *Nigerian Copyright Law and Practice* (2nd ed., Books & Gavel publishing, 2012) 125.

12 Section 10 Copyright Act Cap C28, Law of the Federation of Nigeria, 2004.

13 Asein (n 11) 113.

fixed, tangible expression entitled to copyright protection'.[14] John Asein stated that an author is very often, but not necessarily, a human person.[15] However, the United States Court of Appeals for the ninth circuit has held that an author and owner of a copyrighted work must be a human.[16] The copyright ownership in a work belongs to the person recognised by law as having the legal rights over the work, with economic rights to exploit the work. An author, where different from the owner, must assign his rights to another for the person to be deemed as so in law.[17]

Where the person who is the subject of the photograph is assigned copyright in the work; such person as the copyright owner can validly enforce copyright against a third party who exploits the work without authorisation. The person whose image is painted, drawn, or photographed does not enjoy copyright in the work. In the United States of America, a supermodel Gigi Hadid was sued for posting a photograph of herself without the permission of the photographer who took the photo.[18] A reminder that copyright will protect a specific output of intellectual creativity and not the image.[19] The Copyright Act is silent on image rights in photograph.

Trademarks and the protection of images

There is an increasing trend where celebrities register their names, slogans, and aliases as trademarks in Nigeria. While it is acceptable to register names and slogans as trademarks, the registration of images or pictures of a person as a trademark will, in some way, be viewed as a curious development. More so, nothing in the Trademarks Act suggests that the image of a person can be registered as a trademark.[20] Section 67 of the Trademarks Act defines a trademark as:

> except in relation to a certification trade mark, a mark used or proposed to be used in relation to goods for the purpose of indicating, or so as

14 Ibid *Community for Creative Non-Violence v. Reid*, 490 U.S. 546, 561, 178 USPQ 129, 135 (1973).

15 Asein (n 11) 113.

16 *Naruto v. Slater*, 888 F3d 418 (9th Cir. 2018). The Court, interpreting the United States Copyright Code held that a monkey cannot own a copyright in a selfie picture taken by it.

17 Section 10 Copyright Act Cap C28, Law of the Federation of Nigeria, 2004.

18 *Xclusive-Lee Inc. v. Jelena Noura 'Gigi' Hadid* (1:19-cv-00520) (2019 District Court, Eastern District of New York). Although Pamela K. Chen, United States District Judge eventually dismissed the suit filed by the plaintiff. The learned judge stated that they failed to comply with the procedural prerequisite registration under the US copyright law; the requirement is a statutory condition before a plaintiff can file infringement lawsuits. Consequently, she declined the plaintiff's application to amend the claim as per registration and dismissed their complaint for direct and contributory infringement.

19 Kelsey Farish, 'Do Deepfakes Pose a Golden Opportunity? Considering Whether English Law Should Adopt California's Publicity Right in the Age of the Deepfake' (2020) 15 *Journal of Intellectual Property Law & Practice* 40, 44.

20 Cap. T18 Laws of the Federation of Nigeria 2004.

> to indicate, a connection in the course of trade between the goods and some person having the right either as proprietor or as registered user to use the mark...[21]

The same section defines a mark as including 'a device, brand, heading, label, ticket, name, signature, word, letter, numeral, or any combination thereof'.[22] It may be problematic trying to subsume a picture of a person within the meaning of trademark from the provisions of the Act. Again section 9 of the Trademarks Act listed the name and signature of an individual as the types of marks considered as distinctive trademarks. Section 9 of the Trademarks Act listed items that may suffice as distinctive trademarks. Paragraph (1) (a) of section 9 provides that a mark registrable in Part A of the register must consist of at least one of the listed particulars, which are: the name of a company, individual, or firm, represented in a special or particular manner.

The key qualification to the registration of a name is that the name is to be represented in a special or particular manner. This means that a name *simpliciter* cannot be considered registrable. This is because one person does not bear a name solely. There will be thousands of people bearing the same name. For example, in the United States, a name of a person can be registrable only upon a showing of acquired distinctiveness.[23] Thus, the public must have associated the name with the goods/services that the person represents. The Trademarks Act requires a trademark to be registered in relation to particular goods or classes of goods.[24] It must be used for those goods[25] in default of which the trademark may be liable to be removed from the register of trademarks.[26] These requirements may likely not be fulfilled by celebrities in music, movies, and acting.

Section 4 of the Trademarks Act insists a trademark must be registered in respect of particular goods or classes of goods. When there is an issue regarding the class any of goods fall into, the registrar determines the final decision. The use of 'must' shows the provision mandatory.[27] There were

21 Ibid.
22 Ibid Section 67.
23 Barton Beebe, *Trademark Law; An Open-Source Casebook* version 7 (2020) Digital edition, 49.
24 Section 4 Cap. T18 Laws of the Federation of Nigeria 2004.
25 Ibid section 18, 32 and 67.
26 Ibid section 31.
27 In *Fidelity Bank Plc. v. Monye & Ors. (2012) LPELR-7819(SC)* the Supreme Court held that the Word "MUST" appearing in the provision is a word of absolute obligation and occurs in a section which is concerned with a fundamental principle of justice... it admits no discretion." Instructively, the Court of Appeal held in the case of *Ugwu & Ors v. PDP & Ors (2013) LPELR-21356(CA)* as follows: '*I agree with Learned Senior Advocate for the appellants, and as conceded by the Learned Senior Advocate for the 1st respondent, that generally such mandatory terms, like shall, must and the like, by reason of their mandatory*

34 classes of goods, however in 2007, classes 35–45 covering services were added by the federal minister of trade.[28] In ***Ramhead Industrial & Commercial Co. Ltd v. Ekulo International Ltd* & 2 Ors., the federal high court** stated that 'use must be in relation to goods in the Act and the provision does not include service marks'.[29] The implication of the provision of the Act as well as the decision of the federal high court above is to the effect that a celebrity, either an artiste or actor, cannot validly register a trademark for goods. This is because the classification of goods has no provision that covers their business.[30] This is a major hurdle for celebrities in the registration of their names and images as trademarks. However, we are aware that many celebrities have registered their names and other signature as trademarks in Nigeria.[31]

In practice, service marks are registrable pursuant to the action of the minister earlier mentioned. Celebrities register their names, distinctive slogans, and other signature trademarks in relation to the relevant services they provide. The registration of a mark bestows on the proprietor of the mark, the exclusive right to use the mark for registered goods.[32] Any use of the mark by a third party without the authorisation of the owner amounts to an infringement.[33]

Another hurdle is the exclusive right granted by the registration of a trademark is only for the class of goods/services for which the trademark was registered. It is questionable when a celebrity registers a trademark in a particular class for services, whether the celebrity be legally capable of stopping the use and registration of his name on other goods by a third party? Section 13 of the Trademarks Act suggests that a proprietor of a trademark can only oppose the registration of a similar trademark if the latter trademark is sought to be registered for similar goods or same goods as that of the earlier registered proprietor. Therefore, it seems that where both registrations are

---

nature demand and require that they must be complied with. Compliance with what they command cannot be waived. This point is so settled and elementary that it need not be dwelt on beyond what I have said.' The Court went ahead to hold that *'Mandatory words in a statute are sacrosanct, do not allow for condonation of departures from them and are applied strictly.'*

28 The validity of the Minister's action and the registration of trademarks for services have been questioned in some quarters. This is because the procedure laid down by the law was not followed in the amendment of the goods classification in extending registration of trademarks to service marks. See for example *https://www.linkedin.com/pulse/legality-otherwise-registrantion-service-marks-nigeria-obiabo/*; see also *https://tnp.com.ng/insights/legality-of-service-marks-in-nigeria*

29 Suit No: FHC/L/CS/256/2012 unreported, delivered 7/6/2017.

30 The Nice classification of goods and services for a comprehensive list of goods/services and the classes they fall in; *https://www.wipo.int/classifications/nice/nclpub/en/fr/*

31 Omotola J Ekeinde recently registered her first name as a trademark *https://www.premiumtimesng.com/entertainment/nollywood/443686-actress-omotola-jalade-ekeinde-trademarks-first-name.html,* several other celebrities have also done this; Mr. Macaroni, Kizz Daniel, Mark Angel etc.

32 Ibid section 5.

33 Ibid section 5 (2).

in different classes or for different nature of goods, the registered proprietor will not be able to stop the subsequent applicant.

The Trademarks Act allows defensive registration.[34] A well-known trademark is an invented word or words registered in relation to particular goods/services. It has become so well-known that its use in relation to other goods would likely be taken as indicating a connection in the course of trade between those goods and a person legitimately entitled to the use of the trademark. Due to the goodwill of these marks, mischievous competitors often seek to capitalise and register such marks in a different class. Because of this, the law creates a scope of protection through the defensive registration of trademarks.

Perhaps this concept of defensive registration of a trademark is helpful to a celebrity to register a name, signature, and slogan, among others as a trademark for those classes of goods and services that are likely to be exploited by third parties. This sort of registration will stop third parties from registering the same trademark or similar trademark for those classes of goods and services. A celebrity can register an image in clothing, playthings, hair, and cosmetics even though they do not use the trademark for such purposes. Bestowed on the celebrity is the right to license such registered trademark to a business that may need the mark for commercial purposes.

However, the problem is related to application of a defensive trademark registration that requires identification of a class of goods/services. The use of the trademark in this class should be well-known that use in other classes is inferred to have the same origin as the mark's earlier proprietor. Section 34 (3) of the Trademarks Act forbids trafficking in a trademark.[35] The preceding notwithstanding, section 11 of the Trademarks Act provides that:

> it shall not be lawful to register as a trademark or part of a trademark (a) any matter the use of which would, by reason of it being likely to deceive or cause confusion or otherwise, be disentitled to protection in a court of justice or be contrary to law or morality...[36]

The implication of this is that despite not having a registered trademark for a particular class of goods, the owner of the mark can still stop the use and registration of a trademark based on the grounds that the registration of that mark by a third party is likely to cause confusion or that action of the third party in the registration of the mark is disentitled to protection in a court or that it will be contrary to law and morality.

It will be contrary to morality to allow a person to reap benefits from the use of an image of another without the consent of the person whose image

34 Ibid Section 32.

35 In this context, a situation where a person registers a trademark, without intent to use same, with the view to assigning same or licensing it to other users for a fee.

36 Cap. T18 Laws of the Federation of Nigeria 2004.

is being used. As stated by the court in the case of *The Procter and Gamble Company v. Global Soap and Detergent Industries Ltd. And the Registrar of Trade Marks*,[37] the essence of a trademark is that 'it indicates a connection in the course of trade between the goods and some person having the right to use the name'.

A celebrity whose image, including name, slogan, signature or otherwise, is sought to be registered as a trademark by a third party can oppose the registration of such a trademark vide the provisions of section 11 above. Section 3 of the Trademarks Act also allows a person to sue for passing off where the person has no registered trademark rights. Therefore, though the use of a trademark may not afford full image rights protection, it could still be helpful to protect the name and image of a person.

The Court of Appeal in Rihanna's case,[38] while stating that there is no laid down the rule of law that guides the enforcement of image rights, suggested that a celebrity seeking to control the use of his or her image must rely upon some other cause of action such as breach of contract, breach of confidence, and infringement of copyright or passing off.[39]

Right to privacy in protecting use of image

In the absence of a specific law on the image rights, another principle of law that can be utilised is privacy law. In the United States, attribution to the rights to personality and publicity extends to photographs.[40] The image of the person in the photograph. In Nigeria and the United Kingdom, there can be an extension by way of reference to rights to privacy. No doubt, when it comes to respecting the dignity of a person, privacy ranks high.[41] The Constitution of the Federal Republic of Nigeria, 1999 does not expressly define the term privacy; however, the general privacy rights are provided in section 37.

The section states that 'the privacy of citizens, their homes, correspondence, telephone conversations and telegraphic communications is hereby guaranteed and protected'.[42] Conversely, the protection of image rights of a person, where the same has been used in a way to suggest endorsement of a

37 [2013] 2 NWLR p. 409; see also *Ferodo Ltd. v. Ibeto Ind. Ltd (2004) 5 NWLR (Pt. 866) 317.*

38 Section 31 Cap. T18 Laws of the Federation of Nigeria 2004.

39 Sara Mansoori, "Case Comment: *Fenty v. Arcadia Group Brands Ltd*, Rihanna succeeds in controlling how her image is used" *https://inforrm.org/2015/02/19/case-comment-fenty-v-arcadia-group-brands-ltd-rihanna-succeeds-in-controlling-how-her-image-is-used-sara-mansoori/* accessed 14 October 2020; see also Ewallace, "*Rihanna v. Topshop* -UK Court of Appeal Upholds Decision in Landmark Passing Off Judgment" *https://www.irelandip.com/2015/02/articles/intellectual-property/rihanna-v-topshop-uk-court-of-appeal-upholds-decision-in-landmark-passing-off-judgment/* accessed 14 October 2020.

40 *Healan Laboratories Inc V Topps Chewing Gum Inc,* 202 F2d 866 (2d Cir. 1953).

41 ES Nwauche, 'The Right to Privacy in Nigeria' (2007) Vol. 1(1) Review of Nigerian Law 64.

42 The Constitution of the Federal Republic of Nigeria, 1999, as amended, s.37.

business or products and services, it is not clear how the courts will interpret the right of privacy to protect the individual. It is also not clear how damages will be assessed in favour of the plaintiff.

Although there have been instances where Nigerian celebrities have threatened brand owners and businesses with an action founded on violations of their image rights, these cases never made it to court as the threats were settled between the parties.[43] It is common to think of image rights as mostly accruing to celebrities. The reason for this is not farfetched. The images of celebrities constitute a stream of income for the celebrities when licensed for endorsement deals, advertising, and promotion of businesses because these images attract consumers to the goods and services for which the image is used in its commercialisation.[44] Hence, there is a need to protect the rights of these classes of persons in the use of their images.

Unauthorised use of a person's image in a way that suggests endorsement and advertising may cause confusion and deceive consumers or third parties into believing that the famous person they know has endorsed the use and patronisation of such goods and services. Also, it is possible that unauthorised use of a celebrity's image on a brand may affect the celebrity's contractual relationship with another brand.[45] While most of the decided cases,[46] especially in jurisdictions other than Nigeria, on image rights, may have propelled this belief, it is, however, clear that every person is entitled to enforce improper use of images.

In the recently decided case of *Amudat Adeleke v. Bukola Saraki & 3 Ors*,[47] an individual who is not a celebrity successfully enforced her right against the improper use of her image on election campaign advertorials. When this chapter was written, this case was the only Nigerian case available. The facts of this case relate to breach of privacy rights in relation to election and voting decisions. The applicant was a business entrepreneur who deals in assorted mobile phones and phone accessories at a street market at Victoria Island Lagos. During the electioneering campaigns for the 2019 presidential elections in Nigeria, the director general of the presidential campaign for Peoples Democratic Party led his team for a one-on-one campaign at the market where the applicant operates.[48]

43 In 2016, RMD, a Nigerian actor, threatened Jumia, Nigeria's largest e-commerce site, with a legal action over Jumia's use of his image on Jumia's fashion Instagram page *https://www.herald.ng/rmd-goes-war-jumia-threatens-legal-action/* The matter was settled out of court.

44 S Nwauche, 'The Right to Privacy in Nigeria' (2007) Vol. 1(1) Review of Nigerian Law 64.

45 *Ibid.*

46 *Robyn Rihanna Fenty & Ors. v. Arcadia Group Brands Limited (T/A TOPSHOP) & An*or. [2013] EWHC 2310 (CH); *Proactive Sports Management Ltd. v. Wayne Rooney & Ors* [2010] EWHC 1807 (QB); *Irvine v. Talksport [2002] EWHC 367 (Ch.).*

47 (Unreported) Judgment delivered on 27 April 2020 at the Federal High Court of Lagos in suit number FHC/L/CS/193/2019 *coram* Justice A.O. Faji.

48 One of the major political parties in Nigeria and presently the main opposition party.

During a discussion with the campaign team, the applicant expressed her support for the candidate of the campaign team and agreed to the taking of a picture of her by the team. This picture she believed was for a commemoration of the visit and discussion she had with the campaign team. Some days after, the applicant saw her images on digital billboards and other signposts at strategic public places with the inscription 'I dey vote Atiku/Obi' meaning I will vote for Atiku/Obi.[49] The applicant was dissatisfied with the use of her image and instituted an action at the federal high court to enforce her human rights to privacy.[50]

> A declaration that the unauthorised use, publication and display of the Applicant's image by the 1st respondent as part of the 3rd and 4th respondents' presidential campaign advert as set out in the statement hereto, is unlawful and constitutes a breach and an infringement of the Applicant's fundamental rights, inter alia, to privacy as enshrined, guaranteed and provided for in the 1999 constitution of the Federal Republic of Nigeria.[51]

The applicant was successful in this case and the court granted all her reliefs, including damages in the sum of five million nairas against the respondents.[52] In applying the fundamental right to privacy as a means to enforce the applicant's right to the wrongful use of her image, the court held that since the Constitution did not define the term 'privacy of citizen' or limit the interpretation of same; the phrase should be interpreted 'generally, liberally and expansively to include privacy of a citizen's body, life, person, thought, conscience, feelings, views, decisions (including his plans and choices), desires, health, relationships, character, material possessions, family life, activities, etc.'.[53] The court cited an earlier decision in the case of *Nwali v EBSIEC & Ors*[54] and held, as stated in the quotation below.

> …the term 'privacy of citizens' is not directly obvious on its face. It is very wide as it does not define the specific aspects of the privacy of the citizen it protects. A citizen is ordinarily a human being constituting of his body, his life, his person, thought, conscience, belief, decisions (including his plans and choices), desires, his health, his relationships,

49 Pidgin English translated as 'I am voting Atiku/Obi'. Atiku was the presidential candidate of the People's Democratic Party at the 2019 Presidential election while Peter Obi was the vice-presidential candidate and running mate of Atiku Abubakar.

50 Suit No. FHC/L/CS/193/2019.

51 *Amuda Adeleke v. Bukola Saraki & Ors* (Unreported) Judgment delivered on 27 April 2020 at the Federal High Court of Lagos in suit number FHC/L/CS/193/2019 2.

52 Ibid 50–1.

53 Ibid 41.

54 (2014) LPELR-23682 CA.

> character, possessions, family etc. It includes all his constituents as a human being and implies a right to protect one's thoughts, conscience or religious belief from coercive and unjustified intrusion and one's body from unwarranted invasion. The phrase should thus not be interpreted narrowly; otherwise, the intended practical objective of the section would not be realised. The phrase should, therefore, be interpreted to give it a general meaning and application.

The court had to go far and wide in defining the term 'privacy of citizen' to widen the scope enough to cover instances of improper use of a person's image. There is no stand-alone cause of action or remedy yet for abuse of image rights in Nigeria. Breach of image rights has no *sui generis* mode of enforcement in Nigeria as held in the case of *Amudat Adeleke v. Bukola Saraki* (supra), breach of image rights can be enforced as fundamental human rights to privacy in Nigeria.[55]

A peek into other jurisdictions on authorised use of image

In other jurisdictions, such as in the United Kingdom, breach of image rights could be enforced by some forms of legal actions. Some image rights cases instituted have proceeded on the unlawful 'appropriation' of aspects of an individual's personality. Where a claimant alleges that he has been falsely held out as endorsing goods or services of another person, there appears to be available relief under the torts of passing off; and under the tort of defamation[56] in some cases. Traditionally, the tort of passing off protects intellectual property and applies to persons or businesses in competition. However, the tort has recently been extended to fill the void of image rights legislation in some common law jurisdictions like the United Kingdom.

In the case *Edmund 'Eddie' Irvine v. Talksport*,[57] the high court held that where a celebrity is falsely held out as endorsing a brand or commercial service, the holding out comes within the tort of passing off. The court, however, stated that the claimant must prove that he had a 'significant reputation or goodwill' and that the defendants' actions falsely suggested to a significant section of the relevant market that he endorsed the goods in question. It will also be relevant whether or not individuals commercialise their image prior to the defendant's action.[58] In this case, *Irvine,* the claimant, was a successful Formula 1 driver of Ferrari. He had participated in several documented sponsorship deals and was consequently able to establish and compute the damage to the goodwill of his publicity.

55 Section 37 of the CFRN.

56 *Tolley v. J S Fry & Sons Ltd.* 1 All ER Rep. 131.

57 *Irvine v. Talksport* [2003] EWCA Civ 423; [2003] 2 All ER 881; [2003] EMLR 538.

58 Farish (n 19) 45.

In *Starbucks (HK) Ltd v British Sky Broadcasting Group Plc*,[59] the UK Supreme Court held that mere reputation is insufficient to succeed in an action for passing off. To successfully bring an action in passing off, the claimants must show goodwill in the form of customers within a country or jurisdiction. Although goodwill is an integral part of a successful action of passing off, the claimants will equally need to prove misrepresentation and damages to restrain an unauthorised use of their images.[60]

It is evident from the discussions above that protection and enforcement of image rights lie in a hotchpotch of causes of action ranging from the common law action in passing off, defamation, and breach of the right to identity and right to publicity.[61] As earlier stated, proof of goodwill is an essential element in an action for passing off. If this principle is applied in an action in passing off for breach of image rights, it is likely then that only the celebrities might be successful in such actions. It is, however, possible that any person may easily succeed in an action for the enforcement of the right to privacy. In the Nigerian case of *The Boots Company Limited v. United Niger Imports Limited*,[62] the court enumerated the elements of a passing-off action. The elements that must be proved by a plaintiff for a successful action in passing off were given as follows: (1) proof that ownership has become distinctive of his goods by a substantial number of the public or persons involved in a trade in the relevant market as coming from a particular source; (2) that the defendants used a name, mark, sign so resembling the plaintiff's to deceive or cause confusion in the minds of the common customer; and (3) that the use of the name, mark, sign is likely to cause or has caused injury, actual or probable, to the goodwill of the plaintiff's business.[63]

The problem that may be faced by the image right owner in enforcing his rights under passing off is how to prove that he has garnered goodwill using the image on a set of goods and services. Thus, it will also be challenging to prove that the defendant is engaged 'in a common field' of business. An analysis of the rule in the High Court's decision in the *Robyn Rihanna Fenty & Ors. v. Arcadia Group Brands Limited's*[64] case also supports this assertion.

59 [2015] UKSC 31.

60 Emmanuel K Oke, 'Image Rights and Passing off: Should Reputation Be Enough for Celebrities to Succeed in English Courts?' (2020) 15 *Journal of Intellectual Property Law & Practice* 49, 51–4.

61 The right of publicity is an intellectual property right that protects against the misappropriation of a person's name, likeness or other indicia of personal identity—such as nickname, pseudonym, voice, signature, likeness or photograph—for commercial benefit. International Trademark Association, 'Right of Publicity' *https://www.inta.org/topics/right-of-publicity/* accessed 26 September 2020.

62 (1977) 1 A.N.S.L.R 144.

63 T&A legal, "An Appraisal of Passing off Actions under Nigerian Law" *https://www.mondaq.com/nigeria/trademark/704160/an-appraisal-of-passing-off-actions-under-nigerian-law* accessed 13 October 2020.

64 [2013] EWHC 2310 (CH).

Rihanna owns a fashion line business, Fenty, who is in the same line of business as the defendant. It is likely that the ruling may have been different if Rihanna had no fashion line business. Although the judge was quick to point out in its judgement that 'there is today in England no such taking as a free-standing general right by a famous person (or anyone else) to control the reproduction of their image'.[65] Each case will be decided on the basis of its merits.

Although there is no known Nigerian case on passing off as a means of enforcing the image right, as of the time of writing this chapter, it is a general principle of law in Nigeria that where the existing statue or case law is silent or makes no provision on an aspect of the law, there can be recourse to foreign judgements that will be of persuasive effect.[66] Thus, as it currently stands, recourse will be made to existing UK judicial decisions[67] with regard to the image rights.

Conclusion and recommendations

In this chapter, it is established that image rights has increasingly become a contentious topic, regarding the economic and other interests of celebrities. Who owns these rights? The person who photographs the celebrity or the subject matter of the photograph? There has been an attempt to answer these questions in this chapter, arguing that the bundle of rights in the intellectual property laws of Nigeria reveal the absence of laws specifically relating to image rights.

Copyright, trademarks, passing-off, and privacy rights do not offer full protection and enforcement of a breach of image rights. These heads of law can, however, provide redress for the subject of the image. To gain benefits in the copyright law, the subject of the photograph or artistic work should obtain ownership of the work through an assignment, where possible. It is also recommended that celebrities who wish to register their mark as a trademark should consider registering the same in the classes of services for advertising and business management. This consideration will widen the scope of their trademark registration protecting it from any unauthorised use. Furthermore, if the trademark becomes a well-known mark after such initial registration; the celebrity could consider a defensive registration of the mark in all the relevant classes of goods and services.

For celebrities or other persons who engage independent photographers for their photoshoot, it is advisable to get the rights in those photos assigned to the celebrity, subject of the photo, if the situation permits. This will make

65 L J Kitchin stated that, 'There is in English law no "image right" or "character right" that allows a celebrity to control the use of his or her name or image.'

66 *Agboti v. Balogun & Ors.* (2020) LPELR-49904 (CA).

67 *Fenty* and *Irvine* cases (supra). See also *Hines v Winnick* [1947] Ch. 708; *Marengo v Daily Sketch and Sunday Graphic* (1948) 65 RPC 242; *Clark v Associated Newspapers* [1998] RPC 261.

image rights easier for the celebrity to proceed against any unauthorised use of the picture. Overall, it is proposed that an express body of laws on image rights will eliminate controversies to a large extent. These rights may either be self-standing or may be incorporated in existing laws. In Nigeria, there is a Copyright Bill before the national assembly. There is no provision on image rights in this Bill, thus, creating doubt as to whether this area of law will be legislated on in the nearest future.

16 Intellectual property reform in Nigeria

Bankole Sodipo

Introduction

On March 1, 2021, Nigerian born Dr. Ngozi Okonjo-Iweala became the first female and the first African director general (DG), of the World Trade Organisation (WTO).[1] It then became imperative for Nigeria to review her level of compliance with WTO treaty obligations, especially the Trade-Related Aspects of Intellectual Property (TRIPS), as it will be unconscionable for her to head WTO, and yet the DG's home country is noncompliant. Nonetheless, as a developing country, it behooves the Nigerian government to balance treaty obligations with local needs.

Whilst the debate about the extent to which intellectual property (IP) actually incentivises creativity and inventiveness continues to rage,[2] evidence abounds that copyright-based industries contribute significantly to Nigeria's GDP.[3] With Nigeria's bourgeoning film industry, Nollywood, winning international nominations, Nigerian music stars winning Oscars, Nigerian authors winning Nobel, Booker and other prizes, the need for a homegrown reform of Nigeria's Copyright Act, 1988[4] is accentuated. Reforms are required on, Nigeria's Merchandise Marks Act, 1916, Trade Marks Act, 1965 and the Patents and Designs Act, 1970 that all do not currently meet local needs nor align with the global practices. This chapter pulls together the several thoughts in earlier chapters, identifies the gaps in

1 https://www.wto.org/english/thewto_e/dg_e/dg_e.htm

2 Kate Darlington and Aaron Perzanowski, *Creativity without Law: Challenging the Assumptions of Intellectual Property* (NYU Press, 2017). Jeremy de Beer and Chidi Oguamanam, in Mathew L Reilly (eds), 'Open Minds: Lessons from Nigeria on Intellectual Property, Innovation, and Development' *Open Development: Networked* (2013) 249 *Innovations in International Development*, 259.

3 Samuel Samiai Andrews, 'Reforming Copyright Law for a Developing Africa' (2018–2019) 66 *Journal of the Copyright Society of the U.S.A* 1. Hemen Philip Faga and Ole Ngozi, 'Limits of Copyright Protection in Contemporary Nigeria: Re-Examining the Relevance of the Nigerian Copyright Act in Today's Digital and Computer Age' (2011) 2 *Nnamdi Azikiwe University Journal of International Law* 211.

4 As amended in 1992 and 1999, now Chapter C28, 2004 Laws of the Federation of Nigeria.

DOI: 10.4324/9781003250883-20

Nigeria's IP framework and suggests how these gaps can be plugged. It offers thoughts on many of the issues raised in the earlier chapters and on the random issues calling for reforms, but does not pretend to be an in-depth analysis of the issues.

Attempts at reform

Predictably, given the age of the applicable statutes, several attempts driven largely by the local lobby have pushed for reforms of Nigerian IP laws. In the last two decades, the executive has prepared several IP Bills whilst a number of private member's Bills have also been presented at the National Assembly,[5] but none has birthed a new law. Bills introduced to previous sessions of the National Assembly that are not passed into law before the session ends have to be re-introduced afresh to the current session before it can be passed, irrespective of the stage the bill has reached the National Assembly. Another private members' Bill introduced by Senator Abiru had its first reading in early May 2021, and has been approved by the National assembly.[6] The Bills that are largely locally driven seek to ameliorate the plight of relevant stakeholders.

Plant variety and animal breeders' rights

Agricultural-based industries play a substantial role in employment and they make up a sizeable part of Nigeria's GDP. It is therefore curious that innovation in plant varieties cannot be patented, yet there is insufficient plenitude of rights for plant breeders,[7] talk less, animal breeders. Two statutes govern plant and animal breeding in Nigeria today, the National Crop and Livestock Breeds (Registration, etc.) Act of 1987[8] and the National Agricultural Seeds Act, 1992.[9] I have argued elsewhere that "None of them go far enough. There are no exclusive rights granted to breeders of plants and animal varieties that seek to encourage them to be more innovative and to conduct relevant research".[10]

The last 15 years have witnessed various attempts to introduce a form of plant variety protection in Nigeria. There has been local lobby championed by the Nigerian Agricultural Seeds Council and the Ministry of Agriculture, but the executive Bill still being vetted by the ministry of justice is yet to be introduced

5 See, for example, the Trade Marks Bill SB 375 introduced by Senator Umaru Kurfi (Katsina Central) in 2016, which was never passed in the 7th Assembly.

6 Copyright Bill 2021.

7 Titilayo Adebola, 'Examining Plant Variety Protection in Nigeria: Realities, Obligations and Prospects' (2019) 22 *Journal of World Intellectual Property* 36. Elimma Ezeani, 'Economic and Development Policy-Making in Nigeria' (2012) 56 *Journal of African Law* 109.

8 No. 33 of 1987.

9 No. 72 of 1992.

10 Bankole Sodipo, *Copyright Law: Principles, Practice and Procedure*, Chapter 1.

to the National Assembly.[11] Some foreign concerns are urging for these reforms too. The foreign organisations include the International Union for the Protection of New Plant Varieties (UPOV), the Partnership for Inclusive Agricultural Transformation in Africa (PIATA), Alliance for a Green Revolution in Africa (AGRA), the Rockefeller Foundation and Bill & Melinda Gates Foundation and the United States Agency for International Development (USAID).[12] Similarly, the Ministry of Trade has also championed this cause by preparing Bills for the reform of the entire IP spectrum, with provisions for Plant and Animal Breeds Rights along the lines of the African Union model law.

Debates continue to rage about the involvement of foreign concerns, especially the push for Nigeria to embrace Genetically Modified Organisms (GMOs) with strong sentiments being advanced on opposite sides of the debates.[13] Evidence suggests that some consumers are indifferent and are prepared to consume GMOs[14] and this is supported by many[15] despite possible risks. Suffice it to say that Nigeria's population explosion calls for urgent measures to increase our agricultural yields through innovative farming. It makes good sense to incentivise innovative farmers through IP or akin systems. This is the basis for the urgent call to introduce a legal regime that will guarantee some measure of return on investments by preventing competition from the third parties who may seek to exploit the agriculture-based innovation.

Copyright issues

The lobby for copyright reforms in Nigeria has been locally driven.[16] Issues calling for reform in copyright range from the need to increase penalties

11 https://agra.org/seed-legislation-nigeria-takes-steps-to-secure-the-legacy-of-plant-breeders-and-foundation-seed-producers/#:~:text=we%20make%20Nigeria-,Seed%20legislation%3A%20Nigeria%20takes%20steps%20to%20secure%20the%20legacy%20of,breeders%20and%20foundation%20seed%20producers&text=A%20new%20draft%20law%20known,seeds%20for%20increased%20crop%20production.

12 https://agra.org/seed-legislation-nigeria-takes-steps-to-secure-the-legacy-of-plant-breeders-and-foundation-seed-producers/#:~:text=we%20make%20Nigeria-,Seed%20legislation%3A%20Nigeria%20takes%20steps%20to%20secure%20the%20legacy%20of,breeders%20and%20foundation%20seed%20producers&text=A%20new%20draft%20law%20known,seeds%20for%20increased%20crop%20production.

13 Ademola A Adenle, 'Stakeholders' Perceptions of GM Technology in West Africa: Assessing the Responses of Policymakers and Scientists in Ghana and Nigeria' *Journal of Agricultural and Environmental Ethics* 27, 241–63 (2014). https://doi.org/10.1007/s10806-013-9462-y.

14 For cow-peas, see for example Saket Kushwaha, A Musa, James Lowenberg-DeBoer, and Joan Fulton, 'Consumer Acceptance of GMO Cowpeas In Sub-Sahara Africa' Agricultural and Applied Economics Association (AAEA) > Agricultural and Applied Economics Association (AAEA) Conferences > 2004 Annual meeting, August 1–4, Denver, CO.

15 Olaitan Oluwasey Olusegun and Ifeoluwa Ayokunle Olubiyi, 'Implications of Genetically Modified Crops and Intellectual Property Rights on Agriculture in Developing Countries' (2017) 61 *Journal of African Law* 253.

16 Bankole Sodipo, *Piracy and Counterfeiting: GATT TRIPS and Developing Countries,* Kluwer Law International, London-The Hague-Boston, 1997, (Chapter 1). Bankole Sodipo, "The Nigerian Copyright Act 1988, as it Affects the Entertainment Industry"

against piracy, measures to penalise those who deal with mechanisms that counter protection measures, to what should be eligible for protection. It also includes the extent of the powers of the Nigerian Copyright Commission (NCC), the rights in the digital space, the liability of service providers for unauthorised content on their platforms, challenges with blank tape levies, clarifications on distinctions between authorship and ownership, and the protection of foreign copyright works, arising from some court decisions that have raised some concerns. Other areas of concern in copyright include the extent to which the balance tilts towards the protection of private interests when there is a big deficit in Nigeria's educational needs, issues of performers' rights and improvement in alternative dispute resolution.

Piracy and the powers of the NCC

The NCC has had challenges in meeting its obligations in the enforcement of copyright.[17] Despite the efforts of the NCC at prosecuting pirates, piracy is increasing rather than abating.[18] This can be attributed to at least two of the following reasons. Piracy is an organised crime, it is well-funded. On the other hand, the NCC is not well-funded.[19] The other reason is the non-deterrent level of penalties arising from the devaluation of the Nigerian currency, the Naira, since 1988, when the applicable statute was passed. The penalties that appeared deterrent at that time now look unreasonable. Further, although the validity of the NCC's copyright notification system has been affirmed by some,[20] it may be wise to clarify this in a new statute that confirms that notification is not compulsory neither is it necessary for the eligibility of copyright protection for works. To deal with these, there must be an amendment of the law with heavy penalties. The NCC must also be properly funded.

[1993] 1 *Entertainment Law Review* 17. Desmond Oriakhogba and Alero Fenemigho, 'Development, Concept and Scope of Copyright Protection in Nigeria: An Overview' (2014) 5 *Nnamdi Azikiwe University Journal of International Law and Jurisprudence* 179, Kunle Ola, 'Evolution and Future Trends of Copyright in Nigeria' (2014) 2 *Journal of Open Access Law* 1.

17 Bankole Sodipo, 'The Nigerian Copyright Council and the Administration of Copyright in Nigeria' 1993 *Copyright World*, July/August Issue. Kunle Ola, 'Evolution and Future Trends of Copyright in Nigeria' (2014) 2 *Journal of Open Access Law* 1. Temitope Oloko, 'The Administration and Regulation of Intellectual Property Rights in Nigeria' 15 *Nigerian Law Journal* 148 (2011).

18 Omotayo Awomolo-Enujiugha, 'Piracy and Its Burden on Copyright in Nigeria: Challenges and Solutions' (2020) 23 *Journal of World Intellectual Property* 413. Mary Imelda Obianuju Nwogu, "Copyright Law and the Menace of Piracy in Nigeria" 34 *Journal of Law Policy & Globalization* 113 (2015). Faga and Ngozi (n 3) 211.

19 A visit to the Lagos office of the NCC will immediately reveal its sorry state and the commitment of the federal government to the copyright cause.

20 Adekola Tolulope Anthony and Eze Sunday Chinedu, 'Intellectual Property Rights in Nigeria: A Critical Examination of the Activities of the Nigerian Copyright Commission' 35 *Journal of Law, Policy and Globalization* 56 (2015).

Eligibility, infringements, blank tapes and performers' rights

Presently, copyright may protect a work irrespective of whether the work is created terrestrially in Nigeria outside Nigeria or in the outer space,[21] provided the work meets the conditions for eligibility and it is made by the qualified persons. But it has been argued that gaps in the copyright space, include the extent of protection that should be offered to screenplays[22] or statute. There are debates as to whether statutes are protected by copyright, though the better view as confirmed by case law is that statutes are literary works protected by copyright in Nigeria.[23] The Court of Appeal's decision in *Microsoft Corporation v Franike*[24] that the Act does not protect the copyright work of Microsoft, a US corporation is frightening, though given per incuriam.[25] It is perhaps safer to introduce a provision in a new statute that incorporates that 1972 Copyright (Reciprocal Extension Order) or its equivalent becomes necessary.

There are suggestions that amendments are needed to clarify when infringements of copyright occur[26] and further distinguish between authorship and ownership of copyright[27] but this may not really be necessary![28] There is a need to expand the scope of dispute resolution regimes outside the arena of the courts beyond the Copyright (Dispute Resolution Panel) Rules 2007[29] through an Amendment to the Act.

21 Tare Brisibe, 'Law and Regulation of Activities Related to Outer Space in Nigeria / Weltraumrecht in Nigeria / Droit Spatial en Nigeria' *55 Zeitschrift fur Luft- und Weltraumrecht – German Journal of Air and Space Law*, 554 (2006).

22 Chijioke Okorie, 'Lessons in Protecting and Enforcing Copyright in Screenplays in Nigeria' (2020) 41 *Business Law Review* 55.

23 Bankole Sodipo, 'Are Statutes Literary Works Protected by Copyright in Nigeria?' (2020) 9 *International Journal of Legislative Drafting and Law Reform* 4. *The Attorney General of the Federation and Minister of Justice, Butterworths Publishers (Proprietary) Ltd & Odade Investment Ltd v Iven Tech Limited* (*AG Fed v Iventech*), Unreported SUIT NO: FHC/L/CS/977/2007 delivered on Tuesday 17th December, 2019, Coram Oguntoyinbo J.

24 (2011) LPELR-8987 (CA).

25 Bankole Sodipo, 'Are Foreign Copyright Works Protected in Nigeria?' (2020) 10(2) *Queen Mary Journal of Intellectual Property* 238–54.

26 Bukola Faturoti, 'Re-Importing the Concept of Authorisation of Copyright Infringement to Nigeria from the UK and Australia' (2017) 31 *International Review Law Computers & Technology* 4.

27 Chioma Nwabachili and Chudi Nwabachili, 'Authorship and Ownership of Copyright: A Critical Review' (2015) 34 *Journal of Law Policy & Globalization* 1.

28 For more clarification on this, see For more reading, see: *Copyright Law: Principles, Practice and Procedure* (2nd ed., Swan Publication, 2017). Bankole Sodipo, 'Employees as Authors in Nigeria – Who Owns the Copyright?' *Managing Intellectual Property*, August/September Euromoney, 1991, 44. Bankole Sodipo, 'Ownership of Copyright in Nigeria" Nigerian Copyright Law' *Prospects for National Development*, G O S Amadi, Atim-Ekpo Bassey, A Iwobi, A C Nwaogugu, D I Nwoga (ed.), 19, Nigerian Copyright Commission.

29 N A Inegbedion and J O Odion, 'Recent Legal Developments' (2008) 7 *University of Botswana Law Journal* 185.

The blank tape levy regime aimed at compensating authors for possible exploitation of their works by blank tapes faces its own challenges, for instance, it is uncertain if it accommodates fair dealing principles.[30] The levels of usage of "blank tapes" for works that do not need authorisation in Nigeria is not certain; hence, the regime that forces payment for all the uses may not be sustainable. This may need further scrutiny and possible clarification by the way of amendment.

The significance of the performer's rights in our creative industries, where many performances do not derive from scripted works that satisfy the test of fixation for copyright protection.[31] The view has been expressed that the NCC does little to enforce performer's rights. Although no verifiable data have been offered to support this assertion, it may be necessary to expand the definition of performer to include stand-up comedians and television or radio format shows.

Internet and online issues

There are concerns on the extent to which online resources are protected especially as there have been no amendments to the statute since Nigeria became party to the new WIPO treaties.[32] Right holders have the exclusive right to reproduce the work in a material form,[33] to publish the work,[34] perform the work in public[35] and broadcast or communicate the work to the public by a loudspeaker or any other similar device.[36] It is not conclusive if this will cover online dealings that are often transient and not in a permanent form. I have argued elsewhere that copying under the Act for criminal penalty relates to the permanent form,[37] hence this calls for reform.

The Act defines "copy" to mean

> a reproduction in written form, in the form of a recording or cinematograph film, or in any other material form, so however that an

30 Ifeoluwa Olubiyi, 'Imposition of a Copyright Levy in Nigeria: Legal Justifications and Comparative Analysis' (2014) 4 Journal of *Sustainable Development of Law & Policy* 87.

31 Dorcas Odunaike, 'Performers' Rights and Evolution of Performance in Nigeria' (2016) 53 *Journal of Law Policy & Globalization* 61.

32 Michael Sunday Afelayan, 'Legal Challenges of Intellectual Property and Copyright Protection of Online and Digital Data in Nigeria' (2018) 79 *Journal of Law Policy & Globalization* 139. Fabian Odoh and Godwin Emeka Odoh, 'The Emerging Digital Age and Its Legal Impacts on Copyright Protection in Nigeria: The Need to Strategize' (2019) *Acta Universitatis Danubius. Juridica* 73. Faga and Ngozi (n 3) 211. Abayomi Al-Ameen, 'Copyright in the Era of Internet Adversity: Pre-Empting a New Dawn for Nigeria' (2020) 29 *Information and Communication Technologies Law* 174.

33 S.6(1)(a) (i) of the Act.

34 S.6(1)(a) (ii) of the Act.

35 S.6(1)(a) (iii) of the Act.

36 S.6(1)(a) (vii) of the Act.

37 Bankole Sodipo, 'Fracturing Constitutional Rights: The prosecution of alleged broadcast infringers in Nigeria' 2020 64(1) *Journal of African Law* 1–15.

> object shall not be taken to be a copy of an architectural work unless the object is a building or model.

The Act defines "communication to the public" to include, "in addition to any live performance or delivery, any mode of visual or acoustic presentation, but does not include a broadcast or re-broadcast". These should be reviewed to accommodate transient copying and the right to make available in line with Nigeria's treaty obligations under the WIPO copyright treaties.

Human rights and educational issues

Given the state of Nigeria's economy and its educational infrastructure, it is unclear if the copyright system meets the fundamental rights educational needs for books in a developing country like Nigeria.[38] Although there are exceptions to copyright control, compulsory licensing for educational needs, there is a little evidence that these balancing mechanisms in the copyright system have been utilised to meet Nigeria's educational needs. Before agreeing to law reform, it may be necessary to proceed with some caution, provide some evidence that may instruct the way forward.

Folklore and traditional knowledge

Despite the statutory regime for folklore in Nigeria, challenges remain in the identification, ownership and commonality of folklore in the different parts of Nigeria.[39] Traditional Knowledge suffers greater challengers than folklore as articulated by the copyright statute as there is no canopy of protection for innovation in the health, food, agriculture and similar sectors.[40] In particular, traditional medicines and traditional knowledge deserve sui generis protection.[41] New evidence continues to emerge demonstrating that traditional Nigerian society was a relatively advanced technologically innovation society.[42] To this end, there is an urgent need to build a reliable data

38 Samuel Ugwumba, 'The Case for Integrating Copyright Law with the Constitutional Right to Education in Nigeria and Developing Countries' (2020) 61 *IDEA* 100. Wahab Akanmu Aboyade et al., 'Copyright Infringement and Photocopy Services among University Students and Teachers in Nigeria' (2015) 8(1) *International Journal of Arts & Science* 463, 471. Lea Shaver, 'Copyright and Inequality' (2014–2015) 92 *Washington University Law Review* 117.

39 Bambo Adewopo, 'Protection and Administration of Folklore in Nigeria' (2006) 3 *SCRIPTed: A Journal of Law, Technology and Society*, 1. Ayoyemi Lawal Arowolo, 'African Traditional Intellectual Property Rights, Customary Law, and Legal Pluralism' (2018–2019) 11 *African Journal of Legal Studies* 299.

40 Ezeani (n 7) 109.

41 Ibid.

42 Akinwumi Ogundiran and O Akinlolu Ige, 'Our Ancestors Were Material Scientists': Archaeological and Geochemical Evidence for Indigenous Yoruba Glass Technology'

base of the Nigerian folklore and traditional knowledge. There is a need to amend Nigerian statutes to ensure that those who use Nigerian folklore and traditional knowledge compensate and share benefits with the relevant community or practitioners of the knowledge.

Patents

To a large extent, Nigeria complies with her treaty obligations for patents. Patents are renewable yearly for a total period of 20 years.[43] The Patents and Designs Act does not discriminate against any area technology[44] as product patents are obtainable for pharmaceuticals.

Some view the patent system with some skepticism partly because it was introduced to Nigeria to protect British patents,[45] yet this does not obviate the usefulness of patent specifications for research.[46] The system has been criticised by many as the formal examination system appears to have open the floodgates for patents that would not have been granted if there is a substantive examination system.[47] As such, the National Assembly may consider introducing a substantive examination system.

The COVID-19 pandemic and the emerging vaccines have accentuated the debate on access to essential medicines in Nigeria. The debate about TRIPS flexibilities, that is, mechanisms within TRIPS that may be used by developing countries to secure access to patents for health and other public interests is pertinent. Nigeria already has a compulsory licensing system and a government use regime.[48] There may be need to remove the authorisation for compulsory licence from the purview of the courts given that applications can be tied up through the courts system for the entire 20 years of the term of the relevant patent. It may be noted that the current government use regime may be more flexible than the entire TRIPS flexibilities regime.[49]

The employee invention reward scheme may need to be re-worked as the right to patent an invention should not belong to the employer in all the

(2015) 46(8) *Journal of Black Studies* 751. The level of finesse of the stolen Benin Ife, Nok and Arochukwu cultural properties attest to this.

43 Section 7, PDA.

44 Section 1, PDA.

45 Bankole Sodipo, *Piracy and Counterfeiting: GATT TRIPS and Developing Countries* (Kluwer Law International, London-The Hague-Boston, 1997) (Chapter 1). Bankole Sodipo, 'Government Use of Patented Medicines in Securing Access to Essential Medicines in a Post Covid-19 Nigeria' (2020) 42 *European Intellectual Property Review*. Gaius Ezejiofor, 'The Law of Patents in Nigeria: A Review' (1973) 9 *African Law of Studies* 39.

46 Olusegun Oyedepo, Patent and Economic Development in Nigeria' (2012) 16 *Nigerian Law Journal* 144.

47 Ezejiofor (n 45) 39. S K Date-Bah, 'Transfer of Technology to Nigeria and the Patents and Designs Act 1970' (1981) 25 *Journal of African Law* 80.

48 Ezejiofor (n 45) 39.

49 Bankole Sodipo, 'Government Use of Patented Medicines in Securing Access to Essential Medicines in a Post Covid-19 Nigeria' 42 *European Intellectual Property Review* (2020).

circumstances envisaged by the law. For example, we may wish to revisit section 2(4)(a)(i) of the Patents and Designs Act that provides that the right belongs to the employer

> if his contract of employment does not require him to exercise any inventive activity but he has in making the invention used data or means that his employment has put at his disposal.[50]

There is a measure of on-going research and patentable inventions in Nigeria. There is some evidence that local and international innovation is derived from Nigeria's biodiversity[51] and traditional herbalists, but it is doubtful if stakeholders benefit from this. Nigeria may wish to review her patent laws to have either of the following declarations:

Where the underlying information about the invention is derived from Nigeria's biodiversity or from the practices or knowledge of persons living in Nigeria than either,

- a the right to the patent will be jointly owned by the local community with the biodiversity or the persons whose practices or knowledge has been used or
- b the invention shall not be patentable as the biodiversity or practice or knowledge forms part of the prior art.

There is on-going debate on whether software inventions are patentable, and this is now the subject of litigation.[52] Some posit that software inventions are not patentable because of some foreign laws that preclude such inventions from being patentable. The better view is that given that the statute does not define inventions, a computer invention should be patentable if it meets the criteria for patentability. To this end, it may be wise for the new statute to spell out things that are controversial, so allow for certainty and avoid litigation.

Finally, there is an urgent need to amend the statute to give independence to the Patents Registry by making it part of a Commission similar to the NCC and the Corporate Affairs Commission.

50 Temitope O Oloko, 'An Examination of Article 27 of the TRIPS Agreement in Relation to the Provisions on Patentable Subject Matter under the PDA in Nigeria' https://repository.up.ac.za/bitstream/handle/2263/57031/Oloko_Examination_2016.pdf?sequence=1&isAllowed=y

51 Olawale Ajai, 'Access to Genetic Resources and Biotechnology Regulation in Nigeria' (1997) 6 *Review of European Community and International Environmental Law* 42. Remigius Nwabueze, 'What Can Genomics and Health Biotechnology Do for Developing Countries' (2004–2005) 15 *Albany Law Journal of Science and Technology* 369.

52 *E-Transact Global Limited v Interswitch Limited,* Suit No. FHC/L/CS/961/2016 and *Interswitch Limited v E-Transact Global Limited & Anor* Suit No. FHC/L/CP/784/2016.

Designs

Nigeria's design rights regimes cover textiles, shapes of containers, equipment integrated circuits and the like. They are registrable for three terms of five years each.[53] One of the challenges is that the tenor of the cases that hold that the mould must be tendered in court. Moulds are very expensive and they are needed for manufacture of the products and if courts insist they must have the moulds, it may mean that production will cease.[54] This calls for reforms so that the drawings of the moulds and the photographs and a siting of the mould in court should suffice. It is not certain if our textile or fashion industry regard the design system in Nigeria as adequately providing for them.

Trade mark issues

Trade marks have been protected and litigated in Nigeria for over a 100 years.[55] Trade marks are renewable forever in Nigeria, seven years in the first instance and 14 years thereafter.[56] It is curious that a trade mark proprietor who fails to renew may renew after several years of his failure provided his mark is still on the register. This means that a person who conducts a search and notes that a mark has not been renewed (or even used for say three years) and who opts for a confusingly similar mark may be pursued by a proprietor who renews his mark and institutes an action for infringement. The procedure for the removal of marks for failure to renew must be changed as it creates an unfair position in the market place. Given that, TRIPS require the minimum period of registration to be seven years,[57] Nigeria may consider amending the Act to reduce the renewal period of registration from 14 years to seven years.

The shape of a container or a product, the sound of a product or the smell of products can be sufficiently distinctive to serve to distinguish the products from others. Yet there are challenges to the registration of shapes, sounds and smells in Nigeria. Despite the regulations used in registering shapes as trademarks, there is still a controversy whether services are indeed types of intangible goods to warrant service marks registration in Nigeria without an amendment to the statute. The Act must be amended to close the gaps and enable shapes, sounds, smells and services to be registrable.

53 Chudi Nwabachili and Chioma Nwabachili, 'Challenges to Effective Legal Protection of Industrial Designs in Nigeria' (2015) 33 *Journal of Law, Policy and Globalization* 7.

54 *Uzokwe v. Densy Ind. (Nig) Ltd & Anor* (2002) LPELR-3456(SC) 2002 2 NWLR (Pr. 752) 528; *Nigerian Breweries Plc v Pabod Breweries Ltd & anor.* (2010) LPELR-4609 (CA).

55 For more reading on issues of reform, see, Bankole Sodipo, 'Trade Marks Protection in Nigeria: Infringement and Remedies under the Law' *Nigerian Law Reform Commission Journal*, 2012.

56 Section 23 Trade Marks Act, 1965.

57 Article 18, TRIPS.

The current law does not accommodate geographical indications (GI) of origin or appellations of origin. A GI is

> a sign used on products that have a specific geographical origin and possess qualities or a reputation that are due to that origin. In order to function as a GI, a sign must identify a product as originating in a given place. In addition, the qualities, characteristics or reputation of the product should be essentially due to the place of origin. Since the qualities depend on the geographical place of production, there is a clear link between the product and its original place of production.[58]

There is evidence that we have enormous potentials to boost local products if we have a regime for the geographical indications.[59] We need to introduce this regime in Nigeria as it is a locally beneficial TRIPS obligation.[60]

To curb counterfeiting, the statute must be reviewed to expand the scope of what constitutes infringement and to make attempts and aiding and abetting offences. The statute must increase the penalties for counterfeiting and empower specialised prosecutors similar to the Copyright Inspectors in Nigeria, the officers of the National Office of Food Drug Administration and Control (NAFDAC) in Nigeria and the Trading Standards Officers in the UK. Importation of counterfeit goods must also be prohibited. Dealing with, storing and distributing infringing products whether online or not must be prohibited. We must also improve the administrative measures against the import or export of counterfeit goods by streamlining the notification process and the possibility of release of goods where they are not counterfeit. Nigeria may also consider having a policy on parallel goods rather than leave it to further debate and allow courts to give conflicting decisions. Any effort at reform must also consider resolving the quagmire created by the Ferodo case[61] as it should be possible to register a get-up as a device that includes a word mark and use the same to prevent third parties who use a different name as a mark but adopt identical get up.[62]

The Act may also be amended to give statutory backing to the inspection and seizure order popularly known as the Anton Piller Order as provided under the Copyright Act. The legislature may also consider establishing a formal Tribunal beyond the powers of the Registrar as a tribunal. Reforms may introduce alternative dispute resolution mechanisms. Finally, as was

58 https://www.wipo.int/geo_indications/en/

59 Ayoyemi Lawal-Arowolo, 'Geographical Indications and Cultural Artworks in Nigeria: A Cue from Other Jurisdictions' (2019) 22 *Journal of World Intellectual Property* 364.

60 Articles 22–23, TRIPS.

61 *Ferodo Limited vs Ibeto Industries Limited* (2004) LCN/3262(SC).

62 Ayoyemi Lawal-Arowolo, 'Ferodo Limited and Ferodo Nigeria Limited v. Ibeto Industries Limited: A Critical Review' 1(2) (2012) *NIALS Journal of Intellectual Property* (NJIP) 118-136, 136.

stated with regards to the Patents Registry, a Commission must be established to take over the functions of the Registry like the CAC.

Entertainment and sports industry

Arguably, the Nigerian statutes discussed above do not go far enough to meet the needs of Nigeria's entertainment and sports industries. For instance, unauthorised dealings with the photographs and events of celebrities may not be fully protected by the performer's rights (not being performances as defined by the Copyright Act) or trade mark law. The constitutional right to privacy is in its infancy and whilst it can be developed through case law, it is perhaps time to flesh out the scope of the rights through legislation.

Conclusion

As stated earlier, this chapter was not intended to present a detailed analysis of the issues raised. However, it set out to ignite thinking or corroborate arguments on several issues that have been identified that require urgent reforms in the IP sector in Nigeria. The issues raised must be urgently redressed in any effort at law reform. IP remains a possible guarantee against unfair competition by unscrupulous third parties wishing to reap the benefits of the efforts of others. Nigeria has a booming copyright-based industry and sectors that can benefit from the proper harnessing of the fruits of IP. Reform in the sector has become more urgent as a Nigerian heads the WTO today.

Index

Note: Page numbers followed by "n" denote endnotes.

For Product Safety Concerns and Information please contact our EU
representative GPSR@taylorandfrancis.com
Taylor & Francis Verlag GmbH, Kaufingerstraße 24, 80331 München, Germany

www.ingramcontent.com/pod-product-compliance
Lightning Source LLC
LaVergne TN
LVHW021121300926
849160LV00010B/807
9781032169033